Mastering OpenCV with Python

Use NumPy, Scikit, TensorFlow, and Matplotlib to learn Advanced algorithms for Machine Learning through a set of Practical Projects

Ayush

Orangeava.com

First published: November 2023

Published by: Orange Education Pvt Ltd, AVA™

Address: 9, Daryaganj, Delhi, 110002

ISBN: 978-93-90475-79-7

www.orangeava.com

Dedicated to

My beloved Parents:

Shri Luv Vaishya
Neeti Vaishya

&

And to my adored family, and family,
without whom this journey would not have been possible

About the Author

Ayush brings over 5 years of invaluable expertise in AI, ML, and computer vision to the table. With a passion for technology deployment and a track record of guiding projects from inception to completion, Ayush possesses a unique ability to simplify complex concepts. His career highlights include creating advanced computer vision models, refining algorithms for optimal performance, and leveraging data analytics for actionable insights. With his experience, Ayush has created this invaluable resource to equip readers for success in the world of computer vision.

About the Technical Reviewer

Kaushal Singh, an accomplished Data Scientist and AI researcher with a rich and diverse career spanning 5 years. He is currently working as an Assistant Professor and Training and Placement Officer at the Department of Computer Science and Information Technology, School of Engineering, P P Savani University, Surat, Gujarat, with a passion for harnessing the power of data and artificial intelligence, he made significant contributions to the field through research and technical expertise. Throughout his career, he delved deep into the realms of data science and artificial intelligence, honing his skills in machine learning, deep learning, and data analysis. His proficiency extends to developing state-of-the-art AI models and leveraging data-driven insights to solve complex real-world challenges. He is not only a practitioner but also a dedicated researcher. He authored 8 research papers and 4 Book Chapters published in reputable journals and conferences, making substantial contributions to the advancement of AI technologies. His work particularly shines in areas like natural language processing, computer vision, and predictive analytics. Beyond his research endeavors, he also sought after technical reviewers. His keen eye for detail and extensive domain knowledge make him a valuable asset in ensuring the quality and credibility of technical content in the fields of data science and AI. He consistently provides insightful feedback to fellow researchers and peers. With 5 years of hands-on experience and a commitment to pushing the boundaries of AI, he is trying to continue to shape the landscape of data science and artificial intelligence, driving innovation and excellence in the industry.

Acknowledgements

I want to extend my heartfelt thanks to my parents for their unwavering support and guidance throughout this journey. Their presence has been my anchor, and their belief in my dreams has been my driving force.

Additionally, my deepest gratitude goes out to my family who have been like the sturdy branches of a tree, providing shelter and strength in every season. Their boundless love, patience, and encouragement have been the cornerstone of my endeavors, grounding me when the winds of doubt blew, and lifting me higher when aspirations reached for the sky. Together, they have formed the backdrop against which the narrative of my life and this book unfolds.

I would like to express my sincere appreciation to my current organization for their unwavering support and encouragement. They have not only provided a conducive environment for growth but have also served as invaluable mentors, guiding me through the intricacies of my field. Their belief in my potential has been a driving force and I am profoundly grateful for the opportunities and inspiration they have offered.

Preface

Unlock the captivating world of computer vision with this comprehensive guide that takes you on an enriching journey from novice to expert. Packed with step-by-step tutorials, easy-to-understand explanations, and detailed code examples, this book ensures that you grasp even the most intricate concepts effortlessly. You'll find yourself immersed in the world of computer vision as we demystify complex algorithms and techniques with hands-on, real-world projects that bring your learning to life.

Whether you're a seasoned developer or just starting your coding adventure, our easy-to-follow language and engaging approach make this book your ideal companion. Explore the power of OpenCV, delve into image manipulation, unravel the secrets of feature detection, and seamlessly integrate machine learning into your projects. With this book in your hands, you'll gain the skills and confidence to conquer the dynamic field of computer vision and embark on exciting journeys of your own.

The book comprises 12 chapters that guide you from the fundamentals of computer vision to advanced applications. You'll start with an introduction to computer vision and image manipulation, progress to image processing techniques, and delve into advanced concepts like feature detection and machine learning integration. The final chapter offers practical projects to apply your newfound knowledge.

Chapter 1: This chapter introduces readers to computer vision and OpenCV, covering its latest version (4.7) and essential setup for computer vision projects. It's a crucial starting point for understanding the core concepts and tools needed in the world of computer vision.

Chapter 2: Building on the basics, this chapter explores image essentials and operations, setting the stage for more advanced manipulation techniques. Readers will gain practical skills in image handling and modification.

Chapter 3: Readers delve into image processing operations, including rotations, resizing, and color spaces, gaining crucial skills in image manipulation.

Chapter 4: This chapter explores morphological operations, image smoothing, and blurring techniques, laying the foundation for image enhancement.

Chapter 5: This chapter unlocks the power of image histograms for enhancing images, adjusting contrast, and more, with a focus on practical manipulation.

Chapter 6: Readers master image segmentation and thresholding techniques, essential for isolating objects of interest in images.

Chapter 7: This chapter covers edge detection, contour extraction, and their roles in object recognition, enhancing readers' image analysis skills.

Chapter 8: This chapter emphasizes machine learning applications in image classification and clustering using OpenCV. It introduces decision trees, K-means clustering, and support vector machines, providing a solid foundation for applying these techniques in real-world scenarios.

Chapter 9: In this chapter, readers explore feature detection and description techniques used in image processing. They'll gain hands-on experience with state-of-the-art algorithms, enabling them to tackle complex computer vision challenges effectively.

Chapter 10: This chapter provides a foundational understanding of neural networks and their applications in various fields, including image analysis with OpenCV. Readers will also delve into network architecture, activation functions, and metrics used in neural networks.

Chapter 11: This chapter delves into object detection techniques, offering readers the tools to identify objects of interest in images and videos.

Chapter 12: The final chapter puts readers' knowledge into practice with projects covering automated book inventory, document scanning, face recognition, and drowsiness detection. It's a hands-on culmination of the book's teachings allowing readers to showcase their skills in real-world applications.

Get a Free eBook

We hope you are enjoying your recently purchased book! Your feedback is incredibly valuable to us, and to all other readers looking for great books.

If you found this book helpful or enjoyable, we would truly appreciate it, if you could take a moment to leave a short review with a 5 star rating on Amazon. It helps us grow, and lets other readers discover our books.

As a thank you, we would love to send you a free digital copy of this book, and a **30%** discount code on your next cart value on our official websites:

www.orangeava.com

www.orangeava.in (For Indian Subcontinent)

☑ **Here's how:**

Leave a review for the book on Amazon.

Take a screenshot of your review, and send an email to **info@orangeava.com** (it can be just the confirmation screen).

Once, we receive your screenshot, we will send you the digital file, within 24 hours.

Thank you so much for your support – it means a lot to us!

Downloading the code bundles and colored images

Please follow the link to download the
Code Bundles of the book:

https://github.com/OrangeAVA/Mastering-OpenCV-with-Python

The code bundles and images of the book are also hosted on
https://rebrand.ly/31c5e5

In case there's an update to the code, it will be updated on the existing GitHub repository.

Errata

We take immense pride in our work at **Orange Education Pvt Ltd,** and follow best practices to ensure the accuracy of our content to provide an indulging reading experience to our subscribers. Our readers are our mirrors, and we use their inputs to reflect and improve upon human errors, if any, that may have occurred during the publishing processes involved. To let us maintain the quality and help us reach out to any readers who might be having difficulties due to any unforeseen errors, please write to us at :

errata@orangeava.com

Your support, suggestions, and feedback are highly appreciated.

DID YOU KNOW

Did you know that Orange Education Pvt Ltd offers eBook versions of every book published, with PDF and ePub files available? You can upgrade to the eBook version at **www.orangeava.com** and as a print book customer, you are entitled to a discount on the eBook copy. Get in touch with us at: **info@orangeava.com** for more details.

At **www.orangeava.com**, you can also read a collection of free technical articles, sign up for a range of free newsletters, and receive exclusive discounts and offers on AVA™ Books and eBooks.

PIRACY

If you come across any illegal copies of our works in any form on the internet, we would be grateful if you would provide us with the location address or website name. Please contact us at **info@orangeava.com** with a link to the material.

ARE YOU INTERESTED IN AUTHORING WITH US?

If there is a topic that you have expertise in, and you are interested in either writing or contributing to a book, please write to us at **business@orangeava.com**. We are on a journey to help developers and tech professionals to gain insights on the present technological advancements and innovations happening across the globe and build a community that believes Knowledge is best acquired by sharing and learning with others. Please reach out to us to learn what our audience demands and how you can be part of this educational reform. We also welcome ideas from tech experts and help them build learning and development content for their domains.

REVIEWS

Please leave a review. Once you have read and used this book, why not leave a review on the site that you purchased it from? Potential readers can then see and use your unbiased opinion to make purchase decisions. We at Orange Education would love to know what you think about our products, and our authors can learn from your feedback. Thank you!

For more information about Orange Education, please visit **www.orangeava.com**.

Table of Contents

CHAPTER 1

Introduction to Computer Vision

Introduction

Welcome to the world of computer vision. This book will take you on a journey through the exciting and rapidly evolving world of computer vision and image processing. The book begins by introducing computer vision and the OpenCV library. We will then proceed to cover the essential libraries and the required environment setup for this course.

Structure

In this chapter, we will discuss the following topics:

- Introduction to Computer Vision
- Applications of Computer Vision
- Python
- OpenCV
  - A brief history of OpenCV
  - OpenCV 4.7
- Supporting Libraries
- Environment Setup
  - Installing Python
  - Package Manager
  - Installing Supporting Libraries
  - Installing OpenCV
  - Verifying our Installation
  - IDE
- Documentation

Introduction to Computer Vision

Computer vision aims to provide machines with the ability to recognize and analyze images or videos, just like humans do. By developing algorithms that teach computers to *see*, computer vision has the potential to disrupt a wide range of industries such as healthcare and automotive.

With the improvements in camera quality and increased ease of access to good cameras, the amount of visual data in the world is exploding, and computer vision helps us to make sense of this data and put it to better use.

Engineers today have been able to develop cameras that produce eye-like images. As computers have learned the ability to see, our job is to leverage that information and use it to understand and analyze that data.

Did you know? A typical camera sensor can capture 16.8 million distinct colors because it has a bit depth of 8 bits per color channel. However, the human eye can only perceive around 10 million colors, so not all of these colors can be distinguished by the human eye. Cameras and computer vision systems are capable of capturing and processing more colors than the human eye can see.

Computer vision is a subset of artificial intelligence with visual information at its heart. The field focuses on enabling computers to process, analyze, and interpret image data and generate meaningful insights from it.

With the advancements in technology, computational power and cameras have gotten better with time and the field has emerged as one of the most promising careers of the day. We are able to capture high-quality images and process huge amounts of data at a speed, which was impossible some years back.

Computer vision has a wide array of applications across various sectors. Be it healthcare, defense, transportation, or even entertainment, computer vision has shown great promise in all of these areas. Innovations in the field have made significant contributions to these areas.

Applications of Computer Vision

We are surrounded by computer vision in our daily lives, from the automatic face detection in your smartphone camera to the improvement in image quality in your Instagram posts or Snapchat filters. Computer vision has made a significant impression on our everyday lives.

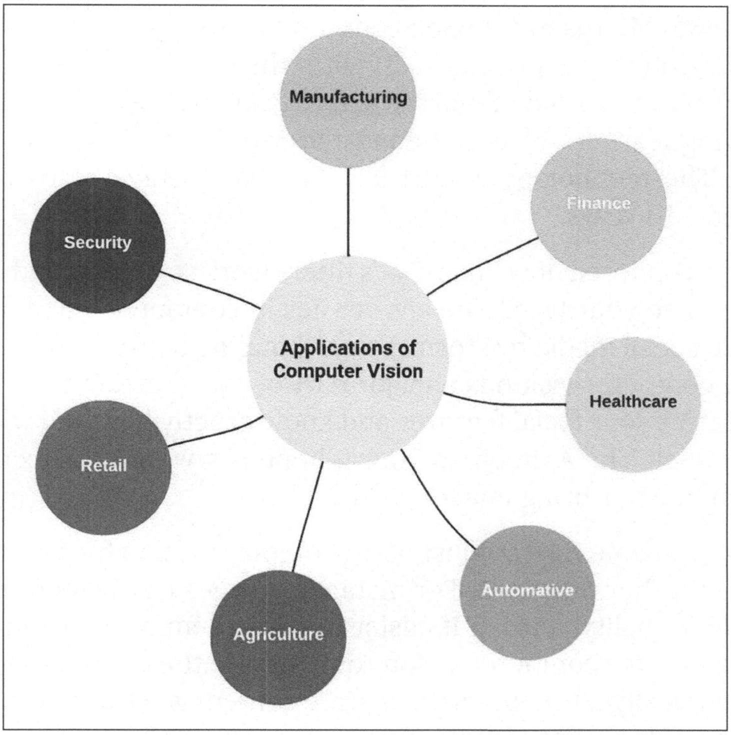

***Figure 1.1**: Applications of Computer Vision*

Computer vision has revolutionized the healthcare field. It has greatly improved the diagnosis speed and helps doctors in providing a much more precise diagnosis. By analyzing the images of the concerned area, it can analyze the skin deformities and help diagnose diseases such as dermatitis and melanoma. Using medical imaging, computer vision can help us get a glimpse of defects in internal organs, by analyzing X-rays or MRI scans, for faster diagnosis or allowing doctors to detect issues like fractures or tumors. Be it using Chest X-rays to detect diseases like tuberculosis or analyzing heart images for detecting heart diseases, computer vision has proved how the medical field can greatly benefit from it.

One of the most promising applications of computer vision has been in aiding visually impaired people. Computer vision has assisted visually impaired people in navigating their surroundings, thereby increasing their independence. Computer vision technologies can analyze the environment and provide audio or tactile feedback to the user. Applications such as navigation assistance, object detection, and face or text recognition have greatly benefitted visually impaired individuals. Furthermore, these technologies are expected to improve even further with time.

Did you know? Microsoft's PeopleLens technology helps visually impaired children and young people interact with their peers more easily. It is a head-worn device that reads aloud the names of known individuals in spatialized audio, allowing learners to understand the relative position and distance of their peers. The technology is currently in a multistage research study for learners aged 5–11 years.

Have you ever wondered how Snapchat's filters work so quickly and accurately in applying effects to your face? The answer lies in computer vision, a technology that has taken social media by storm. From changing backgrounds to enhancing your images, computer vision is a major part of social media these days. These algorithms detect your facial features and know exactly how and where to apply a particular effect. The Animoji on your iPhone is a wonderful example of how computer vision helps bring images to life.

Social media companies are not just using computer vision for fun use cases, but also for various other purposes. For instance, images can be compressed while preserving their quality, making it easier to send them over the internet. Social media companies use computer vision to moderate the content. Algorithms are used to automatically filter out inappropriate content, such as nudity or violence, without the need for human intervention.

Computer vision has not only been used in commercial projects but has also demonstrated its usefulness in more altruistic endeavors, contributing to advancements in various aspects of life on Earth. For example, computer vision has been used for wildlife conservation, which has helped in protecting various endangered species. Surveillance applications have helped solve the poaching problem and have helped maintain a healthy ecosystem in the forests. Similar to wildlife, computer vision has helped in plant life conversation as well. Conservationists have been able to use computer vision to help with their efforts through various use cases such as plant disease detection, species identification, and habitat monitoring.

Apart from these, the possibilities in the field of computer vision are endless. There have been use cases such as video surveillance, face recognition, autonomous vehicles, robotics, agriculture, retail, gaming, and sports. There is no end to the number of applications that computer vision has to offer, and the list will keep on growing in years to come.

With the world moving at such a fast pace. Computer vision offers endless exciting opportunities for budding engineers to help solve real-life problems like never before.

Think about It: What do you think is a computer vision application that can be used to make this world a better place?

Python

To delve into the world of computer vision, we first need to understand the packages and libraries that we are going to use.

Python is a popular language for computer vision tasks due to its ease of use and versatility, which makes it a popular language for a wide number of uses. A large number of libraries and tools designed for image processing make it a remarkable language for computer vision applications. Furthermore, the large community support and cross-platform compatibility make it a preferred choice for anyone stepping into the world of computer vision.

Python 3 is the latest version of Python that has been released. It has included Unicode support, which means developers across the world can use Python in multiple languages. Python 3 handles exceptions in an improved way, which makes it easy for developers to handle errors. Furthermore, better garbage collection and memory management make Python 3 much faster than its predecessors.

Python 3 includes a wealth of image-processing libraries and offers many features that are beneficial for computer vision applications. As a result, it is an excellent language to use in this field.

OpenCV

Open-Source Computer Vision Library (**OpenCV**) is the focal library we are going to be using for image processing applications. OpenCV is originally written in C++ language, although it is compatible with Python using Python bindings. OpenCV, along with Python, provides a strong combination for creating powerful computer vision applications and is frequently used for research and deployment.

Initially released in the year 2000, OpenCV is an open-source library, which has since become one of the most comprehensively used libraries for computer vision. It provides a wide range of features for image processing and is used in various applications such as security, automation, and healthcare.

Another major advantage that favors OpenCV is its compatibility with several programming languages such as Python, Java, and MATLAB. The library is cross-platform as well and can run on numerous systems including Linux, Windows, Mac, Android, and iOS. Additionally, OpenCV is compatible with various computer vision and deep learning frameworks namely TensorFlow and PyTorch (We will be discussing these frameworks in detail as we move on towards further chapters).

OpenCV contains a large collection of pre-built functions that can be used for several development tasks. Functions such as image smoothening, histograms, edge and contour detection, and so on, are inherently built into the OpenCV library, which makes it easy to implement these functions in your computer vision tasks. These functions can be used for an extensive range of operations including feature detection, image segmentation, object detection, and many more. Furthermore, OpenCV incorporates an automatic memory management ability that automates the allocation and the deallocation of memory in image and matrix operations, which simplifies the usage of these functions and enhances their optimization.

Moreover, OpenCV is not only limited to image processing but it also provides a superb interface for video analysis and video processing. It provides functions to use video streams from various sources such as webcams and cameras or remotely located IP cameras as well. Video capabilities allow the development of many use cases that can process videos in real-time.

The ability to process videos in real-time opens a wide range of possible use cases such as video surveillance and self-driving cars. Using object detection and tracking features, OpenCV has significantly improved video surveillance and provides enhanced solutions for security that can outperform the human eye in many scenarios. Computer vision has given rise to another new sector, which is self-driving cars. By using OpenCV's ability to process videos in real-time along with features like object detection and image segmentation, self-driving cars are a reality these days.

Did you know? Tesla's Autopilot system has driven over five billion miles (as of September 2021) on public roads. It has been noted by the National Highway Traffic Safety Administration that Tesla's autopilot features have reduced crash rates as high as up to 40%. Tesla's cars are continuously gathering data from human drivers' driving patterns and behaviors, which is then utilized to enhance the performance of the Autopilot system gradually.

Brief history of OpenCV

OpenCV has gone through various developments over time and four major versions of the library have been released.

OpenCV 1.x was the initial version of the OpenCV library released in 2000. It provided basic computer vision algorithms for image processing such as edge and corner detection, feature detection, and image filtering.

OpenCV 2.x was released in 2009. It added advanced computer vision features such as object detection and object tracking. The 'Mat' data structure was introduced in this version and GPU acceleration for real-time analysis was also added. It added support for multiple platforms, including Windows, Linux, and Mac, which enabled developers to explore OpenCV on the platform of their choice.

OpenCV 3.x was released in 2015. The major introduction in this version was a new deep learning module that included popular deep learning frameworks like TensorFlow and Caffe, allowing the users to use neural networks for various tasks such as object classification, object detection, and so on. By adding support for multithreading and SIMD operations, this was much faster and more efficient than the earlier versions of OpenCV. This version had a modular structure with which users could install only the necessary modules, hence reducing the overall size of the library. It provided advancements to the existing algorithms such as face detection and also included multiple new algorithms for computer vision such as SIFT and SURF feature detectors.

OpenCV 4.x is the latest version of OpenCV, which was released in 2018. It included support for Vulkan graphics, which allowed for more efficient computation on supporting hardware. It has also added more frameworks such as PyTorch and ONNX for improved deep learning support. There were several additions with new computer vision algorithms and features for better image processing along with various performance updates, making the library faster and more efficient. OpenCV 4.x also provides better support for CUDA, which stands for Computer Unified Device Architecture, a parallel processing unit developed by NVidia for improved performance. OpenCV 4.x enables the use of 3D images by adding support for depth cameras.

OpenCV 4.7

The latest version of OpenCV, 4.7, was released on December 28, 2022, and included many features, such as:

- **Improvements in the dnn module**: New network architectures, Huawei CANN Backend, improved OpenVINO support, and performance optimizations.

- **New image and Video codecs**: Iterator-based API for multi-page image formats, libspng, SIMD-acceleration, H264/H265 support on Android, Orbbec RGB-D camera backend, and improved audio input via GStreamer backend CUDA 12 and Video Codec SDK support.
- **New algorithms**: NanoStack and StackBlur.
- New universal intrinsic backend for scalable vector instructions (RISC-V RVV).

OpenCV 5 is in development as of now and there are a few pre-release versions available for testing. However, it will be a few years at least before we can expect a proper release.

Supporting Libraries

OpenCV is a powerful computer vision library, but its capabilities can be further expanded by leveraging third-party libraries that seamlessly integrate with OpenCV.

We will be exploring these libraries in this section.

NumPy

NumPy is a Python library used for numerical computations that enables the use of large multidimensional arrays. It offers a vast array of mathematical functions that can be used on these arrays. It allows us to perform operations such as creating and manipulating arrays, arithmetic operations such as addition and subtraction, and various mathematical functions such as trigonometric, statistical, or logarithmic operations on these arrays.

NumPy enables us to perform mathematical operations very efficiently. It optimizes the use of available computational power by utilizing multi-core CPUs and graphic cards in the system, resulting in faster computation for numerical operations.

Another major feature of the NumPy library is broadcasting. Broadcasting is a powerful NumPy feature as it allows arrays of various sizes and shapes to be used together for arithmetic operations. NumPy does this by automatically increasing or *broadcasting* the size of smaller arrays to match that of the larger ones. This helps us write code effortlessly as it eliminates the need to use loops or any other operations that might be needed for operating on different-sized arrays.

NumPy is often used in conjunction with other computing libraries, which helps users to perform various applications like data analysis and visualization seamlessly. SciPy is a library built on top of NumPy, which provides support for several data analytic tasks like regressions or data modeling. Matplotlib is another library that is often used together with NumPy. Matplotlib is a library that is used for creating high-quality data visualizations. We will be utilizing these libraries extensively as we progress through the course.

Matplotlib

Matplotlib is a widely used library for data visualization and data analysis. It provides a range of plotting functions that help the user create various types of visualizations.

Some of the common types of plots that can be created using Matplotlib include line plots, scatter plots, histograms, and heatmaps. Matplotlib also provides the ability to extensively customize these plots. Users can choose any color they want, the title for their plots, include annotations or tweak the axes within the plots according to their requirements.

Matplotlib also allows the creation of subplots, which are a way of creating multiple plots within a single figure. It also provides many output formats for saving plots such as JPEG, PNG, PDF, and so on.

Matplotlib is often used along with NumPy. Its easy-to-use features and interoperability with other libraries have made it a popular choice among data scientists and researchers for data visualization.

SciPy

SciPy is an open-source library that provides a wide range of functionality for data analysis and visualization. It consists of modules that help users with scientific and mathematical computations and includes modules for statistics, linear algebra, image or signal processing, and so on.

SciPy is built on top of the NumPy library. While NumPy provides functionality to work with n-dimensional arrays and apply some mathematical operations on them, SciPy takes it a bit further by providing more complex and convenient functions for data processing, optimization, and more.

SciPy is seamlessly integrated with other libraries in Python such as NumPy, Scikit-learn, and Matplotlib. This makes SciPy a powerful tool for data analysis as researchers can use it alongside other libraries to create a comprehensive environment for data science.

Scikit-Learn

Scikit-Learn or sklearn is a machine learning library that provides a wide range of machine learning algorithms such as regression, classification, and so on. It also provides users with various data preprocessing and model evaluation tools, making it a complete package for data scientists.

Scikit-learn is built on top of NumPy, SciPy, and Matplotlib, providing easy integration with these libraries, which helps the users to perform a wide range of applications. It can also be integrated with other Python libraries and can be used with frameworks like TensorFlow.

While it is not an image processing library, Scikit-Learn is a powerful tool for machine learning tasks, and we will be using it when implementing machine learning algorithms in later sections of this course.

Scikit-Image

Scikit-Image is an image processing library that provides various algorithms such as image segmentation, filtering, and feature extraction.

Scikit-Image provides similar features to OpenCV. However, it is considered easier to learn and more user-friendly, while OpenCV offers better optimizations and, consequently, better performance.

Similar to Scikit-Learn, this library was built on top of **`numpy,scipy`**, and **`matplotlib`**. As mentioned earlier, OpenCV was built on C++ and has Python bindings.

While we will be using OpenCV primarily in our computer vision journey, Scikit-Image comes in handy sometimes for implementing specific algorithms.

Mahotas

Mahotas is another popular image-processing library that contains various algorithms for computer vision tasks. Mahotas is built on the NumPy library and is proven to be efficient for many image-processing tasks.

Our primary library for image processing is going to be OpenCV. However, we are going to use Mahotas for specific use cases and will use it to complement OpenCV.

Our approach throughout the book will leverage the strengths of each image-processing library.

TensorFlow

TensorFlow is an open-source library for developing artificial intelligence applications based on deep learning. Developers can use TensorFlow to train neural networks for a wide range of use cases such as image recognition and natural language processing.

TensorFlow has a wide range of features, which makes it one of the best frameworks for training neural networks. From creating small, optimized models for mobile applications to large industry-size models, TensorFlow can be used to train models of any size. It also provides several visualization tools to help developers monitor and evaluate their models as they train. Additionally, TensorFlow offers an adaptable architecture, which means users can train models on a variety of platforms such as CPUs or GPUs.

Did You Know? The ChatGPT model was created using TensorFlow. A specific variant of TensorFlow, that is, TensorFlow mesh was used to train this model. Training data consisting of hundreds of GB or several TB is estimated to be used for training. The number of model parameters is not disclosed but is rumored to be around 175 million.

Google has developed **TPUs**, which stands for **Tensor Processing Units**. These are custom-designed integrated circuits designed specifically for machine learning tasks. TPUs are specifically designed to optimize matrix operations, can handle more data in parallel due to higher memory, and consume lower power compared to other chips. The chip is designed to work with TensorFlow, and TensorFlow now includes specific functions to take advantage of TPUs. By using TensorFlow with this hardware, users can significantly improve neural network training times and inference speed for the models.

Try it Out: You can use Google Cloud, a free notebook offered by Google, to experiment with and train neural network models on TPU.

Keras

Keras is an easy-to-use and modular library that helps users to create and experiment with neural networks quickly. Keras is a high-level neural network API, which means users do not have to write complex neural network codes from scratch and can use pre-coded building blocks such as layers and activation functions for their model development.

Keras was initially developed as a standalone library for neural networks. However,

Google acquired Keras in 2015 and, since then, Keras has been integrated into the TensorFlow framework.

While this book focuses primarily on image processing and OpenCV-based approaches, there is a case to be made that neural networks are an important part of the domain, and there is a dedicated chapter to neural networks where we train our very own neural network using TensorFlow and Keras.

Dlib

Dlib is a C++ library containing various applications for computer vision or natural language processing tasks. Dlib provides capabilities for various tasks such as text classification and Support Vector Machines. However, for the scope of this book, we will keep it limited to the computer vision part of the library.

Dlib is widely used in computer vision applications for facial recognition tasks. Dlib's face recognition models are considered as one of the most reliable models for face detection and recognition. Dlib models have been able to demonstrate high accuracy for these applications and were even able to successfully identify and detect faces from challenging video streams.

Dlib 68 face point detector is a popular model for plotting facial landmark points in images and videos. The pre-trained model can detect 68 key points, such as nose, ear, and so on, on the face, which the users can use for face-related computer vision projects.

Environment Setup

Having covered the fundamentals and the essential libraries needed for computer vision, we can proceed with setting up our own customized computer vision environment to execute our codes.

The major steps can be broken down as follows:

1. Installing Python
2. Package Managers (Pip and Conda)
3. OpenCV and supporting libraries
4. Downloading an IDE
5. Testing our environment

Installing Python

The first step will be to download the latest version of Python.

Depending on the operating system, the following steps can be taken to install Python. We will be using the latest release of Python, which is 3.11.2, as of April 2023.

Installing Python on Windows

We will be using the official Python installer to install Python on our Windows systems.

Here are the steps:

Step 1: The Python installer can be downloaded from the official Python website. (https://www.python.org/downloads).

You can download the version that you want depending on your operating system (32-bit or 64-bit). Download the installer to your system by clicking the appropriate link.

Once the download is complete, proceed to launch the installer and begin installing Python on your system.

Step 2: The installer would look like this:

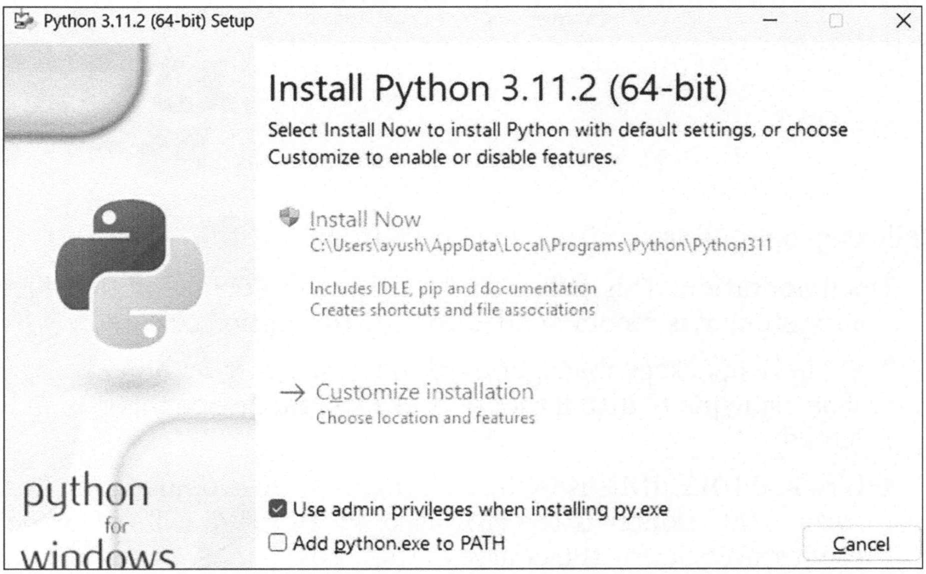

Figure 1.2: *Start menu of the Python Installer*

The **Install Now** option will download Python with all the default features. We will use custom installation to choose the features according to our requirements.

The **Use admin privileges when installing the py.exe** option will be pre-selected, and we will keep it like this.

We will select **Add python.exe to the PATH** option. This will allow Python to run directly through the command line.

Step 3: Selecting the **custom installation** option will lead us to the **Option Features** screen as shown in *Figure* 1.3 (You could skip this step if you selected the default **Install Now** option in the earlier step.):

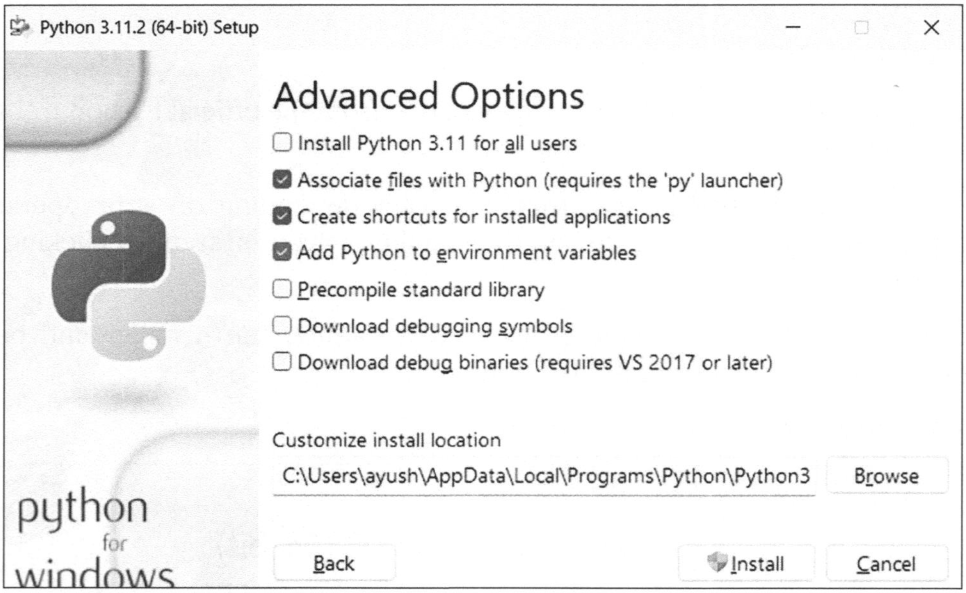

***Figure 1.3**: Advanced Options in the Python Installer*

The following options are available to choose from:

- **Documentation**: This will install the Python documentation files into your system. It is recommended to keep this option selected.
- **Pip**: Pip is a package manager used to install other Python packages. We will be using pip to install a lot of packages, and hence this option will be selected.
- **tcl/tk and IDLE**: IDLE is Python's Integrated Development and Learning Environment. Tkinter is the GUI used by IDLE. We will not be needing these features during the course of this book.
- **Python test suite**: Test Suite to test Python's functionality. We will keep

this checked.

- **py launcher**: Makes it easier to start Python. We will keep this checked.
- **For all users**: We will keep it checked so all users can access Python.

Step 4: We are led to the advanced options screen by clicking **`Next`**. Select the options according to your requirements:

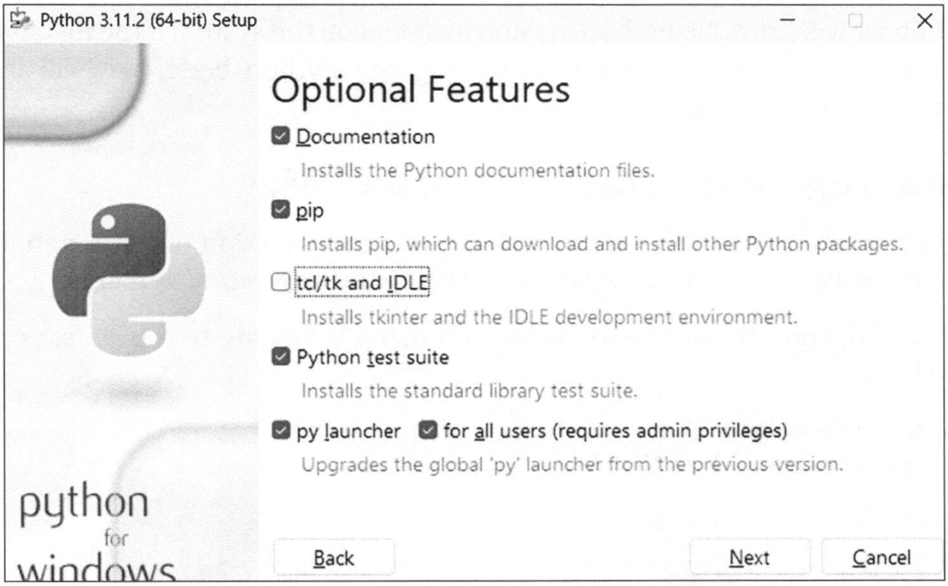

***Figure 1.4**: Optional Features in the Python Installer*

- **Install for all users**: Install Python for all users if there are multiple users on the system.
- **Associate files with Python**: Associate all Python files with this launcher. Recommended to select this option.
- **Create shortcuts for installed applications**: Enables shortcuts for installed applications.
- **Add Python to environment variable**: Recommended as this will enable us to launch Python directly.
- **Precompile standard library**: Compiling the Python standard library modules into bytecode files. Not needed.
- **Download debugging symbols**: Download additional files for debugging. Not needed.
- **Download debug binaries**: Downloads executables files that have been debugged. Not needed.

Add the path where you want to install Python and click **`Next`**.

Step 5: Python will be installed, and a **`Setup was Successful`** message will be displayed. We can verify if Python was installed properly or not now.

Go to the start menu and open the command prompt. In the command prompt, enter the following line:

```
'python -version'
```

The output will print the Python version installed on the system if the installation was successful. Now we can start writing the Python code. We will install additional dependencies before that.

Installing Python on Ubuntu and Mac

Both Ubuntu and macOS come with a pre-installed version of Python, but the specific version may vary depending on the operating system version.

For Ubuntu, you can use the following command to update to the latest version of Python:

```
sudo apt-get update
sudo apt-get install python3
```

For macOS, you can use Homebrew:

```
brew update
brew install python
```

Package Manager

A package manager will help you manage and install Python packages easily. All the libraries we discussed earlier can be installed easily using a package manager.

The most common package manager for Python is Pip. Pip allows users to install or upgrade packages from the PyPI (Python Package Index). It is a command-line tool that comes with Python (Remember, we already installed Pip during our Python installation.). Pip also allows us to create virtual environments for our applications as well.

Another widely used package manager is Conda. It is a cross-platform package manager and can be used to install packages from the Anaconda distribution. Conda supports packages from other sources as well.

For now, we will be using Pip to install most of our packages. Pip already comes with Python, so we don't need to install it separately. You can verify your pip installation by the following command in the command prompt:

```
pip -version
```

Installing libraries

We will first install the necessary libraries that we discussed in the previous section to help us with our computer vision applications.

First, we will install the NumPy library:

```
pip install numpy
```

Followed by the SciPy library:

```
pip install Scipy
```

Next, we will install the Matplotlib to help with our visualization use cases:

```
pip install matplotlib
```

Then, we will install the Scikit-Learn and Scikit-Image libraries:

```
pip install scikit-learn

pip install scikit-image
```

Installing Mahotas

To install Mahotas, launch the command prompt and type the following command:

```
pip install mahotas
```

Installing OpenCV

The next step is to install the OpenCV library. We can use Pip to install all the libraries we need for our computer vision journey.

To install OpenCV, launch the command prompt or Terminal and type the following command:

```
pip install opencv-python
```

This will install the latest version of `opencv` along with all the dependencies required to run the library.

To install a specific version of the OpenCV library, the following command can be used:

```
pip install opencv-python==<version_number>
```

OpenCV-**contrib** is an extended version of the OpenCV library. It contains additional algorithms and not all the features in this library are open source. It can be installed by the following command:

```
pip install opencv-contrib-python
```

Verifying our installation

Once the installation has been completed, we can verify all the libraries by importing them in Python. To do that, open the command prompt or terminal and type Python to enter the Python mode.

Once inside the Python mode, import the libraries by using the following command and print their respective version numbers:

```
import cv2
import numpy as np
import scipy
import matplotlib
import mahotas
import sklearn
import skimage

print(cv2.__version__)
print(np.__version__)
print(scipy.__version__)
print(matplotlib.__version__)
print(mahotas.__version__)
print(sklearn.__version__)
print(skimage.__version__)
```

The output will be the version number of all the necessary libraries installed previously.

IDE

IDE stands for Integrated Development Environment. It is software that helps in the development of applications by providing necessary tools such as an editor, debugger, compiler, and more.

While the preferred IDE is subjective and varies depending on the use cases, for this course, we will be using Spyder. However, there are various other options available for you to use such as PyCharm or Jupyter Notebooks. Feel free to use any other IDE according to your personal preferences.

We can use pip to install Spyder:

```
pip install spyder
```

Spyder can be launched by typing `spyder` in the command prompt/terminal.

Documentation

The documentation is an essential tool to refer to when searching for algorithms or codes while using the OpenCV library. The documentation provides detailed information about the library and all the tutorials with their respective codes can be found in the OpenCV official documentation.

The documentation is available online and can be accessed by visiting the official website at https://docs.opencv.org.

This brings us to the end of *Chapter 1* where we have familiarized ourselves with the fundamental concepts of computer vision and have set up a suitable environment to begin our exploration of codes. Now that we have a better understanding of the fundamentals of computer vision, we can explore its diverse applications and begin creating innovative solutions.

I would like to leave you with a final thought: *What do you think are the best uses of computer vision?* As readers, we all have unique perspectives and experiences that can lead to innovative solutions using this technology. By learning more about computer vision technology in the following chapters, you can equip yourself with the knowledge and skills needed to be a part of the exciting advancements in this field.

Conclusion

Computer vision aims to provide machines with the ability to recognize and analyze images and videos, just like humans do. Computer vision has a wide array of applications in various sectors such as healthcare, automotive, and manufacturing.

Python is a popular language for computer vision tasks due to its ease of use and versatility. OpenCV is an open-source library that has become one of the most comprehensively used libraries for computer vision.

Numpy is a Python library used for numerical computations that enables the use of large multidimensional arrays. Matplotlib is a widely used library for data visualization and data analysis, while TensorFlow is an open-source library for developing deep learning-based artificial intelligence applications.

The OpenCV documentation provides detailed information about the library, and all the tutorials with their respective codes can be found in the OpenCV official documentation.

In the next chapter, we will delve into the fundamentals of images. We will explore the basics of images in detail and discuss pixels in an image. Following that, we will learn how to read, write, and display images using OpenCV. The book will then progress to cover topics like drawing shapes on images using OpenCV, including rectangles, circles, and other basic shapes.

Test Your Understanding

1. Which of the following is NOT a computer vision application?
   A. Object detection
   B. Image classification
   C. Face recognition
   D. Sentiment analysis
2. NumPy is a Python Library for:
   A. Computer Vision
   B. Numerical Computing
   C. Natural Language Processing
   D. Data visualization

3. What can the Matplotlib library be used for?
   A. Data visualization
   B. Numerical Computing
   C. Machine Learning Algorithms
   D. Data augmentation
4. What data type is commonly used to represent images in OpenCV?
   A. List
   B. Mat
   C. Dictionary
   D. String
5. What is NumPy broadcasting?
   A. A way to perform operations on arrays with different shapes
   B. A way to sort elements in a NumPy array
   C. A way to reshape a NumPy array
   D. A way to randomly generate specific-sized NumPy arrays

CHAPTER 2
Getting Started with Images

In this chapter, we will cover the fundamental concepts of images and basic operations. We will start by providing a clear definition of image basics such as pixels. Next, we will delve into an explanation of how to read, display, and save images using the OpenCV library. We will then move on to the practical task of drawing shapes on images using OpenCV, with an emphasis on topics such as rectangles, circles, and other basic shapes.

Structure

In this chapter, we will discuss the following topics:

- Introduction to images and pixels
- Reading, displaying, and writing images
    - Imread
    - Imshow
    - Imwrite
    - Waitkey
- Manipulating images with pixels
    - Accessing individual pixels
    - Accessing a region of interest (ROI)
- Drawing in OpenCV
    - Line
    - Rectangle
    - Circle
    - Text

Introduction to images and pixels

What is an image? In non-technical terms, an image refers to a visual representation of a scene, object, or person, that enables us to better understand the world around us. In the digital context, an image is a multidimensional array of pixels.

Pixels are the building blocks of images. A pixel is the smallest unit of a digital image, containing information about its color and position. When multiple pixels come together in a two-dimensional grid, they form a complete image. Pixels in a digital image are arranged in a grid pattern to create the overall image. Each pixel contains specific color information, and together they form the complete image.

Pixels are commonly used to represent grayscale or color images. Grayscale images are typically represented as a 2D grid of pixels, while colored images are often represented as a multi-dimensional matrix. In a grayscale image, each pixel is assigned a value between 0 and 255, representing the intensity of the image at that point. A value of 0 indicates no intensity, resulting in a black pixel, while a value of 255 represents maximum intensity, resulting in a pure white pixel.

In color images, each pixel is represented by a combination of three or four values, with the most common color space being the RGB color space. In this space, three values representing the intensity of the red, green, and blue color channels are used to represent a single pixel. Each value ranges from 0 to 255 and represents the amount of each color that is present in the pixel. A typical RGB pixel can be represented in the format (red, green, blue).

For instance, a color with (0,0,0) values represents black since all the colors have 0 intensity, while (255,255,255) represents a white image because all colors have their maximum values.

Let's look at a few more examples of how colors are represented in the RGB color space:

- (255,0,0) produces a pure red color since red is at its maximum while green and blue are at 0.
- (0,255,0) produces a pure green color.
- (0,0,255) produces a pure blue color.
- (255,255,0) produces yellow since it is a combination of red and green.
- (128,128,128) represents a grey color.

PPI, or Pixels per Inch, represents the number of pixels present in a single inch of a digital image. A higher PPI means that there are more pixels per inch, resulting in a smoother and more detailed image. Conversely, a lower PPI means that pixels are larger and there are fewer of them per inch, resulting in a less detailed and less sharp image.

Resolution is a term used to describe the total number of pixels that make up an image. The higher the resolution, the more pixels there are, resulting in a more detailed and high-quality image. Resolution is typically measured in **pixels per inch** (**PPI**) or **dots per inch** (**DPI**). When an image has a lower resolution, it means there are fewer pixels and therefore, the image has less detail.

Aspect ratio refers to the proportional relationship between the width and height of an image, which determines the image's overall shape. It is typically expressed as two numbers separated by a colon (for example, 4:3 or 16:9) that represent the width and height of the image or screen. For instance, an image with an aspect ratio of 4:3 would have a width that is 4 units long for every 3 units of height. The aspect ratio is used to ensure that the image fits the display size correctly when displaying images on different devices.

Did you know? The number of pixels in digital images has been increasing rapidly over the years. The first commercially available digital camera, the Dycam Model 1, had a resolution of just 0.01 megapixels, while today's high-end cameras can capture images with resolutions of 100 megapixels or more.

Loading and displaying images

It's time to start working with images! In this book, you'll get hands-on experience as we guide you through the process of exploring and manipulating images. Please be sure to implement the code examples yourself as we move forward, as this will help solidify your understanding of the concepts we'll be covering.

Imread()

To get started with image processing in OpenCV, we'll need to use the imread() function. This function enables us to load images into our programs:

```
cv2.imread(path, flag=cv2.IMREAD_COLOR)
```

Parameters:

- `path`: This is a string which represents the path of the image to be read. It can be an absolute or passive path.
- `flag`: This is an optional parameter. It specifies how the image can be read. has a large number of options but we will be needing only a few of those.
- `cv2.IMREAD_COLOR (1)`: This loads the image in BGR format. It is the default format for the function.
- `cv2.IMREAD_GRAYSCALE (0)`: This loads the image in grayscale.
- `cv2.IMREAD_UNCHANGED (-1)`: This loads the image in its original format, generally used to include the alpha channel.

The integers mentioned here indicate that instead of specifying the full flag name when using the `imread` function, you can simply pass an integer value corresponding to the desired flag:

```
cv2.imread(path, 0)
```

This will load the image in grayscale format.

Imshow

To display an image, we will be using the `imshow` command:

```
cv2.imshow(winname, mat)
```

Parameters:

- `Winname`: This represents the name of the window that the image is displayed in.
- `Mat`: This represents the NumPy array of the image we want to display.

Imwrite

Imwrite is to save images to our system.

```
cv2.imwrite(filename, img, params=None)
```

Parameters:

- **Filename**: A string representing the path of the image to be saved. This can be an absolute or a relative path.
- **Img**: This represents the NumPy array of the image we want to write.
- **Params**: This is an optional parameter that specifies formatting and compression parameters for the image file. For now, the default value of `None` is acceptable.

Example code:

In this exercise, we will be loading an image and displaying the image using the codes we learnt earlier:

```
import cv2

# Using imread to read out image
img = cv2.imread("Pictures/dog.jpg")

# Print the shape of the image
print(img.shape)

# Displaying the image
cv2.imshow("Dog Image", img)

# Wait until a key is pressed
cv2.waitKey(0)

# Close all Windows
cv2.destroyAllWindows()
```

You can use any image for this if you want. The following image can be downloaded from the GitHub repository:

Figure 2.1: *Image to execute imread and imshow codes*

The image should be displayed and the shape of the image is printed.

You might have seen a few new commands in the preceding code.

WaitKey

WaitKey is a function used in OpenCV programs to allow users to display a window for a specific amount of time or until the user presses a key. Without `waitKey`, the image or video would close instantly before the user had time to view it.

It takes only an integer argument, which is the number of milliseconds the window stays open. If the argument given is 0 or not given at all, the function waits for a key press before closing the window.

DestroyAllWindows

DestroyAllWindows is a simple command that will close all the windows that were opened by OpenCV during the execution of our code. This does not take any parameters.

We have successfully run our first OpenCV code and can now read and display images.

Try it out: Try to write the preceding image to your disc now with a different path.

Manipulating images with pixels

In the previous section, we covered how to load and display an image. Now, we can move on to discussing image manipulation techniques and accessing specific points within the image.

Images are stored as NumPy arrays in Python, which means elements of an image can be indexed the same as NumPy arrays. Image indexing allows us to manipulate individual pixels or a certain region of pixels in an image.

Note to remember - Python is a zero-indexed language, which means that the index of the first element in a sequence is 0, not 1.

For example, let's take a 2D image matrix such as this:

3	4	8	1	0	2	7
0	8	7	9	96	4	7

9	6	13	5	7	8	9
7	4	3	5	17	8	9
8	15	4	14	5	6	7
8	7	1	4	2	25	8
9	66	7	5	7	9	0

***Figure 2.2**: 2D Matrix representing an image*

The preceding figure is a 7*7 image matrix.

To access individual elements of an array, the first index specifies the word and the second index is the column of the element.

We can use indexing [0, 0] to access the top-leftmost element of the array, and [6, 6] to access the bottom-right element.

Similarly, let's say we need to find the index of element 13 in the array. What do you think it would be? The answer is [2, 2]. And what about the index of element 14? The answer is [4, 3].

We can move forward now and start manipulating and accessing pixels in images using OpenCV.

Accessing individual pixels

To access a particular pixel of an image, we can use the similar img[row, col] indexing. Accessing a pixel value using this will return a NumPy array with the pixel value in it:

```
pix = img[5,7]
```

This command will assign the pixel's value in row 5 in column 10 to the pix array.

As discussed earlier, if the image is grayscale, it will return a single value. However, if it is an RGB image, we will get three values, with each value corresponding to its respective color channel.

For an RGB image, the preceding code line will return an array containing three values, such as array([32, 43, 3], dtype=uint8). Whereas for a grayscale image, it will simply return a single value, which could be, for example, 30.

We can also modify the values of pixels using indexing. We can assign a value to a particular pixel as follows:

```
img[5,7] = 255
```

If **img** is a grayscale image, this will assign the pixel a value of 255. If the image **img** is in the BGR format, then all three color channel values will be set to 255.

If we want to set a specific value in an RGB image, we can use the color code of that particular color:

```
img[5,7] = [0,255,0]
```

This will set the green channel value to 255 and the other two channels to 0, resulting in a pure green pixel.

Let's try manipulating pixels in our images:

```
import cv2

# Load an image in grayscale mode
img = cv2.imread('ss.jpg')

# Get the pixel value at x=75, y=25
pixel_value = img[25, 75]

#Print this value
print(pixel_value)

#Manipulate value of this pixel
img[25, 75] = 0

#Rechecking value
print(pixel_value)
```

The value has been updated to 0 indicating that our pixel manipulation has been successful.

Next, let's try another code to manipulate whole column values:

```
import cv2

# Load an image
img = cv2.imread('12.jpg')

# Access and manipulate the pixels
for i in range(img.shape[0]):
```

```
        for j in range(img.shape[1]):

            # Checking for every tenth column
            if j % 10 == 0:
                # Setting this value to 0
                img[i,j] = [0,0,0]

# Display our result
cv2.imshow('Person', img)

cv2.waitKey(0)
cv2.destroyAllWindows()
```

Accessing a region of interest (ROI)

We will now discuss how to manipulate whole regions of an image by defining a **Region of Interest** (**ROI**) using indexing. It is often necessary to be able to manipulate a specific region of an image instead of a single pixel or the full image.

To create a rectangular ROI, we can use x and y coordinates, along with `w` and `h` for `width` and `height`. Using this method, we can perform any operation on the defined ROI.

To define an ROI, we can use the following command:

```
roi = img[y:y+h, x:x+w]
```

This will create an ROI by slicing the necessary points of the image into that variable:

```
import cv2

# Load image
img = cv2.imread('ss.jpg')

# Define index values
x=50
y=60
w=75
h=75

# Extract ROI from the image
roi = img[y:y+h,x:x+w]
```

```
# Print shape of the extracted ROI
print(roi.shape)

# Assigning a colour to a different ROI
img[100:150,150:200] = (255,255,0)

# Display the image with the ROI and rectangle
cv2.imshow('Extracted ROI rectangle', roi)
cv2.imshow('Image with ROI colour', img)
cv2.waitKey(0)
cv2.destroyAllWindows()
```

The command carries out two operations on regions of interest. First, a rectangular portion of the image is extracted and saved in a variable. This can be used if we want to use indexing to extract a section from an image. The ROI region in our primary image is given a color in the second section.

Drawing in OpenCV

In this section, we'll learn how to draw shapes with OpenCV. We can design a wide range of shapes using OpenCV, including lines, circles, rectangles, and polygons, and we can customize their size and color. Using OpenCV, text can be added to photos as well. Shapes can be used for several things, including annotating photographs and emphasizing particular areas of them.

We will begin by creating a blank canvas on which we can draw various shapes. Alternatively, you can also load an image and draw the shapes on it.

To create a canvas for drawing shapes, we can use NumPy to create a NumPy array. Using various methods, we can then draw on this NumPy canvas:

```
canvas = np.zeros((600, 600, 3), dtype=np.uint8)
```

We use the **np.zeros** function to create our canvas. It is a NumPy function that creates a NumPy array of zeros with a specific shape and data type. In this case, we create an array of shapes (600,500,3) with the 'np.uint8' data type. This data type corresponds to an 8-bit unsigned integer with a range of values ranging from 0 to 255.

Now that we have our canvas, we can start drawing shapes on them. The first shape that we discuss is the line.

Line

We create lines on our images using the **`cv2.line`** command. This command offers multiple parameters, allowing us to customize lines to suit our specific needs and requirements.

Parameters:

- **Img**: The image where the line will be drawn.
- **Pt1**: The starting coordinates of the line. This will be in tuple (x,y) format.
- **Pt2**: End coordinates of the line. This will be in tuple (x,y) format.
- **Color**: The color of the line. This will be in tuple (B, G, R) format.
- **Thickness**: The thickness of the line in pixels. This is an optional argument with a default value of 1.
- **lineType**: The type of the line. We will not be using this parameter and can leave it to the default value.
- **Shift**: Number of fractional bits in the line coordinates. We will not be using this parameter and can leave it to the default value of 0.

```
cv2.line(img, pt1, pt2, color, thickness=1, lineType = cv2.
LINE_8, shift = 0)
```

Let us try creating a few lines now:

```
import numpy as np
import cv2
# Create a black canvas
canvas = np.zeros((600, 500, 3), dtype=np.uint8)

# Define the vertices of the triangle
p1 = (250, 100)
p2 = (100, 400)
p3 = (400, 400)

# Draw the lines using cv2.line()
cv2.line(canvas, p1, p2, (0, 255, 0), 1)
cv2.line(canvas, p3, p1, (255, 0, 0), 3)
cv2.line(canvas, p2, p3, (255, 255, 255), 10)

# Display the image
cv2.imshow("Triangle", canvas)
cv2.waitKey(0)
cv2.destroyAllWindows()
```

In the preceding code snippet, we create a triangle using three connecting lines. We first define the coordinates of the lines and then specify different colors and thicknesses for each line.

The first line is from point P1 to P2 with green color and thickness of 1 px. Similarly, line 2 is from point P3 to P1 with a blue color and thickness of 3 px and line 3 goes from point P2 to P3 with white color and thickness of 10 px:

***Figure 2.3**: Output: 3 lines with different parameters*

Rectangle

Drawing rectangles is similar to drawing a line in OpenCV. We can use the **`cv2.rectangle`** command to create rectangles in OpenCV:

```
Cv2.rectangle(img, pt1, pt2, color, thickness=1, lineType=cv2.
LINE_8, shift=0)
```

Parameters:

- **Img**: The image where the line will be drawn.
- **Pt1**: The top left corner point of the rectangle. This will be in tuple (x,y) format.
- **Pt2**: The bottom right point of the rectangle. This will be in tuple (x,y) format.
- **Color**: The color of the rectangle being drawn. This will be in tuple (B, G, R) format.
- **Thickness**: The thickness of the rectangle border in pixels. This is an optional argument with a default value of 1. If the thickness of the rectangle is negative, it will fill the rectangle.

- **lineType**: The type of the line. We will not be using this parameter and can leave it to the default value.
- **Shift**: Number of fractional bits in the line coordinates. We will not be using this parameter and can leave it to the default value of 0.

Now, based on the preceding explanation, let's try to create this image:

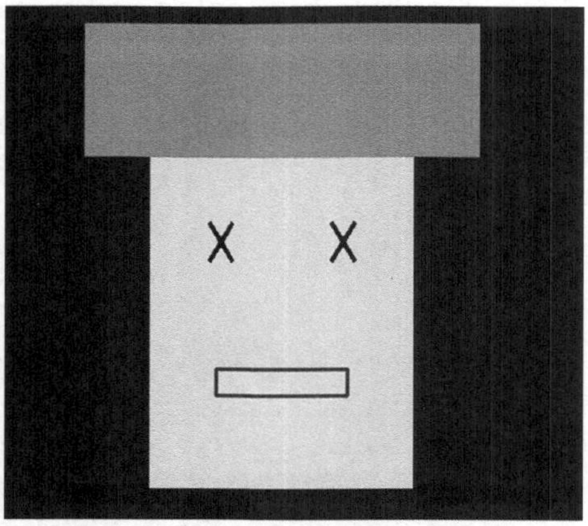

***Figure 2.4**: Recreating this image using OpenCV*

The code is as follows if you need any help:

```
import numpy as np
import cv2

# Create a black image
img = np.zeros((600, 500, 3), dtype=np.uint8)

# Draw the figure using rectangles and lines
# Face
cv2.rectangle(img, (150, 150), (350, 400), (242, 199, 155),
thickness=-1)

# Cap
cv2.rectangle(img, (100, 50), (400, 150), (198, 131, 56), thick-
ness=-1)

# Mouth
cv2.rectangle(img, (200, 310), (300, 330), (128, 0, 128), thick-
ness=2)

# Draw the eyes on the face as X shapes
cv2.line(img, (195, 200), (212, 228), (0, 0, 0), thickness=2)
```

```
cv2.line(img, (212, 200), (195, 228), (0, 0, 0), thickness=2)
cv2.line(img, (288, 200), (305, 228), (0, 0, 0), thickness=2)
cv2.line(img, (305, 200), (288, 228), (0, 0, 0), thickness=2)

# Display the image
cv2.imshow("Robo", img)
cv2.waitKey(0)
cv2.destroyAllWindows()
```

We recreate the preceding image by using three rectangles and four lines. Rectangles are used to create the mouth cap and face of the robot and the lines are used to create his eyes. We define three rectangles and set the thickness parameter to -1 to fill the cap and face colors. Then we use four lines to draw the eyes of the robot.

Circle

The **`cv2.circle()`** function is used to draw a circle on an image:

```
Cv2.circle(img, center, radius, color, thickness=1, lineType =
cv2.LINE_8, shift=0)
```

Parameters:

- **Img**: The image where the line will be drawn.
- **Center**: The cent point of the circle. This will be in tuple (x,y) format.
- **Radius**: Radius of the circle
- **Color**: The color of the circle. This will be in tuple (B, G, R) format.
- **Thickness**: The thickness of the circle border in pixels. This is an optional argument with a default value of 1. If the thickness of the rectangle is negative, it will fill the circle.
- **lineType**: The type of the line. We will not be using this parameter and can leave it to the default value.
- **Shift**: Number of fractional bits in the line coordinates. We will not be using this parameter and can leave it to the default value of 0.

Let's try creating a few circles ourselves:

```
Import numpy as np
import cv2

# Create an empty canvas
canvas = np.zeros((500, 500, 3), dtype=np.uint8)
```

```
# Define the center point
center = (250, 250)

# Define the radii of the circles
radius1 = 50
radius2 = 100
radius3 = 150

# Define the colors of the circles
color1 = (0, 0, 255)
color2 = (255, 0, 0)
color3 = (0, 255, 0)

# Define the thickness of the circles
thickness1 = -1
thickness2 = 2
thickness3 = 10

# Draw the circles on the canvas
cv2.circle(canvas, center, radius1, color1, thickness1)
cv2.circle(canvas, center, radius2, color2, thickness2)
cv2.circle(canvas, center, radius3, color3, thickness3)

# Display the image
cv2.imshow("Image", canvas)
cv2.waitKey(0)
cv2.destroyAllWindows()
```

By implementing the preceding code, we create three circles with varying colors and thickness, while the center circle is filled with color.

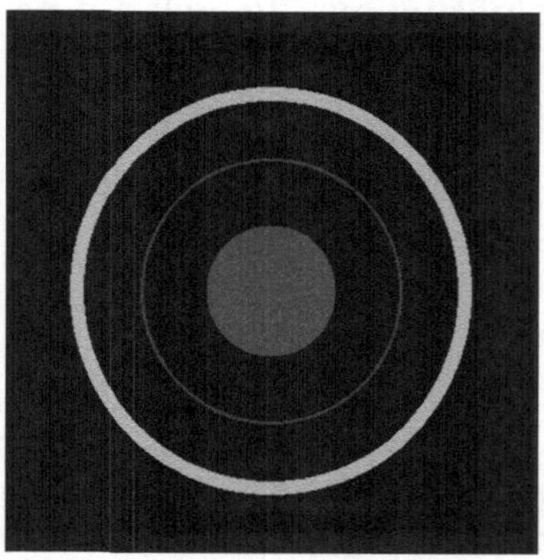

***Figure 2.5**: Output: 3 circles with different parameters*

Text

We use the function **cv2.putText()** to add text to images:

```
Cv2.putText(img, text, org, fontFace='cv2.FONT_HERSHEY_SIMPLEX',
fontScale=0, color=(0,0,0), thickness=1, lineType='cv2.LINE_AA',
bottomLeftOrigin=False)
```

Parameters:

- **Img**: The image where the line will be drawn.
- **Text**: The text string to be drawn.
- **org**: The coordinates of the bottom-left corner of the text.
- **fontFace**: The font type of the text. This is an optional argument with a default value of **cv2.FONT_HERSHEY_SIMPLEX**.
- **fontScale**: Font scale factor that is multiplied by the font-specific base size. This is an optional argument with a default value of 1.
- **Color**: The color of the text. This will be in tuple (B, G, R) format. This is an optional argument with a default value of (0,0,0).
- **Thickness**: The thickness of the lines in the text. This is an optional argument with a default value of 1. If the thickness is negative, it will fill the text.
- **lineType**: The type of the line. We will not be using this parameter and can leave it to the default value.
- **bottomLeftOrigin**: This is a flag that indicates the position of the text. This is an optional parameter, and the default value is **False** which will place the text at the top-left corner. **True** will put it at the bottom-left position.

```
import numpy as np
import cv2

# create a blank image
img = np.zeros((600, 500, 3), dtype=np.uint8)

# define the text to be displayed
text = "Hello World!"

# set the text color and position
color = (255, 0, 0)
pos = (50, 200)

# display the text using cv2.putText()
```

```
cv2.putText(img, text, pos, cv2.FONT_HERSHEY_SIMPLEX, 2, color, 3)

# display the image
cv2.imshow("Image with text", img)
cv2.waitKey(0)
cv2.destroyAllWindows()
```

***Figure 2.6**: Text output*

This brings us to the end of this chapter, where we have explored the fundamental concepts of images and basic operations using OpenCV. We have covered important topics such as pixels, reading and displaying images, and drawing shapes on images. With this foundational knowledge, we are now better equipped to dive deeper into image-processing techniques in the following chapters.

Conclusion

This chapter provided a solid introduction to the fundamental concepts of images and basic operations. We defined key concepts such as pixels and explained how to read, display, and save images using the OpenCV library. Additionally, we explored the practical task of drawing shapes on images, with a focus on basic shapes like rectangles and circles. This foundation will be invaluable for building more complex image-processing applications in the future.

In the next chapter, we will explore translation-based operations like rotation and resizing and show readers how to control the size and orientation of resulting images using OpenCV. We will then cover arithmetic operations on images, such as addition, subtraction, and division. Additionally, we will explore bitwise operations on images, including AND, OR, and XOR. The chapter will also provide an in-depth look at the channels of an image and the various color spaces that images can be represented in, such as RGB, grayscale, and HSV. Readers will learn how to work with these different color spaces to manipulate and enhance their images.

Points to remember

- An image can be represented as a collection of pixels ordered in a multidimensional array. Each element of the array corresponds to the value of a single pixel in the image.
- imread() reads an image file from the disk, while imshow() displays the image and imwrite() saves the image to the disk.
- Waitkey allows users to display a window for a specific amount of time or until the user presses a key.
- DestroyAllWindows() is used to close all the windows that were opened by OpenCV during the execution of our code.
- Python is a zero-indexed language, which means that the index of the first element in a sequence is 0, not 1.
- To access a particular pixel of an image, we can use img[row, col] indexing and img[y:y+h, x:x+w] indexing to access any ROI in an image.
- Cv2.line is used to draw lines in OpenCV while cv2.rectangle is used for rectangles and cv2.circle is used to draw circles.
- Cv2.puttext is used to draw text on our images.

Test your understanding

1. Whatis a pixel?
   A. The brightness of the image
   B. The smallest unit of an image
   C. A type of image format
   D. Measurement of the clarity of an image
2. Image resolution can be used to describe:
   A. The size of the image
   B. The amount of color in the image
   C. The amount of details in the image
   D. To measure the brightness of the image

3. With which OpenCV function is the waitKey() function generally used?

   A. imshow()

   B. imwrite()

   C. imread()

   D. cvtColor()

4. What is the value of the "thickness" parameter value for filling a rectangle with color while using cv2.rectangle()?

   A. 0

   B. -1

   C. 1

   D. FIll

5. What is the function to add text to images?

   A. cv2.text()

   B. cv2.putText()

   C. String str

   D. cv2.add()

CHAPTER 3

Image Processing Fundamentals

In this chapter, we will cover various operations in image processing, starting with translation-based operations such as rotation and resizing. Readers will learn how to rotate and resize images using OpenCV, as well as how to control the size and orientation of the resulting images. The chapter then covers arithmetic operations on images, such as addition, subtraction, and division. Continuing with the theme of image operations, the chapter covers bitwise operations on images, such as AND, OR, and XOR. Finally, the chapter concludes by discussing the channels of an image and various color spaces in which an image can be represented.

Structure

In this chapter, we will discuss the following topics:

- Geometric transformations on images
    - Image translation
    - Rotation
    - Scaling
    - Flipping
    - Shearing
    - Cropping
- Arithmetic operations on images
    - Addition
    - Subtraction
    - Multiplication
    - Division

- Bitwise operations on images
    - AND
    - OR
    - XOR
    - NOT
- Channels and color spaces

Geometric transformations

Image transformations enable us to modify an image in multiple ways. They play a crucial role in computer vision and allow us to alter the image size or orientation for various computer vision tasks. These operations are used extensively for computer vision tasks and will be a fundamental part of all our computer vision applications. These transformations are essential in computer vision applications such as object recognition, image segmentation, and facial recognition.

In technical terms, image processing involves transforming the coordinates of image points from one coordinate system to another. Using various transformation functions, it is possible to map pixel coordinates in the original image to new coordinates in the transformed image, resulting in different types of transformations.

As we move forward with this chapter, we will explore various image transformation techniques, including rotation, scaling, and more, beginning with image translation.

Image translation

Image translation is the process of shifting an image in horizontal and vertical directions. Using image translation we can move our image on the x and y axis by a specified amount.

To perform image translation, a translation matrix is applied to the image that maps the original coordinates to the new, shifted coordinates.

Image translation is a simple and effective technique that can be combined with other image processing techniques to achieve the desired outcome. It has various use cases, such as aligning two images together or stitching images in panoramic shots. Image translation is also commonly used to augment data when creating a dataset for training deep learning models.

Image translations can be performed by applying affine transformations to an input image. An affine transformation is a linear transformation applied to an image, which can alter its size and aspect while preserving the position and shape of the object. An important characteristic of affine transformations is that they preserve the parallelism of lines.

We use the **`cv2.warpAffine`** function in OpenCV to apply affine transformations:

```
cv2.warpAffine(src, M, dsize, dst, flags=INTER_LINEAR,
borderMode=BORDER_CONSTANT, borderValue=0)
```

Parameters:

src: The source image on which transformations will be applied.

M: The transformation matrix.

dsize: Size of the output image.

dst: **`dst`** is an optional output image that stores the result of transformation. The **`dst`** image must be of the same size and type as the input image src. If the **`dst`** image is not provided, the OpenCV function will create an output image of the same size and type as the input image and return it as the output.

Flags: It is an optional parameter that specifies the interpolation method to be used.

borderMode: This specifies how to handle the pixels that fall outside the image boundaries. It is a with default value as **`cv2.BORDER_CONSTANT`**.

borderValue: This is used only with **`cv2.BORDER_CONSTANT`** mode and specifies the constant value used to pad the image. It is an with default value as 0.

The code for image translation is as follows:

```
import cv2
import numpy as np

img = cv2.imread("input.jpg")

# Define the translation matrix
tx = 50   # x-direction
ty = 100  # y-direction
```

```
M = np.float32([[1, 0, tx], [0, 1, ty]])

# Apply the translation to the image
rows, cols, _ = img.shape
translated_img = cv2.warpAffine(img, M, (cols, rows))

cv2.imshow("Original Image", img)
cv2.imshow("Translated Image", translated_img)
cv2.waitKey(0)
cv2.destroyAllWindows()
```

The code produces the following output:

***Figure 3.1:** Image Translation Output*

Rotation

Image rotation is the process of rotating an image by an angle around its center point. It is a widely used operation in image processing and can be used in a variety of image processing applications.

There are two ways to perform image rotation, and while one method is sufficient, it is important to discuss both options for a comprehensive understanding of the topic.

The first is the cv2.rotate function for image rotation. The drawback of using this function is that it can only rotate the image by 90 degrees in a clockwise or anticlockwise direction. It does not allow us to choose an arbitrary angle to rotate the image. The **`cv2.rotate`** function can be implemented as:

cv2.rotate(src, rotateCode, dst)

Parameters:

src: The source image on which transformations will be applied.

rotateCode: This parameter specifies the direction and angle in which the image should be rotated. The possible values for **`rotateCode`** are:

- **cv2.ROTATE_90_CLOCKWISE:** Rotates the image 90 degrees in clockwise direction.
- **cv2.ROTATE_90_COUNTERCLOCKWISE**: Rotates the image 90 degrees in counter clockwise direction.
- **cv2.ROTATE_180**: Rotates the image by 180 degrees.

dst: **`dst`** is an optional output image that stores the result of transformation. The **`dst`** image must be of the same size and type as the input image **`src`**. If the **`dst`** image is not provided, the OpenCV function will create an output image of the same size and type as the input image and return it as the output.

We can rotate our image as follows by the following code:

```
import cv2

img = cv2.imread('image.jpg')

# Rotate clockwise by 90 degrees
rot_img_90cw = cv2.rotate(img, cv2.ROTATE_90_CLOCKWISE)

# Rotate counterclockwise by 90 degrees
rot_img_90ccw = cv2.rotate(img, cv2.ROTATE_90_COUNTERCLOCKWISE)

# Rotate by 180 degrees
rot_img_180 = cv2.rotate(img, cv2.ROTATE_180)

cv2.imshow('Original', img)
cv2.imshow('Rotated 90 CW', rot_img_90cw)
cv2.imshow('Rotated 90 CCW', rot_img_90ccw)
cv2.imshow('Rotated 180', rot_img_180)
cv2.waitKey(0)
cv2.destroyAllWindows()
```

The code produces the following output:

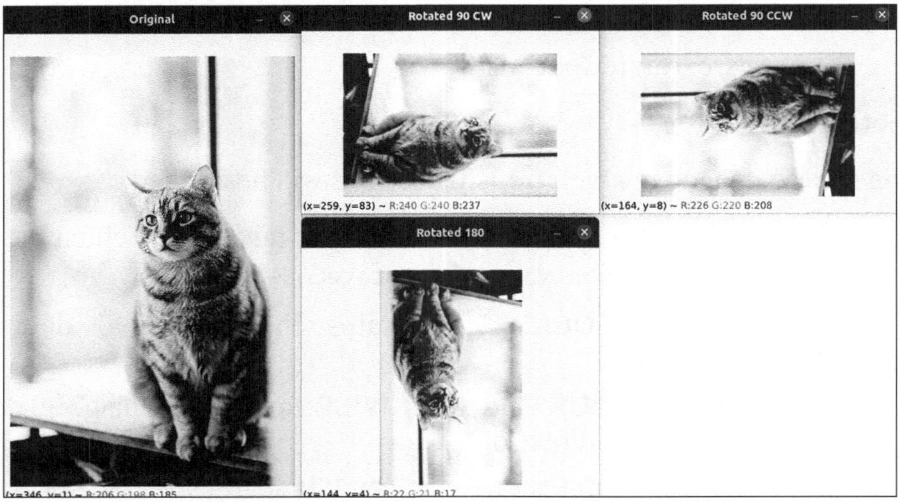

Figure 3.2: *Image Rotation Output*

Another method we use for image rotation is by using the **`cv2.warpAffine`** function discussed earlier. This method allows us to choose any arbitrary angle and the center point to rotate the image.

We use another function, **`cv2.getRotationMatrix2D,`** to generate the rotation matrix used with the **`cv2.warpAffine`** function. While creating a matrix for picture translation on our own is simple, it is helpful to use a dedicated function to create a matrix for rotation:

```
cv2.getRotationMatrix2D(center=None, angle, scale=1)
```

Parameters:

center: The center point(x,y) of the image rotation. The default value for is None. If a point is not specified, the function will use the center point of the image.

angle: The angle of rotation in degrees. Positive values indicate counter-clockwise direction, while negative values correspond to clockwise rotation.

scale: The scale parameters is used to scale the size of the image by a factor. The default value for in 1, which means the output image is the same as the size of the input image.

Let's try going through some code for rotation:

```
import cv2
import numpy as np
```

```
img = cv2.imread('111.png')
rows, cols = img.shape[:2]

# Get rotation matrices.
M1 = cv2.getRotationMatrix2D((100,100), 30, 1)

M2 = cv2.getRotationMatrix2D((cols/2,rows/2), 45, 2)

M3 = cv2.getRotationMatrix2D((cols/2,rows/2), -90, 1)

# Perform rotation
rotated1 = cv2.warpAffine(img, M1, (cols, rows))
rotated2 = cv2.warpAffine(img, M2, (cols, rows))
rotated3 = cv2.warpAffine(img, M3, (cols, rows))

cv2.imshow('Original Image', img)
cv2.imshow('Rotated Image 1', rotated1)
cv2.imshow('Rotated Image 2', rotated2)
cv2.imshow('Rotated Image 3', rotated3)
cv2.waitKey(0)
cv2.destroyAllWindows()
```

The code produces the following output:

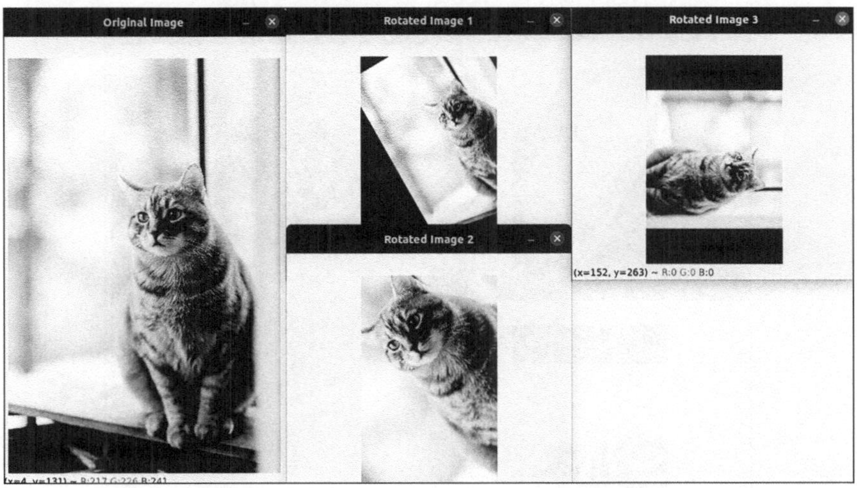

Figure 3.3: *Image Rotation Output*

The preceding code performs three rotations on the image. The initial rotation matrix M1 designates the image's center point as (100,100), meaning that the image will be rotated 30 degrees anticlockwise from this position. The second rotation rotates the image 45 degrees anticlockwise using the image's center point as the pivot. Since we set the scaling factor to 2, the image will double in size. In the final rotation, we assign a negative number to the angle to indicate that the rotation is 90 degrees clockwise.

Think about it. The code has a minor issue that needs to be addressed. Let's take a moment to consider if there are any improvements that can be made. Hint: Try printing sizes of the output images.

We have used the scaling factor of 2 for our image. Earlier, we discussed the importance of specifying the output image size in the **`warpAffine`** function. In this instance, we set the output picture size to match the size of the input image. To obtain our scaled image, we must replace these numbers with new ones.

We can update our code with the following lines:

```
#new values for the output
scale = 2
new_cols = int(cols * scale)
new_rows = int(rows * scale)

# Create output image with the new size
rotated2 = cv2.warpAffine(img, M2, (new_cols, new_rows))
```

The code produces the following output images with rotation:

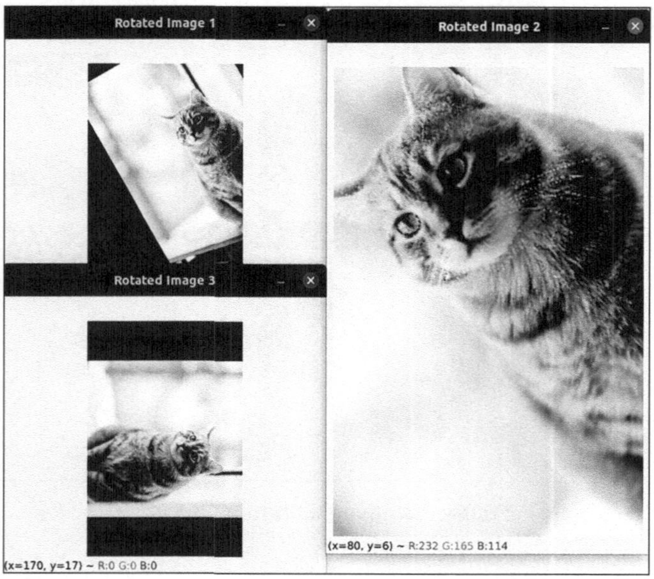

Figure 3.4: *Image Rotation Output with the updated size*

Scaling

Image scaling is a common task in image processing that allows us to resize images according to our requirements. When resizing an image, it is important to maintain the aspect ratio of the image to avoid producing a distorted image.

We use the `cv2.resize()` function to resize images using OpenCV:

```
cv2.resize(src, dst, dsize, fx=0, fy=0, interpolation=cv2.INTER_
LINEAR)
```

Parameters:

- **src:** The source image on which transformations will be applied.
- **dst: dst** is an optional output image that stores the result of transformation. The **dst** image must be of the same size and type as the input image **src**. If the **dst** image is not provided, the OpenCV function will create an output image of the same size and type as the input image and return it as the output.
- **dsize:** The size of the output image after resizing.
- **fx:** The scaling factor along the horizontal axis.
- **fy:** The scaling factor along the vertical axis.

If `dsize` is not specified, it will automatically be calculated using the scaling factors fx and fy.

dsize = (int(src.shape[1] * fx), int(src.shape[0] * fy)).

- **interpolation:** Interpolation refers to the technique used to estimate the new pixel values after applying geometric transformations. Following values can be used for this parameter:
  - **cv2.INTER_NEAREST:** nearest neighbor interpolation.
  - **cv2.INTER_LINEAR:** bilinear interpolation.
  - **cv2.INTER_CUBIC:** bicubic interpolation over 4×4 pixel neighborhood.
  - **cv2.INTER_AREA:** resampling using pixel area relation. It is the recommended interpolation method when shrinking an image.
  - **cv2.INTER_LANCZOS4:** Lanczos interpolation over 8x8 pixel neighborhood.

The default value is **`cv2.INTER_LINEAR`**:

```
import cv2
```

```
img = cv2.imread('input_image.jpg')

# Resize the image to half its size
resized_img = cv2.resize(img, (0,0), fx=0.5, fy=0.5)

# Resize the image to a specific width and height
resized_img = cv2.resize(img, (640, 480))

cv2.imshow('Original Image', img)
cv2.imshow('Resized Image', resized_img)
cv2.waitKey(0)
cv2.destroyAllWindows()
```

In the preceding code, we load an image and resize it in two ways. First, we shrink the image to half its original size using the scaling factors **fx** and **fy**, both set to 0.5 for both the horizontal and vertical values. In this case, the **dsize** parameter is 0 as it will be automatically calculated based on the **fx** and **fy** values.

Next, we resize the image by providing specific values for height and width, and, in this case, **fx** and **fy** are not needed as we have specified values for the **dsize** parameter.

Note: If you specify both 'fx' and 'fy' along with the 'dsize' parameter in the cv2. resize() function, the 'dsize' parameter will be ignored, and the output size will be calculated based on 'fx' and 'fy' scaling factors.

Image scaling can also be implemented using the **cv2.warpAffine** function:

```
import cv2
import numpy as np

img = cv2.imread('cat.jpg')

# Define the new size
new_size = (400, 400)

# Compute the scaling factors for x and y axis
sx = new_size[0]/img.shape[1]
sy = new_size[1]/img.shape[0]

# Define the transformation matrix
M = np.float32([[sx, 0, 0], [0, sy, 0]])
```

```
# Apply the affine transformation
resized_img = cv2.warpAffine(img, M, new_size)

cv2.imshow('Original Image', img)
cv2.imshow('Resized Image', resized_img)
cv2.waitKey(0)
cv2.destroyAllWindows()
```

The code produces the following output:

***Figure* 3.5:** *Image Resize Output*

Flipping

Image flipping is used to flip an image horizontally or vertically. We can use the cv2.flip function to implement image flipping:

```
cv2.flip(src, dst, flipCode=1)
```

Parameters:

- **src:** The source image to be flipped
- **dst:** Output Variable
- **flipCode:** A flag that specifies how to flip the array. The following values can be used with this parameter.
  - **'0':** Vertical flip. Image is flipped around the x-axis.
  - **'1':** Horizontal flip. Image is flipped around the y-axis
  - **'-1':** Image is flipped around both axes

The default value for is 1:

```
import cv2

img = cv2.imread('111.png')

# Flip the image horizontally
x_flip = cv2.flip(img, 1)

# Flip the image vertically
y_flip = cv2.flip(img, 0)

# Flip the image on both axes
xy_flip = cv2.flip(img, -1)

cv2.imshow('Original Image', img)
cv2.imshow('Horizontal flip', x_flip)
cv2.imshow('Vertical flip', y_flip)
cv2.imshow('Both axes', xy_flip)
cv2.waitKey(0)
cv2.destroyAllWindows()
```

The code produces the following output demonstrating image flipping:

Figure 3.6: *Image Flip Output*

Shearing

Image Shearing is a linear transformation that distorts an image along one of its axes. When an image is sheared along the x-axis, the pixels in the image are shifted horizontally. This causes the image to look skewed in the x direction. Similarly, when the image is sheared along the y-axis, the pixels in the image are shifted vertically, causing it to look skewed in the y direction. Parallel lines are not preserved in image shearing.

We will use the **`cv2.warpAffine`** function to implement image shearing:

```
import cv2
import numpy as np

img = cv2.imread("image.jpg")

# shearing parameters
shear_factor_x = 0.2
shear_factor_y = 0.3

# Obtain shearing matrices
M_x = np.array([[1, shear_factor_x, 0],
                [0, 1, 0]])
M_y = np.array([[1, 0, 0],
                [shear_factor_y, 1, 0]])

# Apply shearing transformations
rows, cols = img.shape[:2]
sheared_img_x = cv2.warpAffine(img, M_x, (cols + int(rows * shear_
factor_x), rows))
sheared_img_xy = cv2.warpAffine(sheared_img_x, M_y, (cols + in-
t(rows * shear_factor_x), rows + int(cols * shear_factor_y)))

cv2.imshow("Original Image", img)
cv2.imshow("Sheared Image (X axis)", sheared_img_x)
cv2.imshow("Sheared Image (X and Y axis)", sheared_img_xy)
cv2.waitKey(0)
cv2.destroyAllWindows()
```

The code produces the following image shearing output:

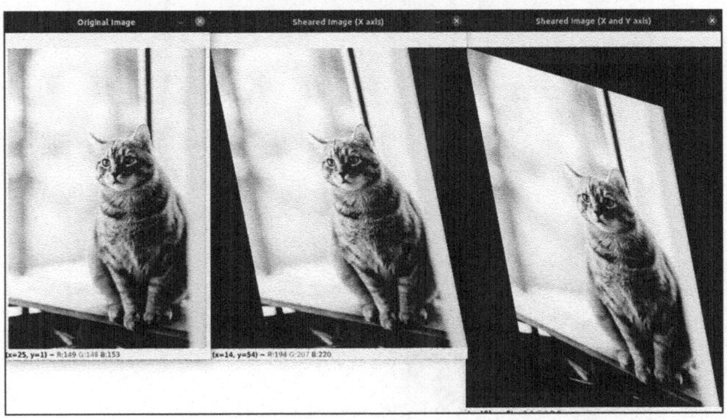

Figure 3.7: *Image Shearing Output*

Cropping

Image cropping is the process of selecting a rectangular portion of an image. Cropping can be considered a type of geometric transformation, where a section of the source image is removed to produce a new image. In the original image, a rectangular region of interest (ROI) is chosen, and only the pixels in that region are kept, with the remaining pixels being discarded.

Cropping an image in OpenCV can be achieved by using image slicing, as we discussed in the previous chapter. Since this has already been covered, we will not go into further detail. Here is a short code snippet for a quick review:

```
import cv2

img = cv2.imread("image.jpg")

# Define ROI coordinates
x1, y1 = 100, 100 # top-left corner
x2, y2 = 300, 400 # bottom-right corner

# Crop image
cropped_img = img[y1:y2, x1:x2]

cv2.imshow("Original Image", img)
cv2.imshow("Cropped Image", cropped_img)
cv2.waitKey(0)
cv2.destroyAllWindows()
```

The code produces the following output showing image cropping:

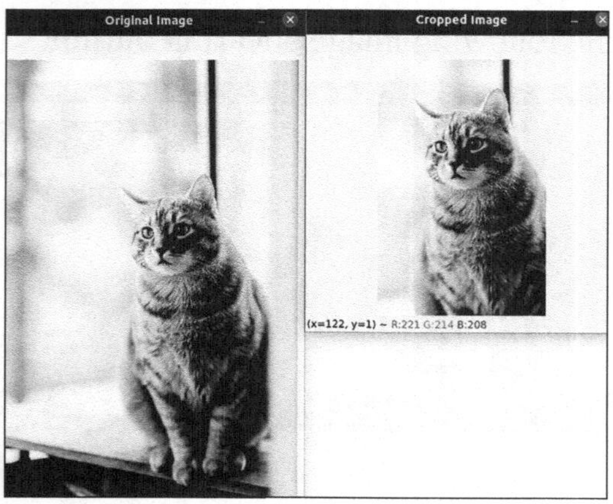

Figure 3.8: *Image Cropping Output*

Arithmetic Operations

Arithmetic operations are a fundamental concept in image processing. These operations involve performing basic mathematical operations on images to generate new images with different properties. These operations are performed on the pixel values and allow us to extract useful information from the images.

Arithmetic operations on images can be used for a variety of applications such as adjusting the brightness or contrast of an image. Another major use case of arithmetic operations is that they enable us to blend two or more images together.

There are several types of arithmetic operations that can be performed on images. Some of the basic arithmetic operations are addition, subtraction, multiplication, and division.

One of the major challenges in performing arithmetic operations on images is the pixel values falling outside the range of 0-255. This can occur due to reasons such as the addition or subtraction of a large value to an image and can lead to major issues such as information loss and image distortions.

Clipping is a technique used to address the issue of pixel values falling outside the valid range of 0-255. This involves setting any pixel value above 255 to 255 and any pixel value below 0 to 0, ensuring that all pixel values fall within the valid range. Another solution is to use wrapping, whereby if a value exceeds 255, it wraps around to 0 instead of going above 255. For example, a value of 270 will be set to 255 if it is clipped but will be wrapped around to 15 in the other case.

The choice of which technique to use ultimately depends on the specific needs of the image processing task at hand.

We begin by discussing image addition and how the overflow of pixel values is managed in image addition using cv2 versus normal Python addition on NumPy values.

Addition

Image addition is a basic arithmetic operation that involves adding pixel values of two or more images to produce a single image. The main advantage of image addition is that it allows us to implement more complex operations such as image blending or masking. Image blending involves combining two images in different ratios to generate an output image, while masking involves overlaying a binary mask on an image to work on selected image regions. We will discuss these topics as we move further along the chapter.

We use the **`cv2.add()`** function to perform addition using the OpenCV library:

```
cv2.add(src1, src2, dst, mask, dtype)
```

Parameters:

- **src1 and src2:** The source images to be added. Both images should be of the same type and size.
- **dst:** Output Variable.
- **mask:** Masking allows us to choose specific pixels where the operation has to be performed. This is an . If it is left blank, the operation is performed on all the pixels.
- **dtype:** The data type of the output. This is an optional parameter that defaults to the input data type if left blank.

We will now attempt to add images by implementing the **`cv2.add`** function. In addition, we will also compare how overflow values are handled in NumPy addition:

```
import numpy as np
import cv2

# Initialize two sample 3x3 images
img1 = np.array([[10, 20, 30],
                 [40, 50, 60],
                 [70, 80, 90]], dtype=np.uint8)
img2 = np.array([[100, 200, 150],
                 [50, 250, 100],
                 [150, 200, 50]], dtype=np.uint8)

# Add the images
cv2_add = cv2.add(img1, img2)
print("cv2.add() result:\n", cv2_add)

# Add the images using numpy addition
numpy_add = img1 + img2
print("Numpy addition result:\n", numpy_add)
```

This code produces the following output:

cv2.add() result:

```
[[110 220 180]
[ 90 255 160]
[220 255 140]]
Numpy addition result:
[[110 220 180]
[ 90  44 160]
[220  24 140]]
```

In the preceding code, we initialize two 3x3 matrices with random values ranging from 0-255, which represent our images.

The **`cv2.add()`** function is then used to add **`img1`** and **`img2,`** and the result is stored in **`cv2_add`**. Any pixel value that is greater than 255 is set to 255 (the maximum value that can be stored in a uint8 datatype), while any pixel value less than 0 is set to 0. Thus, the values at indexes [1,1] and [2,1] are set to 255, as they added up to 300 and 280, respectively.

Next, we perform addition using the NumPy operation. In this case, the values are not clipped to 255 but are wrapped around, as discussed earlier. Thus, the values for [1,1] and [2,1] indexes are 44 and 24, respectively.

Next, we will discuss the weighted addition of images, which means that each image has a different contribution to the final output, and these contributions are not equal, as shared earlier.

We use the **`cv2.addWeighted()`** function for this:

```
cv2.addWeighted(src1, alpha=1.0, src2, beta=0.0, gamma=0.0, dst,
dtype)
```

Parameters:

- **src1 and src2:** The source images to be added. Both images should be of the same type and size.
- **alpha:** Weight of the first image. The range of alpha is 0 to 1, where 0 means the first image will not contribute to the output, and 1 means that the first image will have the maximum contribution to the output. The default value for **alpha** is 1.
- **beta:** Weight of the second image. The range of beta is between 0 and 1, similar to the alpha parameters. The default value for **beta** is 0.

- **gamma:** A scalar value that can be added to all the pixels after the weighted sum is calculated. This is an with default value as 0.
- **dst:** Output array.
- **dtype:** The data type of the output. This is an optional parameter that defaults to the input data type if left blank.

```
import cv2
import numpy as np

img1 = cv2.imread('image1.jpg')
img2 = cv2.imread('image2.jpg')

# Add the two images with different weights
result = cv2.addWeighted(img1, 0.7, img2, 0.3, 0)

cv2.imshow('Result', result)
cv2.waitKey(0)
cv2.destroyAllWindows()
```

The code produces the following output:

Figure 3.9: *Image Blending Output*

The preceding code loads two images and adds them with different weights. The value of the **`alpha`** parameter is set to 0.7, and the **`beta`** parameter is 0.3, which means **`img1`** has a 70% contribution while **`img2`** has a 30% contribution to the final output. The **`gamma`** value is set to 0, indicating that no scalar is added to the initial result.

Subtraction

Next, we will discuss image subtraction. We use the **`cv2.subtract()`** function for image subtraction in OpenCV. This function is very similar to the **`cv2.add()`** function we discussed earlier.

This function takes two images as inputs and subtracts the pixel values of the second image from the first image. Any negative values resulting from the subtraction are set to 0, as discussed earlier:

```
cv2.subtract(src1, src2, dst, mask, dtype)
```

Parameters:

- **src1 and src2:** The source images to be subtracted. Both images should be of the same type and size. The **src2** image is subtracted from **src1** image.
- **dst:** Output variable.
- **mask:** Masking allows us to choose specific pixels where the operation has to be performed. This is an. If it is left blank, the operation is performed on all the pixels.
- **dtype:** The data type of the output. This is an optional parameter that defaults to the input data type if left blank.

Multiplication and division

Multiplication of images involves multiplying each pixel value of one image with the corresponding pixel value of another image. Similarly, the division of images involves dividing each pixel value of one image with the corresponding pixel value of another image.

Since both image multiplication and division have similar syntax and documentation, we will be discussing them together and implementing them using a single code for brevity:

```
cv2.multiply(src1, src2, dst, scale=1.0, dtype)

cv2.divide(src1, src2, dst, scale=1.0, dtype)
```

Parameters:

- **src1 and src2:** The source images to be multiplied or divided.

- **dst:** Output variable.
- **scale:** The scale factor in **cv2.multiply()** is a scalar value that is multiplied with the product of the corresponding pixel values of the input images. The scale parameter in **cv2.divide** is used to divide the numerator (source image) by a scalar value. It is an optional parameter and its default value is 1.0.
- **dtype:** The data type of the output. This is an optional parameter that defaults to the input data type if left bank.

Bitwise operations

Bitwise operations can be used to combine two images or to extract and modify specific parts of these images. While bitwise operations may seem low-level and simple, they are essential in image processing. Bitwise operations might look similar to arithmetic operations, but they are not exactly arithmetic operations.

Arithmetic operations typically involve manipulating the numeric values of pixels in an image using mathematical operations such as addition, subtraction, multiplication, and division. Bitwise operations, on the other hand, involve manipulating the individual bits of the pixel values in an image. These operations are based on the logical operations of AND, OR, XOR, and NOT.

Bitwise operations are performed on the binary representation of these pixel values. Binary operations can be performed on both binary or grayscale/colored images. Binary images have a pixel value of 0 and 1, so bitwise operations on these are very straightforward. In grayscale images, pixel values are in the range of 0-255 in a single channel, while for colored images, there are multiple channels where each channel is processed separately and then combined.

The four primary bitwise operations are AND, OR, XOR and NOT. We will discuss these operations in detail, but since their syntax and documentation are similar, we will keep them together for the sake of brevity.

AND

Bitwise AND Is a binary operation that takes two images and performs the logical AND operation on them. This operation results in an image where the resultant pixel is 1 only if the corresponding pixel on both images is 1. If any of the bits in the input image is 0, the resulting pixel value is 0.

The primary use of bitwise AND operation is masking. It can be used to apply a binary mask on images to extract certain regions of an image. Bitwise AND can also be used for object tracking or for use cases such as image segmentation and image sharpening. The syntax for this operation is:

```
cv2.bitwise_and(src1, src2, dst, mask)
```

OR

Bitwise OR is a binary operation that takes two images and performs the logical OR operation on them. This operation results in an image where the resultant pixel is 1 if either of the corresponding pixels on both images is 1. If both of the bits on the input images are 0, the resulting pixel value is 0.

The primary use case of bitwise OR is image blending; two images can be blended together using this operation. This can also be used for image segmentation or many other use cases, such as the addition of random noise to images. The syntax for this operation is:

```
cv2.bitwise_or(src1, src2, dst, mask)
```

XOR

Bitwise XOR is a binary operation that takes two images and performs the logical XOR (exclusive OR) operation on them. This operation results in an image where the resultant pixel is 1 if only one of the corresponding pixels on the input images is 1. If both of the bits on the input images are 0 or 1, the resulting pixel value is 0.

Bitwise XOR can be used for image encryption by using a key. It can also be used for use cases such as edge detection and histogram equalization, which is a concept we will delve deeper into as we move further along the book. The syntax for this operation is:

```
cv2.bitwise_xor(src1, src2, dst, mask)
```

NOT

Bitwise NOT is a unary operation that takes a single image and performs the logical NOT operation on it. This operation results in an image where all the values of the images are reversed. All pixel values corresponding to 0 are set to 1, and all pixel values corresponding to 1 are set to 0 during the bitwise NOT operation.

The primary use case of this operation is image inversion. Apart from that, this can also be used for masking and image thresholding. The syntax for this operation is:

```
cv2.bitwise_not(src, dst, mask)
```

Since the parameters for all the operations are similar, we can discuss them together.

Parameters:

- **src1 and src:** The source images to be used for bitwise operations.
- **dst:** Output variable.
- **mask:** This is optional mask used to specify which pixels of the input images should be processed. The default value is None, meaning the full image will be used:

```
import cv2
import numpy as np

# Create two black and white images
img1 = np.zeros((400, 400), dtype=np.uint8)
img2 = np.zeros((400, 400), dtype=np.uint8)

# Draw a rectangle on img1
cv2.rectangle(img1, (50, 50), (350, 350), (255, 255, 255), -1)

# Draw a circle on img2
cv2.circle(img2, (200, 200), 150, (255, 255, 255), -1)

# Perform bitwise AND
bitwise_and = cv2.bitwise_and(img1, img2)

# Perform bitwise OR
bitwise_or = cv2.bitwise_or(img1, img2)

# Perform bitwise XOR
bitwise_xor = cv2.bitwise_xor(img1, img2)

# Perform bitwise NOT on img1
bitwise_not = cv2.bitwise_not(img1)

cv2.imshow('img1', img1)
cv2.imshow('img2', img2)
cv2.imshow('AND', bitwise_and)
cv2.imshow('OR', bitwise_or)
cv2.imshow('XOR', bitwise_xor)
cv2.imshow('NOT of img1', bitwise_not)
cv2.waitKey(0)
cv2.destroyAllWindows()
```

The code produces the following output showing various bitwise operations:

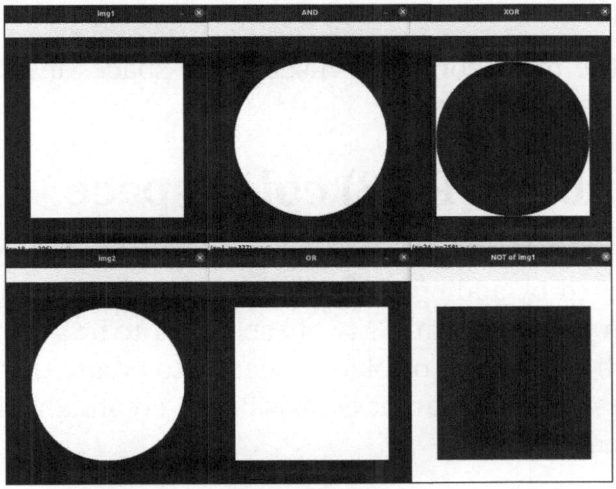

Figure 3.10: *Image Bitwise Operations Output*

Channels and color spaces

In OpenCV, images are represented as a matrix of pixel values. The number of channels in an image is the number of matrices used to represent the image. For example, a grayscale image has one channel, while a color image typically has three channels (red, green, and blue). Channels in an image allow us to separate color components of an image and process them separately for additional information.

A color space represents a specific way of describing colors with a mathematical model. Color values are defined as a combination of primary colors and how these primary colors are combined to create a particular color, depending on the color space. Until now, we have been working with the RGB color space, which is a color model that represents all colors using a combination of three channels: red, green, and blue. We will explore common color spaces as we move on further in the topic. We will also discuss grayscale images, which, while not a color space, are very important in image processing.

Color spaces can be better explained by comparing them to a real-life example. Imagine a painter trying to mix and create new colors for a painting. The painter can produce a wide spectrum of colors by choosing multiple paint tubes and combining them in different ratios. Paint can be blended to generate different colors, such as pink when red and white are combined and green when yellow and blue are combined. Similarly, different color spaces allow us to modify the brightness or saturation of colors and create new colors using different combinations of primary colors.

We will discuss the most commonly used color spaces in detail. We start by discussing the RGB color space.

Red Green Blue (RGB) color space

RGB color space contains red, blue and green channels to represent an image. The image is created by adding these three colors in the required amounts to create a particular color. The intensity of each color to be generated determines how much of each red, green, or blue is needed to create that particular color. By combining these three colors it is possible to create a wide array of colors needed for our images.

Each channel in the RGB color space has values ranging from 0 to 255, which describe the intensity of a particular color. A value of 0 represents no color or complete darkness, while a value of 255 represents the maximum intensity or full brightness of that color. For example, pure red is represented by (255, 0, 0) in the RGB color space, where the red channel is at its maximum value (255) and the green and blue channels are both set to 0. Similarly, pure blue is represented by (0,0,255) and pure green can be represented by (0,255,0).

For example, the color pure yellow is represented as (255, 255, 0), which means that the values of the Red channel are 255, the Green channel is 255, and the Blue channel is 0.

Some of the other colors are represented as:

Color	RGB Code	R	G	B
Orange	(255,165,0)	255	165	0
Brown	(165,42,42)	165	42	42
Light Gray	(211,211,211)	211	211	211
Dark Gray	(64,64,64)	64	64	64

We can also access and manipulate each individual value if we want to change colors. In the preceding table, we find the light gray color represented as (211, 211, 211). If we decrease these values, the colors will begin to darken, resulting in a darker gray.

Similarly, if we reduce the red channel of orange (255, 165, 0) – for example, by changing it to (200, 165, 0) – the color will become less intense and shift towards a shade that has less red, while still retaining its orange character.

Another important use of these values is that we can use them to detect a specific color or a range of colors in an image. We can use the red values of each pixel in an image to find red objects like red flowers. For example, if the red values (R) in an image are greater than a certain number (let's say 200), we can say those pixels likely belong to red objects, and we can use this technique to detect red flowers in the image.

RGB color space is often not considered to be intuitive because it is difficult to recreate colors using this color space. Mixing red, blue, and green in ratios might not result in the expected color, and it is often difficult to recreate the exact combination of these three. Despite its limitations, the RGB color space is widely used in various applications, including image processing, and it will be frequently utilized throughout our journey in this field.

Let us try to visualize these channels of an image with the help of some code:

```
import cv2

img = cv2.imread("ss.jpg")

im1=img.copy()
im2=img.copy()
im3=img.copy()

im1[:,:,0]=0
im1[:,:,1]=0

im2[:,:,2]=0
im2[:,:,1]=0

im3[:,:,2]=0
im3[:,:,0]=0

cv2.imshow("Original Image",img)
cv2.imshow("Red channel",im1)
cv2.imshow("Blue channel",im2)
cv2.imshow("Green channel",im3)

cv2.waitKey(0)
```

```
cv2.destroyAllWindows()
```

The code produces the following output:

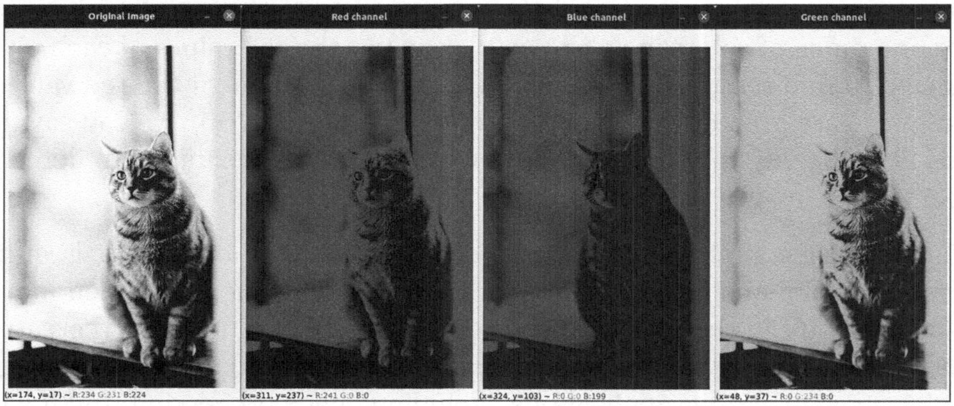

***Figure 3.11**: Image Channels in an RGB image*

The preceding code displays the three channels of the image separately. First, we set the red and green channel values to 0 in **im1**. This only outputs the blue channel of the image since the other channels have been set to 0. Similarly, we can do this for the other two channels by setting the values of the other channels to 0 in **im2** and **im3**.

RGB is a widely used color model in computer graphics, digital imaging, and video production to show images on electronic devices such as televisions, computer monitors, and mobile devices. RGB is also used for the most common tasks in OpenCV; however, the channels are reversed in this case to create a BGR color space.

Blue Green Red (BGR) color space

BGR color space is the RGB color space reversed. This is the most commonly used color space in OpenCV. There is no other difference with respect to RGB color space except for the positioning of channels. The only reason BGR is used by OpenCV is that BGR was used as the default format for some hardware and software systems, and this convention has been carried over into some modern image processing libraries like OpenCV. Matplotlib uses RGB color space, so we will make sure to change the color space of the image before trying to display an OpenCV Image using matplotlib.

The next color space we will explore is the HSV color space.

Hue Saturation Value (HSV) color space

Hue Saturation and Value are the three components of this color space. Let's have a better understanding of each of these channels:

- **Hue**: Hue refers to the pure color that we perceive. Hue is essentially a pure color without any white or black added to it. So, for example, all types of Blue, whether dark blue or light blue, will have the same blue hue.

  The Hue value ranges from 0 to 360 degrees, representing a full circle of colors. Red is located at 0 degrees, green at 120 degrees, and blue at 240 degrees. The Hue component in OpenCV's HSV color space is a uint8 value from 0 to 255, but the actual hue range is 0 to 360 degrees. To fit this range in an 8-bit integer, values are scaled down to 0-179, where each value corresponds to a specific hue.
- **Saturation**: Saturation represents the intensity of the color. The saturation value is represented as a percentage from 0% to 100%. A 100% saturation value will represent that the color is fully saturated, meaning that it has the maximum possible intensity. A 0% saturation will have no color and will be a pure white pixel.
- **Value**: Value is the amount of white or black added to the hue. It represents the lightness or the darkness of the color. This is also represented as a percentage, ranging from 0% to 100%. A value of 0% represents the darkest possible color (black), while a value of 100% represents the lightest possible color (white).

Unlike the RGB color space, HSV color space is not based on the simple addition of three primary colors. Compared to the RGB or BGR color spaces, the HSV color space has the benefit of separating color information from brightness information. This makes it simpler to adjust colors without altering the brightness of an image.

Now that we have explored two color spaces, we can try changing the color spaces of an image. We will use the cv2.cvtColor function to change the color spaces of an image.

cvtColor()

```
cv2.cvtColor(src, code, dst, dstCn=0)
```

Parameters:

- **src:** The source image to be converted.

- **code**: This represents the type of conversion you want to perform. This parameter defines the current color space of the image and specifies the desired color space to which the image needs to be converted.

There are a lot of possible options for . A few of them are as follows:

- **cv2.COLOR_BGR2HSV:** Converts an image from BGR to HSV.
- **cv2.COLOR_BGR2GRAY:** Converts an image from BGR to grayscale.
- **cv2.COLOR_HSV2BGR:** Converts an image from HSV to BGR.
- **cv2.COLOR_BGR2RGB:** Converts an image from BGR to RGB.
- **dst:** Output Variable
- **dstCn**: This is the number of channels in the output image. The default value is 0, which matches the number of channels in the input image.

Let's try this using some code:

```
import cv2

img_bgr = cv2.imread(‘img.jpg’)

# BGR to grayscale
img_gray = cv2.cvtColor(img_bgr, cv2.COLOR_BGR2GRAY)


cv2.imshow(Original Image’, img_bgr)
cv2.imshow(‘Grayscale Image’, img_gray)
cv2.waitKey(0)
cv2.destroyAllWindows()
```

The code produces the following output:

Figure 3.12: *cvtColor Output*

Hue Saturation Lightness (HSL) color space

HSL Or Hue Saturation Lightness is another color model used in image processing. The color space is similar to HSV color space, but there's a slight difference in how they calculate brightness.

Hue and Saturation channels are similar to the HSV color space. However, the value channel is replaced by the Lightness channel in this space. The L channel in HSL is intended to imitate the way humans perceive brightness and is more closely linked to the way people perceive brightness than the V channel in HSV. In contrast, the Value channel in HSV space represents the maximum value of the R, G, and B color components:

- **Hue**: Hue refers to the pure color that we perceive. This is similar to the description in the HSV channel.
- **Saturation**: Saturation represents the intensity of the color. This is also similar to the description in the HSV channel.
- **Lightness**: Lightness is the measure of how bright or dark the color is, with 0% lightness being black and 100% lightness being white. This is useful for brightening or darkening images as well as for adding creative touches to them.

Increasing the lightness value makes colors lighter and closer to white, while decreasing it darkens the colors. At a lightness value of 50%, colors remain in their original state. Values below 50% darken the colors, and values above 50% make them lighter.

For example, let us take the Gray color represented in HSL color space as HSL: Hue = 0°, Saturation = 0%, Lightness = 50%.

If we increase the lightness value, The gray becomes lighter, moving closer to white while still being recognizable as a shade of gray. Similarly, if we decrease the lightness value, the gray will become darker as it moves closer to black.

In general, HSL and HSV color spaces have their own unique benefits and can be useful in different scenarios depending on the task being performed. The decision to use either of them largely depends on the specific requirements of the task.

LAB color space

The LAB color space was designed to resemble the human vision system closely. This color space mimics how the human eye perceives color and thus mimics the human eye more closely than any other color space. The LAB color space is also known as CIE LAB color space because it was developed by the **International Commission of Illumination** (**CIE**) in 1976 to create a standardized color model.

The LAB color space consists of three dimensions:

- **L channel (Lightness)**: The L channel represents the lightness dimension. It describes the brightness of the image. The values are in the range of 0 to 100 where 0 is the lowest brightness(black) and 100 is the brightest (white).
- **a channel (Green - Red)**: This defines pure green color on one side and pure red color on the opposite side. The values for this dimension range from -128 to +127 and define the color between green to red channels. Negative values represent shades of green, and as we move on to the positive values, shades of red get defined by these values.
- **b channel (Blue - Yellow)**: This defines pure blue color on one side and pure red color on the opposite side. The values for this dimension range from -128 to +127 and define the color between blue to yellow channels. Negative values represent shades of blue, and as we move on to the positive values, shades of yellow get defined by these values.

The color model is designed in such a way that it is independent of any particular device or technology, making it more universal and applicable in various fields.

YCbCr color space

The YCbCr color space is a color encoding system that represents colors as a combination of brightness (luma) and two color-difference signals (chroma). This color space separates luminance (brightness) and chrominance (color) information, allowing for more efficient compression of images.

YCbCr color space is similar to the RGB color space, but it uses luminance (Y), blue-difference (Cb), and red-difference (Cr) components instead of red, green, and blue. Y represents the image's brightness, while Cb and Cr represent the difference between the color and the brightness.

- **Y channel:** This channel represents the brightness of the color and is sometimes referred to as the luminance channel.
- **Cb and Cr channels:** These channels represent the color information of the image. The Cb channel represents the blue-difference, and the Cr channel represents the red-difference.

Grayscale

Images in grayscale are represented in a single channel only and contain values from 0 to 255. This value indicated the amount of light on the pixel. A value of 0 means there is no light on the pixel, and hence the pixel's color is black. Meanwhile, a value of 255 represents the maximum and has a value of white. All the values in between are different shades of grey.

Grayscale is technically not a color space since it is a single-channel representation of an image and does not have any color information.

We will be converting our images to grayscale for image processing many times in the course of this book. However, there is something to remember. In most standard algorithms for converting RGB to grayscale, the red, green, and blue channels are not given equal weights. This is because the human eye is more sensitive to green light than to red or blue light, so green is typically given more weight in the conversion process. One common method is to use the formula:

Grayscale = 0.2989 * Red + 0.5870 * Green + 0.1140 * Blue

Conclusion

This chapter discussed several important operations in image processing using OpenCV. We started with translation-based operations such as rotation and resizing, where we learned how to manipulate the size and orientation of images. We then covered arithmetic operations, including addition, subtraction, and division, and bitwise operations like AND, OR, and XOR. Finally, we delved into the topic of image channels and color spaces, exploring various ways an image can be represented to aid in image processing tasks.

In the next chapter, we will be exploring morphological operations on images. We will start by discussing dilation and erosion, and how they can be used to manipulate the shape and structure of images. We will also cover the opening and closing of images, which are more advanced morphological operations. Additionally, we will delve into image smoothing and blurring, and explore various types of image blur along with their properties. Throughout the chapter, readers will learn how to apply these operations and adjust their properties to achieve desired effects using OpenCV.

Points to Remember

- Image transformation allows us to alter the image size or orientation for various computer vision tasks.
- Arithmetic operations involve performing basic mathematical operations on images to generate new images with different properties.
- Arithmetic operations involve manipulating the numeric values of pixels

in an image using mathematical operations such as addition, subtraction, multiplication, and division.

- OpenCV weighted addition of images allows us to add images such that each image has a different contribution to the final output.
- Bitwise operations involve manipulating the individual bits of the pixel values in an image, while arithmetic operations involve performing basic mathematical operations on images.
- The number of channels in an image is the number of matrices used to represent the image.
- Color spaces are mathematical models that represent colors using coordinates, allowing for easier manipulation and processing of color information.
- Grayscale images are created by applying the formula **0.2989 * Red + 0.5870 * Green + 0.1140 * Blue** to the RGB color channels, with each channel contributing to the final image with a different weight.

Test Your Understanding

1. The function commonly used for image scaling is

   A. cv2.rotate()

   B. cv2.resize()

   C. cv2.flip()

   D. cv2.cvtColor()

2. Which technique is used to address the issue of pixel values falling outside of the valid range of 0-255 in images?

   A. Blurring

   B. Clipping

   C. Sharpening

   D. Thresholding

3. Which of the following is not a bitwise operator used in image processing?

   A. NOT operator

   B. OR operator

   C. XOR operator

   D. IF operator

4. Which of the following color spaces is used to separate the luminance and chrominance information of an image?

   A. RGB color space

   B. BGR color space

   C. YCbCr color space

   D. HSV color space

5. Which of the following formulas is used to convert a color image to a grayscale?

   A. 0.2989 * Red + 0.5870 * Green + 0.1140 * Blue

   B. 0.5870 * Red + 0.1140 * Green + 0.2989 * Blue

   C. 0.1140 * Red + 0.2989 * Green + 0.5870 * Blue

   D. 0.3333 * Red + 0.3333 * Green + 0.3333 * Blue

CHAPTER 4
Image Operations

In this chapter, we will cover the topic of morphological operations on images. We will start with an introduction to dilation and erosion and demonstrate how these operations can be used to manipulate the shape and structure of images. Later on in the chapter, we will dive into more advanced morphological operations, such as the opening and closing of images. Additionally, we will cover the topic of image smoothing and blurring, where we will explore various types of image blur and their properties. We will discuss the commonly used average and median blur techniques and their applications. After that, we will move on to more complex blurs such as Gaussian and bilateral filtering. Throughout the chapter, we will use OpenCV to apply these blurs to images and show readers how to adjust the blur properties to achieve the desired effects.

Structure

In this chapter, we will discuss the following topics:

- Morphological operations on images
    - Erosion
    - Dilation
    - Opening and closing
    - Morphological gradient
    - Tophat and Black hat
- Image smoothing and blurring
    - Average blur
    - Median blur
    - Gaussian blur
    - Bilateral filter

Morphological operations on images

Morphological operations are a fundamental set of operations in image processing that allow us to manipulate the shape and structure of images. Morphological operations are mathematical in nature and provide a useful set of tools allowing us to extract information or remove noise from the images among many other use cases.

Morphological operations are generally performed on binary images. Morphological operations are performed using a structuring element, or kernel, by applying it to an input image and producing a different image as an output. The nature of the structuring element decides the output of the operation and can be accordingly manipulated to produce the required output.

The structuring element is a shape smaller than the input image that is placed on top of each pixel of the input image and the operation is applied by sliding it through the image:

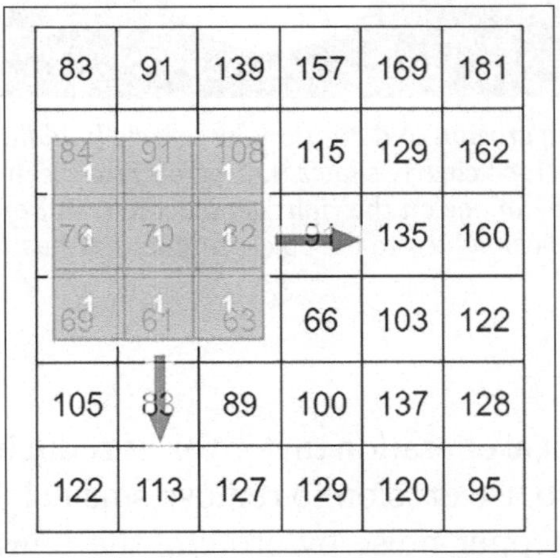

Figure 4.1: A 3x3 *structuring element placed on an image. The structuring element is applied to each pixel in a left-to-right and top-to-bottom traversal order*

The shape and size of the structuring element will determine the type of operation performed on the input image. A small structuring element will result in subtle differences in the output image while a structuring element of larger size will have more visible and major differences in the resulting image.

The structuring element is generally a binary matrix consisting of 0s and 1s where the 1 values define the shape of the structuring element. The shape of a structuring element can be anything from a simple line, square or rectangle to complex shapes like a diamond or ellipse. The choice of the type of structural element to be used depends upon the desired output and the individual use case on hand.

The basic morphological operations used in image processing are dilation and erosion. Based on these operations additional operations such as opening or closing can be achieved by applying the aforementioned operations in a certain order. Dilation involves increasing the size of the object in an image by adding pixels to its boundary. Conversely, erosion involves reducing the size of the object by removing pixels near the boundary. We can see the differences with the help of the following figure:

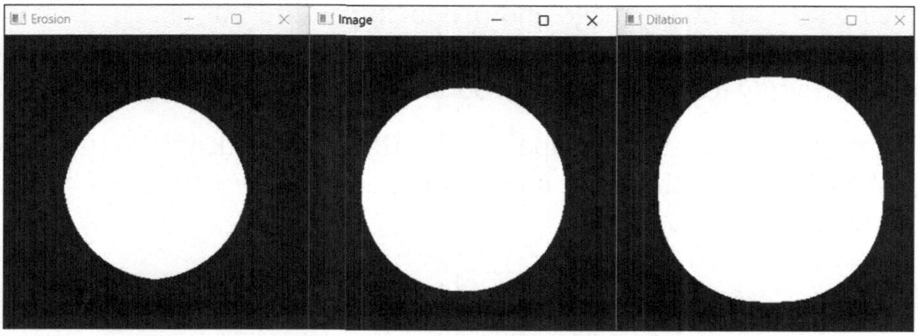

Figure 4.2: *Image showing erosion and dilation on a circle (middle image). The image on the left is the eroded output, which clearly shows that pixels have been removed from the object's boundary. In contrast, the image on the right depicts the result of dilation, demonstrating that pixels have been added to the object and its size has visibly increased.*

Erosion

Erosion is a morphological operation that involves reducing the size of the object in an image. We can also use erosion to remove small objects in our image, such as removing salt and pepper noise by eroding the unwanted noise pixels. We can compare erosion to polishing the surface of an object to make it smoother by removing the small bumps and scratches, similar to how erosion in OpenCV removes small details from an object to create a smoother image.

As mentioned earlier, the size of an object in an image is reduced by removing pixels near the boundary of that object. Erosion can be used to remove noise from the image by removing the small and redundant noisy pixels in the image. Erosion can also be used to separate connected regions in objects that are touching each other, as these might be considered as a single object in image processing and might result in incorrect results. We can also use erosion to smoothen the boundaries of an object in an image or as a precursor for various image processing applications.

Erosion works by initializing a structuring element and passing this structuring element over each pixel of the image. The area under the structuring element is considered for the operation:

- If all the pixels inside the area are greater than zero, then the value is changed to 255.
- If the pixels within the area are not all greater than zero, they are set to zero.

The process is repeated for all the pixels of the image. Essentially, if any cell in the kernel is black, the center pixel in consideration will turn black as well.

It is important to note that pixels with a value of one are only considered as structuring elements. In the following figure, there is a 3x3 matrix denoting a structuring element. The pixels with values as one are only considered. The structuring element in this case consists of five pixels with a value of one, arranged in the shape of a plus sign (+):

0	1	0
1	1	1
0	1	0

Figure 4.3: *A 3x3 kernel with certain values set to one denotes the structuring element values to be considered.*

For a better explanation of the concept, we can take a small matrix signifying an image and apply a sample 3x3 kernel to it. Let us try to visualize how erosion operation works on a 10x10 matrix:

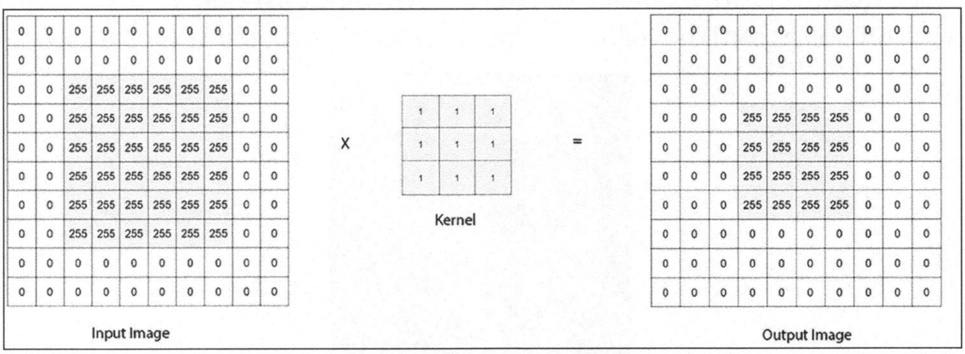

Figure 4.4: *An input image of size 10x10 is eroded using a 3x3 kernel to produce an output image*

cv2.Erode()

```
cv2.erode(src, kernel="3x3 numpy array with all elements as 1", dst, anchor=(-1,-1), iterations=1, borderType=cv2.BORDER_CONSTANT, borderValue=0)
```

Parameters:

- `src`: The source image to be used for erosion.
- `kernel`: This is the structuring element to be used for erosion. This is an . The default value for this is a 3*3 structuring element with all values set as 1.
- `dst`: Output variable.
- `anchor`: The anchor is the pixel used as the reference point for the operation to be performed on the surrounding pixels. The anchor is usually specified by its position in the structuring element used for the operation. This is an optional parameter with a default value of (-1,-1) meaning that the anchor is at the center of the kernel.
- `iterations`: The number of times erosion will be applied to the image. This is with the default value defined as 1.
- `borderType`: This is the pixel extrapolation method, an optional parameter with a default value of **`cv2.BORDER_CONSTANT`**.
- `borderValue`. This is used only with cv2.BORDER_CONSTANT mode and specifies the constant value used to pad the image. It has a default value of 0.
- **Erosion** should be applied carefully as overusing this function can result in information loss on the image and important features of the image might disappear. Erosion can be used to remove small objects from the image however over-applying the function will lead to the removal of more significant objects in the image.

Let's try to demonstrate this using some code. We will try to remove the unnecessary objects and noise from the following figure to demonstrate how erosion works:

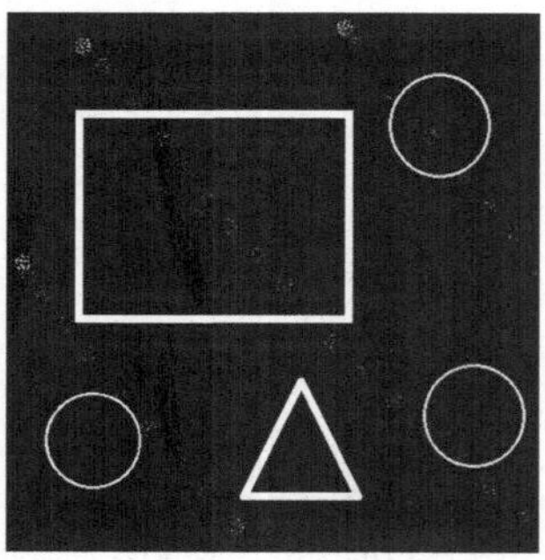

***Figure 4.5**: A random image we will be using to apply erosion*

```
import cv2
import numpy as np

img = cv2.imread("test.jpg")

# Apply erosion once to remove noise
kernel = np.ones((5,5),np.uint8)
img1 = cv2.erode(img, kernel, iterations=1)

# Apply erosion multiple times to show bad result
img2 = cv2.erode(img, kernel, iterations=10)

cv2.imshow('Original Image', img)
cv2.imshow('Erosion', img1)
cv2.imshow('Over Erosion', img2)
cv2.waitKey(0)
cv2.destroyAllWindows()
```

The preceding code outputs the following images:

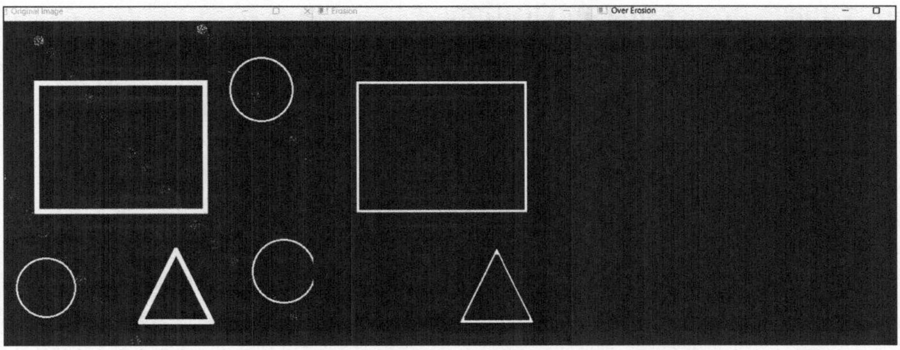

Figure 4.6: *The figure shows three images. The leftmost is our input image. The second image shows the output after applying erosion once. The rightmost image displays the result of over-erosion. The image is blank as all the objects have been eroded away.*

In the preceding code, we first load our image and apply erosion two times. In the first erosion, we iterate keeping the number of iterations as one. We can see that the operation has removed noise from our image. We can also see that the circles have been removed indicating that erosion can be used to eliminate unwanted objects from our image.

We then apply a second erosion operation. This time we keep the number of iterations as ten. We can observe that the image has over eroded, and all the objects of our image have disappeared completely. This shows how we need to be careful about erosion and how applying erosion multiple times can lead to information loss.

Dilation

Dilation is a morphological operation that involves increasing the size of the object in the image. It is the opposite of erosion. Dilation can be used to enhance the boundaries of an object in an image or fill the gaps between two objects. Similar to how we compared erosion, we can do the same with dilation by comparing it with painting a wall. Using a thick brush while painting will cause the paint to spread beyond the boundary, just like dilation will make the objects in the image larger than they were before.

Opposite to erosion, dilation increases the size of an object by adding pixels near the boundaries of that object. By using a larger structuring element, dilation can also be used to fill gaps or holes in the image as it adds pixels to the boundaries. We can use dilation to enhance the edges of an object. Dilation can enhance edges with thin lines or gaps, resulting in an object with more clearly defined boundaries. Similar to erosion, dilation is also often used as a precursor to various image processing applications.

Similar to erosion, dilation also works by initializing a structuring element and passing this structuring element over each pixel of the image. The area of the image lying under the structuring element is operated:

- If any of the pixels inside are greater than 0, then the value is changed to 255.
- If there are no pixels inside the area of the structuring element, the point is set to 0.

The process is repeated for all the pixels of the image until the sliding window has passed through the entire image.

Now, we have a dilated image where each object in the original image has expanded or grown based on the structuring element, making the objects appear larger or more connected in the resulting image.

Let us try to visualize how erosion operation works on a 10x10 matrix. We can initialize a matrix signifying an image and apply a sample 3x3 kernel to it:

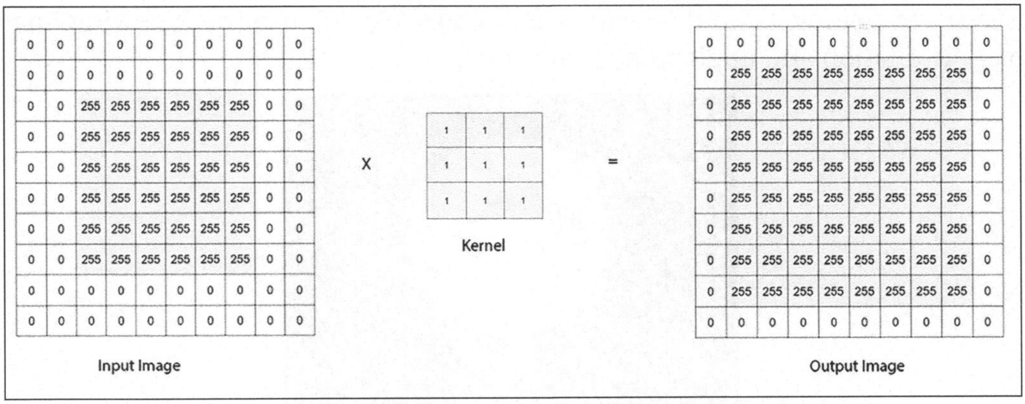

Figure 4.7: *An input image of size 10x10 is dilated using a 3x3 kernel to produce an output image*

cv2.Dilate()

```
cv2.dilate(src, kernel="3x3 numpy array with all elements as 1", dst, an-
chor=(-1,-1), iterations=1, borderType=cv2.BORDER_CONSTANT, borderValue=0)
```

Parameters:

- `src`: The source image to be used for erosion.
- `kernel`: This is the structuring element to be used for erosion. This is an . The default value for this is a 3*3 structuring element with all values set as 1.
- `dst`: Output variable.
- `anchor`: The anchor is the pixel used as the reference point for the operation to be performed on the surrounding pixels. The anchor is usually specified by its position in the structuring element used for the operation. This is an optional parameter with a default value of (-1,-1) meaning that the anchor is at the center of the kernel.
- `iterations`: The number of times erosion will be applied to the image. This is with the default value defined as 1.
- `borderType`: This is the pixel extrapolation method, an optional parameter with a default value of **`cv2.BORDER_CONSTANT`**.
- `borderValue`. This is used only with **`cv2.BORDER_CONSTANT`** mode and specifies the constant value used to pad the image. It has a default value of 0.

Dilation should also be used carefully as overusing this function can result in the creation of artefacts in an image. If dilation is applied too many times or the structuring element is too large, it will merge adjacent objects together, resulting in incorrect results.

Let's try to demonstrate this using some code. We will use the following image to apply dilation and implement some code:

***Figure 4.8**: An image we will be using to apply dilation*

```
import cv2
import numpy as np


img = cv2.imread("test2.jpg")

# Apply erosion once to remove noise
kernel = np.ones((5,5),np.uint8)
img1 = cv2.dilate(img, kernel, iterations=1)

# Apply erosion multiple times to show bad result
img2 = cv2.dilate(img, kernel, iterations=5)

cv2.imshow('Original Image', img)
cv2.imshow('Dilation', img1)
cv2.imshow('Over Dilation', img2)
cv2.waitKey(0)
cv2.destroyAllWindows()
```

This will result in the following output images:

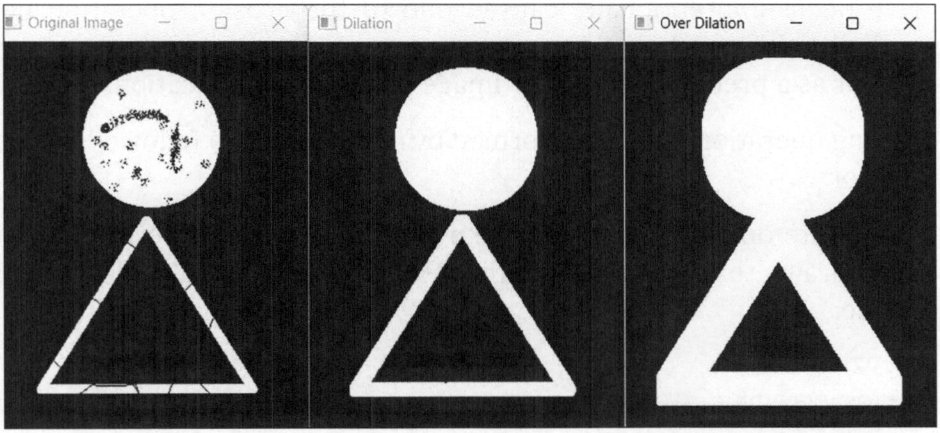

***Figure 4.9**: The figure shows three images. The leftmost is our input image. The second image shows the output after applying dilation. We can see that the noise has been removed from the circle and irregular edges have been joined in the triangle. The rightmost image displays the result of over-dilation. The objects have joined together to create a single object.*

In the preceding code, we apply dilation two times. In the first operation, we can observe that the dilation operation has removed the noise from the circle object in the image. We also see that the irregular edges in the triangle have been joined together in the operation. This shows how dilation can be used to remove noise from certain objects and how irregular shapes can be completed using dilation.

In the second iteration, we apply dilation for five iterations. We observe that the operation has joined the two objects showing how over-dilation can join unwanted objects together and has to be carefully applied during image processing applications.

The rest of the morphological operations are based on different combinations of erosion and dilation operations with the original image.

Opening

Opening is a morphological operation that is a sequence of erosion and dilation operations. Erosion followed by Dilation is referred to as an opening operation in image processing. This is called an opening operation as it "opens" up the main object in the image by removing unwanted objects or noise from the image and then restoring the object to its original size.

Performing erosion first on the image will result in the removal of small objects or noise in the image. Following this, the dilation operation will close any gaps that have been unintentionally caused due to the erosion operation before. Opening operation can help us to remove unwanted noise, separate objects in an image, or as a precursor for other image processing applications.

The opening operation can be performed by coding erosion followed by dilation in our editor.

To demonstrate opening, we will write a code to remove noise from an image containing drawn text. We will draw the text and also manually add some noise to this code:

```
import cv2
import numpy as np

# Generate a 300x300 image with a black background
img = np.zeros((200, 450), np.uint8)

# Draw the text "OPENING" on the image
font = cv2.FONT_HERSHEY_SIMPLEX
cv2.putText(img, "OPENING", (15, 125), font, 3, (255, 255, 255), 5)

# Add noise to the image
noise = np.zeros((200, 450), np.uint8)
cv2.randn(noise, 0, 50)
noisy= cv2.add(img, noise)

# Define a 5x5 kernel for the erosion and dilation operations
kernel = np.ones((5, 5), np.uint8)

# Perform erosion
erosion = cv2.erode(img, kernel, iterations=1)

# Perform dilation on eroded image
opening = cv2.dilate(erosion, kernel, iterations=1)

cv2.imshow("Original Image", img)
cv2.imshow("Noisy Image", noisy)
cv2.imshow("erosion", erosion)
cv2.imshow("Opening Result", opening)
cv2.waitKey(0)
cv2.destroyAllWindows()
```

The preceding code results in the following output:

***Figure 4.10**: The figure shows four images. The first image is our original image. The image on the top right shows our generated noisy image. The bottom left image shows our result after erosion. Note: that the noise has disappeared but the text size has also been reduced. The bottom right shows our final result after applying dilation to restore the thickness of our text.*

In the preceding code, we first create a blank canvas and draw the text **`OPENING`** inside it. We then manually add some noise to our image. This is done by creating another image, drawing some random noise on it and adding both images. We then proceed to the morphological operations.

As discussed earlier, during the opening operation, erosion takes place first, this operation removes the noise from the image. However, it has also reduced the width of the text and it is not properly visible. To rectify this, the opening operation uses a dilation operation which increases the text size, and our object becomes properly visible again.

We will now use the inbuilt opening function to implement this operation in a single line. The **`cv2.Morphologyex()`** function enables us to do this operation.

Cv2.morphologyex()

```
cv2.morphologyEx(src, dst, op, kernel,  anchor=(-1,-1),
iterations=1, borderType=cv2.BORDER_CONSTANT, borderValue=0)
```

Parameters:

- **`src`**: The source image to be used for erosion.
- **`dst`**: Output variable.

- **op**: This specifies the type of operation to be performed in the image. The possible values for this parameter are:
    - **cv2.MORPH_OPEN**: opening operation
    - **cv2.MORPH_CLOSE**: closing operation
    - **cv2.MORPH_GRADIENT**: morphological gradient
    - **cv2.MORPH_TOPHAT**: top hat transform
    - **cv2.MORPH_BLACKHAT**: black hat transform
- **kernel**: This is the structuring element to be used for erosion. This is an. The default value is a 3*3 structuring element with all values set as 1.
- **anchor**: Reference point for the operation. This is an optional parameter with a default value of (-1,-1) meaning that the anchor is at the of the kernel.
- **iterations**: The number of times erosion will be applied to the image. This is with the default value defined as 1.
- **borderType**: This is the pixel extrapolation method, an optional parameter with a default value of **cv2.BORDER_CONSTANT**.
- **borderValue**. This is used only with **cv2.BORDER_CONSTANT** mode and specifies the constant value used to pad the image. It has a default value of 0.

```
import cv2
import numpy as np

# Generate a 300x300 image with a black background
img = np.zeros((200, 450), np.uint8)

# Draw the text "OPENING" on the image
font = cv2.FONT_HERSHEY_SIMPLEX
cv2.putText(img, "OPENING", (15, 125), font, 3, (255, 255, 255), 5)

# Add noise to the image
noise = np.zeros((200, 450), np.uint8)
cv2.randn(noise, 0, 50)
img2 = cv2.add(img, noise)

# Define a 5x5 kernel for the opening operation
kernel = np.ones((5, 5), np.uint8)

# Perform the opening operation on the image
opening = cv2.morphologyEx(img, cv2.MORPH_OPEN, kernel)
```

```
cv2.imshow("Noisy Image", noise))
cv2.imshow("Opening Result", opening)
cv2.waitKey(0)
cv2.destroyAllWindows()
```

We get the following output:

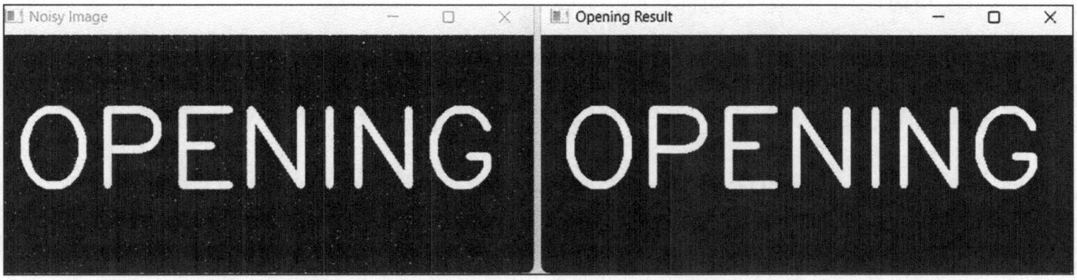

***Figure 4.11**: Output of opening operation using cv2.morphologyEx() function. The left image shows our noisy image and the right image is our final result after the operation.*

In this code, instead of using erosion and dilation operations separately, we use the **`cv2.morphologyEx()`** function with the **`cv2.MORPH_OPEN`** parameters to perform our opening operation. We draw the same input image and can see that the results are similar to when we performed the opening operation by using erosion and dilation separately.

Closing

Closing is a morphological operation that is a sequence of dilation and erosion operations. Dilation followed by erosion is referred to as a closing operation in image processing. It is called a closing operation because it *closes* the gaps and holes in an object within an image by expanding the object.

Performing dilation on the image results in the gaps and holes being filled. The object size has also increased. However, as pixels have been added to the object boundary, to rectify this, erosion is used which shrinks the object again by removing pixels from the boundary. As a result, the gaps and the holes remain closed and the object in the image maintains its shape and size.

Similar to the opening operation, the closing can be performed by performing dilation followed by erosion. We can also use the aforementioned **`cv2.morphologyEx`** function as this will allow us to implement the operation in a single line. We will use the **`cv2.MORPH_CLOSE`** parameter in the operation type parameter in this function to perform a closing operation.

Let's try performing the closing operation on an image:

```
import cv2
import numpy as np

img = np.zeros((200, 450), np.uint8)

# Draw the text "CLOSING" on the image
font = cv2.FONT_HERSHEY_SIMPLEX
cv2.putText(img, "CLOSING", (15, 125), font, 3, (255, 255, 255), 5)

noisy_img = img.copy()

# Create noise using difference of two images
noise = np.zeros_like(img)
for I in range(1000):
    x, y = np.random.randint(0, img.shape[1]), np.random.randint(0, img.
shape[0])
    cv2.circle(noisy_img, (x, y), 1, (0, 0, 0), -1, lineType=cv2.LINE_
AA)

# Define kernel for closing operation
kernel = np.ones((5, 5), np.uint8)

# Perform closing operation
dilated_img = cv2.dilate(noisy_img, kernel)
closed_img = cv2.erode(dilated_img, kernel)

cv2.imshow"""Original Imag""",img)
cv2.imshow"""Noisy Imag""", noisy_img)
cv2.imshow"""Dilate""", dilated_img)
cv2.imshow"""Close""", closed_img)
cv2.waitKey(0)
cv2.destroyAllWindows()
```

The preceding code demonstrates the closing operation by performing dilate and erosion operations separately. We get the following output:

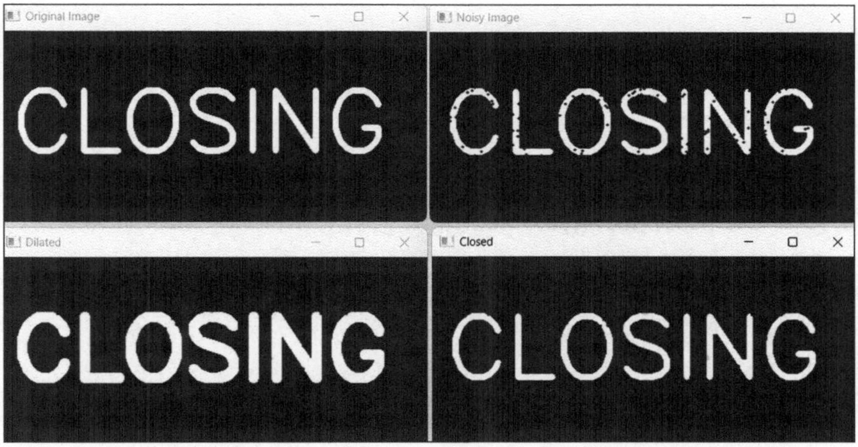

Figure 4.12: *The figure shows four images. The first image is our original image. The image on the top right shows our generated noisy image. The bottom left image shows our result after dilation. Note: that the noise has disappeared, but the text thickness has increased. The bottom right shows our final result after applying erosion to restore the thickness of our text.*

Similar to what we did earlier, we generate artificial noise in our drawn text. We distort the text by placing *gaps* on our image by drawing small black circles on it. For closing, we perform the dilation operation first, which closes out gaps but also thickens the text a lot. The following erosion function then takes care of it and the text returns to its original size.

We can also use the **cv2.morphologyEx()** function with the **MORPH_CLOSE** parameter to perform the closing operation:

```
import cv2
import numpy as np

img = np.zeros((200, 450), np.uint8)

# Draw the text "OPENING" on the image
font = cv2.FONT_HERSHEY_SIMPLEX
cv2.putText(img, "CLOSING", (15, 125), font, 3, (255, 255, 255), 5)

noisy_img = img.copy()

# Create noise using difference of two images
noise = np.zeros_like(img)
for i in range(1000):
    x, y = np.random.randint(0, img.shape[1]), np.random.randint(0, img.
shape[0])
    cv2.circle(noisy_img, (x, y), 1, (0, 0, 0), -1, lineType=cv2.LINE_
```

```
AA)

# Define kernel for closing operation
kernel = np.ones((5, 5), np.uint8)

# Apply closing operation
closed_img = cv2.morphologyEx(noisy_img, cv2.MORPH_CLOSE, kernel)

cv2.imshow("Noisy Image", noisy_img)
cv2.imshow("Closed", closed_img)
cv2.waitKey(0)
cv2.destroyAllWindows()
```

This results in the following output:

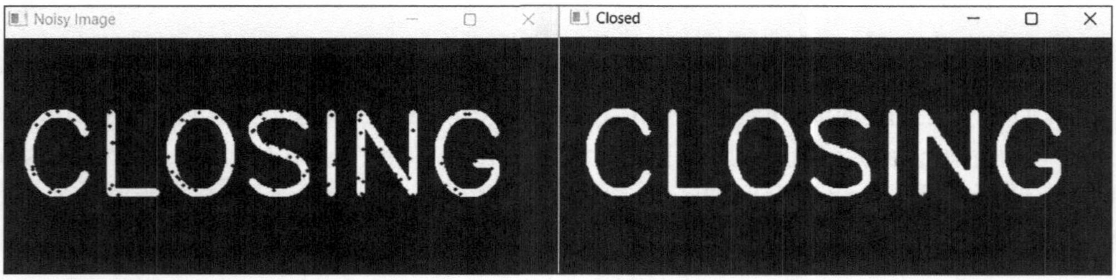

***Figure 4.13**: Output of closing operation using cv2.morphologyEx() function. The left image shows our noisy image, and the right image is our final result after the operation.*

Morphological gradient

The next operation we will discuss is the morphological gradient. The morphological gradient is the difference between dilation and erosion operations on an image.

Both operations are applied to the source image and the gradient is calculated by subtracting the eroded image from the dilated image. Our object, in reference to the dilated image, will have been expanded while our object in the eroded image would have been reduced in size. By subtracting the images, we end up with the boundary of our object in the image.

The size of the kernel will affect the output by defining the thickness of the boundary of our object in the image. If we use a larger kernel in the operation, we will get a thicker boundary, while using a smaller kernel will result in a thinner boundary. We will compare this when we implement this in the following code.

The main objective of the morphological gradient is to highlight the boundary of the object in our images. Apart from edge detection, morphological gradients can also help us in segmenting images or extracting objects from the image as the edges are much more prominent than before.

The morphological gradient can be expressed as follows:

Morphological Gradient (G) = Dilation (D) - Erosion (E)

Where:

Dilation (D) is the result of the dilation operation on the input image.

Erosion (E) is the result of the erosion operation on the input image.

Morphological Gradient (G) represents the difference between the dilation and erosion results.

As discussed in opening and closing, this can be mathematically done, or we can use the **cv2.morphologyEx** function to implement this. We will use the **cv2.MORPH_GRADIENT** parameter in the operation type parameters in this function to perform a morphological gradient operation:

```
import cv2
import numpy as np

# Read the input image
img = cv2.imread('img.jpg', 0)

# Define the kernel
kernel = np.ones((3,3), np.uint8)

# Apply morphological gradient
gradient = cv2.morphologyEx(img, cv2.MORPH_GRADIENT, kernel)

# Display the result
cv2.imshow("Image", img)
cv2.imshow('Morphological Gradient', gradient)
cv2.waitKey(0)
cv2.destroyAllWindows()
```

This results in the following output:

***Figure 4.14**: Output of morphological gradient operation using cv2.morphologyEx() function. The left image shows our grayscale image, and the right image is our final result after the operation showing the boundaries of the objects in the image.*

Using our morphological boundary operation, we are able to extract the boundary out of the objects in our image. Readers can try using different kernel sizes to extract edges of various sizes from the image.

Top hat

The Top hat operation, also known as the white hat operation, is used to highlight the bright regions in an image. The Top hat operation is the difference between the opening of an image and the original image.

As discussed earlier, we obtain the opened image by subtracting the eroded image from the dilated image. Subtracting this opened image from the original image results in our top hat operation. The opening operation has removed the small objects from our image. When we subtract the original image from this image, these are the only objects left in the resulting image and thus appear as bright spots. The rest of the image is subtracted as it was and results in values closer to 0 giving a black region as output.

This allows this operation to be used in various applications where the minute features need to be highlighted. It has various medical applications such as the detection of blood vessels or nuclei in cell images as these regions can be easily enhanced and thus segmented from the original image for further examination. We can also use this method to detect small objects in an image or for applications such as analyzing textures or detecting dents or cracks on a surface.

We will use the **`cv2.morphologyEx`** function with the **`cv2.MORPH_TOPHAT`** parameter in the operation type parameters to perform top hat operations:

```
import cv2
```

```
import numpy as np

# Read input image in grayscale
img = cv2.imread("galaxy.jpg", cv2.IMREAD_GRAYSCALE)

# Define a rectangular structuring element for the top hat operation
kernel = cv2.getStructuringElement(cv2.MORPH_RECT, (3, 3))

# Perform the top hat operation
tophat = cv2.morphologyEx(img, cv2.MORPH_TOPHAT, kernel)

cv2.imshow("Original Image", img)
cv2.imshow("Top Hat Result", tophat)
cv2.waitKey(0)
cv2.destroyAllWindows()
```

The preceding code results in the following output:

Figure 4.15: *Output of tophat operation using cv2.morphologyEx() function. The left image shows our original image and the right image is our final result after the operation. The tophat operation has enhanced the bright spots (stars in this case) in our resultant image.*

In the preceding output, we can see the results of the tophat operation. We use the **`MORPH_TOPHAT`** parameter in the **`cv2.morphologyEx()`** function to implement our top hat operation. As can be observed from the result, the top hat operation has enhanced the small details in the image. The small white stars in the galaxy image are extracted from the image separately and large objects have been removed from the resultant image.

Bottom hat

The bottom hat operation, also known as the black hat operation, is the opposite of the top hat operation and is used to highlight the dark regions of an image.

The top hat operation is the difference between the closing of an image and the original image.

The closed image is obtained by subtracting the dilated image from the eroded image. Subtracting this closed image from the original image results in our bottom hat operation. The closing operation has expanded the dark regions and closed the gaps in them. Opposite to the top hat operation, when we subtract the original image from this image, bright regions are removed, and these dark regions are the only objects left in the resulting image and thus appear as dark spots.

Black hat operations have a wide array of uses in image processing, as they highlight the edges and boundaries of objects. These capabilities of black hat operations allow them to be used for various tasks such as image segmentation and edge detection. Text written against dark backgrounds or handwritten letters or words can be identified using black hat operations.

We will use the **`cv2.morphologyEx`** function with the **`cv2.MORPH_BLACKHAT`** parameter in the operation type parameters to perform bottom hat operations:

```
import cv2
import numpy as np

# Read input image in grayscale
img = cv2.imread("img.jpg", cv2.IMREAD_GRAYSCALE)

# Define a rectangular structuring element for the top hat operation
kernel = cv2.getStructuringElement(cv2.MORPH_RECT, (3, 3))

# Perform the top hat operation

bottomhat = cv2.morphologyEx(img, cv2.MORPH_BLACKHAT, kernel)

cv2.imshow("Original Image", img)
cv2.imshow("Top Hat Result", bottomhat)
cv2.waitKey(0)
cv2.destroyAllWindows()
```

***Figure 4.16**: Output of bottom hat operation using cv2.morphologyEx() function. The left image shows our original image, and the right image is our final result after the operation. The image has been able to highlight white text on black background.*

The bottom hat operation results in the preceding result. The black hat transformation highlights white objects in a dark background in an image.

Smoothing and blurring

Image smoothing and blurring are similar techniques in image processing used to remove noise or reduce sharpness from images. These smoothing and blurring are used interchangeably however, there is a slight difference between them.

Image smoothing is the process of removing noise from an image while preserving the edges inside the image. We implement image smoothing by using a low-pass filter on the image. A low-pass filter allows the low-frequency components of an image to pass through while blocking the high-frequency components.

Image blurring is the process of reducing the sharpness of the image. We implement image blurring by using a high-pass filter on the image. A high-pass filter blocks the low-frequency components of an image while allowing the high-frequency components to pass through.

Various filters are used for image smoothing or blurring processes. We will discuss four main filters, average, median, gaussian and bilateral filters in detail as we move along in the chapter.

While image blurring is useful in reducing noise and creating a smoother image, it is important to note that it also results in a loss of image detail and edges. These techniques have to be used carefully to avoid any loss of information loss in the images.

Average blurring

Average blurring is a simple and fast blurring technique used frequently in image processing. Average blurring helps us to remove noise from the image by reducing the high-frequency contents of an image, resulting in a smoother image.

Average blurring is a type of blurring where the value of each pixel is replaced by the average value of pixels surrounding it. A kernel is used to describe the area to be considered for calculating the average value for the pixel in consideration. The kernel is iterated over the image pixel by pixel and the value for each pixel is calculated, resulting in an overall blurred image.

The average filter, also called a box filter, is a linear filter used to implement average blurring. For best results, the size of the filter is taken in odd dimensions such as 3, 5 or 7 and while we are allowed to use rectangular shape kernels, the shape is generally kept a square. The values for each pixel in this filter are the same and the sum of coefficients in this filter is equal to 1. The size of the filter describes how blurred the resultant image should be. As the size of the filter increases, the amount of blurring in the image also increases. Conversely, using a smaller filter will result in less blurring of the image.

Let us compare two kernels of sizes 3 and 7:

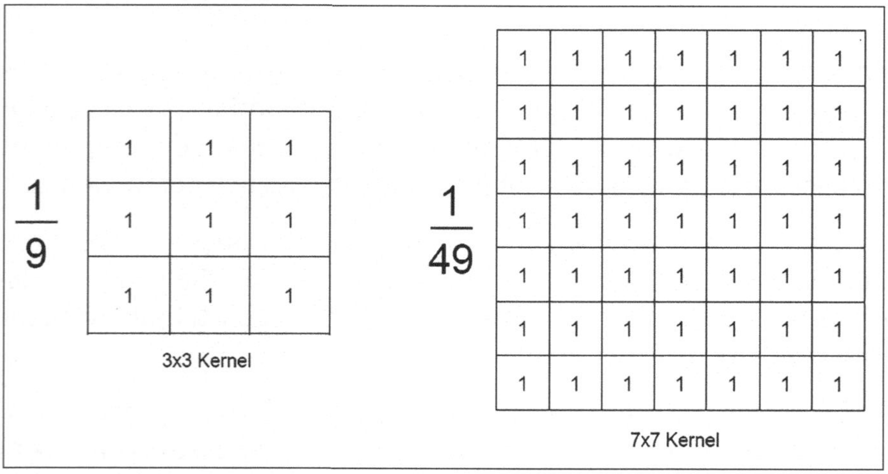

Figure 4.17: *3x3 and 7x7 kernels used for average blurring*

The 3x3 kernel will result in a less blurred image than the 7x7 kernel. This is because the smaller kernel will take a smaller area into account for averaging compared to the larger kernel. Using a smaller kernel will involve averaging fewer pixels around each center pixel. As a result, the center pixel value is determined using nearby pixels that are closer in distance compared to a larger kernel, resulting in less blurring of the image.

Let us demonstrate how a 3x3 averaging filter is applied to a 9x9 image:

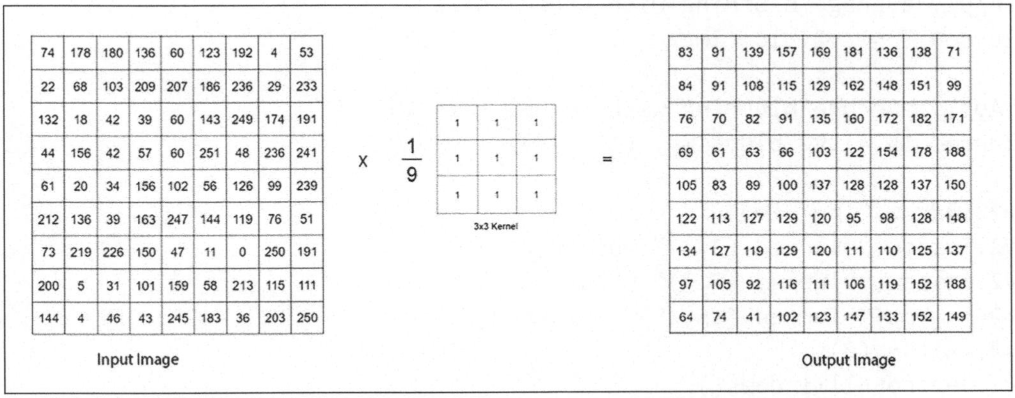

Figure 4.18: *By applying a 3x3 kernel to the image and performing an average blurring operation, the resulting image on the right is produced.*

We will use the cv2.blur function to implement blurring.

Cv2.blur()

```
cv2.blur(src, ksize=(3,3), dst, anchor=(-1,-1), borderType='cv2.BORDER_
DEFAULT')
```

Parameters:

- `src`: The source image to be blurred.
- `kernel`: Size of the kernel to be used for the average filter. This is an optional parameter. The default value for this is a 3*3 filter with each value equal to 1/9.
- `dst`: Output variable.
- **anchor**: The anchor is the pixel used as the reference point for the operation to be performed on the surrounding pixels. This is an optional parameter with a default value of (-1,-1) meaning that the anchor is at the of the kernel.
- **borderType**: This is the pixel extrapolation method, an optional parameter with a default value of **cv2.BORDER_CONSTANT**.

```
import cv2
```

```
img = cv2.imread('1.jpg')

# Apply average blurring with kernel size 3
blurred_3 = cv2.blur(img, (3, 3))

# Apply average blurring with kernel size 7
blurred_7 = cv2.blur(img, (7, 7))

# Apply average blurring with kernel size 15
blurred_15 = cv2.blur(img, (15, 15))

cv2.imshow("img",img)
cv2.imshow("blurred (3,3)", blurred_3)
cv2.imshow("blurred (7,7)", blurred_7)
cv2.imshow("blurred (15,15)", blurred_15)
cv2.waitKey(0)
cv2.destroyAllWindows()
```

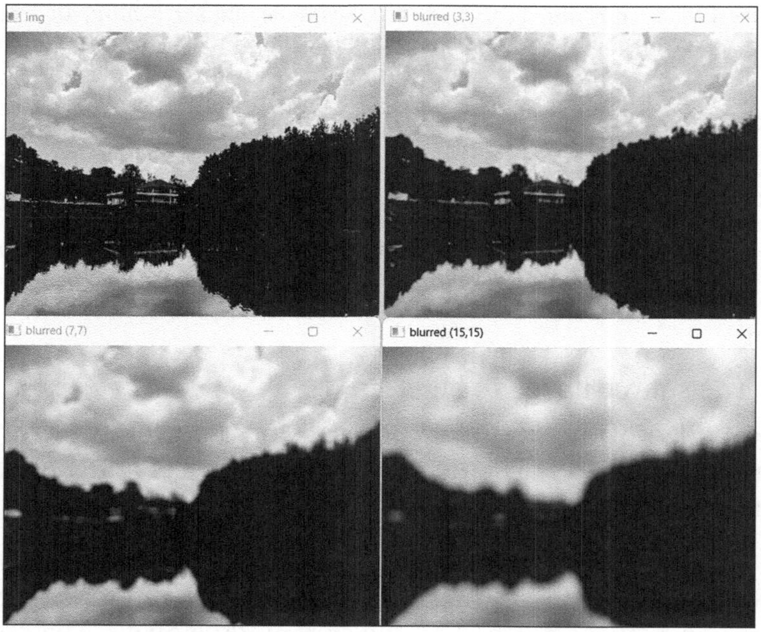

Figure 4.19: *Application of cv2.blur() function on our image. As the kernel size increases, we can observe that the image gets blurrier.*

In the preceding code, we implement average blurring using the **`cv2.blur()`** function. We use three different kernel sizes in our blur function to compare the differences with respect to each kernel size. We start by implementing a blur function with a kernel size of (3,3), we then implement a blur operation with a kernel size of (7,7) and finally a blur operation with a large kernel size of (15,15). We then display the results and can infer that as we increase the size of the kernel, the image gets more blurred.

While Average blur is an efficient and easy-to-use approach for image blurring and can help us get rid of high-frequency noise such as salt and pepper noise, it is essential to note that over-blurring can result in information loss and result in incorrect outputs. It is essential to be wary of the kernel sizes to be used during the operation as an excessive kernel size will result in our image getting extremely blurred resulting in information loss.

Next, we discuss median blurring.

Median blur

Median blurring is another popular blurring algorithm we use in image processing. Unlike average blurring, where we take the average value of the surrounding pixels, in median blurring the median value of the pixels inside the kernel region is used for the center pixel.

Similar to average blurring, we use a kernel for median blurring with an odd dimensional filter size. The filter in median blurring has to be square and we cannot use a rectangular size filter like we did in average blurring.

Median blurring has a major advantage over average blurring in that the edges are often preserved during median blurring, which is not the case when taking the average value of the whole kernel. This is because the median value is not affected that much by outliers and thus, if there are a few extreme values in the neighboring pixels, it cannot affect the overall result in such a significant way.

We use the **`cv2.medianBlur()`** function to implement median blurring in our code.

cv2.medianBlur()

```
cv2.medianBlur(src, ksize, dst)
```

Parameters:

- **`src`**: The source image to be blurred.
- **`kernel`**: Size of the kernel to be used for the average filter. Note: Unlike **`cv2.blur()`**, **`cv2.medianBlur()`** takes an integer as input to denote the size of the square, rather than the full filter size.
- **`dst`**: Output variable.

```
import cv2

img = cv2.imread('image.jpg')

# Apply median blur with kernel size 3x3
median_3 = cv2.medianBlur(img, 3)

# Apply median blur with kernel size 7x7
median_7 = cv2.medianBlur(img, 7)

# Apply median blur with kernel size 15x15
median_15 = cv2.medianBlur(img, 15)

cv2.imshow('Original', img)
cv2.imshow('Median Blur 3', median_3)
cv2.imshow('Median Blur 7', median_7)
cv2.imshow('Median Blur 15', median_15)
cv2.waitKey(0)
cv2.destroyAllWindows()
```

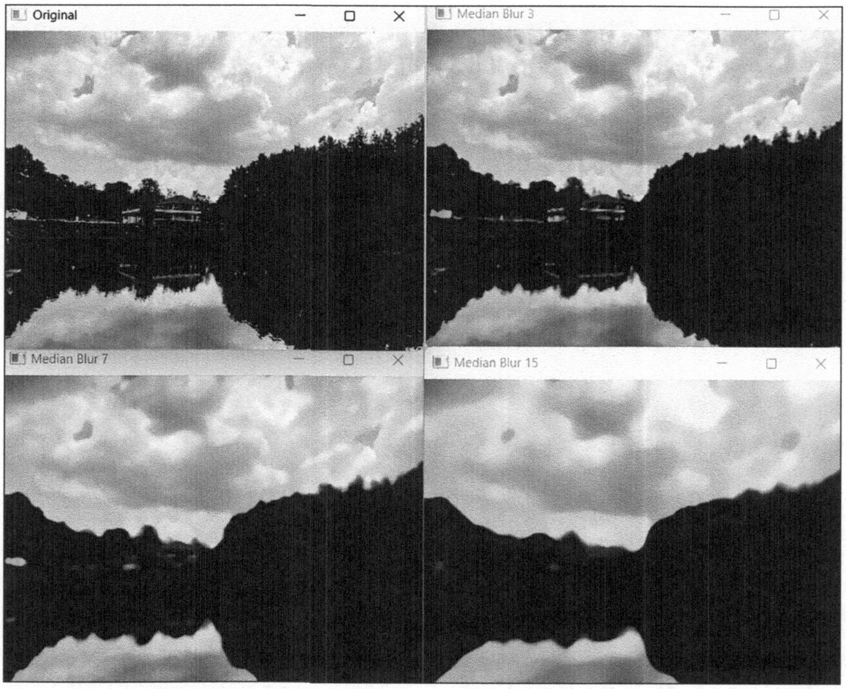

Figure 4.20: *Application of cv2.mediaBlur() function on our image. As the kernel size increases, we can observe that the image gets blurrier, however, some edges are preserved compared to the average blurring operation.*

In the preceding code, we take an image and apply median blur with three different kernel sizes of 3, 7 and 15, similar to what we did in average blurring. Try comparing the results for averaging blur and median blur. We can notice that the median blur has been able to preserve edges more compared to the average blur.

Median blur is particularly useful in removing salt and pepper noise from the image. It is a noise containing randomly occurring white and black pixels in an image:

```
import cv2
import numpy as np

noisy_img = cv2.imread('22.jpg')

# Apply Median Blur
denoised_img = cv2.medianBlur(noisy_img, 3)

cv2.imshow('Noisy Image', noisy_img)
cv2.imshow('Denoised Image', denoised_img)
cv2.waitKey(0)
cv2.destroyAllWindows()
```

***Figure 4.21**: The **left** image is our input image containing salt and pepper noise. Applying median blur removes this noise and produces a clean image on the right.*

The preceding code loads an image which has salt and pepper noise. Applying median blur to the image removes this noise efficiently.

It is important to note that median blur also has a few disadvantages. This is a computationally expensive operation as it takes a bit of time to get the median and hence the operation will be slower compared to average blurring. If not taken care of with the kernel sizes, substantial information loss can also be observed in this operation.

The next blurring method we discuss is Gaussian blurring.

Gaussian blur

The next blurring operation we will discuss is the Gaussian blurring. Similar to the blurring methods we saw earlier, gaussian blurring will also use a kernel in its operation. Gaussian blurring uses a special type of kernel called the Gaussian kernel for the process.

The Gaussian kernel is a matrix of weights applied to each pixel in an image. The kernel is defined in such a way that the center of the kernel has the highest value or weight, and as we move away from the center the weights start to decrease. This effectively means that when we apply this kernel to a pixel, the blurring operation takes place in such a way that the pixels nearer to the center pixel have more contribution to the overall value compared to pixels that are further away from it.

The Gaussian kernel is defined using the formula:

$$G(x,y) = \frac{1}{\sqrt{2\pi\sigma^2}} e^{-\frac{x^2+y^2}{2\sigma^2}}$$

***Figure 4.22**: Gaussian Filter formula*

X and y are the coordinates of each matrix and sigma defines the standard deviation that controls the width of the distribution. A higher value of sigma produces a wider distribution, resulting in more smoothing or blurring of the image.

Based on the preceding formula, a Gaussian kernel of size 5 with a sigma value of 1.5 will look like this:

0.003765	0.015019	0.023792	0.015019	0.003765
0.015019	0.059912	0.094907	0.059912	0.015019
0.023792	0.094907	0.150342	0.094907	0.023792
0.015019	0.059912	0.094907	0.059912	0.015019
0.003765	0.015019	0.023792	0.015019	0.003765

***Figure 4.23**: 5x5 Gaussian filter generated using the preceding formula, taking the sigma value as 1.5*

Gaussian blurring is useful to remove various types of noise from the image, but the main effect of Gaussian blurring can be seen in Gaussian noise. Gaussian noise is a noise that follows the Gaussian probability distribution. Gaussian images will make our images look grainy.

We use the **`cv2.gaussianBlur()`** function to implement Gaussian blurring in our code.

cv2.gaussianBlur()

```
cv2.gaussianblur(src, ksize=0, dst, sigmaX=0, sigmaY=0, borderType='cv2.
BORDER_DEFAULT')
```

Parameters:

- **`src`**: The source image to be blurred.
- **`ksize`**: Kernel size of the gaussian kernel. This value is a tuple. The default value is (0,0) which means that the size is computed based on the **`sigmaX`** and **`sigmaY`** values.
- **dst**: Output variable.
- **`sigmaX`**: The standard deviation of the Gaussian kernel in the X direction.

It is an optional parameter, and the default value is 0. In case of 0, it will be calculated based on kernel size.

- **sigmaY**: The standard deviation of the Gaussian kernel in the Y direction. It is an optional parameter with a default value of 0. In case of 0, it will be made equal to the **sigmaX** value.
- **borderType**: This is the pixel extrapolation method, an optional parameter with a default value of **cv2.BORDER_CONSTANT**.

```
import cv2

image = cv2.imread(‘img.jpg’)

# apply Gaussian blur with kernel size (5,5) and standard deviation of 0
gaussian_blur = cv2.GaussianBlur(image, (5, 5), 0)

# display the original and blurred images side by side
cv2.imshow(‘Original Image’, image)
cv2.imshow(‘Gaussian Blurred Image’, gaussian_blur)

# wait for a key press and then close all windows
cv2.waitKey(0)
cv2.destroyAllWindows()
```

Figure 4.24: *Left: Original Image with texture. Applying Gaussian blur removes some texture while preserving edges producing an image on the right.*

In the preceding code, we use Gaussian blur to remove noise from our image. As we can see, the texture has been removed from the image while preserving the edges of the text image.

Bilateral filter

A bilateral filter is a non-linear filter that allows us to blur images while preserving the edges of objects in the image. This makes it a popular choice for a wide range of image processing applications such as denoising and edge detection.

The filters we discussed earlier only consider the spatial distance between the pixels in consideration. However, a Bilateral filter is a special type of filter as it considers both the spatial distance and the difference between the intensity values of neighboring pixels. Edges are basically large differences in intensity values, a bilateral filter is able to take that into consideration and hence handles these differences accordingly (We will discuss edges in detail as we move along the book). This feature allows the filter to preserve the edges in an image while reducing noise.

This filter works on an image by computing a weighted average of the intensity values of the pixels within an area around the center pixel. These weights are defined by two factors, the spatial distance and the intensity value between the pixels. Spatial distance is the Euclidean distance between the two pixels and intensity is just the absolute difference between the intensity values of these pixels.

A Gaussian function is used to calculate these two parameters. The Gaussian function is applied separately to both parameters. The standard deviation in the Gaussian function controls what values are given to each pixel in the filter. The larger the standard deviation, the more weight is given to both neighboring pixels with larger differences in intensity and those that are farther away from the center pixel. By applying separate Gaussian functions to the two parameters, the bilateral filter will help us by being able to balance the importance of spatial distance and intensity difference in the computation of the weighted average:

$$BF[I]_P = \frac{1}{W_P} \sum_{q \in S} G\sigma_s(\| p - q \|) G\sigma_r(Ip - Iq)\, Iq$$

Figure 4.25: *Bilateral Filter formula comprising both the spatial and intensity components*

The bilateral filter is implemented using the **`cv2.bilateralFIlter()`** function in OpenCV.

cv2.bilateralFilter()

`cv2.bilateralFilter(src, d, sigmaColor, sigmaSpace, dst, borderType='cv2.BORDER_DEFAULT')`

Parameters:

- `src`: The source image to be blurred.
- `d`: This is the diameter of the pixel neighborhood to be used in the bilateral filter.
- `sigmaColor`: Standard deviation value of the bilateral filter in the color space. A larger value will mean that pixels with large differences in intensity values will be mixed.
- `sigmaSpace`: Standard deviation value of the bilateral filter in the coordinate space. A larger value will mean that pixels with large differences in distance will be mixed.
- **dst**: Output variable.
- **borderType**: This is the pixel extrapolation method, an optional parameter with a default value of **cv2.BORDER_CONSTANT**:

```
import cv2

img = cv2.imread('image.jpg')

# Apply bilateral filter with high sigma values
filtered_img_high = cv2.bilateralFilter(img, 15, 200, 200)

# Apply bilateral filter with low sigma values
filtered_img_low = cv2.bilateralFilter(img, 15, 50, 50)

cv2.imshow('Original', img)
cv2.imshow('Filtered (high)', filtered_img_high)
cv2.imshow('Filtered (low)', filtered_img_low)
cv2.waitKey(0)
cv2.destroyAllWindows()
```

Figure 4.26: *Bilateral Filter output. The image starts to get blurred as we increase the sigma values, however, we can observe that the edges are significantly preserved compared to other blurring methods discussed earlier.*

In this example, we load an image and apply the bilateral filter twice, once with high **`sigmaColor`** and **`sigmaSpace`** values of 200, and once with low **`sigmaColor`** and **`sigmaSpace`** values of 50. The resulting filtered images are then displayed side by side for comparison. We can see that larger values of **`sigmaColor`** and **`sigmaSpace`** result in a more blurred image, smaller values for these parameters will result in a sharper image while preserving the edges of our object.

A bilateral filter is a powerful tool we can use in our image-processing applications. However, we need to keep in mind that this is a computationally expensive operation and is significantly slower than the other methods discussed earlier.

Conclusion

In this chapter, we have discussed the topic of morphological operations on images, starting with the basic dilation and erosion operations. We demonstrated how these operations can be used to manipulate the shape and structure of images and control the resulting size and shape. We also covered more advanced morphological operations such as the opening and closing of images. Additionally, we explored various image smoothing and blurring techniques, including the commonly used average and median blur, as well as more complex blurs like Gaussian and bilateral filtering, and demonstrated how to apply these techniques using OpenCV.

In the next chapter, we will explore the topic of histograms and their uses in image processing. We will begin by defining histograms and showing how they can be used to represent the distribution of pixel intensities in an image. We will demonstrate how histograms can be used to enhance images, adjust contrast, and perform other advanced image processing techniques. Additionally, we will cover how to manipulate histogram plots and use histograms with masks to select specific areas of an image for processing.

Points to remember

- Erosion is a morphological operation that is used to decrease the size of objects in an image, while dilation, on the other hand, is an operation that increases the size of objects in an image.
- Opening is a morphological operation that involves a sequence of erosion followed by dilation operations, while closing is an operation that involves a sequence of dilation followed by erosion.
- The morphological gradient is the difference between dilation and erosion operations on an image.
- Top hat and bottom hat are morphological operations that highlight the bright and dark regions of an image, respectively, by subtracting the original image from the opened and closed versions of the image.
- Average blur is a simple and fast technique for smoothing out an image by replacing each pixel value with the average value of its neighboring pixels in a kernel window.
- Median blur is a non-linear image filtering technique that replaces each pixel value with the median value of its neighboring pixels in a kernel window, which is effective in removing salt-and-pepper noise while preserving edges in the image.
- Gaussian blur is a linear image filtering technique that convolves the image with a Gaussian kernel, which results in smoothing the image by reducing high-frequency noise while preserving edges and details.
- The bilateral filter is a non-linear smoothing filter that preserves edges while reducing noise in an image.

Test your understanding

1. What does the Erosion function do to an image?

   A. Increases the size of the objects

   B. Decreases the size of the objects

   C. Highlights bright regions of an image

   D. Blurs an image by an average value

2. How is the closing operation performed in an image?

   A. Dilation followed by erosion

   B. Erosion followed by dilation

C. Subtracting eroded image from the dilated image

D. Subtracting eroded image from the original image

3. What does the tophat operation do?

A. Highlights the white objects in an image

B. Enhances the dark regions in an image

C. Enhances the boundary of the objects

D. Removes noise from the image

4. Which of the following types of noise is median blur most effective at removing?

A. Speckle noise

B. Gaussian noise

C. Salt and pepper noise

D. Chromatic noise

5. What is the main purpose of using a bilateral filter?

A. To remove salt and pepper noise

B. To smoothen an image while preserving edges

C. To enhance bright portions of an image

D. To enhance the boundary of objects in an image

Chapter 5

Image Histograms

We begin this chapter with a definition of histograms and explore the uses of histograms for image processing. We then move on to learn how histograms can be used to represent the distribution of pixel intensities in an image, and how this information can be used to enhance images, adjust contrast, and perform other advanced image processing techniques. We cover how to manipulate histogram plots and how histograms can be used with masks to select specific areas of an image for processing. Towards the end of this chapter, we will learn about histogram equalization and its techniques.

Structure

In this chapter, we will discuss the following topics:

- Introduction to Histograms
- Matplotlib helper functions
- Histogram for colored images
- Two-dimensional histograms
- Histogram with masks
- Histogram equalization
    - Introduction to histogram equalization
    - Histogram equalization on colored images
    - Adaptive histogram equalization
    - Contrast limited adaptive histogram equalization
- Histograms for feature extraction

Introduction to histograms

A histogram is a representation of the distribution of pixel intensities in an image. In simpler words, a histogram displays the count or sum of pixels with each intensity value in an image. The number of pixels with each intensity value is counted and displayed as a plot for better visualization.

The histogram values are plotted on a line graph with the help of the matplotlib library. The x-axis on this graph represents the range of intensity values, while the y-axis is used to represent the count of pixels for the corresponding intensity value. The higher values in the graph will represent more pixels with the intensity values, while lower values will denote fewer pixels for those intensity values.

A histogram generally looks like this:

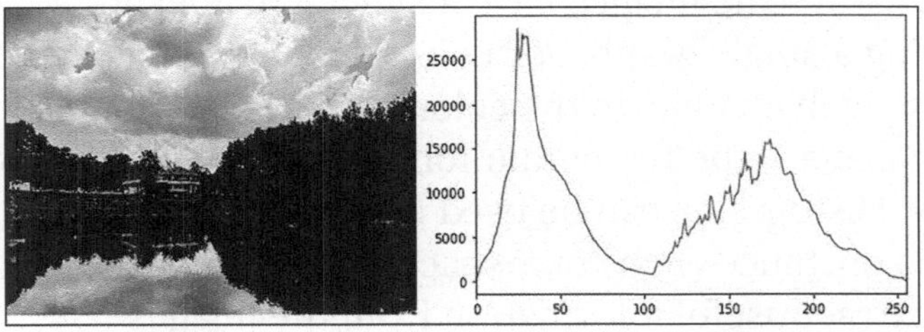

Figure 5.1: *A grayscale image with the corresponding histogram where the x-axis represents the intensity values, and the y-axis represents the number of pixels with those intensity values.*

In the histogram, the x-axis represents the different intensity values ranging from 0 (pure black) to 255 (pure white), while the y-axis represents the number of pixels that have each intensity value. The peaks in the histogram mean that the corresponding intensity values have a higher frequency of pixels. Here we see two peaks in the image in the ranges of ~ 30-45 and ~ 160-175 showing us that the number of pixels with these intensities is higher. Similarly, lower values in the histogram mean that pixels of those intensities are fewer in the image.

OpenCV creates a histogram by dividing the intensities into fixed intervals called bins. Histograms group the different intensity values of an image into bins. For instance, if we consider an image with intensity values between 0 to 255, dividing them into 8 bins will create 8 different groups, with each group containing 32 intensity values. These groups can be represented as ranges, such as 0-32, 32-64, 224-256, and so on. Similarly, for representing each value separately, we can keep the number of bins as 256. Following this, a cumulative distribution function (CDF) is obtained by adding up the frequencies of bins, starting from the lowest bin up to the current bin. The CDF reflects the cumulative probability of encountering a value that is less than or equal to the value represented by the current bin.

In a histogram, "bins" represent the intervals or ranges into which the data is divided. It is used to count the frequency of values falling within those intervals. The number of bins decides how detailed the histogram is. More bins mean we can see smaller differences in the data.

The "bin range" sets limits for the data intervals in a histogram. In a grayscale image histogram with 256 bins, each bin represents a different shade of gray, from 0 (black) to 255 (white). When we change the bin range like selecting a range from 100 to 120, we are narrowing down to specific gray shades in that range. This helps us see how often those specific shades appear in the image. This gives us a closer look at certain details in the pixel distribution.

In these examples, we have used a grayscale image to introduce ourselves to histograms, however, histograms can be calculated for both grayscale and colored images. Grayscale images have a single channel and histograms can be represented using a single graph. For colored images, a separate histogram will be calculated for each channel in the color space. For instance, In the RGB color space, we will calculate the histogram for each color channel (Red, Green, and Blue) separately. Histograms can be used for various other color spaces such as HSV, LAB, and so on. Since each color space has different properties, histograms can help us to extract useful information from the images.

Histograms are used in a variety of image-processing applications. We can use histograms to enhance our images by improving the overall brightness and contrast of our images. Histograms can also be used for thresholding images, where a threshold value is selected based on the distribution of pixel intensities. We can use this value to segment the image into different regions based on intensity values. By visualizing the distribution of pixel intensities in an image, histograms can help identify regions of interest, improve image quality, and facilitate various other image processing tasks.

We will use the cv2.calcHist function to calculate histograms using OpenCV.

cv2.calcHist()

```
cv2.calcHist(images, channels=[0], mask=None, histSize=[256],
ranges=[0,256])
```

Parameters:

- `images`: List of input images in form of arrays.
- `channels`: List of indices of channels used to compute the histogram. For a grayscale image the value is [0], while for RGB images values will

be [0,1,2] representing each channel. This is an image with default value as [0].

- **mask**: Binary mask to specify region of interest for histogram calculation. The default value is None, which will consider the whole image.
- **histSize**: Array of histogram sizes (number of bins) for each channel. The default value for this parameter is [256].
- **ranges**: List of ranges for each channel specifying the minimum and maximum values for each channel. The default value for this parameter is [0,256].

Let us try creating our own histograms for an image for a better understanding of the concepts:

```
import cv2
import numpy as np
import matplotlib.pyplot as plt

img = cv2.imread(image.jpg')

gray_img = cv2.cvtColor(img, cv2.COLOR_BGR2GRAY)

# Define number of bins for the histogram
num_bins = 8

# Define the range for each bin
bin_range = [0, 256]

# Calculate the histogram with 256 bins
hist = cv2.calcHist([gray_img], [0], None, [num_bins], bin_range)


# Calculate the histogram with 8 bins
hist2 = cv2.calcHist([gray_img], [0], None, [256], bin_range)


# Plot the histogram using matplotlib
plt.plot(hist)
plt.xlim([0, 255])
plt.show()


plt.plot(hist2)
plt.xlim([0, num_bins-1])
plt.show()
```

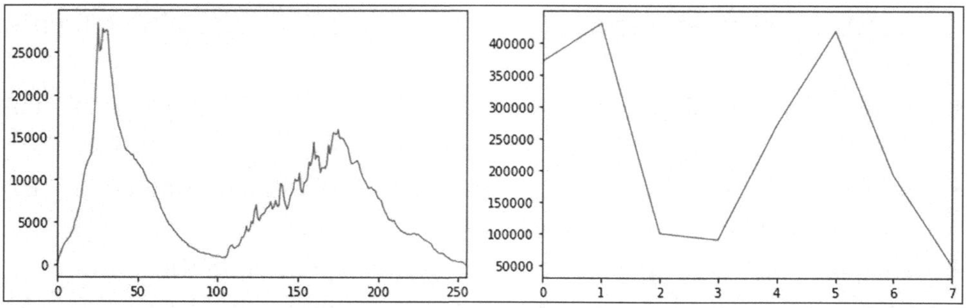

Figure 5.2: *Two histograms with 256 bins (left) and 8 bins (right). The histogram with 256 bins is much more detailed while the smaller histogram provides a generalized overview of the image.*

The above code calculates two histograms of bin sizes 8 and 256, respectively. First, we define a variable **num_bins** to define 8 bins and the bin range [0,256]. We use **cv2.calcHist()** function to calculate histograms for both 8 and 256 bins, respectively producing two graphs as shown in *Figure* 5.2.

The histogram with 256 provides a more fine-grained analysis of the image. Each pixel intensity is marked separately in the histogram, and thus the histogram is more detailed and captures the subtle variations in the intensity values. The histogram with 8 bins is more coarse-grained analysis of the image. The intensity data is divided into 8 bins, and this provides a more generalized overview of the intensity data. Overall, a smaller bin size can provide a quicker overview of the data, while a larger bin size will produce a more detailed representation of the data.

Before we move on further into histograms, let us take an overview of the matplotlib functions we will be using for our plots.

Matplotlib helper functions

Matplotlib is a Python library for creating visualizations and data plots, offering a wide variety of functions to generate a diverse range of graphs and charts. We will be using matplotlib to visualize our histograms.

We will not be delving deeper into matplotlib syntax, but for the sake of our discussion, we will have a look at the functions we have used:

- **plt.plot()**: We can use the **plt.plot()** function to visualize any types of graphs or charts that we might want. This takes arguments to define the data points and the type of plot we want. To draw histograms using **plt.plot** we case simply use **plt.plot(hist)**.
- **plt.xlim()** and **plt.ylim()**: These functions set the x and y-limits of the plot. They both take two arguments, **xmin** and **xmax**, **ymin** and **ymax** to define

the minimum and maximum range across the x and y axis respectively. We can use these functions such as **plt.xlim([xmin, xmax])** and **plt.ylim([ymin,ymax])**.

- **plt.show()**: This function allows the created graphs to be displayed on the screen. It also allows interaction such as zooming and saving the plots. We can use **plt.show()** to display our plots.
- **plt.xlabel()** and **plt.ylabel()**: These functions are used to set the labels for the x-axis and the y-axis respectively in a matplotlib plot.
- **plt.title()**: This function is used to set the title of a matplotlib plot by providing a name or caption for the plot.
- **plt.imshow()**: This function is used to display an image or a matrix as a 2D plot. It is commonly used in matplotlib to visualize images by representing pixel intensities with colors.
- **plt.colorbar()**: This adds a color bar to the plot, providing a mapping between the numerical values and the colors in the matplotlib plot.

These are some rudimentary matplotlib functions we will be using in our computer vision tasks. Any additional information needed for these functions or any new functions that are introduced as we move further along the chapter can be found in the matplotlib documentation.

Histogram for colored images

Histograms for colored images are very similar to computing a histogram for grayscale images. The only difference is that colored images have to be split into individual channels and the histogram for each channel is computed independently.

We use the same function **cv2.calcHist()** to compute histograms for images. Since **cv2.calcHist()** can only process one channel at a time, we need to split a color image into its individual channels, such as red, green, and blue, and compute their histograms separately:

```
import cv2
import numpy as np
import matplotlib.pyplot as plt

img = cv2.imread('image.jpg')

# Split the image into its three color channels
b, g, r = cv2.split(img)

# Set the histogram parameters
```

```
histSize = 256
histRange = (0, 256)

# Compute the histograms for each color channel
b_hist = cv2.calcHist([b], [0], None, [histSize], histRange)
g_hist = cv2.calcHist([g], [0], None, [histSize], histRange)
r_hist = cv2.calcHist([r], [0], None, [histSize], histRange)

plt.plot(b_hist, color='b')
plt.plot(g_hist, color='g')
plt.plot(r_hist, color='r')
plt.xlim([0, 256])
plt.show()
```

The output for the preceding image is as follows:

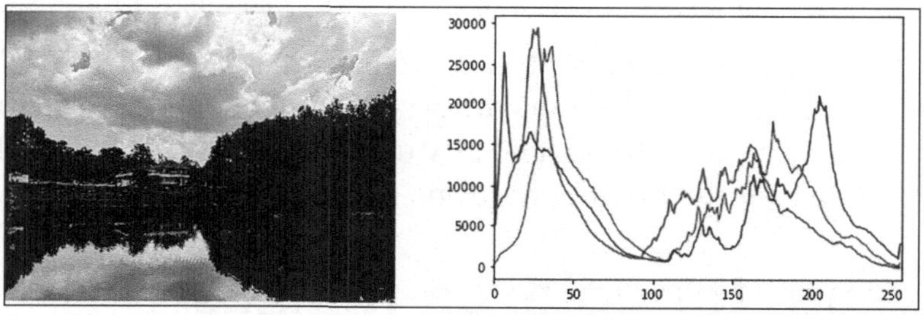

***Figure 5.3**: Histogram for the corresponding BGR image. We can observe that there are separate lines on the graph representing each channel.*

The three lines in the chart represent a line for each of the red, green, and blue channels.

To understand the histogram better, we take another image and compute the histogram for that:

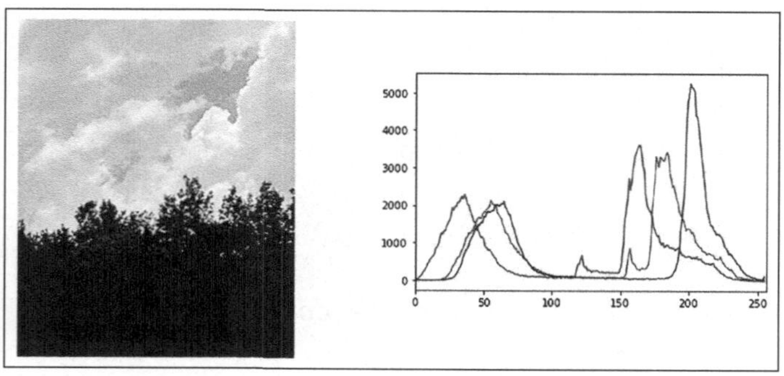

***Figure 5.4**: Histogram for a subregion of the earlier image. The histogram lines have changed significantly. This can be used to extract region-specific information from an image.*

Each line in the plot represents a histogram for the corresponding channel in the images (see *Figure* 5.4). In the first image, we observe a histogram with two peaks, one corresponding to lighter intensity values and the other to darker intensity values. It is evident that the image primarily consists of darker regions rather than lighter regions.

In the second image, we focus on a specific sub-region of the image. Here, we notice that the histogram exhibits a prominent peak in the higher intensity values, indicating the presence of lighter regions compared to darker areas.

Two-dimensional histograms

Two-dimensional histograms are used to capture the joint distribution of two channels in an image. We can use two-dimensional histograms to analyze the relations between these two channels, which could help us determine the color intensity or spatial relationships between the two channels.

2D histograms are visualized as a two-dimensional plot where each variable can be represented on the x and y axis, respectively. A single pixel on the two-dimensional histogram plot represents the frequency or quantity of occurrences of a specific combination of x and y values in the image. This provides information about how much of that particular value is present in the image along both the x and y axes. Just like our traditional histograms, two-dimensional histograms use bins for both channels. Since it is a 2D histogram, 256 bins for each channel will result in overall 256*256 = 65536 unique data points.

Let's create a 2D histogram for an image and try to analyze that histogram for better understanding:

```
import cv2
import numpy as np
import matplotlib.pyplot as plt

image = cv2.imread(image.jpg')

# Convert the image to the HSV color space
hsv_image = cv2.cvtColor(image, cv2.COLOR_BGR2HSV)

# Split the image channels
h, s, v = cv2.split(hsv_image)

# Define the number of bins for each channel
bins = [50, 50]
```

```
# Compute the 2D histogram
histogram = cv2.calcHist([h, s], [0, 1], None, bins, [0, 180, 0, 256])

plt.imshow(histogram, interpolation='nearest', origin='upper', as-
pect='auto', cmap='jet')
plt.colorbar()
plt.xlabel('Hue')
plt.ylabel('Saturation')
plt.title('2D Histogram')
plt.show()
```

The above code produces the following output:

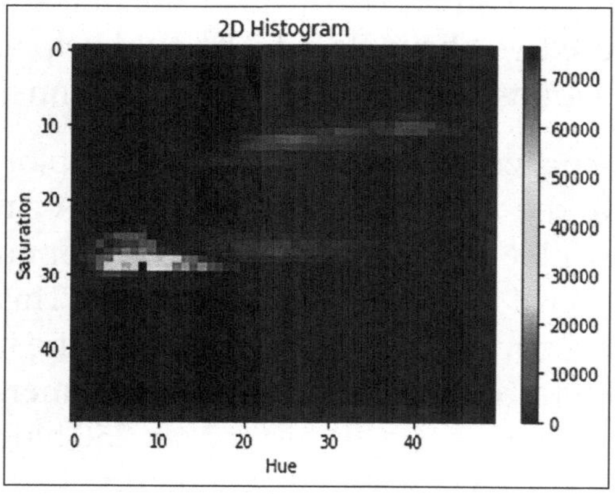

***Figure 5.5**: A two-dimensional histogram representing the hue and saturation channels on the x-axis and y-axis respectively.*

This is a 2D representation of two channels of an image. We have converted the image to an HSV channel and visualized a histogram for the hue and saturation channels. Using the above histogram, we can see the relation between two channels. As seen on the vertical color scale on the right side of the image, it starts with blue values, indicating very low values, and progresses to dark red, representing the maximum intensity.

We can observe that there is a red pixel in the histogram around bin 9 in the hue channel and bin 31 in the saturation channel. This means that there are around 7000 occurrences of pixels lying under these respective bins. We can also observe that typically, the yellow values in the hue channel here are distributed across 5-15 bins, while the saturation channel tends to have values concentrated around bin numbers 30-35. Yellow values correspond to around 5000 in the scale, indicating that the pixels lying under these bins have 5000 occurrences.

Similarly, we can create histograms for relationships in other channels as well:

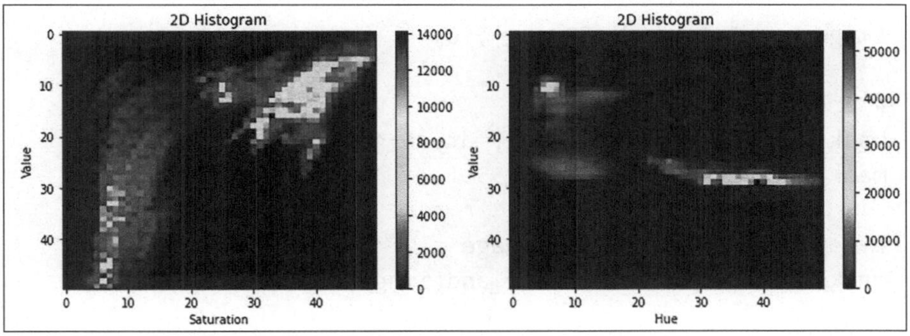

***Figure 5.6**: Two-dimensional histograms for the relation between other channels of the image. Saturation-Value and Hue-Value on the x-axis and y-axis respectively.*

Histogram with masks

In the previous sections, we discussed that masks can be used on images to selectively compute histograms for a specific region of an image. The mask parameter in the **`cv2.calcHist()`** function can be used to specify the mask for our histogram computation area.

Masks serve as specialized filters in image processing. For instance, when working with a photo and wanting to isolate a specific element, such as a person's face, masks are employed to hide the unwanted portions, allowing us to concentrate solely on the face. If we want to analyze only the mouth portion of a person's face, we can create a mask that isolates or covers everything except the mouth area.

Now, why do we use masks in histograms? Masks help us answer specific questions about an image. For example, we can use a mask to find out how much of a certain color is in just the sky of a landscape photo. Masks allow us to select and work on exactly what we want to study in an image, which can be really useful.

The advantage of using masks in histograms is that they give us more control and precision in our analysis. Instead of looking at the whole picture, we can zero in on particular areas and get detailed information about just those parts.

In the following code, we will compute a histogram for an image by creating a binary mask using OpenCV:

```
import cv2
import numpy as np
```

```
import matplotlib.pyplot as plt

image = cv2.imread('23.jpg', 0)

# Create a binary mask
mask = np.zeros_like(image, dtype=np.uint8)
mask[100:300, 100:300] = 255

# Apply the mask to the image
masked_image = cv2.bitwise_and(image, mask)

# Calculate and plot the histogram
histogram = cv2.calcHist([image], [0], masked_image, [256], [0,
256])
plt.plot(histogram)

cv2.imshow('Original Image', image)
cv2.imshow('Masked Image', masked_image)
cv2.waitKey(0)
cv2.destroyAllWindows()
```

The output images and their corresponding histograms are shown in *Figure* 5.7 and *Figure* 5.8 respectively:

Figure 5.7: *The original and masked image.*

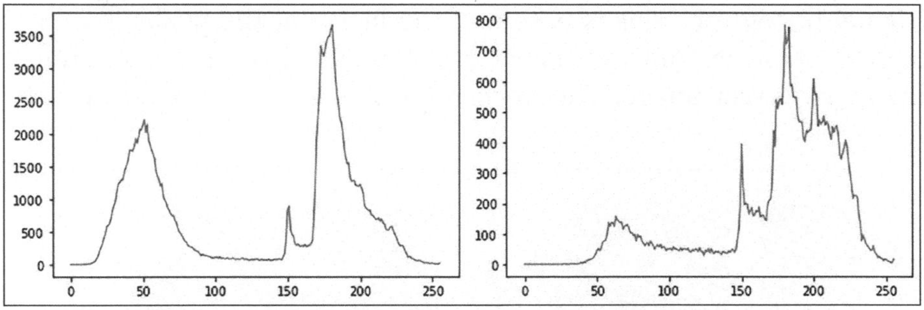

Figure 5.8: *Histograms for the original and the masked image.*

The above code applies a mask on a grayscale image. Similar to how histograms are processed for color images, masks can also be applied in the same way using channel-wise histogram computation.

Histogram equalization

Histogram equalization is the process of improving the contrast of an image. The unevenly distributed intensity values in an image are stretched out, creating a more even intensity distribution over the image. This method effectively improves the global contrast of the image.

The underlying process to perform histogram equalization is to first calculate and plot the histogram for an image. The resultant histogram often has uneven peaks, creating an imbalanced distribution of pixel intensities across the image. A modified image is then created by evening out these intensity values, thereby resulting in a uniform histogram and improving the contrast of the image:

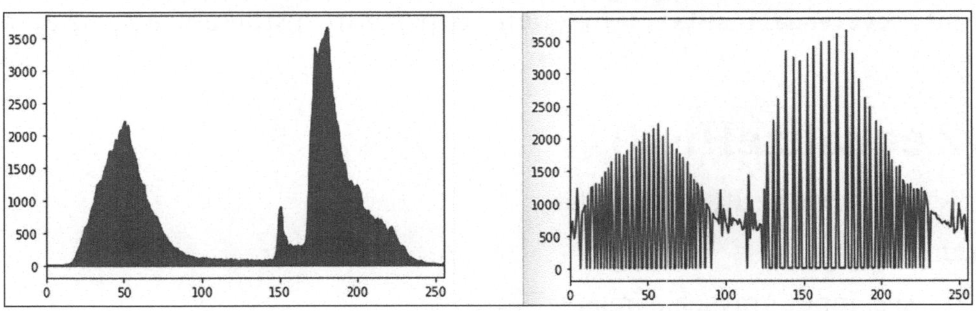

Figure 5.9: *Histograms before (left) and after(right) equalization. Histogram Equalization has smoothened out the peaks in the original histogram, leading to an image with better contrast.*

The preceding charts represent histograms before and after applying histogram equalization. We can see that the process has been able to smooth out the peaks to some level, and the resulting histogram is a smoother chart compared to the original histogram. This is based on the fact that the peaks in a histogram correspond to lower-contrast images and smoothing out the histogram results in a higher-contrast image. The images for the above histogram can be seen here:

Figure 5.10: *Images before (left) and after(right) histogram equalization. Histogram Equalization has effectively enhanced the image by significantly improving its contrast and overall visual quality.*

Our histogram equalization process has been able to increase the contrast of the image. The brighter areas of the image become whiter, and the darker areas become more pronounced, resulting in a significantly improved image.

We use **`cv2.equalizeHist()`** function to perform histogram equalization in OpenCV.

cv2.equalizeHist()

```
cv2.equalizeHist(src, dst)
```

Parameters:

- **`src`**: Input grayscale image
- **`dst`**: Output Array

Let's try histogram Equalization using some code:

```
import cv2
import numpy as np
```

```
import matplotlib.pyplot as plt

img = cv2.imread('img.jpg', 0)

# Calculate histogram
hist_input = cv2.calcHist([img],[0],None,[256],[0,256])

# Perform histogram equalization
equalized = cv2.equalizeHist(img)

# Calculate histogram of equalized image
hist_equalized = cv2.calcHist([equalized],[0],None,[256],[0,256])

# Save equalized image to file
cv2.imshow("Original Image", img)
cv2.imshow("Equalized_image", equalized)
cv2.waitKey(0)
cv2.destroyAllWindows()

# Plot histograms using matplotlib
plt.plot(hist_input, color='blue')
plt.fill_between(range(len(hist_input)), hist_input.flatten(), col-
or='blue')
plt.xlim([0,255])
plt.show()

plt.plot(hist_equalized, color='blue')
plt.xlim([0,255])
plt.show()
```

This code produces the charts and images as output that we saw earlier in the code. We use the **cv2.equalizeHist()** function directly on the image. To display histogram charts before and after histogram equalization, we have calculated histograms separately. We use OpenCV to display our input and equalized images and matplotlib lib to visualize our histogram charts.

The histogram equalization process can be done using a number of algorithms. In the preceding example, we have used the standard histogram equalization method. This is a global image transformation that applies the same transformation to all the pixels of the image. While this technique is good for improving the overall contrast of images, it will not work properly on images containing local variations in the intensity distribution.

To be able to better handle the local variations in the intensity distribution, we will use adaptive histogram techniques. These methods apply different transformations to different regions of the image effectively being able to handle local variations in the intensity properly. We will discuss these in detail as we move along with the chapter.

Histogram equalization on colored images

Histogram equalization can be performed on colored images as well. The process is very similar to what we saw earlier. Histogram equalization is performed on each channel of a multi-channel image and the same function **`cv2.equalizeHist()`** can be used to perform histogram equalization.

However, there are some important considerations to be noted about histogram equalization on colored images. While we can perform histogram equalization on RGB or BGR images, it is recommended not to use this color space for histogram equalization. This is because RGB color space does not separate the brightness from the color information in the images, so performing histogram equalization on this channel will produce distorted results. The following image shows the output of histogram equalization in RGB color space:

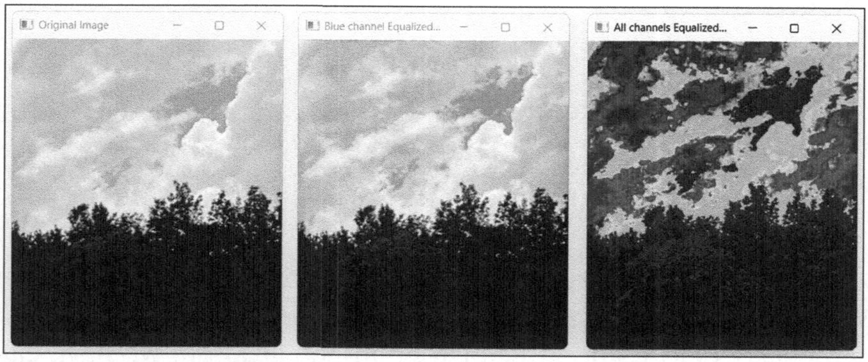

***Figure 5.11**: Histogram Equalization on the RGB/BGR color space. The middle image illustrates the histogram equalization process applied to a single channel, while the image on the right demonstrates the application of histogram equalization to all channels. However, it is worth noting that using histogram equalization on the RGB color space can lead to distorted results, making it an impractical approach.*

It is recommended to perform histogram equalization in color space that separates the brightness from color information. We can use the Value channel in the HSV color space, the Lightness channel in the HSL color space, or the Luminance channel in the Lab Color space for histogram equalization.

Let's try histogram equalization using some code:

```
import cv2

img = cv2.imread('image.jpg')

img_hsv = cv2.cvtColor(img, cv2.COLOR_BGR2HSV)
h, s, v = cv2.split(img_hsv)

# Perform histogram equalization on the value channel
v_eq = cv2.equalizeHist(v)

# Merge the equalized value channel back into the HSV image
img_hsv_eq = cv2.merge((h, s, v_eq))

# Convert the equalized HSV image back to the original color
space
img_eq = cv2.cvtColor(img_hsv_eq, cv2.COLOR_HSV2BGR)

cv2.imshow('Original Image', img)
cv2.imshow('Equalized Image', img_eq)
cv2.waitKey(0)
cv2.destroyAllWindows()
```

The preceding code results in the following output:

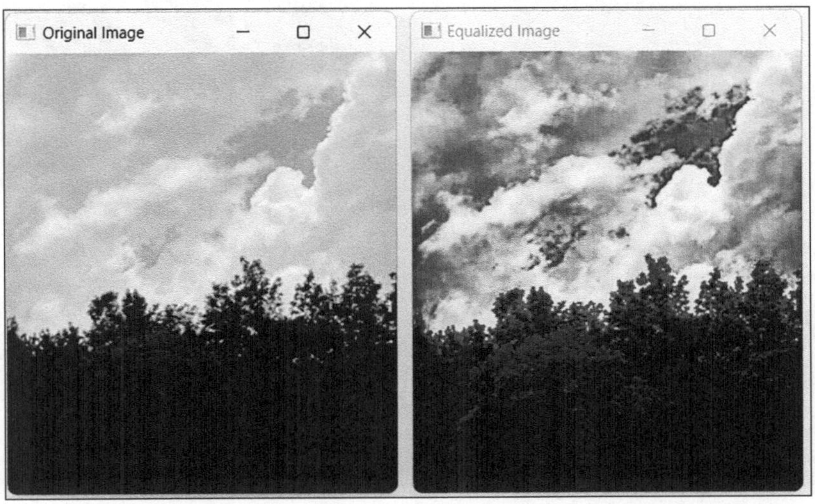

***Figure 5.12**: Histogram Equalization on the Value channel in the HSV color space. The application of histogram equalization has greatly improved the image, resulting in a significant enhancement of its visual quality and contrast.*

In the preceding code, we have converted our image into the HSV color space and equalized the Value channel. As it is clearly visible, histogram equalization has significantly enhanced the image.

Adaptive histogram equalization

Adaptive histogram equalization is used to perform equalization while considering local variations in the intensity distributions of the image. Unlike the standard histogram equalization, which applies a global transformation of the image, adaptive equalization applies the same technique independently to small local regions of the image. Adaptive histogram equalization techniques thus help us in improving contrast in images with local variations in intensity.

While a rudimentary version of adaptive histogram equalization can be implemented by dividing the images into smaller parts and processing them independently, they generally do not give good results. This is because the basic AHE will not take into consideration the overall global contrast of the image and will increase the noise in the smaller regions with low contrast. Additionally, all the boundaries of these smaller grids will be visible due to the sudden change in intensity and the final output will not be an acceptable image, as shown in *Figure 5.13*:

Figure 5.13: *Adaptive Histogram Equalization by manually dividing the image into a grid and applying separate operations on each sub-region. AHE can result in a very poor output (right) because basic AHE doesn't consider global contrast and enhances the noise in the image.*

To handle the underlying drawbacks of the basic AHE, more advanced techniques have been developed for adaptive histogram equalization. CLAHE is one of the most used techniques for adaptive histogram equalization.

Contrast limited adaptive histogram equalization (CLAHE)

Contrast limited adaptive histogram equalization or CLAHE, is an extension of the adaptive histogram equalization technique. As discussed previously, AHE often results in undesirable results, especially in low-contrast regions. One of the major issues in the vanilla AHE model was that there was a major contrast difference in nearby grid sub-regions of the image. CLAHE helps to circumvent some of these issues and handles histogram equalization in a much better way.

The main advantage CLAHE offers is that it limits the contrast. It does so by introducing a contrast limit parameter that controls the region-wise amount of contrast enhancement in the image. By applying limits on contrast, CLAHE prevents the excess amplification of noise in the image.

CLAHE works by dividing the image into small sub-regions and then computing the histogram for each region. The histogram values are clipped based on the predefined contrast limit parameter. The **cumulative distribution function** (**CDF**) for the clipped histogram is calculated, and it is then used to map the pixel intensities in each tile for achieving contrast enhancement. The sub-regions are then combined to create the enhanced output image.

CLAHE uses two parameters, **`clipLimit`** and **`titleGridSize`**, to specify the contrast limit parameter and grid size for the image. Increasing the **`clipLimit`** will allow more contrast enhancement in the image, allowing for a more pronounced enhancement of contrast; however, it might also result in over-amplification of noise. A smaller **`clipLimit`** will result in more subtle changes in the image. A larger **`titleGridSize`** parameter will divide the image into larger sub-regions resulting in more global contrast adjustment and will maintain a smoother transition on the boundaries. A smaller **`titleGridSize`** will have more localized contrast adjustments and will enhance smaller details in the image.

We use **`cv2.createCLAHE()`** function in OpenCV for applying CLAHE to our images.

cv2.createCLAHE()

```
cv2.createCLAHE(clipLimit=40, tileGridSize=(8,8))
```

Parameters:

- **`clipLimit`**: This parameter controls the contrast enhancement in the image. This is a maximum value for each histogram bin and any value above the **`clipLimit`** is clipped. A higher value will mean more contrast enhancement. The default value for this parameter is 40.
- **`titleGridSize`**: This is the size of the grid that the image will be divided into. This is a tuple (x,y) denoting the number of tiles in row and column. The default value for this parameter is (8,8) which will divide the image into 8 rows and 8 columns.

Let's try to infer how CLAHE works by applying the operation using different values for the parameters:

```
import cv2

# Load image in grayscale
img = cv2.imread('image.jpg', 0)

# Create CLAHE object
clahe = cv2.createCLAHE(clipLimit=2.0, tileGridSize=(8,8))

clahe2 = cv2.createCLAHE(clipLimit=20.0, tileGridSize=(8,8))

clahe3 = cv2.createCLAHE(clipLimit=2.0, tileGridSize=(24,24))

# Apply CLAHE to image
clahe_img = clahe.apply(img)
clahe_img2 = clahe2.apply(img)
clahe_img3 = clahe3.apply(img)

cv2.imshow('Original', img)
cv2.imshow('CLAHE 1', clahe_img)
cv2.imshow('CLAHE 2', clahe_img2)
cv2.imshow('CLAHE 3', clahe_img3)
cv2.waitKey(0)
cv2.destroyAllWindows()
```

Output:

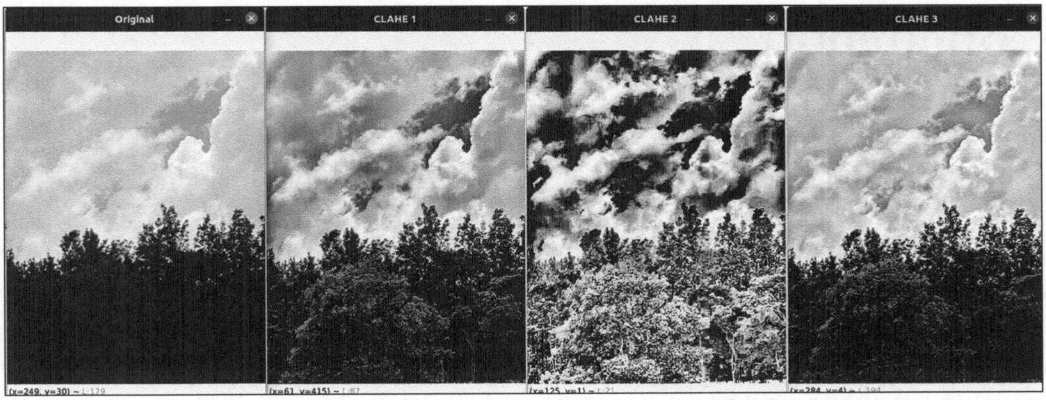

***Figure 5.14**: Contrast Limited Adaptive Histogram Equalization with different parameters.*

We use CLAHE with three different parameters in the above code. The first operation is implemented using **`clipLimit`** of 2 and **`titleGridSize`** of (8,8). The output for this "CLAHE 1" produces a sufficiently enhanced image. Next, to understand the impact of the **`clipLimit`** parameter, we increase its value sufficiently to 20. It is noticeable that increasing the contrast limit has significantly increased the contrast variation in the image "CLAHE 2". Finally, we try changing the **`titleGridSize`** parameter, by increasing it to (24,24). We can observe that the overall image is much smoothed out, and global contrast values have been considered.

Histograms for feature extraction

Histograms provide insights into the intensity distribution of an image and the frequency of the various characteristics and attributes of an image. This makes histograms an effective tool for feature extraction in images. We can use histograms to capture the color and texture of images and use this information for various purposes, such as image segmentation or image retrieval.

Histogram of Oriented Gradients (HOG) features capture the distribution of gradient orientations in an image and are used for various tasks such as face detection, human activity recognition, and gesture recognition. We will discuss HOG in detail as we move along with the chapter.

Features extracted using histograms can be used for various applications, such as content-based image retrieval, handwritten digit recognition and many other computer vision use cases, making them a very effective and widely used feature of image processing applications.

Conclusion

In this chapter, we explored the fundamentals of histograms and their applications in image processing. We started by understanding the concept of histograms and how they represent the distribution of pixel intensities in an image. Moving forward, we delved into advanced techniques such as histograms for colored images. Additionally, we explored the power of two-dimensional histograms to capture joint distributions and relationships between different channels. Lastly, we learned about histogram equalization methods, including adaptive histogram equalization and contrast limited adaptive histogram equalization, which is valuable for enhancing image contrast and improving visual quality.

In the next chapter, we will delve into the fascinating field of image segmentation. We will start by understanding the concept of image segmentation, which involves dividing an image into multiple segments or regions. Various techniques for image segmentation will be explored, providing readers with a comprehensive understanding of this important process. We will then explore multiple thresholding techniques, including global thresholding, adaptive thresholding, and Otsu's thresholding while highlighting their unique features and applications.

Points to remember

- A histogram displays the count or sum of pixels with each intensity value in an image. The number of pixels with each intensity value is counted and displayed as a plot for visualization.
- Matplotlib is a library for creating visualizations and data plots, offering a wide variety of functions to generate a diverse range of graphs and charts.
- Histograms for colored images are similar to computing a histogram for grayscale images. The colored images have to be split into individual channels, and the histogram for each channel is computed independently.
- Two-dimensional histograms are used to capture the joint distribution of two channels in an image, which can be used to analyze the relations between these two channels.
- The mask parameter in the cv2.calcHist() function can be used on images to selectively compute histograms for a specific region of an image.
- Histogram Equalization is the process of improving the contrast of an image. The unevenly distributed intensity values in an image are stretched out, creating a more even intensity distribution over the image.

- CLAHE (Contrast Limited Adaptive Histogram Equalization) is a technique used to enhance image contrast while limiting the amplification of noise.
- Features extracted using histograms can be used for various applications, such as content-based image retrieval, handwritten digit recognition and many other computer vision applications.

Test your understanding

1. Which of the following statements about histograms is true?
   A. Histograms can only be used on grayscale images
   B. Histograms are used to adjust the brightness of the image
   C. Histograms provide information about the spatial information of pixels in an image
   D. Histograms provide the distribution for pixel color intensities in an image
2. Histogram equalization is used to:
   A. Improve the contrast of an image
   B. Improve the brightness of an image
   C. Apply histograms to a specific region of an image
   D. Apply histograms on colored images
3. What is the primary purpose of a two-dimensional histogram?
   A. To represent the distribution of pixel intensities in an image
   B. To represent a joint distribution of two channels in an image
   C. To generate spatial information about the image
   D. To improve the brightness of an image
4. What does the x-axis of a histogram represent?
   A. The channels of an image
   B. The frequency of the data
   C. The range of the data
   D. The count of pixels in the image

5. What is the one major advantage of using CLAHE?
    A. Preserves local details while preserving contrast
    B. Enhances image brightness
    C. Focuses on global contrast only
    D. Reduces noise in an image

Chapter 6
Image Segmentation

In this chapter, we will explore image segmentation. Image segmentation involves dividing an image into meaningful regions or segments, and it is essential for tasks like object recognition and image editing. We will cover basic techniques such as thresholding and its types. We will also discuss advanced methods like the GrabCut algorithm, which combines user input with graph cuts for more accurate segmentations. Additionally, we will explore clustering-based segmentation and deep learning-based techniques, which utilize clustering algorithms and convolutional neural networks respectively, to achieve precise segmentations. By the end of this chapter, you will have a comprehensive understanding of various segmentation approaches and their applications.

Structure

In this chapter, we will discuss the following topics:

- Introduction to image segmentation
- Basic segmentation techniques
    - Thresholding
        - Simple thresholding
        - Adaptive thresholding
        - Otsu's thresholding
    - Edge and Contour based segmentation
- Advanced segmentation techniques
    - Watershed algorithm
    - GrabCut algorithm
    - Clustering based segmentation
- Deep Learning-based segmentation techniques

Introduction to Image Segmentation

Image segmentation is the process of dividing an image into multiple parts or regions for a more detailed understanding of the image. The primary purpose of image segmentation is to separate objects of interest from the background. Image segmentation is a powerful feature used to extract valuable information from the images.

Using image segmentation, we can effectively extract objects of interest from the background or divide an image into multiple parts with different categories, enabling enhanced analysis and understanding of the image contents. One very important use case of image segmentation is self-driving cars. Using image segmentation, self-driving cars can separate and categorize various objects in the frame such as traffic lights, pedestrians, roads, or vehicles. This information can help the algorithm understand the environment and enable safe autonomous driving.

Pixel-based segmentation operates at the pixel level and assigns categories to individual pixels in an image. Some of the pixel-based segmentation techniques include thresholding, clustering, or edge detection. Region-based segmentation divides the image into regions based on similarities such as color or texture. Region-based segmentation techniques include region growing and watershed segmentation.

Semantic segmentation is the process of assigning a label to every pixel in an image. The various objects in the image are divided into categories and labelled accordingly, with each class having a different color. For reference, in the preceding autonomous driving car example, all the vehicles on the road will be categorized together and labeled with the same color. Similarly, all the remaining pixels will be labeled into different categories such as roads, traffic lights or pedestrians, with each class having a separate color.

Instance segmentation helps us to differentiate each object in the image separately irrespective of the class it belongs to. All the objects in instance segmentation are distinguished separately and are not divided into the same class as we do in semantic segmentation. In the autonomous car example, all the vehicles in the image will be divided into individual objects and not as a single class enabling the identification of individual objects. Similarly, all the occurrences of objects of pedestrians, traffic lights and roads will be segmented separately.

Panoptic segmentation is a combination of semantic and instance segmentation. Pixels are assigned a class and each object in the class is also segmented separately, allowing us to both distinguish and identify individual instances within the scene.

In this chapter, we will be discussing a range of segmentation techniques. We will begin with basic fundamental segmentation techniques such as thresholding and contour detection. We then move on to more advanced segmentation techniques such as the watershed algorithm and the GrabCut method. Although there is a dedicated chapter on deep learning techniques, we will touch upon segmentation using deep learning briefly in this chapter. However, as the focus of this book is not on deep learning, we will provide a high-level overview without delving into extensive details.

Basic Segmentation Techniques

Let's start by discussing some basic segmentation techniques. Basic segmentation techniques include thresholding, which involves dividing an image based on intensity values; simple thresholding uses a fixed global threshold, while adaptive thresholding adjusts the threshold locally. Otsu's thresholding automatically determines the optimal threshold by minimizing the intra-class variance.

Edge and contour-based segmentation techniques focus on extracting boundaries and contours to identify and separate objects in an image, often using techniques like edge detection, region growing, or active contours.

These techniques form the foundation of many more advanced segmentation algorithms and play a crucial role in various applications.

Image thresholding

Image thresholding is a segmentation technique used to divide an image into various categories based on the intensity values of the pixels. Image thresholding helps us to binarize an image. A binary image has values that are either 0 or 255, unlike a grayscale image, where the pixel values can range from 0 to 255.

Thresholding is performed by comparing the individual pixel intensity values to a predefined threshold value. If a pixel's value is greater than or equal to the threshold value, it is assigned to one category (typically 255 or white). On the other hand, if the pixel value is lower than the threshold, it is assigned to another category (typically 0 or black):

Figure 6.1: *Left: Grayscale image containing pixels in the range of 0-255. Right: Corresponding binary image containing only either 0 or 255 pixels.*

Thresholding has several important uses in image processing. The most important use case of thresholding is image segmentation. By choosing appropriate methods and values, thresholding can be used to separate foreground objects from the background. Thresholding is used for image binarization tasks and is often used as a preprocessing step for more advanced image processing algorithms. Thresholding can help us apply various operations, such as noise reduction or edge detection, to achieve better results.

Thresholding can be accomplished using a variety of techniques. The most fundamental form of thresholding is binary thresholding, where a global threshold value is set, and all the image pixels are modified based on this value. Another technique is adaptive thresholding, which involves dividing the image into multiple regions, with each region having a separate threshold value. This approach provides a more localized and adaptive result based on the characteristics of each region. Otsu's thresholding is another technique that automatically calculates the threshold value based on the image histogram. This method determines the most effective threshold value by analyzing the histogram distribution of the image.

We discuss these methods in detail as we move along the chapter:

Simple Thresholding

Simple or Binary thresholding is a very simple thresholding to divide the image into two parts. Binary thresholding works by comparing the pixel intensity values, by a predefined value and categorizing each pixel of the image accordingly. Pixels having intensity values greater than or equal to the threshold value are set to 255, while the pixels having lower values are set to 0.

The threshold value is selected based on the requirements of the task at hand. In binary thresholding, this threshold value has to be manually set by the user. This value is between 0 and 255 and has to be carefully selected. Selecting a lower threshold value, such as 10, will assign a value of 255 to pixels that exceed 10, leading to a predominantly white image. Conversely, choosing a significantly higher threshold value will assign a value of 0 to most pixels, resulting in a predominantly black image:

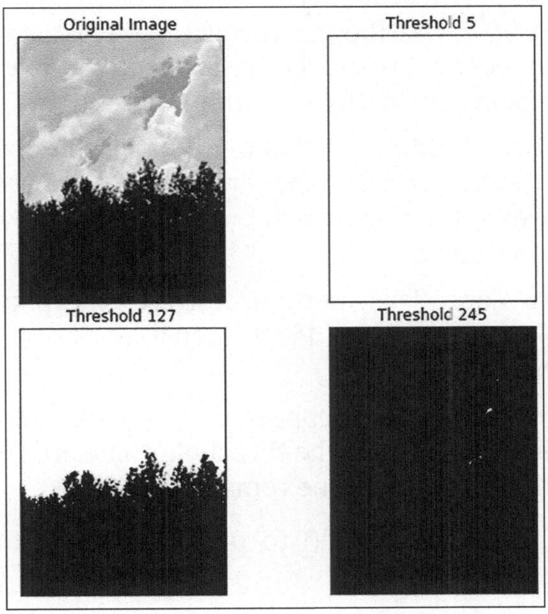

Figure 6.2: *Simple thresholding outputs using different threshold values*

In the preceding image, the image is thresholded with three different threshold values. The image with 5 as the threshold value is completely white. This is because the algorithm has set all the values in the range of 5-255 to 255, resulting in an almost full white output. Similarly, the operation with a 245-threshold value has set all the pixels below 245 to 0, resulting in an almost black image. Choosing a value such as 127, has divided the image into two acceptable segmented parts as the values in the range 127-255 are set to 255 and values below 127 have been set to 0. Typically, the threshold value to be used will be defined by the use case at hand.

Binary thresholding can be used for various applications such as object extraction or image segmentation. Setting an appropriate threshold value can help us extract the object from the background or divide the image into multiple regions. Image binarization can often help us in tasks such as Optical Character Recognition or Barcode Reading as it can make it easier to extract information while increasing accuracy.

Simple thresholding can be performed using various techniques:

- **Binary Thresholding**: This is the simple binary segmentation where the image pixels are segmented into two categories based on the threshold values. Pixel intensity values above this value are set to the maximum value, and values below or equal are set to 0.
- **Inverse Binary Thresholding**: This is exactly the opposite of binary thresholding. It is the flipped result of the binary thresholding. Pixel intensities above the threshold value are set to 0 while the pixel intensities below or equal are set to the maximum value.
- **Truncated Thresholding**: In this method, all the pixel intensities above the threshold value are set to the threshold value instead of the maximum value. The pixel intensities remain unchanged if they are below or equal to the threshold value.
- **Threshold to Zero**: This method converts the pixel intensities below the threshold value to zero. Pixel intensities above the threshold value remain unchanged.
- **Inverse Threshold to Zero**: Opposite of the Threshold to Zero parameter. Pixel intensity values above the threshold value are set to 0. Values below or equal to the threshold value remain unchanged.

We use the function cv2.threshold() to perform simple thresholding on our images.

cv2.threshold()

```
retval, threshold = cv2.threshold(src, thresh, maxval=255,
type='cv2.THRESH_BINARY', dst])
```

Parameters:

Inputs

- **src**: Input image for thresholding.

- **thress**: The threshold value to be used to binarize the image. Pixels higher than this value will be assigned the value defined in **maxval** parameter, while pixels equal or lower to the value will be assigned a 0 value.
- **maxval**: The maximum value to be assigned to the pixels that are greater than the threshold value. The default value for this parameter is 255.
- **type**: The type of thresholding operation to be performed:
  - **cv2.THRESH_BINARY**: Binary thresholding, where pixel values above the threshold are set to **maxval**, and those below or equal to the threshold are set to 0.
  - **cv2.THRESH_BINARY_INV**: Inverse of binary thresholding. Pixel values above the threshold are set to 0, and those below or equal to the threshold are set to **maxval**.
  - **cv2.THRESH_TRUNC**: Truncated thresholding, where pixel values above the threshold are set to the threshold value itself, and values below the threshold remain unchanged.
  - **cv2.THRESH_TOZERO**: Thresholding to zero, where pixel values below the threshold are set to 0, and those above or equal to the threshold remain unchanged.
  - **cv2.THRESH_TOZERO_INV**: Inverse thresholding to zero. Pixel values above the threshold are set to 0, and those below or equal to the threshold remain unchanged.

The default value for this parameter is '**cv2.THRESH_BINARY**:

- **dst**: Output array

Outputs

- **retval**: The threshold value used in the operation is stored in this variable.
- **threshold**: This variable contains the thresholded image output after the operation.

Implementing a simple thresholding code:

```
import cv2
import matplotlib.pyplot as plt

image = cv2.imread('img.jpg', cv2.IMREAD_GRAYSCALE)

# Apply binary threshold
_, binary = cv2.threshold(image, 127, 255, cv2.THRESH_BINARY)

# Apply binary inverse threshold
```

```
_, binary_inv = cv2.threshold(image, 127, 255, cv2.THRESH_BINARY_INV)

# Apply truncation threshold
_, trunc = cv2.threshold(image, 127, 255, cv2.THRESH_TRUNC)

# Apply to zero threshold
_, to_zero = cv2.threshold(image, 127, 255, cv2.THRESH_TOZERO)

# Apply to zero inverse threshold
_, to_zero_inv = cv2.threshold(image, 127, 255, cv2.THRESH_TOZERO_INV)

# Set figure size
plt.figure(figsize=(10, 8))

plt.subplot(231), plt.imshow(image, cmap='gray')
plt.title('Original Image', fontsize=10), plt.xticks([]), plt.yticks([])
plt.subplot(232), plt.imshow(binary, cmap='gray')
plt.title('Binary Threshold', fontsize=10), plt.xticks([]), plt.yt-
icks([])
plt.subplot(233), plt.imshow(binary_inv, cmap='gray')
plt.title('Binary Inverse Threshold', fontsize=10), plt.xticks([]), plt.
yticks([])
plt.subplot(234), plt.imshow(trunc, cmap='gray')
plt.title('Truncation Threshold', fontsize=10), plt.xticks([]), plt.
yticks([])
plt.subplot(235), plt.imshow(to_zero, cmap='gray')
plt.title('Threshold To Zero', fontsize=10), plt.xticks([]), plt.yt-
icks([])
plt.subplot(236), plt.imshow(to_zero_inv, cmap='gray')
plt.title('Threshold To Zero Inverse', fontsize=10), plt.xticks([]),
plt.yticks([])

plt.show()
```

The preceding results in the following output:

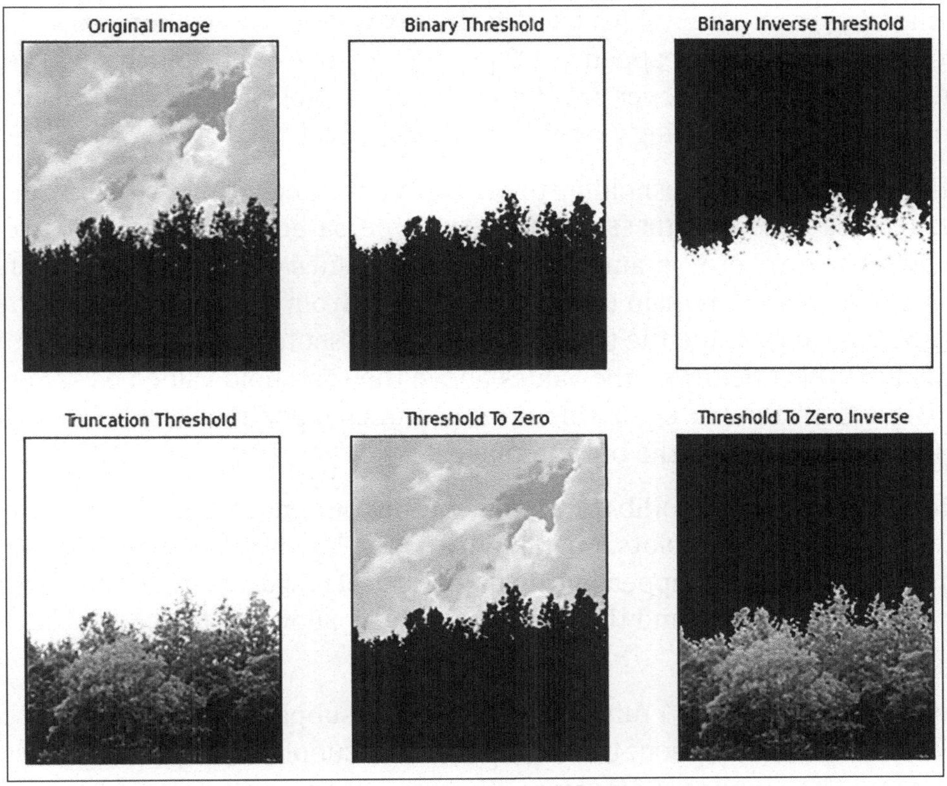

***Figure 6.3**: Output of each thresholding mode in the simple thresholding function*

In the preceding code, we use simple thresholding and demonstrate the results from all the thresholding modes. As seen here, our input image can be broadly classified into two parts, the trees and the sky. We start by converting our input image to grayscale since **`cv2.threshold()`** takes a grayscale as its input.

We start by using a simple binary thresholding by using the **`cv2.THRESH_BINARY`** type parameters and keeping the threshold value to 127. The _ parameter here denotes that the output **`retval`** threshold value will not be stored, and we can ignore it since we do not need the value. As seen from the binary threshold result in the output image, the operation has segmented the input image into two parts and has been able to successfully segment the trees from the sky in the image. We then use **`cv2.THRESH_BINARY_INV`** type with the same threshold value and can see that the thresholding operation has reversed the results from the simple binary operation in the output image.

The next is truncation thresholding using **`cv2.THRESH_TRUNC`** value. The threshold value is set to 127, which means any value in the image will be set to 127 and any pixels below this value will remain unchanged. As seen from the truncation thresholding result, the values lying in the sky region will be more than 127 and hence all the values are capped at 127 producing an overall whitish sky. The tree values are darker and hence will be below 127, which truncation thresholding keeps unchanged, resulting in trees remaining intact.

We then perform the thresholding to zero operation and its inverse using the **cv2.THRESH_TOZERO** and **cv2.THRESH_TOZERO_INV** type parameter values respectively. The threshold to zero parameter will set any values below 127 to zero and all the above values will remain unchanged. As seen from the output image, the sky remains unchanged, and the tree's value has been set to 0. The inverse operation simply flips this operation, the values above the threshold value i.e. 127 are set to 0 while the below or equal values remain unchanged resulting in a black sky and unchanged trees in the output image.

We have also used matplotlib this time to output our images. Matplotlib provides the functionality of subplots, enabling us to display multiple images in a more organized and visually appealing manner. The **plt.figure()** function creates a new figure for plotting, and the figsize parameter allows us to specify the shape of the figure in inches.

We use the **plt.subplot()** function to create our subplot. In the preceding code, the values 231 236 represent the arrangement of subplots in a grid of 2 rows and 3 columns. The number 231 indicates that the subsequent plot will be placed in the first position of a 2x3 grid. Similarly, 232 represents the second position, 233 represents the third position, and so on.

The **cmap** parameter is used to specify the colormap for our images. We use **gray** since we are using grayscale images. The **plt.title()** is used to provide a title for each subplot and the '**fontsize**' parameter specifies its font size. The **plt.xticks()** and **plt.yticks()** functions in Matplotlib are used to customize the tick locations and labels on the *x*-axis and *y*-axis, respectively, of a plot. Keeping these values empty will not add any markers on the x or y axes as seen in our figure. Lastly, the **plt.show()** parameter is used to display our figure.

Adaptive Thresholding

Adaptive thresholding is an advanced and more localized version of the simple thresholding techniques. Simple thresholding uses a global thresholding value on the whole image which might not work properly on images with large variations in image intensities and often results in an inaccurate segmentation of the image. Adaptive thresholding on the other hand takes a more localized approach to handle these variations in image intensities.

Adaptive thresholding involves dividing the image into small regions and applying a different threshold value for each sub-region of the image. Unlike simple thresholding, we do not need to provide the thresholding value manually while using adaptive thresholding. Adaptive thresholding uses statistical methods, mean and Gaussian to calculate the thresholding value for the image.

Adaptive thresholding is particularly helpful when the lighting conditions on the image are not uniform and the image has a lot of intensity variations. This allows for a more accurate segmentation of the image and optimal results can be achieved by using other parameters in the adaptive thresholding function in the OpenCV library.

With OpenCV, we can adjust the size of the block used to calculate the threshold value, which includes the pixel neighborhood for computing mean or Gaussian values and the C value which is a constant value that is subtracted from the mean or Gaussian values. Mean Adaptive Thresholding computes the mean intensity value within each tile as the threshold, suitable for images with uniform lighting. Gaussian Adaptive Thresholding uses a weighted average based on a Gaussian distribution, providing a smooth threshold transition for images with uneven lighting or contrast variations.

We use the **cv2.adaptiveThreshold()** function in OpenCV to implement adaptive thresholding.

cv2.adaptiveThreshold()

```
cv2.adaptiveThreshold(src, maxValue, adaptiveMethod, thresholdType,
blockSize, C)
```

Parameters:

- **src**: The source image on which transformations will be applied.
- **maxval**: The maximum value to be assigned to the pixels that are greater than the threshold value. The default value for this parameter is 255.
- **adaptiveMethod**: The method used to calculate the threshold value.
  - **cv2.ADAPTIVE_THRESH_MEAN_C**: Mean Adaptive Thresholding
  - **cv2.ADAPTIVE_THRESH_GAUSSIAN_C**: Gaussian Adaptive Thresholding

The default value for this parameter is '**cv2.ADAPTIVE_THRESH_MEAN_C**.

- **thresholdType**: The type of thresholded result we want:
  - **cv2.THRESH_BINARY**: Binary Image
  - **cv2.THRESH_BINARY_INV**: Inverted Binary Image

- **blockSize**: The size of the neighborhood to be considered for calculating the threshold value. This should be an odd number and the default value for this parameter is 3.
- **C**: A constant value that is subtracted from the mean or Gaussian average. The default value for this parameter is 0 indicating that no value will be subtracted.

To understand adaptive thresholding better, we will use an image with more variations in local intensities with our code:

```
import cv2
import matplotlib.pyplot as plt

image = cv2.imread('flower.jpg', 0)

# Apply simple thresholding
_, thresh_simple = cv2.threshold(image, 127, 255, cv2.THRESH_BINARY)

# Apply adaptive thresholding with method=cv2.ADAPTIVE_THRESH_MEAN_C
thresh_adaptive = cv2.adaptiveThreshold(image, 255, cv2.ADAPTIVE_THRESH_
MEAN_C, cv2.THRESH_BINARY, 11, 2)

# Create subplots for original image and thresholded images
plt.figure(figsize=(12, 4))

# Display the original image
plt.subplot(131)
plt.imshow(image, cmap='gray')
plt.title('Original Image', fontsize=10),plt.xticks([]),plt.yticks([])

# Display the simple thresholded image
plt.subplot(132)
plt.imshow(thresh_simple, cmap='gray')
plt.title('Simple Threshold', fontsize=10),plt.xticks([]),plt.yticks([])

# Display the adaptive thresholded image
plt.subplot(133)
plt.imshow(thresh_adaptive, cmap='gray')
plt.title('Adaptive Threshold', fontsize=10),plt.xticks([]),plt.yt-
icks([])

# Show the plot
plt.tight_layout()
```

```
plt.show()
```

The preceding code produces the following output:

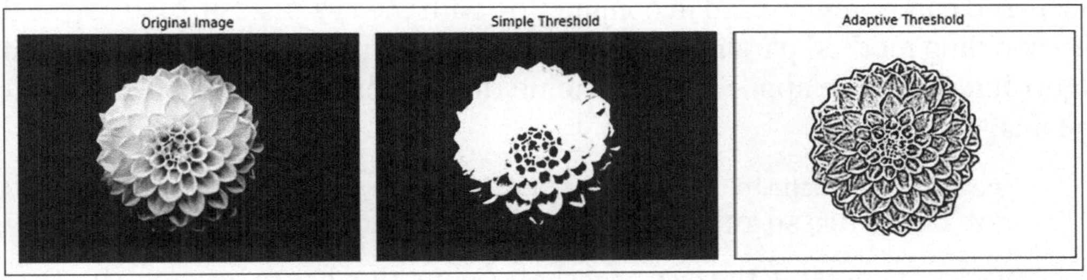

Figure 6.4: *Image thresholding using Simple and Adaptive Thresholding methods. Adaptive thresholding has been able to successfully create a better result.*

We have chosen a flower image as our input image because it exhibits numerous local intensity variations. We begin by applying simple thresholding to the image as a baseline for comparison and then proceed to implement adaptive thresholding. From the results, it is evident that simple thresholding leads to a distorted image, whereas adaptive thresholding results in a significantly clearer thresholded image of the flower.

We use the **`cv2.adaptiveThreshold()`** function keeping the **`adaptiveMethod`** as **`cv2.ADAPTIVE_THRESH_MEAN_C`**, **`thresholdType`** as **`cv2.THRESH_BINARY`**, **`blocksize`** as 11 and C value as 2. I'll leave it up to the reader to try and experiment with these parameters in order to achieve better results.

We use matplotlib subplots to plot the results. The **`plt.tight_layout()`** function is used to automatically adjust the subplot parameters to improve the spacing between subplots and ensure that the content fits within the figure.

Otsu's Thresholding

Otsu's thresholding is used to automatically calculate the threshold value for image segmentation and eliminates the need to manually search for an effective threshold value. Otsu's thresholding calculates the best possible threshold value for the image by using the histogram of the grayscale image.

Otsu's thresholding works best on images where there are two clearly defined peaks in the histogram of the image and finds the best possible threshold value to separate these peaks. The method works by maximizing the inter-class variance between the foreground and background regions of the image. Otsu's method iterates over all the possible threshold values and chooses the value with the maximum variance in the image. Once the threshold value is calculated, binary thresholding can be applied to the image using this threshold value.

Otsu's thresholding is implemented using the **cv2.threshold()** function discussed earlier and is used in conjunction with the **cv2.THRESH_OTSU** flag as the thresholding method parameter. This flag indicates that the Otsu's thresholding algorithm should be applied to determine the optimal threshold value based on the image histogram.

```
retval, threshold = cv2.threshold(image, 0, 255, cv2.THRESH_BINA-
RY + cv2.THRESH_OTSU)
```

The **thresh** parameter in the **cv2.threshold()** function has to be kept 0 for Otsu's thresholding to work. If the **thresh** value is specified it will take precedence over the Otsu's calculated thresholding value and the calculated value using Otsu's method will be ignored. We can use the **retval** parameter to check the threshold value used by Otsu's method for the operation.

Otsu's thresholding can be used with any of the thresholding type parameters discussed in the preceding simple thresholding section, that is, **cv2.THRESH_BINARY**, **cv2.THRESH_BINARY_INV**, **cv2.THRESH_TRUNC**, **cv2.THRESH_TOZERO** or **cv2.THRESH_TOZERO_INV**:

```
import cv2
import matplotlib.pyplot as plt

image = cv2.imread('image.jpg', 0)
# Apply simple thresholding with a threshold value of 127
_, thresholded_image_simple = cv2.threshold(image, 127, 255, cv2.THRESH_
BINARY)

# Apply Otsu's thresholding
retval, thresholded_image_otsu = cv2.threshold(image, 0, 255, cv2.
THRESH_BINARY + cv2.THRESH_OTSU)

# Display the original, simple thresholding, and Otsu's thresholding
results
plt.subplot(131), plt.imshow(image, cmap='gray')
plt.title('Original Image'), plt.xticks([]), plt.yticks([])
plt.subplot(132), plt.imshow(thresholded_image_simple, cmap='gray')
plt.title('Simple Thresholding'), plt.xticks([]), plt.yticks([])
plt.subplot(133), plt.imshow(thresholded_image_otsu, cmap='gray')
plt.title("Otsu's Thresholding"), plt.xticks([]), plt.yticks([])
```

```
plt.tight_layout()
plt.show()
```

***Figure 6.5**: Image thresholding using Simple and Otsu's Thresholding methods. Otsu's thresholding has been able to find a suitable value for thresholding to achieve the optimum result.*

In the above code, we use binary segmentation with a threshold value of 127 and Otsu's thresholding. As it is evident from the preceding results, simple thresholding produces a distorted result while adding Otsu's method produces a significantly better result. On checking the **`retval`** parameter, Otsu's method has calculated the optimum threshold value as 105 resulting in a significantly better segmentation.

Edge and contour-based segmentation

Edge-based segmentation is used to extract boundaries or edges from an image. They work by identifying areas in the image with significant contrast by looking for large variations in color or texture intensities. These changes represent transitions between different objects or regions within the image.

Edge-based techniques work by first applying an edge detection algorithm to map out the boundaries in an image. Edge detection algorithms, such as the Canny edge detector or Sobel operator, are applied to highlight these transitions and generate a binary edge map. Once an edge is detected a binary map is created the edge pixels are assigned a value of 1, representing the presence of an edge, while the non-edge pixels are assigned a value of 0. This binary edge map serves as a mask that outlines the boundaries of objects or regions in the image.

Contour-based segmentation is a technique used to identify and extract boundaries or contours of objects or regions in an image. We start contour-based segmentation with edge detection, where edges are detected using algorithms like Canny or Sobel. These edge pixels are then connected to form continuous curves or contours. Once the contours are detected, we can use them for further processing. Common operations in contour-based segmentation include filtering contours based on area, perimeter, or aspect ratio, approximating contours to simplify shape, and analyzing contour hierarchy.

Contour-based segmentation is particularly useful when dealing with objects or regions that have distinct boundaries and well-defined shapes. In practical implementations, contour-based segmentation is often combined with other techniques, such as thresholding or region growing, to achieve more accurate and robust segmentation results.

Edges and contours are vital concepts in image processing, and to explore them further, the next chapter is entirely dedicated to their detailed analysis. In the upcoming chapter, we will delve into the implementation and practical aspects of edges and contours, providing a comprehensive understanding of these techniques.

Advanced Segmentation Techniques

Now, let's explore some advanced segmentation techniques. The watershed algorithm is a powerful technique that treats grayscale images as topographic maps, where the intensity values represent elevations. It starts by flooding the regions from local minima and gradually merging them based on the watershed lines, resulting in segmenting objects accurately.

The GrabCut algorithm, on the other hand, is an interactive segmentation technique that combines color and texture information with user-provided hints to iteratively refine the foreground and background regions. Lastly, clustering-based segmentation methods, such as k-means or mean-shift clustering, group similar pixels together based on feature similarity, allowing for the identification of distinct regions or objects in an image.

These advanced techniques offer more sophisticated approaches to handle complex segmentation tasks in various applications, including image editing and medical imaging.

Watershed Algorithm

The watershed algorithm is a powerful image segmentation technique inspired by water flowing through a terrain. The watershed algorithm is designed to mimic the filling of basins in a terrain with water, with each basin representing a different region or object. The algorithm uses gradient or intensity information to detect boundaries and regions in the image. The Watershed algorithm is particularly useful when extracting objects that are very close or touching each other. It is a widely applied technique with diverse applications in fields such as medical image analysis or object recognition.

In simple terms, this is how we can implement the Watershed algorithm:

NOTE: Some of the keywords mentioned in the following steps, such as gradients and Sobel kernels, have not been discussed yet. We will delve into these topics in detail as we progress through the course of this book. You can use the provided steps to gain an understanding of how the algorithm works overall, without delving too deeply into its implementation details. Additionally, OpenCV handles many aspects of the process for us, eliminating the need to manually code each component.

- **Gradient**: We start by checking the changes in brightness or colors in the image to identify the boundaries or edges between the edges. We use gradient operators such as sobel or Scharr kernels to detect the edges and highlight the transitions between regions with distinct intensities.
- **Object Markers**: Based on the gradient information received, we mark the points on the image that might be potential objects. This can be done manually, or techniques like thresholding or region growing can be used for this.
- **Labels**: The markers are then assigned a different label to represent each object separately.
- **Watershed Algorithm**: Now that we have identified the potential objects, we can use the watershed concept on the image. As discussed above, we can imagine these markers as basins and start pouring water on them and filling up the areas from these object markers. The water starts from these markers and goes up to the boundaries of other objects.
- **Watershed Lines**: When the water keeps on flowing, eventually they will meet at the boundaries of two potential objects. These boundaries can be thought of as lines representing segmented boundaries of different objects.
- **Post-processing**: We have the initial boundaries or segmentation from the watershed algorithm. However, the results might not be as we expect them to be. We can use some post-processing steps to merge small regions together or remove noise from the image.

It is important to note that watershed algorithms can often result in multiple small regions resulting in over-segmentation. Hence, the post-processing steps need to be applied to increase the segmentation quality and achieve the desired results:

```
import cv2
import numpy as np
import matplotlib.pyplot as plt

# Load the input image
image = cv2.imread('coin.jpg')
original = image.copy()

gray = cv2.cvtColor(image, cv2.COLOR_BGR2GRAY)

# Apply thresholding to create a binary image
ret, binary = cv2.threshold(gray, 245, 255, cv2.THRESH_BINARY_
INV)

# Perform morphological operations to remove noise and enhance
regions
kernel = np.ones((3, 3), np.uint8)
opening = cv2.morphologyEx(binary, cv2.MORPH_OPEN, kernel, itera-
tions=1)
sure_bg = cv2.dilate(opening, kernel, iterations=5)

# Perform distance transform to identify markers
dist_transform = cv2.distanceTransform(opening, cv2.DIST_L2, 5)
ret, sure_fg = cv2.threshold(dist_transform, 0.5 * dist_trans-
form.max(), 255, 0)
# Identify unknown regions
sure_fg = np.uint8(sure_fg)
unknown = cv2.subtract(sure_bg, sure_fg)

# Create markers for the watershed algorithm
ret, markers = cv2.connectedComponents(sure_fg)
markers += 1
markers[unknown == 255] = 0

# Apply the Watershed algorithm
cv2.watershed(image, markers)
image[markers == -1] = [0, 0, 255]

# Convert images to RGB for display
gray_rgb = cv2.cvtColor(gray, cv2.COLOR_GRAY2RGB)
image_rgb = cv2.cvtColor(image, cv2.COLOR_BGR2RGB)
original_rgb = cv2.cvtColor(original, cv2.COLOR_BGR2RGB)
```

```
# Display the intermediate steps and final result
titles = ['Input Image', 'Binary Threshold', 'Morphological Oper-
ations','Distance Transform', 'Markers', 'Final Result']
images = [original_rgb,  binary, sure_bg,dist_transform, markers,
image_rgb]

for i in range(len(titles)):
    plt.subplot(2, 3, i+1)
    plt.imshow(images[i], cmap='gray')
    plt.title(titles[i])
    plt.xticks([]), plt.yticks([])

plt.tight_layout()
plt.show()
```

The preceding code produces the following result:

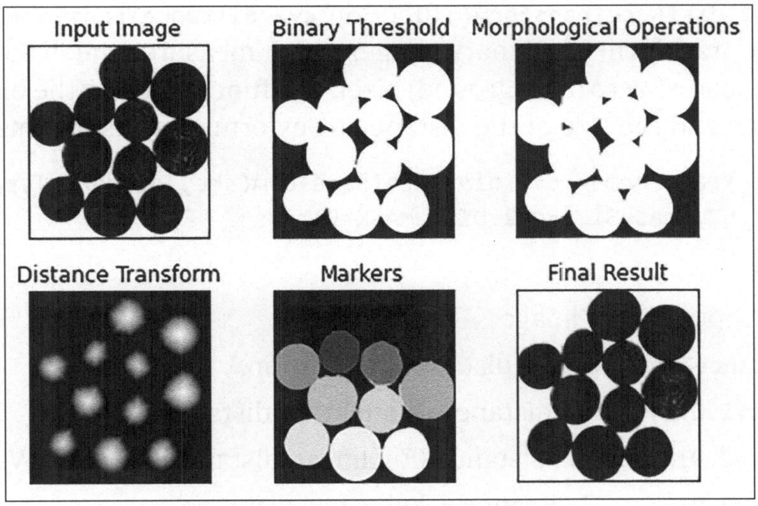

***Figure 6.6**: Watershed algorithm result in steps*

The provided code is a simple implementation of coin segmentation using the watershed algorithm. We start by applying some pre-processing to enhance the original image for our operation. We start by converting the input image to grayscale. Then, a binary thresholding technique is applied to convert our image into binary separating the coins from the background. We then apply morphological operations to enhance the regions of interest in our image:

Figure 6.7: *Input image and the morphed image after preprocessing to be used for watershed algorithm*

To identify the foreground regions accurately, a distance transform is applied using the **cv2.distanceTransform()** function. **cv2.distanceTransform()** measures the distance transform of a binary image, which measures the distance of each pixel to the nearest zero (background) pixel. The function takes the binary image, distance type and the size of the distance transform mask as parameters:

```
dist_transform = cv2.distanceTransform(src, distanceType=cv2.
DIST_L2, maskSize=cv2.DIST_MASK_5)
```

Parameters:

- **src**: Input binary image
- **distanceType**: Type of distance calculation.
    - **cv2.DIST_L1**: L1 distance (Manhattan distance)
    - **cv2.DIST_L2**: L2 distance (Euclidean distance) - Default Value
    - **cv2.DIST_C**: C distance (Chebyshev distance)
- **maskSize**: Size of the distance transform mask:
    - **cv2.DIST_MASK_3**: 3x3 mask
    - **cv2.DIST_MASK_5**: 5x5 mask - Default Value
    - **cv2.DIST_MASK_PRECISE**: Precise mask

Here we have used the L2 distance transform and calculated it using the mask size of 5. We then apply a threshold value to the distance transform result to identify the foreground regions. The threshold value is set to 50% of the maximum distance value.

The unknown regions, which are neither identified as foreground nor background, are determined by subtracting the foreground from the background. This is done using the **cv2.subtract** function, and the result is stored in the unknown variable:

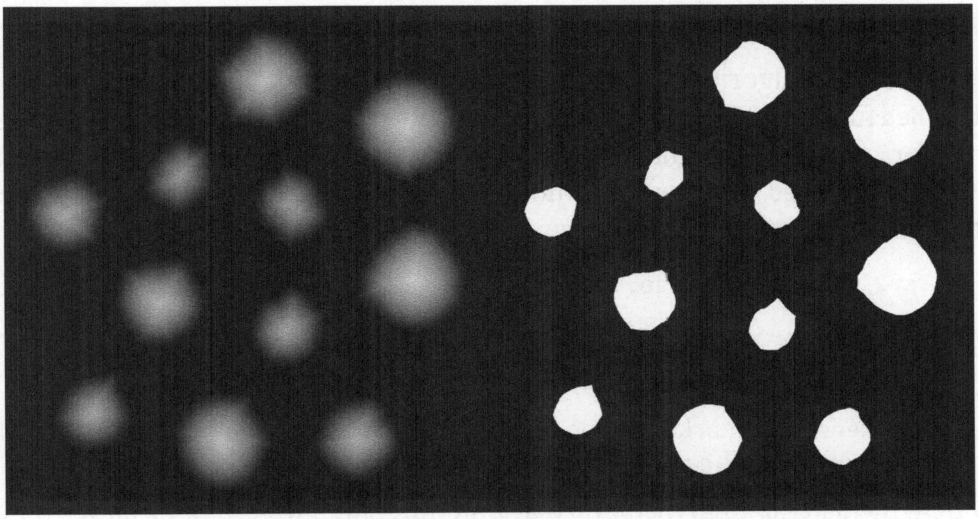

Figure 6.8: *The distance transform image and the sure foreground image depicting objects in the image*

We now apply markers to each object in the image. To label the connected components in the foreground, we utilize the **cv2.connectedComponents** function. **cv2.connectedComponents** is a function used for connected component labeling, which assigns a unique label to each connected component in an image. The function takes the binary image as input and returns the labeled image along with the total number of labels:

```
num_labels, labeled_image = cv2.connectedComponents(binary_image,
connectivity=8, ltype=cv2.CV_32S)
```

Parameters:

- **image**: Input binary image
- **connectivity**: An integer value specifying the connectivity of the pixels. It determines which neighboring pixels are considered connected. Possible values are
- **4**: 4 connected neighbors
- **8**: 8 connected neighbors - Default value
- **ltype**: An optional output label image type

- **cv2.CV_32S**: Represents a 32-bit signed integer label image - Default value
- **cv2.CV_16S**: Represents a 16-bit signed integer label image

By adding 1 to all labels, we ensure that the background region is labeled as 0, and the foreground regions are labeled with positive values. These marker regions represent different objects or regions of interest that we aim to segment.

The watershed algorithm is then applied to the input image using the **cv2.watershed** function. The **cv2.watershed** function applies the watershed algorithm to perform image segmentation based on the provided markers. The result of the **cv2.watershed** function is a modified image where each region is labeled with a unique color or intensity value.

```
cv2.watershed(image, markers)
```

Parameters:

- **image**: The input image on which the watershed algorithm is applied.
- **markers**: The marker image used by the watershed algorithm. It should be a 2D array of the same size as the input image.

We then display the final result by marking the segmented regions with a unique color, such as red used here. This highlights the boundaries between the coins and the background, enabling a clear visual separation.

Figure 6.9: *Final Output of the watershed algorithm. The algorithm has been able to successfully segment all the coins and a red boundary is drawn across each coin*

Overall, the Watershed algorithm provides a powerful approach to image segmentation by leveraging the concept of water-filling basins. It offers the ability to capture fine details and locate boundaries between regions, making it valuable in various applications such as object detection, image analysis, and medical imaging.

GrabCut algorithm

GrabCut is an advanced algorithm, which aims to separate the foreground from the background by giving a rough estimate of the foreground object to be segmented. The user roughly marks the foreground region in the GrabCut algorithm. GrabCut then iteratively refines the segmentation by estimating the color distribution and updating the foreground and background regions until convergence.

The GrabCut algorithm begins by defining a rough outline around the target object. It then utilizes the color information inside and outside the outline to distinguish between the object and the background. Through iterative refinement using color and texture cues, the algorithm progressively improves the segmentation until a satisfactory result is achieved.

The algorithm is based on graph cuts and uses complex non-image processing operations such as Gaussian Mixture Models and graph cuts. Understanding the concepts behind GrabCut requires in-depth knowledge that goes beyond the scope of this course, making it less beneficial to study extensively. OpenCV comes to our rescue by providing a pre-defined implementation of GrabCut, saving us the need to develop it from scratch.

In simple terms, the steps involved in the GrabCut algorithm are:

NOTE: GrabCut incorporates advanced concepts such as Gaussian Mixture Models and graph cuts, which involve complex mathematical principles. While these concepts are beyond the scope of this discussion, it is important to understand that GrabCut leverages these techniques to achieve accurate segmentation. Additionally, investing time and effort in comprehending these complex concepts may not yield significant benefits for most practical applications of GrabCut. Fortunately, OpenCV provides a convenient GrabCut function that encapsulates the underlying complexity, allowing users to utilize the algorithm effectively without delving into its intricate implementation details.

- **Foreground initialization**: The algorithm starts with initializing a bounding box or a masked region for the object in the image. The pixels outside this area are the background pixels and the pixels inside the area are unknown since the bounding box or masked region is just a rough estimate of the object.
- **Gaussian Mixture Model (GMM)**: A Gaussian Mixture model is used to estimate the color distribution of foreground and background regions in the image. The GMM model learns from the color distribution of the

background pixels and classifies the unknown pixels as either foreground or background based on their color distribution.

- **Graph Construction**: Using the GMM model, a graph is constructed where nodes represent pixels and edges represent connections between pixels. The edges are assigned weights based on the GMM parameters. These weights reflect the similarity or dissimilarity between the pixel intensities, helping to capture the relationships between adjacent pixels in the image.
- **GraphCut optimization**: The algorithm applies the GraphCut technique to optimize the segmentation by minimizing the cost function.
- **Iterative Refinement**: The algorithm iteratively updates the foreground and background models by adjusting the GMM parameters using the pixels classified in each iteration. Once the algorithm converges, the final segmentation is obtained.

We use **`cv2.grabCut()`** function in OpenCV to implement GrabCut segmentation on our images.

cv2.grabCut()

```
cv2.grabCut(img, mask, rect, bgdModel, fgdModel, iterCount=5,
mode='cv2.GC_INIT_WITH_RECT')
```

Parameters:

- **`img`**: The source image on which GrabCut will be performed.
- **`mask`**: The mask parameter in **`cv2.grabCut()`** is an input/output mask image that defines the initial foreground in the image. The algorithm updates this mask during the iterations as it refines the segmentation. This is a single-channel image of the same size as img.
- **`rect`**: The rect parameter in **`cv2.grabCut()`** is an optional parameter that defines a rectangular region of interest (ROI) within the image. It is an alternative way to provide an initial estimation of the foreground and background regions. Instead of manually marking the foreground and background in the mask, you can specify a rectangle using the rect parameter.
- **`bgdModel`**: This is a temporary array used by the algorithm to store the background model. It is a float64 numpy array of size 1*65.
- **`fgdModel`**: This is a temporary array used by the algorithm to store the foreground model. It is a float64 numpy array of size 1*65.
- **`iterCount`**: This parameter defines the number of iterations that the algorithm should run. Increasing this parameter will result in better

results, but the execution time will increase as well. The default value for this parameter is 5.

- **mode**: This parameter defines the mode of operation for the GrabCut algorithm. The possible values for this parameter are:
    - **cv2.GC_INIT_WITH_RECT**: This mode uses the rectangle or the 'rect' parameter to initialize the algorithm.
    - **cv2.GC_INIT_WITH_MASK**: This mode uses the provided mask or the 'mask' parameter for initialization.

The default value for this parameter is **cv2.GC_INIT_WITH_RECT**.

Implementing the GrabCut algorithm on our image:

```
import cv2
import numpy as np
import matplotlib.pyplot as plt
image = cv2.imread('dog.jpg')

# Create a mask with same shape as the image, initialized with zeros
mask = np.zeros(image.shape[:2], np.uint8)

# Create the background and foreground model
bgdModel = np.zeros((1, 65), np.float64)
fgdModel = np.zeros((1, 65), np.float64)
# Define the region of interest (ROI) as a rectangle
rect = (140,232,300,560)

# Apply GrabCut
cv2.grabCut(image, mask, rect, bgdModel, fgdModel, iterCount=5,
mode=cv2.GC_INIT_WITH_RECT)

# Assign 0 and 2 to the background and possible background regions in
the mask
mask2 = np.where((mask == 0) | (mask == 2), 0, 1).astype('uint8')

# Apply the mask to the original image to extract the foreground
result = image * mask2[:, :, np.newaxis]

# Convert images from BGR to RGB to display images using matplotlib
image = cv2.cvtColor(image,cv2.COLOR_BGR2RGB)
result = cv2.cvtColor(result,cv2.COLOR_BGR2RGB)
```

```
# Display the original image and the simple thresholded image side by
side
plt.subplot(131), plt.imshow(image, cmap='gray')
plt.title('Original Image'), plt.xticks([]), plt.yticks([])
plt.subplot(132), plt.imshow(result, cmap='gray')
plt.title('Grabcut'), plt.xticks([]), plt.yticks([])

plt.tight_layout()
plt.show()
```

The preceding code results in the following output:

***Figure 6.10**: Output of the GrabCut algorithm*

The preceding image shows the result of the GrabCut algorithm. The algorithm has been able to segment the dog suitably. As mentioned earlier, the GrabCut algorithm uses either a mask or a bounding box rectangle as an input. In this case, we manually define the rectangle by identifying the points that enclose our foreground object and using the **cv2.GC_INIT_WITH_RECT** value in the **mode** parameter. Alternatively, we could have used a mask image to specify the foreground region. We also create empty arrays **fgdModel** and **bdgModel** of the size 1*65 to be used with the GrabCut function.

The rectangular "mask" represents the initial estimation of the foreground and background regions. It is created by specifying a rectangle that encloses the foreground object in the image. In the original mask generated by the GrabCut algorithm, the pixel values 0, 1, 2, and 3 are used to represent different regions:

- Pixel values 0 and 2 correspond to the background region.
- Pixel values 1 and 3 correspond to the foreground (object) region.

The `mask2` is generated by assigning the pixel values of 0 and 2 in the original `mask` to 0 in the new `mask2`, while all other pixel values are assigned to 1. This is done using the numpy function to create a binary mask where 0 represents background or possible background regions, and 1 represents foreground or possible foreground regions.

By applying this mask to the original image, the result is obtained, which only includes the foreground region and removes the background.

The GrabCut algorithm leverages both color information and spatial constraints to robustly segment objects from complex backgrounds. It provides an effective and interactive approach for foreground extraction, making it useful in applications such as image editing, object recognition, and computer vision tasks.

Clustering-based Segmentation

As the name suggests, the clustering-based segmentation technique groups pixels or regions into various clusters where each cluster represents a separate segment or object. Using various clustering algorithms, an image is divided into multiple parts based on their feature similarity.

In clustering-based algorithms, the pixels are treated as data points in a high-dimensional feature space. The algorithm uses distance or similarity metrics such as Euclidean distance and concise similarity to compare pixels and analyze the similarity between them to group them into various clusters.

Clustering-based segmentation can be effective in scenarios where the image contains objects or regions with distinct visual properties, such as different colors or textures. However, it may struggle with complex scenes or regions that exhibit significant variations within the same object class.

Various clustering-based algorithms can be used for segmentation, such as KMeans clustering, mean shift clustering or model-based clustering. KMeans clustering is one of the most popular and efficient clustering algorithms in use these days. However, KMeans clustering expects us to provide the number of clusters in advance. We will be discussing more about KMeans in detail and implementing some code as we move along to the Machine Learning with Computer Vision chapter of the course.

Overall, clustering-based segmentation offers a flexible method to divide images into meaningful segments based on similarity, enabling the detection and differentiation of distinct regions or objects within an image. By utilizing clustering algorithms, this approach allows for effective grouping of pixels or regions based on their shared characteristics, facilitating the extraction of meaningful information and facilitating various image analysis tasks.

Deep Learning-based Segmentation

Deep learning-based segmentation is one of the most advanced and state-of-the-art segmentation techniques and is known for its high accuracy and reliability. The advantage of deep learning models is their ability to learn complex features from images by themselves and there is no need to use any manual segmentation operation.

Deep learning segmentation involves training deep neural networks on large, annotated datasets with mappings between input images and their corresponding segmentation masks. These deep neural networks learn to automatically extract relevant features from the input images and make predictions about the class or label of each pixel or region in the image, enabling them to accurately segment objects or regions of interest.

Deep learning segmentation networks require a large amount of labeled data and a long training time to train and give decent results. However, many widely available pre-trained models can be used for implementing image segmentation using deep learning. Some of the deep learning segmentation networks such as U-Net and RCNN have been able to achieve state-of-the-art performance in terms of segmentation accuracy and precision.

Deep learning training is a complex and resource-intensive process that typically involves a substantial amount of data and extensive computational resources. While deep learning is beyond the scope of this book, we will delve into neural networks in a subsequent chapter, where we will explore practical applications and learn how to perform DL-based inferences.

Conclusion

This chapter provided an overview of various image segmentation techniques. We explored basic approaches such as thresholding, which involves separating objects based on specific intensity values. Additionally, we discussed advanced methods including the GrabCut algorithm, clustering-based segmentation, and deep learning-based techniques. These approaches enable us to extract meaningful regions and boundaries from images, facilitating tasks like object recognition and image editing. By understanding and applying these segmentation techniques, we can gain deeper insights into visual content and enhance computer vision applications.

In the next chapter, we will delve into image kernels, gradients, and their role in edge detection. We will explore the Canny edge detector algorithm in detail, followed by an exploration of contour extraction using OpenCV. Additionally, we will introduce advanced feature detection techniques like SIFT and SURF.

Points to Remember

- Image segmentation is the process of dividing an image into meaningful and distinct regions or segments, enabling us to analyze and understand images at a more granular level.
- Thresholding is a technique used to separate objects from the background in an image by setting a specific threshold value.
- Simple thresholding uses a fixed threshold value, adaptive thresholding adjusts the threshold value based on local image characteristics, and Otsu's thresholding calculates an optimal threshold value by maximizing the between-class variance.
- Edge and contour-based segmentation techniques identify object boundaries by detecting abrupt changes in intensity or gradient within an image.
- The watershed algorithm is designed to mimic the filling of basins in a terrain with water with each basin representing a different region or object.
- In the GrabCut algorithm, the initial foreground region is marked, and the segmentation is iteratively refined by estimating the color distribution and updating the foreground and background regions until convergence.
- Clustering-based segmentation techniques groups pixels or regions into various clusters where each cluster represents a separate segment or object.
- Deep learning-based segmentation techniques employ deep neural networks to automatically extract features and accurately segment objects or regions in images, eliminating the need for manual feature engineering.

Test your understanding

1. Which of the following is not a type or method in the cv2.threshold of OpenCV?
   A. cv2.THRESH_BINARY
   B. cv2.THRESH_TRUNC
   C. cv2.THRESH_ADAPTIVE
   D. cv2.THRESH_TOZERO
2. Otsu's thresholding is a?
   A. Fixed thresholding technique
   B. Adaptive thresholding technique
   C. Technique that maximizes the between-class variance
   D. Contour-based segmentation technique
3. Which of the following statements about the GrabCut algorithm is correct?
   A. GrabCut is a contour-based segmentation technique.
   B. It uses a fixed value for segmentation.
   C. It is designed to mimic the filling of basins in terrain with water.
   D. It requires manual initialization of foreground and background regions.
4. What is the main concept behind the watershed algorithm?
   A. Maximizing the between-class variance
   B. Assigning pixels to different clusters based on similarity
   C. Identifying abrupt changes in intensity or gradient
   D. Simulating a flooding process to separate objects
5. Which of the following statements is false regarding deep learning-based segmentation?
   A. They require large amounts of data.
   B. They are considered state-of-the-art.
   C. They have long training times.
   D. They require manual engineering.

Chapter 7

Edges and Contours

In this chapter, we will explore edge detection and contour extraction. We will begin by understanding edges and how image gradients can be computed. The Sobel, Scharr, and Laplacian filters will be introduced as effective tools for detecting edges and transitions within images. The chapter will then shift its focus to the Canny edge detector, a powerful tool known for its precise edge detection capabilities.

Moving on, we will delve into contour detection and will cover various aspects of contour analysis, including contour visualization, contour hierarchy, contour moments, and the properties of contours. Furthermore, we will discuss contour approximation techniques and explore methods for filtering and selecting contours based on specific criteria.

Structure

In this chapter, we will discuss the following topics:

- Introduction to edges
- Image gradients
- Filters for image gradients
  - Sobel filter
  - Scharr filter
  - Laplacian filter
- Canny edge detector
- Introduction to contours
- Extracting and visualizing contours
- Contour hierarchy
- Contour moments
- Properties of contours
- Contour approximation
- Contour filtering and selection

Introduction to edges

In image processing terms, an Edge refers to a significant and sudden change in the intensity of color in an image. It represents the boundary between the different regions or objects in an image.

Edges are characterized by a sharp contrast in pixel values and often indicate important features or structures. They are commonly represented as lines or curves and play a crucial role in many computer vision and image analysis tasks, including object detection, segmentation, and feature extraction.

Edge detection is a fundamental technique in image processing and computer vision that aims to identify and extract the boundaries or edges of objects or regions within an image. The process of edge detection involves analyzing the changes in intensity or color values between adjacent pixels in an image.

Edge detection algorithms can be categorized into different types, such as intensity based-method gradient-based methods or Laplacian-based methods. Each algorithm has its own advantages, limitations, and parameters that can be adjusted to achieve desired edge detection results.

Image gradients

Image gradients are a fundamental concept in computer vision. Image gradient is the change in directional intensity in an image or we can say that the gradients provide information about the intensity variations in an image. Image gradients are primarily used for edge detection operations.

Image gradients are like a map that shows how steep or gentle the changes are in an image. They help us spot the edges and boundaries between objects:

- When the gradient is high, it means there's a quick change in color or brightness, often indicating an edge or an important detail.
- When it's low, it means the colors or shades are more consistent, like a smooth, flat area in the image.

So, image gradients help us find important features and shapes within pictures.

To understand image gradients better, we can take the help of a 3×3 matrix M. The center pixel marked in red will be our reference pixel for gradient computation:

20	35	81
90	10	50
45	40	32

***Figure 7.1**: A 3x3 Matrix with center Pixel* P(x,y) = 10

For reference, let's assume our center Pixel P is at x and y coordinates. We can write:

P(x,y) = 10

Similarly, to calculate the neighbors of our reference pixel P, we can use the following notation:

Pixel on top - P(x, y-1) = 35

Pixel on bottom - P(x, y+1) = 40

Pixel on left - P (x-1, y) = 90

Pixel on right - P(x+1, y) = 50

Gradient Magnitude: Gradient magnitude represents the strength of the intensity change at a specific point in an image. The magnitude quantities how much the pixel values vary from one point to another in an image. A higher magnitude will denote a larger change in intensity values while a lower change will denote a small change in the intensity values.

In Matrix M, the change of intensity in the horizontal direction can be given by the difference in intensity of the pixel on the right to the pixel on the left:

Gradient in X-direction = Pixel on Right - Pixel on Left

$$Gx = P(x+1, y) - P(x-1, y)$$

Similarly, the vertical change in intensity can be quantified as the difference between the pixel on the bottom and the pixel on the top:

Gradient in Y-direction = Pixel on Bottom - Pixel on Top

$$Gy = P(x, y+1) - P(x, y-1)$$

Now that we have the Gradient in X and Y direction, we can calculate the overall gradient by using the Pythagoras algorithm as:

$$G = sqrt(Gx **2 + Gy **2)$$

Gradient magnitudes are used for edge computation extensively. High gradient magnitudes will represent strong edges in an image. By analyzing the magnitude of the gradient, it is possible to identify regions of interest and perform tasks like edge detection and image enhancement.

Gradient Orientation: Gradient Orientation denotes the direction of change in the intensity values in an image. Gradient Orientation gives us the angle of change in intensity in an image. So if the intensity increases from left to right, the gradient orientation would be aligned with the horizontal axis (0 degrees or π radians). If the intensity decreases from top to bottom, the gradient orientation would be aligned with the vertical axis (90 degrees or $\pi/2$ radians).

Using the gradient magnitude values of Gx and Gy, the gradient orientation in an image can be calculated using mathematical operations such as the arctan function which calculates the angle between the x and y gradient vectors. Thus, we can calculate the gradient direction by:

$$Theta = atan(Gy, Gx) * 180 / pi$$

By analyzing the gradient orientation, it is possible to extract valuable information about the spatial structure and boundaries within an image. Edge detection algorithms rely on gradient orientation to identify the orientation of edges in the image.

We have used a 3x3 matrix to successfully understand how image gradients work. To calculate on the whole images, we will be using gradient filters. We will discuss the three gradient filters provided by OpenCV, Sobel, Scharr and the Laplacian gradient filters.

Filters for image gradients

Gradient filters such as Sobel, Scharr, and Laplacian, play a crucial role in image processing by capturing and highlighting changes in pixel intensity, enabling tasks such as edge detection and feature extraction.

Sobel Filters

Sobel filters are a very commonly used type of spatial filter that calculate the gradients in an image by performing convolution operations. They are primarily used for edge detection due to their simplicity and effectiveness in capturing edge information.

The Sobel filter consists of two types of kernels, one for computing the image gradients in the horizontal or the X direction and the other for computing the gradients in vertical or the Y direction.

The **`SobelX`** and **`SobelY`** filters have predefined values:

-1	0	1
-2	0	2
-1	0	1

Sobel Filter X

-1	-2	1
0	0	0
1	2	1

Sobel Filter Y

***Figure 7.2**: Left: Sobel Filter X, Right: Sobel Filter Y*

To compute the image gradient using these filters, the image is convolved with these kernels. The convolution operation takes place by sliding the kernel over each pixel of the image and multiplying the kernel with it. This effectively calculates the weighted sum of intensities in the neighborhood of the pixel in reference defined by the kernel.

The **`SobelX`** kernel calculates the image gradients in the X direction and emphasizes the vertical edges in the image. The **`SobelX`** kernel enhances vertical edges by assigning negative values to one side and positive values to the other side. This creates a larger difference in values, effectively enhancing the vertical edges in the image. This arrangement accentuates the contrast between the two sides of the vertical edges.

Similarly, the **SobelY** operator calculates the image gradients in the Y direction and emphasizes the horizontal edges in an image. The **SobelY** kernel assigns negative and positive values but in the horizontal direction. This creates a difference in values enhancing the horizontal edges in the image, thus enhancing the contrast between the two sides of the horizontal edges.

Together both of the kernels make an effective gradient computation mechanism effectively calculating the gradient magnitude and orientation in the image.

We can use the **cv2.Sobel()** function in OpenCV to calculate the image gradients using the Sobel operator.

cv2.Sobel()

```
dst = cv2.Sobel(src, ddepth, dx, dy, ksize=3, scale=1, delta=0,
borderType=cv2.BORDER_DEFAULT)
```

Parameters:

- **src**: Input image.
- **ddepth**: Data type of the output image such as **cv2.CV_64F** (64-bit floating-point) or **cv2.CV_16S** (16-bit signed integer). The default value for this parameter will be same the data type of the input image.
- **dx**: Order of the derivatives in the X direction. This can be set to 0 or 1. This is set to 1 to calculate the SobelX parameter or the gradients in the X direction.
- **dy**: Order of the derivatives in the Y direction. This can be set to 0 or 1. This is set to 1 to calculate the SobelY parameter or the gradients in the Y direction.
- Keeping both **dx** and **dy** as 1 will calculate the full gradients for the image.
- **ksize**: Size of the Sobel Kernel to be used. The value for this parameter is an odd integer. The default value for this parameter is 3 indicating a 3x3 kernel.
- **scale**: Scale factor for the computed values. The default value for this parameter is 1 meaning no scaling has been applied.
- **delta**: Additional value added to the computer values. The default value for this parameter is 0.

The Sobel operator can be implemented as:

```
import cv2
image = cv2.imread('1.png', cv2.IMREAD_GRAYSCALE)
# Compute the gradient along x and y directions
```

```
gradient_x = cv2.Sobel(image, cv2.CV_64F, 1, 0, ksize=3)
gradient_y = cv2.Sobel(image, cv2.CV_64F, 0, 1, ksize=3)
cv2.imshow("Gradient X",gradient_x)
cv2.imshow("Gradient Y",gradient_y)
cv2.waitKey(0)
cv2.destroyAllWindows()
```

The code produces the following output:

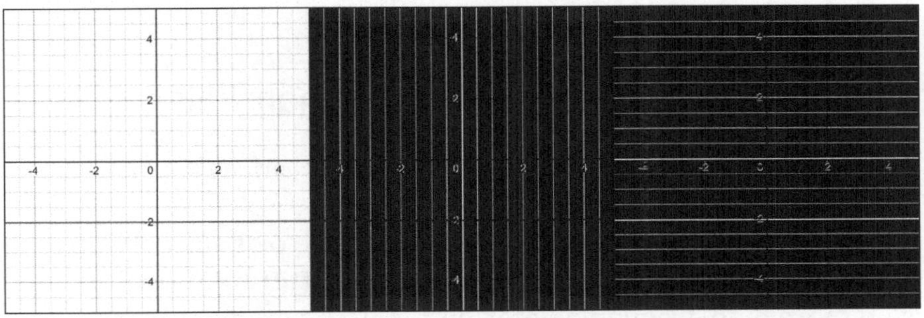

***Figure 7.3**: Input image (left) and outputs for Sobel X and Y Filter. Output for Sobel X filter enhances the vertical edges (center) and Sobel Y filter enhances the horizontal edges (right) in the image.*

In the preceding code, we take a checkered pattern image to execute the Sobel filter since there are distinct vertical and horizontal lines on the image helping us to better visualize both Sobel Kernels. We use the **`cv2.Sobel()`** function discussed earlier with a **`ksize`** value of 3. The output for the Sobel X kernel has emphasized the vertical lines in the image while the Sobel Y kernel has emphasized the horizontal lines in the image.

In summary, the Sobel kernel is a computationally inexpensive method designed to enhance edges by assigning negative and positive values to different sides of the edges. They are applied through convolution operations to emphasize edges in the corresponding directions, which are then used for tasks such as edge detection, image enhancement, and feature extraction.

Scharr Operator

The Scharr operators are a variation of the Sobel operators used for gradient calculation. They are used to provide a more accurate and rotationally symmetric gradient estimate when compared to the Sobel Operators.

Scharr operators are limited to 3x3 kernel size. Similar to the Sobel operators we have separate Scharr kernels for the X and Y direction. The Scharr kernels are as follows:

-3	0	3
-10	0	10
-3	0	3

Scharr Filter X

-3	-10	-3
0	0	0
3	10	3

Scharr Filter Y

Figure 7.4: *Left: Scharr Filter X, Right: Scharr Filter Y*

Scharr kernels provide more emphasis on the central rows and columns compared to the Sobel operators, which helps in achieving better rotational symmetry and preserving more high-frequency information in the gradient estimation.

Sobel operators and Scharr operators are both used for finding image gradients. However, Scharr operators are sometimes preferred over Sobel operators for a couple of reasons, even though they serve a similar purpose:

- **Improved sensitivity**: Scharr operators are more sensitive to subtle changes in image gradients compared to Sobel operators. They can detect edges and details that Sobel might miss, making them a better choice when you need precise edge detection.
- **Better rotation invariance**: Sobel operators are sensitive to the orientation of edges, which means they might perform differently depending on whether the edge is horizontal, vertical, or diagonal. Scharr operators are designed to be more rotationally invariant meaning they perform consistently across various edge orientations.

So, while Sobel operators are quite useful for basic gradient calculations, Scharr operators offer improved accuracy and performance in scenarios were detecting fine details and dealing with edges at different angles is important.

We can use the **`cv2.Scharr()`** function to implement our Scharr Operators.

```
dst = cv2.Scharr(src, ddepth, dx, dy, scale=1, delta=0, borderType=cv2.
BORDER_DEFAULT)
```

The parameters in the Scharr operator are similar to the parameters in the Sobel parameter. The only difference is that the **`cv2.Scharr`** function is missing the **`ksize`** parameter since the kernel size of the Scharr operator is fixed at 3.

We can also use the **cv2.Sobel** function to implement Scharr operators. The **ksize** parameter is set to -1, which indicates that the size of the Sobel kernel is automatically determined based on the provided **dx** and **dy** values. By setting **ksize** to -1, OpenCV internally uses a 3×3 Sobel kernel, which approximates the Scharr operators:

```
import cv2

image = cv2.imread('image.jpg', cv2.IMREAD_GRAYSCALE)

# Compute Scharr X gradient using the cv2.Scharr function
gradient_x = cv2.Scharr(image, cv2.CV_32F, 1, 0)

# Compute Scharr-like Y gradient using the cv2.sobel function
gradient_y = cv2.Sobel(image, cv2.CV_32F, 0, 1, ksize=-1)

cv2.imshow("Gradient X", gradient_x)
cv2.imshow("Gradient Y", gradient_y)
cv2.waitKey(0)
cv2.destroyAllWindows()
```

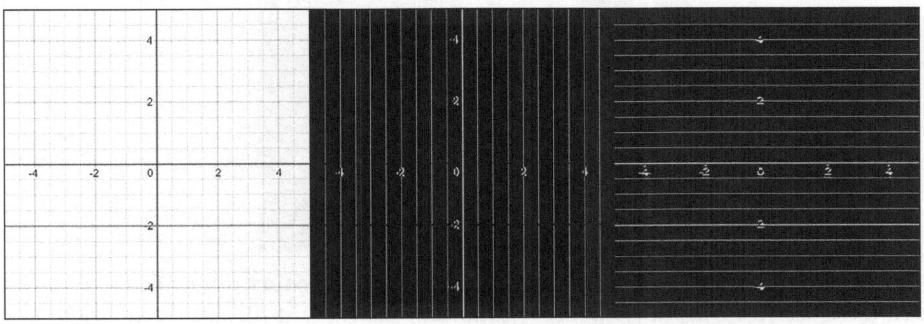

Figure 7.5: *Input image (left) and outputs for Scharr X and Y Filter. Output for Scharr X filter enhances the vertical edges (center) and Scharr Y filter enhances the horizontal edges (right) in the image.*

In the above code, we use both cv2.Scharr and cv2.Sobel functions to implement Scharr operators. We use cv2.Scharr to generate the X gradient and cv2.Sobel to generate "Scharr like" gradients in the Y direction.

We can also manually enter the kernel values to implement our Scharr operators:

```
import cv2
```

```
import numpy as np

image = cv2.imread('objects.jpg', cv2.IMREAD_GRAYSCALE)

# Define Scharr-like kernels
scharr_x = np.array([[-3, 0, 3], [-10, 0, 10], [-3, 0, 3]], dtype=np.
float32)
scharr_y = np.array([[-3, -10, -3], [0, 0, 0], [3, 10, 3]], dtype=np.
float32)

# Compute Scharr-like gradients
gradient_x = cv2.filter2D(image, cv2.CV_32F, scharr_x)
gradient_y = cv2.filter2D(image, cv2.CV_32F, scharr_y)
gradient = np.sqrt(gradient_x**2 + gradient_y**2)


cv2.imshow("Gradient X", gradient_x)
cv2.imshow("Gradient Y", gradient_y)
cv2.imshow("Gradient ", gradient)
cv2.waitKey(0)
cv2.destroyAllWindows()
```

Figure 7.6: *Input image (left) and outputs manually applying Scharr filter. (Top Right): Output for Scharr X,(Bottom Left): Output for Scharr Y, (Bottom Right): Overall calculated gradient output.*

In this example, we first initialize our kernels using NumPy arrays. Then we use **cv2.filter2D()** function to apply kernels to an image. We then use the X and Y gradients to calculate the overall gradient for the image.

cv2.filter2D

```
dst = cv2.filter2D(src, ddepth, kernel, anchor=(-1,-1), delta=0,
borderType=cv2.BORDER_DEFAULT)
```

Parameters:

- `src`: Source Image
- `ddepth`: Output Data type
- `kernel`: The kernel or filter that will be applied to the input image.
- `anchor`: The anchor points of the kernel. It specifies the relative position within the kernel. By default, (-1, -1) is used, which means the anchor is at the kernel center.
- `delta`: An optional value added to the filtered result. By default, it is set to 0.

We can use the above method to apply filters on an image for a multitude of use cases. Why don't you go ahead and try the manual implementation for the Sobel kernels we discussed earlier?

The Scharr operators are advantageous over the Sobel operators in certain aspects. They offer better rotational symmetry, which makes them more suitable for scenarios where edge orientations vary. Additionally, the Scharr operators preserve more high-frequency information, making them useful for applications that require fine detail retention.

However, the Sobel operators provide more flexibility with kernel sizes and separate x and y gradients, allowing for more precise control over the gradient computation. The choice between Scharr and Sobel operators depends on the specific requirements of the application and the desired gradient characteristics.

Laplacian Operators

Laplacian is another operator used to compute the gradients in an image to detect edges and regions of high-intensity changes in an image.

The Laplacian operator is a second-order derivative operator that measures the rate of change of intensity in the image. First-order filters identify edges in an image by detecting local maximum or minimum values. In contrast, the Laplacian operator detects edges at points of inflection, which occur when the intensity value transitions from negative to positive or vice versa.

The Laplacian operator is represented by a 3×3 kernel and the central element of the kernel is assigned a negative value (-4 or -8) and the surrounding elements have positive values (1 or 2). This configuration enhances the edges and intensity transitions in the image.

The Laplacian operator not only detects edges in an image but also provides additional information about the nature of these edges. It classifies edges into two types: inward edges and outward edges. Inward edges are regions where the intensity values transition from higher to lower values, while outward edges are regions where the intensity values transition from lower to higher values.

Internally, the Laplacian operator utilizes the Sobel operator to perform its computations. The Sobel operator calculates the gradients of an image and these derivatives are then used to compute the second-order derivatives necessary for the Laplacian operator:

$$Laplace(f) = \frac{\partial^2 f}{\partial x^2} + \frac{\partial^2 f}{\partial y^2}$$

Figure 7.7: *Laplacian Operator Formula*

The formula to calculate the Laplacian operator is given above. This is used when the **`ksize`** parameter is greater than 1. If **`ksize`** is kept as 1, the Laplacian is computed with the following 3×3 kernel:

0	1	0
1	4	1
0	1	0

3x3 Laplacian

Figure 7.8: 3×3 *Laplacian Filter*

The Laplacian operator in OpenCV is applied by using the cv2.laplacian function.

```
dst = cv2.Laplacian(src, ddepth, ksize=1, scale=1, delta=0,
borderType=cv2.BORDER_DEFAULT)
```

The parameters for **`cv2.laplacian()`** function are similar to the ones we have previously discussed, so they do not need any further discussion.

Let's try some code on Laplacian operators:

```
import cv2
```

```
image = cv2.imread("12.jpg", cv2.IMREAD_GRAYSCALE)

# Apply Laplacian with default ksize
laplacian_default = cv2.Laplacian(image, cv2.CV_64F)

# Apply Laplacian with higher ksize (e.g., 11)
laplacian_higher = cv2.Laplacian(image, cv2.CV_64F, ksize=7)

# Convert the results to unsigned 8-bit for visualization
laplacian_default = cv2.convertScaleAbs(laplacian_default)
laplacian_higher = cv2.convertScaleAbs(laplacian_higher)

# Display the original image and the Laplacian results
cv2.imshow("Original Image", image)
cv2.imshow("Laplacian (Default ksize)", laplacian_default)
cv2.imshow("Laplacian (Higher ksize)", laplacian_higher)
cv2.waitKey(0)
cv2.destroyAllWindows()
```

The code produces the following output:

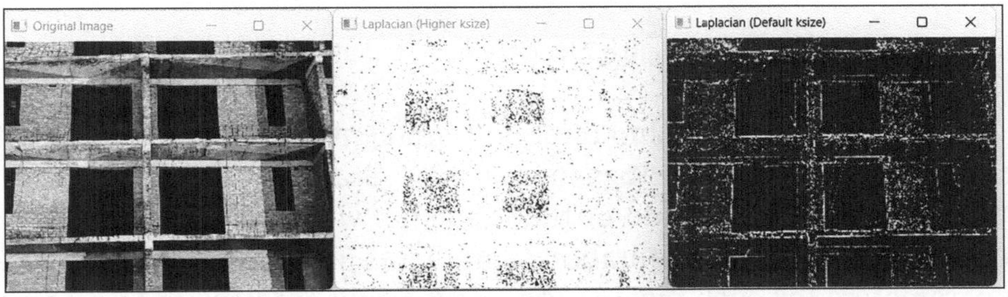

Figure 7.9: *Laplacian Output*

In summary, the Laplacian operator detects and classifies edges as inward or outward by computing the second-order derivatives directly. It captures both horizontal and vertical intensity changes, providing valuable edge information without relying on the Sobel operator.

Canny Edge Detector

The canny edge detector is a widely used algorithm for edge detection in image processing. The algorithm was developed in 1986 by John F. Canny and has since become a pivotal advancement in the field of computer vision and image processing. The Canny edge detector aims to accurately identify the boundaries of objects in an image while minimizing noise and false detections.

The Canny edge detector provides reliable and precise edge detection results by leveraging a set of carefully designed steps. The Canny edge detection algorithm begins by applying Gaussian smoothing to the image, effectively reducing noise and blurring the edges. Next, the algorithm calculates the gradient magnitude and direction to identify areas of rapid intensity changes. Non-maximum suppression is then performed to thin out the edges, followed by hysteresis thresholding to classify pixels as strong or weak edges. Finally, edge tracking connects weak edges to strong edges, resulting in the precise and reliable edge detection provided by the Canny algorithm.

The detailed explanation for the aforementioned steps is as follows:

Step 1: Gaussian smoothing: The image is converted into grayscale and gaussian blur is applied on the image to reduce noise. Smoothing the image will allow us to remove some details from the image, since we are not interested in the small details and want to extract the main boundaries in the image:

$$G(x,y) = \frac{1}{\sqrt{2\pi\sigma^2}} e^{-\frac{x^2+y^2}{2\sigma^2}}$$

Figure 7.10: *Gaussian Formula*

Step 2: Gradient Magnitude and direction:Gradients in an image represent the rate of change in pixel intensities in an image. Gradient magnitude represents the strength or the magnitude of the gradients while gradient direction talks about the direction or the orientation of gradients in the image. We will calculate these parameters for each pixel in the image using gradient operators such as Sobel or Scharr.

Step 3: Non-Max Suppression: Non max suppression in Canny Edge Detection is a process used for thinning the edges and thus accurately representing the true edges in an image. The algorithm keeps only the significant edges by preserving only the local maximum responses and thinning out any non-maximum responses.

Non-max suppression works by iterating over each pixel in an image and comparing its values with the gradient magnitudes of neighboring pixels in the direction perpendicular to the edge indicated by the gradient direction. Non max suppression works by performing the following steps:

- Compute the gradient magnitude and direction of the image using gradient operators such as the Sobel or Sharr operators.

- Iterate over each pixel in the gradient magnitude image.
- Compare the gradient magnitude of the current pixel with its neighboring pixels in the gradient direction.
- If the current pixel has a greater magnitude than its neighbors, it is considered as a candidate for an edge pixel. If the current pixel has a lower magnitude than its neighbors, then the pixel is ignored.
- The value for this pixel is then set to its gradient magnitude value indicating that it is a local minimum response. PIxels that are not considered as local maxima are set to 0.

By performing non-maximum suppression, the algorithm ensures that only pixels with maximum gradient magnitudes along the edges are retained, while suppressing weaker responses that do not correspond to the sharpest edges.

Step 4: Hysteresis Thresholding: There are still a few regions in the image that are not edges and need to be removed. To do that, we first choose two threshold values - a higher and a lower threshold value and use these to classify pixels into strong, weak, or non edges. These threshold values have to be chosen carefully as a large range between these values will keep a lot of false edges while a narrow range might eliminate some real edges from the output.

Pixels with thresholds higher than the upper threshold value are classified as strong edges and these pixels are kept. Pixels with lower values than the lower threshold are considered to be non-edges and these pixels are discarded as edges.

Any values lying between the upper and lower threshold values are classified as weak edges. If the weak edge pixels are connected to a strong edge, these pixels are kept and marked as edge. Otherwise, these values are discarded. This is known as edge tracking by hysteresis and helps to extend and connect edges that may have been broken during thresholding.

Output: The result is an edge map where edges are represented as white and all non-edge areas are depicted as black.

The following code implements the Canny edge detection algorithm in a step-by-step manner as previously discussed. Feel free to skip the following detailed implementation code if you prefer the OpenCV predefined function for the Canny edge detector, which we will delve into after examining this code. However, it is advisable to learn the Canny edge detection process step by step as well:

```
import cv2
import numpy as np
```

```
image = cv2.imread('image.jpg', cv2.IMREAD_GRAYSCALE)

blurred = cv2.GaussianBlur(image, (5, 5), 0)

# Compute the gradients using Sobel operators
gradient_x = cv2.Sobel(blurred, cv2.CV_64F, 1, 0, ksize=3)
gradient_y = cv2.Sobel(blurred, cv2.CV_64F, 0, 1, ksize=3)

# Compute the magnitude and direction of the gradients
gradient_magnitude = np.sqrt(gradient_x**2 + gradient_y**2)
gradient_direction = np.arctan2(gradient_y, gradient_x)
cv2.imwrite('gradient_magnitude.jpg', gradient_magnitude)
cv2.imwrite('gradient_direction.jpg', gradient_direction)

# Perform non-maximum suppression
suppressed = np.copy(gradient_magnitude)
for i in range(1, suppressed.shape[0] - 1):
    for j in range(1, suppressed.shape[1] - 1):
        direction = gradient_direction[i, j] * 180. / np.pi
        if (0 <= direction < 22.5) or (157.5 <= direction <= 180):
            if suppressed[i, j] <= suppressed[i, j + 1] or suppressed[i,
j] <= suppressed[i, j - 1]:
                suppressed[i, j] = 0
        elif (22.5 <= direction < 67.5):
            if suppressed[i, j] <= suppressed[i - 1, j + 1] or sup-
pressed[i, j] <= suppressed[i + 1, j - 1]:
                suppressed[i, j] = 0
        elif (67.5 <= direction < 112.5):
            if suppressed[i, j] <= suppressed[i - 1, j] or suppressed[i,
j] <= suppressed[i + 1, j]:
                suppressed[i, j] = 0
        else:
            if suppressed[i, j] <= suppressed[i - 1, j - 1] or
suppressed[i, j] <= suppressed[i + 1, j + 1]:
                suppressed[i, j] = 0
cv2.imwrite('suppressed.jpg', suppressed)

# Perform thresholding to classify pixels as strong or weak edges
low_threshold = 30
high_threshold = 100
edges = np.zeros_like(suppressed)
edges[suppressed >= high_threshold] = 255
edges[suppressed <= low_threshold] = 0
weak_edges = np.logical_and(suppressed > low_threshold, suppressed <
high_threshold)
```

```
# Perform edge tracking by connecting weak edges to strong edges
strong_edges_i, strong_edges_j = np.where(edges == 255)
for i, j in zip(strong_edges_i, strong_edges_j):
    if np.any(weak_edges[i - 1:i + 2, j - 1:j + 2]):
        edges[i - 1:i + 2, j - 1:j + 2] = 255
cv2.imwrite('edges.jpg', edges)

cv2.imshow('Canny Edges', edges)
cv2.waitKey(0)
cv2.destroyAllWindows()
```

The final output for the code is as follows:

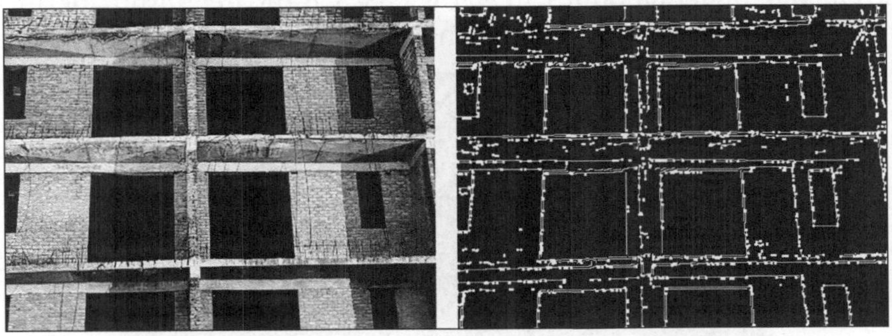

Figure 7.11: *Input and Final Output images for Canny Edge Detector*

The above code works by first loading an image and applying gaussian smoothing to it. We then compute the gradients for the image using the Sobel operator discussed earlier. Gradient Magnitude and the gradient direction are then calculated using the arithmetic formulas of each:

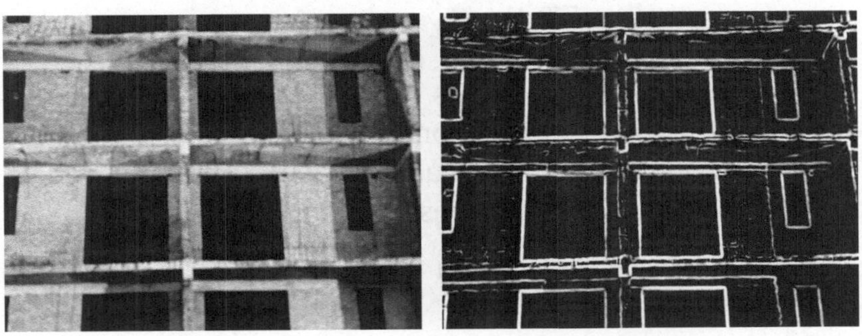

Figure 7.12: *Grayscale image (left) and Gradient magnitude (right) calculation*

We then move on to the non max suppression part of the code. We create a copy of the gradient magnitude image called suppressed and iterate over each pixel in this image except the borders. Hence the -1 in for loops. The gradient direction at the current pixel, represented by direction, is calculated by converting the angle from radians to degrees using the formula direction = gradient_direction[i, j] * 180. / np.pi.

For horizontal edges (0 to 22.5 degrees and 157.5 to 180 degrees), the code compares the gradient magnitude of the current pixel with its right and left neighbors. For diagonal edges (22.5 to 67.5 degrees), the code compares the gradient magnitude of the current pixel with its diagonal neighbors. For vertical edges (67.5 to 112.5 degrees), the code compares the gradient magnitude of the current pixel with its top and bottom neighbors and for the other diagonal edges (112.5 to 157.5 degrees), the code compares the gradient magnitude of the current pixel with its diagonal neighbors. In all the cases, If the magnitude of the current pixel is smaller or equal to either of its neighbors, we set it to zero:

***Figure* 7.13**: *Non Max suppression output*

The values chosen for the directions (22.5, 67.5, 112.5, 157.5) represent the thresholds to determine the orientation of the edges. These values are based on the four main directions (horizontal, diagonal, vertical, and diagonal) and provide a range to check for the suppression condition.

We can also express these values as (0 <= direction < np.pi / 4) for horizontal edges, (np.pi / 4 <= direction < 3 * np.pi / 4) for diagonal edges, (3 * np.pi / 4 <= direction < 5 * np.pi / 4) for vertical edges, and (5 * np.pi / 4 <= direction < 7 * np.pi / 4) for diagonal edges.

The lower and upper threshold values are chosen as 30 and 100 respectively for hysteresis thresholding. Strong and non-edges are chosen and set to 255 and 0 respectively. We use edge tracking to sort the weak edges into either keeping or discarding them.

For each strong edge pixel, the code checks if any of its neighboring pixels within a 3x3 window, defined by weak_edges[i - 1:i + 2, j - 1:j + 2], are classified as weak edges. The **`np.any()`** function checks if there is at least one True value within the specified window If there is at least one weak edge pixel found in the neighborhood, the corresponding region in the edges image is set to 255, indicating a connected edge:

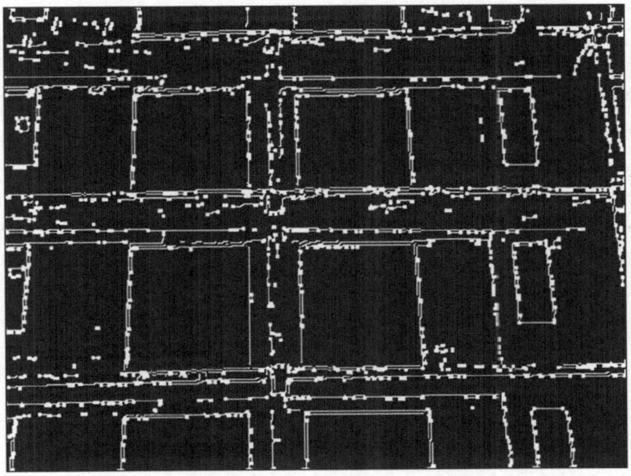

***Figure 7.14**: Final Output Image*

The final edges are obtained after the above operation has iterated through all the strong edge pixels.

For a simpler and more convenient approach, OpenCV provides the cv2.Canny function, which offers a predefined implementation of the Canny edge detection algorithm. This function allows you to perform Canny edge detection without the need for manually coding the steps explained above.

cv2.Canny()

```
cv2.Canny(image, threshold1, threshold2, edges, apertureSize=3,
L2gradient=false)
```

Parameters:

- **`image`**: The input image (Grayscale) on which Canny edge detection will be performed.
- **`threshold1`**: Lower threshold value. Any gradient value below threshold1 is considered a non-edge and will be discarded. If the parameter is explicitly set to threshold1=None, it will default to the value of 100.
- **`threshold2`**: Higher threshold value. Any gradient value above threshold2

is considered a strong edge and will be preserved. TIf the parameter is explicitly set to threshold1=None, it will default to the value of 200.

- Gradient values between threshold1 and threshold2 are treated as weak edges.
- **edges**: Output Array. The edges parameter in the **cv2.Canny** function represents the output image or array where the detected edges will be stored. After applying the Canny edge detection algorithm, the resulting binary image representing the edges will be stored in the edges array.
- **apertureSize**: Size of the Sobel kernel used for the gradient calculation. The value for this can be either 3, 5 or 7. The default value for this parameter is 3.
- **L2gradient**: A Boolean value indicating whether to use the L2-norm for gradient calculation. If True, it calculates the magnitude using the Euclidean distance. If False, it uses the L1-norm (sum of absolute values). The default value for this parameter is **false**.

The following code implements canny edge detection using the **cv2.Canny()** function:

```
import cv2

image = cv2.imread('image.jpg', cv2.IMREAD_GRAYSCALE)

# Apply Canny edge detection
edges = cv2.Canny(image, threshold1=100, threshold2=200)

cv2.imshow('Edges', edges)
cv2.waitKey(0)
cv2.destroyAllWindows()
```

The output for the preceding code is as follows:

***Figure 7.15**: Input and Output images on using cv2.Canny() function for edge detection*

Observe the notable reduction in code complexity achieved by the **cv2.canny** function in OpenCV, as it significantly streamlines our implementation. You can go ahead and try to experiment with different parameters of the **cv2.Canny** function to obtain diverse results.

In conclusion, the Canny edge detector is a powerful technique in computer vision and image processing, known for its ability to provide accurate and reliable edge detection results.

Introduction to Contours

Contours are the continuous curves or boundaries representing the shape of objects inside an image. Contours are an important part of image processing and provide us information about the shape and structure of objects in an image. While contours are continuous curves or boundaries they are represented as a list of points that form a closed curve.

Various properties of contours such as shape, area, or perimeter can be used to analyze and extract meaningful information for objects in an image. Advanced properties on contours such as aspect ratio or convex hull can provide additional insights and information about the contours, enabling more sophisticated analysis and interpretation of the objects within an image.

Contours play a crucial role in computer vision. Contours provide a way to extract the shape and boundary information of objects within an image. They are widely used for object detection and recognition tasks, where the goal is to identify and locate specific objects or patterns in an image. Contours can be leveraged for image segmentation tasks as they can help separate objects from the background or each other. By analyzing various properties of contours such as shape, area, or perimeter among many others, we can generate a lot of insights about the objects in an image. Overall, The analysis and interpretation of contours enable advanced computer vision systems to understand and interact with the visual world more effectively.

Contour Hierarchy

Contour hierarchy refers to the hierarchical relationship between contours detected in an image. It provides information about the connectivity and organization of contours, such as parent-child relationships and the presence of holes within objects.

The contour hierarchy is represented by a NumPy array, where each element corresponds to a contour. Each contour element contains four values: [The index of the next contour at the same hierarchical level, the index of the previous contour at the same hierarchical level, the index of the first child contour, and the index of the parent contour]:

- The index of the next contour at the same level points to the next contour in the hierarchy. Value is -1 if there is no next contour.
- The index of the previous contour at the same level points to the previous contour. Value is -1 if there is no previous contour.
- The index of the first child contour points to the first child contour of the current contour. Value is -1 if there is no child contour.
- The index of the parent contour points to the parent contour. Value is -1 if the contour is a top-level contour.

For example, let us take an image with three contours: a large outer contour (parent), a smaller inner contour (child), and another contour at the same hierarchical level as the outer contour.

The contours and hierarchy will look like this:

Contours: [0, 1, 2]

Hierarchy: [[**-1**,- **1**,**1**,**-1**],[**-1**,**-1**,**-1**,**0**],[**-1**,**0**,**-1**,**-1**]]

Here, the contours with their corresponding hierarchy can be explained as follows:

- **Contour 0 (outer contour)**:

Next contour at the same level: Contour 1

Previous contour at the same level: -1 (no previous contour)

First child contour: Contour 2

Parent contour: -1 (top-level contour)

- **Contour 1 (inner contour)**:

Next contour at the same level: -1 (no next contour)

Previous contour at the same level: -1 (no previous contour)

First child contour: -1 (no child contour)

Parent contour: Contour 0

- **Contour 2 (same level as outer contour):**

Next contour at the same level: -1 (no next contour)

Previous contour at the same level: 0

First child contour: -1 (no child contour)

Parent contour: -1 (top-level contour)

Extracting and Visualizing Contours

To find and draw contours, OpenCV provides us with a function for the identification of contours and another function for the drawing of contours on an image. We will be using **`cv2.findContours`** function to find contours of objects in an image and **`cv2.drawContours`** function to visualize these contours on an image.

cv2.findContours()

```
contours, hierarchy = cv2.findContours(image, mode=cv2.RETR_EXTERNAL,
method=cv2.CHAIN_APPROX_SIMPLE, contours=None, hierarchy=None,
offset=None)
```

Parameters:

image: The image from which contours will be extracted.

mode: The contour retrieval mode. The possible values for this parameter are:

- **`cv2.RETR_EXTERNAL`**: Retrieves only the external contours - Default value.
- **`cv2.RETR_LIST`**: Retrieves all the contours without hierarchical relationships.
- **`cv2.RETR_TREE`**: Retrieves all the contours and creates a full hierarchy of nested contours.
- **`method`**: The method for contour approximation:
- **`cv2.CHAIN_APPROX_SIMPLE`**: Compressed horizontal, vertical and diagonal segments of the contours resulting in a simplified representation of the contours. - Default value.
- **`cv2.CHAIN_APPROX_NONE`**: Stores all the contours without any suppression.
- **`cv2.CHAIN_APPROX_TC89_L1`** and **`cv2.CHAIN_APPROX_TC89_KCOS`**: These methods use the Teh-Chin chain approximation algorithm. It provides more accurate results and smoother curves by using the Douglas-Peucker

algorithm with additional modifications. These methods are suitable when you require higher accuracy and smoother contours.

- **`contours`**: Parameter to store the contour hierarchy information. Default value of None will create a new list.
- **`hierarchy`**: The contour hierarchy represents the relationships between contours, such as parent-child relationships. This parameter takes a NumPy array to store the contour hierarchy information. Default value of None will create a new array.

The mode argument in the cv2.findContours() function determines the contour retrieval mode, specifying how the contours are retrieved from the image. The **`cv2.RETR_EXTERNAL`** mode will retrieve only the external contours meaning it will ignore any internal contours and no contour hierarchy will be generated. The **`cv2.RETR_LIST`** mode will retrieve all the contours in the image but there will be no contour hierarchy. Each contour will be an independent object in the list with no information about parent-child relationships. The CV2.RETR_TREE will return all the contours in the image with a full hierarchy of nested contours.

The method argument will determine the contour approximation method. This specifies how the contour's shape is approximated. The cv2.CHAIN_APPROX_SIMPLE method removes the redundant points resulting in contours shape with fewer points and thus reducing memory consumption. We can use this method when no detailed information is required about the shape information. The **`cv2.CHAIN_APPROX_NONE`** method will store all the points without any compression. This will result in a large number of points but can be used when we need a precise shape of the objects. The contour approximation methods **`cv2.CHAIN_APPROX_TC89_L1`** and **`cv2.CHAIN_APPROX_TC89_KCOS`** utilize the Teh-Chin chain approximation algorithm. These methods result in more accurate and smoother contours compared to **`cv2.CHAIN_APPROX_SIMPLE`**. However, the detailed explanation of the algorithms and their specific effects on contour approximation are beyond the scope of this book.

Now that we have understood how to extract contours in an image, we will go through the **`cv2.drawContours()`** function to draw and visualize these contours on our images.

cv2.drawContours()

```
cv2.drawContours(image, contours, contourIdx, color=(0,0,255),
thickness=1, lineType=cv2.LINE_8, hierarchy=None, maxLevel=sys.maxsize,
offset=(0,0))
```

Parameters:

- `image`: The image of on which contours will be drawn.
- `contours`: The list of contours to be drawn.
- `contourIdx`: The index of contours to be drawn. To draw all the contours -1 is used
- `color`: Color of the contours to be drawn. The value is in BGR format for colored images and scalar for grayscale image. The default value is (0,0,255) indicating a red contour.
- `thickness`: The thickness of the contour lines. Negative values in this parameter will fill the contour.
- `lineType`: The type of line to be drawn. The possible values for this parameter are:
    - `cv2.LINE_4`: 4 connected line indicating contour segment is connected to its previous and next segments.
    - `cv2.LINE_8`: 8 connected Line indicating contour segment is connected to its previous, next and the diagonal segments - Default value.
    - `cv2.LINE_AA`: Anti-aliased line create a smoother line compared to other types by using an anti-aliasing algorithm to reduce jagged edges.

maxLevel: Specifies the contour hierarchy to be drawn. The possible values for this parameter are:

- `0`: Draw only the specified contour. Child and higher-level contours will not be drawn.
- `1`: Draw the specified contour and its immediate child contours. Higher-level contours will not be drawn.
- `2`: Draw the specified contour, its immediate child contours, and the child contours of those child contours. Higher-level contours will not be drawn.
- `sys.maxsize`: Draw all levels of the contour hierarchy. This includes the specified contour, its child contours, and all higher-level contours. - Default value.

Let's try some basic contour finding and drawing codes using the functions discussed above:

```
import cv2
import numpy as np
```

```
image = cv2.imread('objects.jpg')
gray = cv2.cvtColor(image, cv2.COLOR_BGR2GRAY)

# Apply thresholding to create a binary image
_, thresh = cv2.threshold(gray, 200, 255, cv2.THRESH_BINARY)

# Find contours
contours, _ = cv2.findContours(thresh, cv2.RETR_TREE, cv2.CHAIN_APPROX_
SIMPLE)

# Create a copy of the original image
contour_image = image.copy()

# Draw contours on the copy of the original image
cv2.drawContours(contour_image, contours, -1, (0, 255, 0), 2)

cv2.imshow('Original Image', image)
cv2.imshow('Contours', contour_image)
cv2.waitKey(0)
cv2.destroyAllWindows()
```

The input and output for the preceding code are as follows:

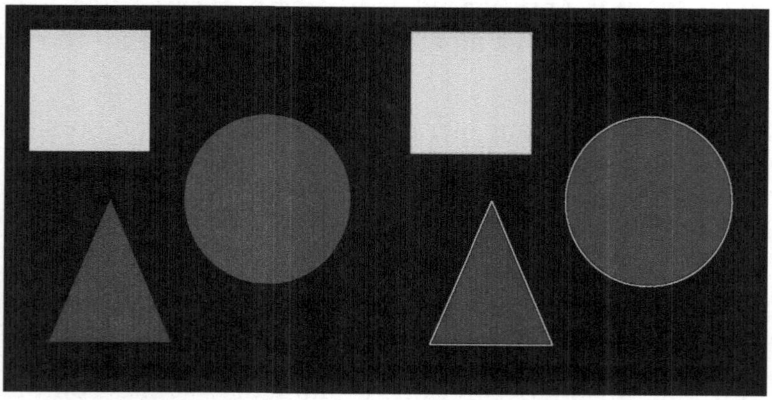

Figure 7.16: *Input image (left) and output image with contours (right)*

The preceding code finds and draws contours across each object in the image as shown in the image.

Contour Moments

Contour moments are statistical measures that describe various characteristics of a contour or shape. These moments provide valuable information about the spatial distribution, size, shape, and orientation of objects in an image.

By analyzing contour moments, we can extract important features and properties of objects, which can be used for various tasks such as object recognition, shape matching, and classification.

There are different types of contour moments that capture different aspects of the shape.

The most commonly used moments are:

- **Area**: Represents the total area enclosed by the contour.
- **Centroid**: Indicates the center of mass or the average position of the contour.
- **Moments of Inertia**: Provide information about the object's resistance to rotation around its centroid.
- **Orientation**: Describes the angle at which the major axis of the object is aligned.
- **Hu Moments**: A set of seven invariant moments that are robust to translation, rotation, and scale changes.

Contour moments can be calculated using mathematical formulas based on the coordinates. Also, OpenCV provides functions to compute moments directly from the contour or the binary image containing the contour.

cv2.Moments()

```
cv2.moments(contour, binaryImage=False)
```

Parameters:

- **`contour`**: Input contour.
- **`binaryImage`**: Flag to indicate whether the input contour is a binary image. If set to True, the input contour is treated as a binary image where non-zero pixels represent the object. If set to **`False`**, the input contour is treated as a contour. The default value is False indicating that the function assumes that the input contour is a contour, not a binary image.

The function returns a dictionary containing various moment values calculated for the given contour or binary image. The dictionary includes keys such as 'm00', 'm10', 'm01', 'm20', 'm02', 'm11', 'mu20', 'mu02', 'mu11', 'nu20', 'nu02', 'nu11', and more. These keys represent different moments and central moments.

Some of the commonly used contour moments are:

- **'m00'**: The zeroth-order moment, represents the total area of the contour or binary image.
- **'m10', 'm01'**: First-order moments, also known as the centroid moments. 'm10' represents the sum of the x-coordinates of all the pixels in the contour, and 'm01' represents the sum of the y-coordinates of all the pixels. These moments are used to calculate the centroid of the contour or binary image.
- **'m20', 'm02', 'm11'**: Second-order moments. 'm20' represents the sum of the squared x-coordinates of all the pixels, 'm02' represents the sum of the squared y-coordinates, and 'm11' represents the sum of the products of x and y coordinates. These moments are used to compute the moments of inertia, which provide information about the shape and orientation of the contour or binary image.
- **'mu20', 'mu02', 'mu11'**: Central moments, which are calculated with respect to the centroid of the contour or binary image. They are normalized versions of the second-order moments and are less sensitive to translation.
- **'nu20', 'nu02', 'nu11'**: Normalized central moments, which are scaled versions of the central moments. They are normalized by dividing them by a power of the zeroth-order moment. These moments provide scale-invariant properties.

These values describe different statistical properties of the contour or binary image, providing information about its shape, position, orientation, and size. By analyzing these moments, we can extract valuable features and characteristics of objects in an image.

Properties of Contours

Contour properties provide quantitative information about the shape, size, and spatial characteristics of objects within an image, allowing for tasks such as object classification, shape analysis, and measurement in computer vision and image processing applications.

Area

The area property measures the area enclosed under the contour boundary. The area lying under a contour is measured using the **`cv2.contourArea()`** function. This function returns the underlying area in the number of pixels.

cv2.contourArea()

```
contourArea(contour, oriented=False)
```

Parameters:

- **`contour`**: Input contour represented as a numpy array.
- **`oriented`**: Parameter representing if the output area should have a signed representation. The default value is **`False`**.

Perimeter

The perimeter refers to the total length of the contour boundary. It represents the sum of line segments that form the contour.

To calculate the perimeter in OpenCV, **`cv2.ArcLength()`** function is used:

```
arcLength(curve, closed)
```

Parameters:

- **`contour`**: Input curve for which you want to calculate the arc length.
- **`closed`**: The parameter indicates whether the curve is closed or not. When set to **`True`**, it assumes the curve is closed, and the first and last points are connected. If set to **`False`**, it treats the curve as an open curve.

Centroid/Center Of mass

The centroid or the Center of Mass property refers to the geometric center point of the contour shape. It is basically the average position of all the contours.

In OpenCV, the centroid can be calculated using Moments of a contour. The moments refer to statistical properties of a contour shape. The **`cv2.moments()`** function in OpenCV can be used to calculate the moments of a contour, and the centroid can be extracted from there.

We will consider the moments needed for calculating the centroid:

- **`m10`**: Moment representing the weighted sum of the x-coordinates of the pixels.
- **`m01`**: Moment representing the weighted sum of the y-coordinates of the pixels.
- **`m00`**: Represents the total area defined by the contour.

The centroid of a contour can be calculated using the following formula:

CentroidX = m10 / m00

CentroidY = m01 / m00

Centroid = (CentroidX, CentroidY)

Using the three properties let's try to calculate these parameters for our image and draw them:

```
import cv2
import numpy as np

image = cv2.imread('objects.jpg')
gray = cv2.cvtColor(image, cv2.COLOR_BGR2GRAY)

# Apply thresholding to obtain a binary image
_, binary = cv2.threshold(gray, 22, 255, cv2.THRESH_BINARY)

# Find contours in the binary image
contours, _ = cv2.findContours(binary, cv2.RETR_EXTERNAL, cv2.CHAIN_
APPROX_SIMPLE)

# Iterate over the contours
for contour in contours:
    # Calculate the area of the contour
    area = int(cv2.contourArea(contour))

    # Calculate the perimeter of the contour
    perimeter = int(cv2.arcLength(contour, True))

    # Calculate the centroid of the contour
    M = cv2.moments(contour)
    centroid_x = int(M['m10'] / M['m00'])
    centroid_y = int(M['m01'] / M['m00'])

    print("Area:", area)
    print("Perimeter:", perimeter)
    print("Centroid (x, y):", centroid_x, centroid_y)

    # Draw the contour, centroid, and text on the image
    cv2.drawContours(image, [contour], 0, (0, 255, 0), 2)
    cv2.circle(image, (centroid_x, centroid_y), 5, (0, 0, 0), -1)
    cv2.putText(image, f"Area: {area}", (centroid_x - 50, centroid_y
- 20), cv2.FONT_HERSHEY_SIMPLEX, 0.5, (255, 255, 255), 2)
    cv2.putText(image, f"Perimeter: {perimeter}", (centroid_x - 80,
centroid_y + 30), cv2.FONT_HERSHEY_SIMPLEX, 0.5, (255, 255, 255), 2)
```

```
cv2.imshow("Object Image", image)
cv2.waitKey(0)
cv2.destroyAllWindows()
```

The output for this code is as follows:

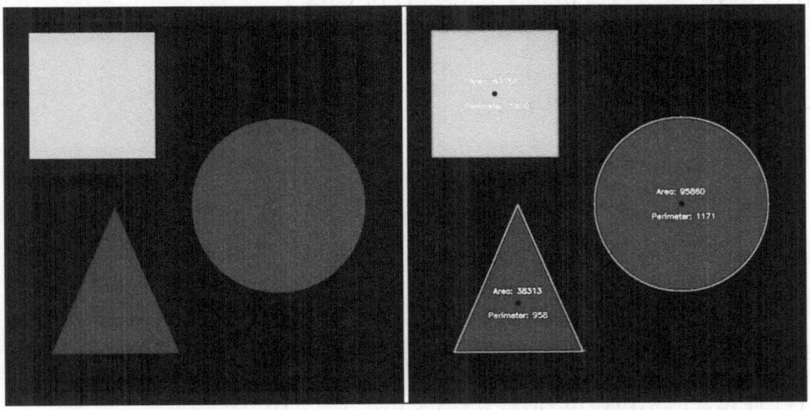

***Figure** 7.17: Input image (left) and output image with the centroid, area and perimeter(right)*

In the preceding code, we first load our image with three objects and apply thresholding to the image to convert it to binary. We then use **cv2.findContours()** function to extract all the contours from the image and loop through each contour.

For each contour, we find the area using **cv2.contourArea()** function and perimeter using the **cv2.arcLength()** function. We calculate the contour moments and use these to obtain our centroid for the contour object.

We then use **cv2.drawContours()** function to visualize these contours on our image. We use **cv2.circle()** function to draw a circle to visualize our centroid point location and **cv2.putText()** to draw the area and parameter values on the image.

Bounding Rectangle

A bounding rectangle refers to the smallest rectangle that can completely enclose an object in an image. The bounding rectangle is typically represented as the top-left coordinates as (x,y) followed by the width and height of the rectangle.

The bounding rectangle can be used for a number of OpenCV tasks as it provides a simple way to describe the location and extent of an object within an image, which can be further utilized for analysis or further processing.

In OpenCV, the bounding rectangle of a contour can be obtained using the **`cv2.boundingRect()`** function.

cv2.boundingRect()

```
x,y,width,height = cv2.boundingRect(contour)
```

Parameters:

- **`contour`**: Input contour

Output:

- **`x`**: x-coordinate of the top-left corner of the bounding rectangle.
- **`y`**: y-coordinate of the top-left corner of the bounding rectangle.
- **`width`**: Width of the bounding rectangle.
- **`height`**: Height of the bounding rectangle.

Let's try to create bounding boxes on some rectangles:

```
import cv2
import numpy as np

image = cv2.imread('rectangles.jpg')

# Convert the image to grayscale
gray = cv2.cvtColor(image, cv2.COLOR_BGR2GRAY)

# Apply thresholding to create a binary image
_, thresh = cv2.threshold(gray, 40, 255, cv2.THRESH_BINARY)

# Find contours
contours, _ = cv2.findContours(thresh, cv2.RETR_EXTERNAL, cv2.CHAIN_
APPROX_SIMPLE)

# Create a copy of the original image
bounding_rect_image = image.copy()

for contour in contours:
    # Get the bounding rectangle for the contour
    x, y, w, h = cv2.boundingRect(contour)

    # Draw a rectangle around the object
    cv2.rectangle(bounding_rect_image, (x, y), (x + w, y + h), (0, 255,
0), 2)

cv2.imshow('Original Image', gray)
```

```
cv2.imshow('Bounding Rectangles', bounding_rect_image)
cv2.waitKey(0)
cv2.destroyAllWindows()
```

The preceding code produces the following output:

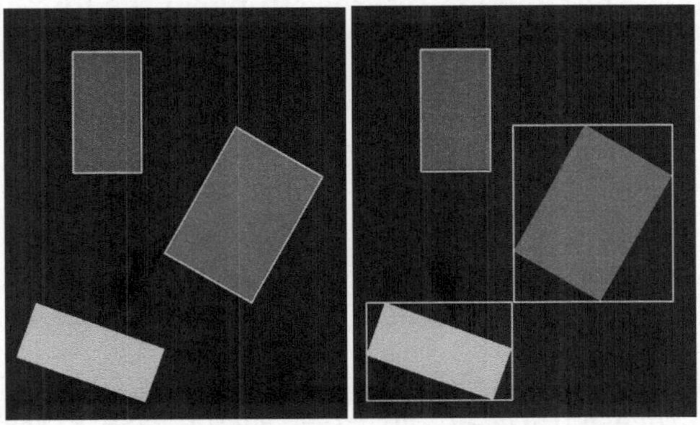

Figure 7.18: *Input image (left) and output image with bounding boxes (right)*

In the preceding code, we have thresholded the image, extracted the contours and looped through each extracted contour to apply the **`cv2.boundingRect()`** function and visualized it on the objects in the image.

The code has been able to successfully create bounding boxes around rectangles in the image. However, upon closer observation, it becomes evident that although these bounding boxes adequately cover the objects, they may not necessarily represent the minimum bounding boxes when considering the object's shape and rotation.

To create bounding boxes that perfectly encapsulate the objects and create a minimum bounding box we use the **`cv2.minAreaRect()`** function in OpenCV.

cv2.minAreaRect()

```
((x,y), (width,height), angle) = cv2.minAreaRect(points)
```

Parameters:

- **`points`**: Input contour

Output:

- **`x`**: x-coordinate of the top-left corner of the bounding rectangle.
- **`y`**: y-coordinate of the top-left corner of the bounding rectangle.
- **`width`**: Width of the bounding rectangle.

- **height**: Height of the bounding rectangle.
- **angle**: Angle of the bounding box.

The **cv2.minAreaRect()** function calculates the minimum area bounding box for a given contour. The function returns a tuple in the format of (center, size, angle).

Let's try to apply this function on the same Figure 7.17:

```
import cv2
import numpy as np

image = cv2.imread('tects.jpg')
gray = cv2.cvtColor(image, cv2.COLOR_BGR2GRAY)

# Apply thresholding to create a binary image
_, thresh = cv2.threshold(gray, 40, 255, cv2.THRESH_BINARY)

# Find contours
contours, _ = cv2.findContours(thresh, cv2.RETR_EXTERNAL, cv2.CHAIN_
APPROX_SIMPLE)

# Create a copy of the original image
bounding_rect_image = image.copy()

# Loop through the contours
for contour in contours:
    # Get the bounding rectangle for the contour
    rect = cv2.minAreaRect(contour)

    # Draw a rectangle around the object
    box = cv2.boxPoints(rect)
    box = np.int0(box)

    # Draw the minimum bounding rectangle on the image
    cv2.drawContours(image, [box], 0, (0, 255, 0), 2)


cv2.imshow('Original Image', gray)
cv2.imshow('Bounding Rectangles', image)
cv2.waitKey(0)
cv2.destroyAllWindows()
```

This code produces the following output:

***Figure 7.19**: Input image (left) and output image with minimum enclosing rectangles (right)*

As we can observe from the results, the function has been able to successfully create minimum enclosing rectangles on our objects.

We have used a **`cv2.boxPoints()`** function in the code above. It is a simple function that takes input box parameters in the format of ((x,y), (width,height), angle) and returns the coordinates of the four corners of the corresponding box rectangle.

cv2.boxPoints()

`cv2.boxPoints(box)`

Parameters:

- **`box`**: Input box in format - ((x,y), (width,height), angle)

Output:

`points`: Four points representing the corners of the rectangle.

We then used these points in the **`drawContours()`** function to visualize them on our input image.

Aspect Ratio

The aspect ratio is a property of contours that describes the proportional relationship between the width and height of a bounding rectangle that encloses the contour.

The aspect ratio is calculated as the ratio of the width to the height of the bounding rectangle:

Aspect Ratio = Width / Height

A contour with an aspect ratio close to 1 indicates a shape that is nearly square or circular, while a contour with an aspect ratio significantly different from 1 suggests a more elongated or stretched shape.

The aspect ratio property can be useful for various operations such as shape analysis or object classification. We can use aspect ratio to differentiate between different classes of objects based on their proportional attributes. In a very simple example, rectangles can be separated from squares in an image using aspect ratios since squares will have aspect ratio values around one.

To calculate the aspect ratio of a contour in OpenCV, we need to first obtain the bounding rectangle of the contour using the **`cv2.boundingRect()`** function discussed earlier. Then, we can calculate the aspect ratio by dividing the width of the bounding rectangle by its height.

Extent

Extent represents how much space or area a shape covers within a given boundary. It tells us how well the shape fills up the available space inside a rectangle that encloses it.

Extent is calculated as the ratio between the area of the contour and the area of the bounding rectangle that encloses it:

Extent = (Contour Area) / (Bounding Rectangle Area)

Extent can be used in object recognition tasks particularly where we need to distinguish between objects that may have similar shapes but differ in terms of their area distribution.

Let's try aspect ration and extend using some code. In this code, we have an image consisting of circles and rectangles. We will use aspect ratio and extent properties individually to classify these objects:

Figure 7.20: *Image to be used in the following code*

```
import cv2
import numpy as np

image = cv2.imread('image.jpg')
image_copy = image.copy()
gray = cv2.cvtColor(image, cv2.COLOR_BGR2GRAY)

_, binary = cv2.threshold(gray, 20, 255, cv2.THRESH_BINARY)

# Find contours in the binary image
contours, _ = cv2.findContours(binary, cv2.RETR_EXTERNAL, cv2.CHAIN_
APPROX_SIMPLE)

for contour in contours:
    # Calculate aspect ratio using minimum area rectangle
    rect = cv2.minAreaRect(contour)
    width, height = rect[1]
    aspect_ratio = int(width) / int(height)

    # Calculate extent
    area = cv2.contourArea(contour)
    bounding_area = width * height
    extent = area / bounding_area

    # Classify object based on aspect ratio
    if aspect_ratio >= 1.05 or aspect_ratio <=0.95:
        # Rectangle
        cv2.drawContours(image, [contour], 0, (255, 0, 255), 2)
        cv2.putText(image, 'Rectangle', (int(rect[0][0]), int(rect[0]
```

```
[1])), cv2.FONT_HERSHEY_SIMPLEX, 0.4, (255, 255, 255), 1)

    else:
        # Circle
        cv2.drawContours(image, [contour], 0, (0, 255, 255), 2)
        cv2.putText(image, ‘Circle’, (int(rect[0][0]), int(rect[0][1])),
cv2.FONT_HERSHEY_SIMPLEX, 0.4, (255, 255, 255),1)


    # Classify object based on extent
    if extent <= 1.05 and extent >= 0.95:
        # Rectangle
        print(1)
        cv2.drawContours(image_copy, [contour], 0, (255, 0, 255), 2)
        cv2.putText(image_copy, ‘Rectangle’, (int(rect[0][0]), in-
t(rect[0][1])), cv2.FONT_HERSHEY_SIMPLEX, 0.4, (255, 255, 255), 1)

    else:
        # Circle
        print(2)
        cv2.drawContours(image_copy, [contour], 0, (0, 255, 255), 2)
        cv2.putText(image_copy, ‘Circle’, (int(rect[0][0]), int(rect[0]
[1])), cv2.FONT_HERSHEY_SIMPLEX, 0.4, (255, 255, 255),1)

cv2.imshow(‘Aspect Ratio Classification’, image)
cv2.imshow(‘Extent Classification’, image_copy)
cv2.waitKey(0)
cv2.destroyAllWindows()
```

The preceding code produces the following outputs:

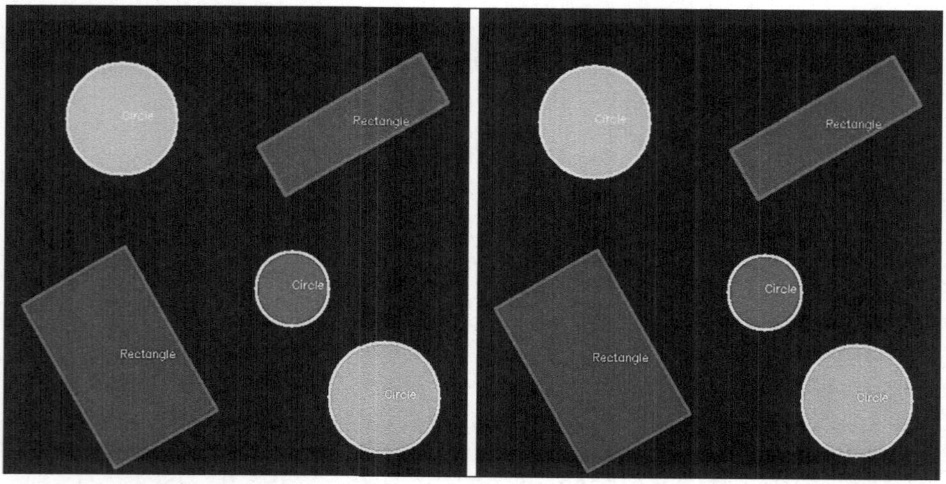

Figure 7.21: *Outputs using aspect ratio (left) and extend (right) based classification. Both the properties give the correct result producing the same images as outputs.*

In the preceding code, we use aspect ratio and extent individually to classify our objects. We start by the initial process of loading an image, grayscale, thresholding and finding contours in our image. We then loop through the contours and calculate the aspect ratios and extent values for each.

Aspect ratio is calculated by creating a minimum area enclosing bounding box using the cv2.minAreaRect and dividing its width by height. We can determine the aspect ratio of a circle as approximately 1, while for a rectangle, it will either be greater or less than 1. To accommodate small mathematical errors, we use a tolerance range of 0.95 to 1.05 in our IF conditions. Based on the aspect ratios we classify the objects accordingly and visualize contours along with the label in our image.

Extent is calculated by dividing the contour area by the bounding box area. For a rectangle, we can observe that the aspect ratio will be approximately 1, while for circles, the aspect ratio will be lower than 1 due to the remaining area in the bounding box. With this understanding, we set the conditions at 0.95 and 1.05 to account for small variations and use IF conditions to visualize the contours and labels.

We can observe that both the outputs are exactly the same. Classification using aspect ratio and extent has worked as intended, producing accurate results.

Convex Hull

Convex Hull refers to the smallest convex polygon or shape that completely encloses a given set of points. In simple words, the convex hull is a boundary that wraps around all the points, forming the smallest possible shape with straight edges ensuring that all the points are included.

We will use **`cv2.convexHull`** to compute the convex hull of a set of points.

cv2.convexHull()

```
hull = cv2.convexHull(points, hull=None, clockwise=False,
returnPoints=True)
```

Parameters:

- **`points`**: Input contour points.
- **`hull`**: Output convex hull represented as a NumPy array. The default value is None indicating a new array allocation.
- **`clockwise`**: Orientation flag. If **`True`**, the output convex hull is oriented

clockwise. The default value is **False** indicating it is oriented counter clockwise.

- **returnPoints**: If **True**, the function returns the coordinates of the points forming the convex hull. If **False**, it returns indices of the points. By default, it is **True**.

```
import cv2
import numpy as np
import matplotlib.pyplot as plt

image = cv2.imread('box.jpg')
image_copy = image.copy()
gray = cv2.cvtColor(image, cv2.COLOR_BGR2GRAY)

_, threshold = cv2.threshold(gray, 180, 255, cv2.THRESH_BINARY_INV)

# Find contours in the binary image
contours, _ = cv2.findContours(threshold, cv2.RETR_EXTERNAL, cv2.CHAIN_
APPROX_SIMPLE)

for contour in contours:
    # Apply convex hull on the contour
    hull = cv2.convexHull(contour)

    # Reshape the hull points for polylines
    hull_points = hull.reshape((-1, 1, 2))

    # Draw the convex hull lines on the image
    cv2.polylines(image, [hull_points], True, (0, 255, 0), 2)
    cv2.drawContours(image2, [contour], 0, (255, 0, 255), 2)

cv2.imwrite("Convex.jpg ", image)
cv2.imwrite("AllContours.jpg ", image_copy)

plt.title('Convex Hull')
plt.show()
```

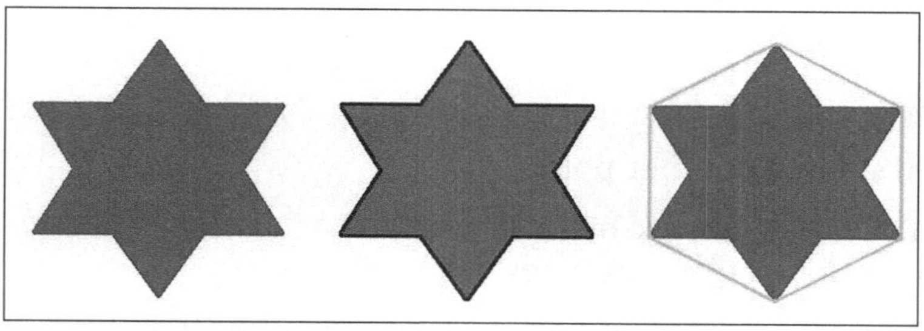

Figure 7.22: *Input image (left), contours (center) and the convex hull visualization (right)*

The preceding code uses a convex hull on our input image. We use the aforementioned **`cv2.convexHull()`** function on our extracted contours. We also duplicate the image and plot normal contours for comparison. As seen from the outputs above, we can observe that the **`drawContours`** function has created the exact boundary around all the irregularities in the shape. However, the convex hull function has created more of a rubber band like boundary around our object.

We have used the **`cv2.polyLines`** function in the preceding code. **`cv2.polylines()`** is a function used to draw one or more polylines on an image. A polyline is a collection of connected line segments. We can define the function as follows:

cv2.polyLines()

```
cv2.polylines(img, pts, isClosed=False, color=(0,0,255), thickness=1,
lineType=cv2.LINE_8, shift=0)
```

Parameters:

- **`img`**: Input image on which to draw the polylines.
- **`pts`**: Array of points specifying the polylines.
- **`isClosed`**: Boolean flag indicating whether the polylines should be closed. The default value is **`False`** indicating that the polyline will not be closed, meaning the last point will not be connected to the first point.
- **`color`**: Color of the polylines. The default values is (0, 0, 255) representing red color.
- **`thickness`**: Thickness of the polyline line. The default value is 1
- **`lineType`**: Type of the line to be drawn. The default value is **`cv2.LINE_8`**.
- **`shift`**: Number of fractional bits in the point coordinates. The default value is 0.

Solidity

Solidity is a measure of how closely a shape matches its convex hull, which is the smallest possible convex shape that completely encloses the object. In layman terms, Solidity refers to how solid or filled a shape appears.

If the solidity value is closer to 1, it means that the shape is mostly filled and doesn't have many holes or concave parts. On the other hand, if the solidity value is closer to 0, it means that the shape has many holes or concave regions, making it less solid.

Solidity is calculated by dividing the contour area by the area of its convex hull representing the proportion of the area covered by the convex hull:

Solidity = (Contour Area) / (Convex Hull Area)

Solidity can be useful in various applications. For example, in object recognition, it can help distinguish between solid objects and objects with holes or concavities or can also be used to filter out irregular shapes or noise in image segmentation tasks.

Contour Approximation

Contour Approximation is a technique used to simplify representation of contours of objects in an image. Contour approximation aims to simplify the contours by reducing the number of points needed to describe them. It does that by smoothing out the contours and removing unnecessary details thus making it simpler to describe them. The process aims to keep the original shape and important features of the contours while removing any small irregularities from the contours.

By reducing the number of points required for representing contours, contour approximation can significantly reduce the processing time and resources required for the process. Removal of small irregularities from the contours results in a smoother representation of an object's boundary.

Contour approximation is a multistep process:

Step 1: Extract Contours: First we need to extract the contours of objects in an image. We need to apply pre-processing steps such as thresholding first followed by a contour detection algorithm to obtain our contours.

Step 2: Set Approximation Accuracy: The contour approximation algorithm requires a parameter called epsilon, which determines the approximation accuracy. This parameter controls the accuracy of contour approximation. A smaller value of epsilon will result in a more accurate approximation but with more points, while a larger epsilon will result in a less accurate approximation but with fewer points.

Step 3: Contour Approximation Algorithm: Algorithms such as the Douglas-Peucker Algorithm are used for contour approximation. It works by iteratively simplifying the contour using a distance threshold. The algorithm starts by identifying the point with the maximum distance from the line segment connecting the first and last points of the contour. If the distance is above the threshold, that point is considered significant and kept as part of the simplified contour. The algorithm then recursively applies this process to the two resulting segments until the entire contour is approximated.

Once the contour approximation is done, additional post-processing steps can be performed depending on the specific application. This may include filtering out small contours or performing additional analysis on the detected contours.

OpenCV provides a direct function **cv2.approxPolyDP()** to perform contour approximation.

cv2.approxPolyDP()

```
cv2.approxPolyDP(curve, epsilon=0.01, closed=True)
```

Parameters:

- **curve**: Input contour.
- **epsilon**: Maximum distance between the original curve and its approximation. Default value for this parameter is 0.01.
- **closed**: A boolean value indicating whether the curve is closed or not. Default value for this parameter is **True** indicating a closed curve.

```
import cv2
import numpy as np


image = cv2.imread('box.jpg')
image2 = image.copy()
gray = cv2.cvtColor(image, cv2.COLOR_BGR2GRAY)

_, threshold = cv2.threshold(gray, 127, 255, cv2.THRESH_BINARY)

# Find contours
contours, _ = cv2.findContours(threshold, cv2.RETR_LIST, cv2.CHAIN_
APPROX_SIMPLE)


for contour in contours:
    # Perform contour approximation
    epsilon = 0.05 * cv2.arcLength(contour, True)
    approx = cv2.approxPolyDP(contour, epsilon, True)

    # Draw the contour and its approximation
    cv2.drawContours(image, [approx], 0, (0, 0, 0), 1)
    cv2.drawContours(image2, [contour], 0, (0, 0, 255), 1)
```

```
cv2.imshow('Contour Approximation', image)
cv2.imshow('Contour Approximation 2', image2)
cv2.waitKey(0)
cv2.destroyAllWindows()
```

The preceding output produces the following result:

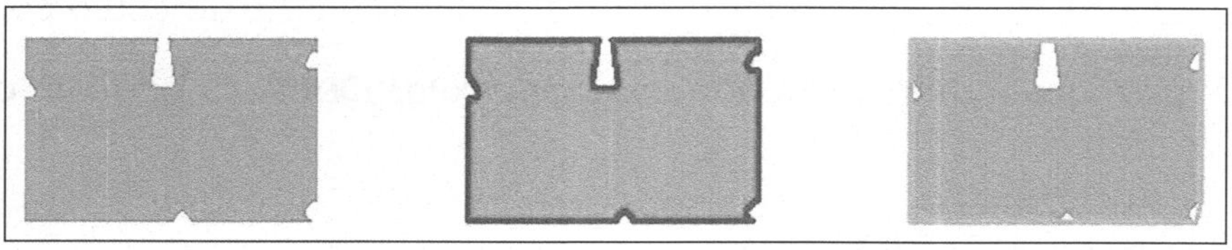

Figure 7.23: *Input image (left) with contours (center) and contour approximation results (right)*

To summarize, contour approximation is an effective technique to reduce the number of points required to describe a contour. The overall shape and structure of the objects in an image are maintained while removing the unnecessary irregularities from the object boundaries.

Contour Filtering and Selection

Contour filtering and selection is a topic that explores techniques to refine and select contours based on specific criteria. It involves applying filters to eliminate unwanted contours and focusing on the most relevant or significant contours for further analysis or processing.

By applying filters based on properties like area, perimeter, aspect ratio, or shape characteristics, we can effectively narrow down the set of contours to those that meet our desired criteria. This allows us to extract and work with the contours that are most relevant to our application, enabling more accurate and targeted analysis of objects or regions of interest within an image.

Some of the criteria that can be used for contour filtering and selection are as follows:

- **Area-based filtering**: This technique involves filtering contours based on their area. Contours with areas below or above certain thresholds can be discarded, helping to remove noise or small irrelevant regions.
- **Perimeter-based filtering**: This technique filters contours based on their perimeter. Contours with perimeters outside a specified range can be removed, effectively eliminating contours that are too small or too large.

- **Aspect Ratio filtering**: Contours can be filtered based on their aspect ratio and is useful for selecting contours that exhibit specific elongation or compactness characteristics.
- **Shape property filtering**: Technique using various other properties discussed earlier such as convex hull, extent and solidity as well to filter contours. Filtering can be done on contours based on these properties allowing for selecting contours that meet specific shape criteria.

Let's try some contour-based filtering on the following image using methods discussed above:

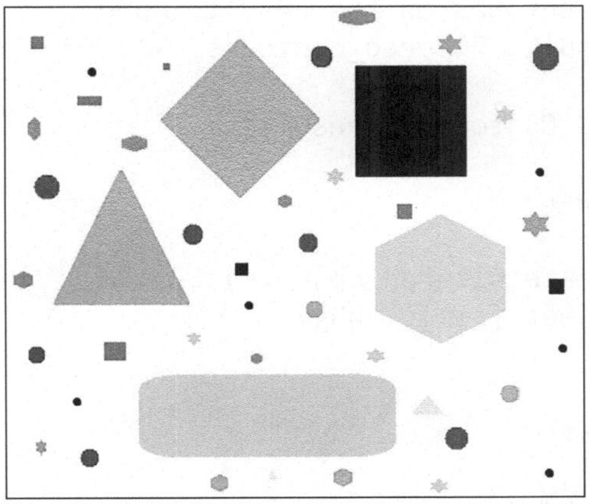

***Figure 7.24**: Input image with noise to be used for Contour Filtering and Selection*

We will use the preceding image for contour filtering and selection. We will use the image to extract out the main objects from the image removing the small objects or the noise:

```
import cv2
import numpy as np

image = cv2.imread('filter.jpg')
gray = cv2.cvtColor(image, cv2.COLOR_BGR2GRAY)

ret, thresh = cv2.threshold(gray, 240, 255, cv2.THRESH_BINARY_INV)

# Find contours
contours, _ = cv2.findContours(thresh, cv2.RETR_TREE, cv2.CHAIN_APPROX_
SIMPLE)

# Filter contours based on area
filtered_contours = []
filtered_objects = []
for contour in contours:
```

```
    area = cv2.contourArea(contour)
    if area > 1000:  # Set minimum area threshold as needed
        filtered_contours.append(contour)
        x, y, w, h = cv2.boundingRect(contour)
        filtered_objects.append(image[y:y+h, x:x+w])

print(len(filtered_contours))

# Create a blank image of the same size as the original image
result = np.zeros_like(image)

# Draw the filtered contours on the result image
cv2.drawContours(result, filtered_contours, -1, (0, 255, 0), 2)

cv2.imshow('Filtered Contours', result)
cv2.waitKey(0)
cv2.destroyAllWindows()

for i, obj in enumerate(filtered_objects):
    cv2.imshow(f'Object {i+1}', obj)

cv2.waitKey(0)
cv2.destroyAllWindows()
```

The output for this code is:

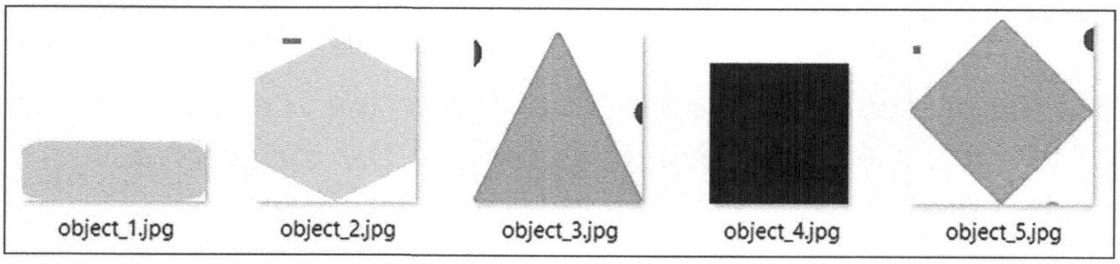

Figure 7.25: *Outputs for Contour Selection and Filtering. All the filtered objects have been saved as separate images.*

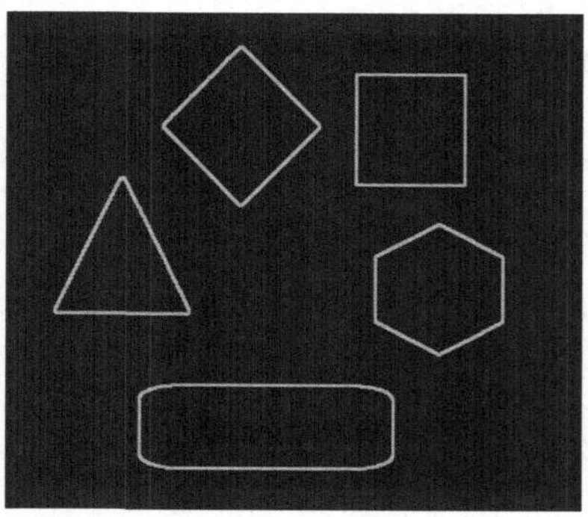

Figure 7.26: *Output for Contour Selection and Filtering representing boundaries or contours of the selected objects.*

Using contour detection we first extract all the contours from the image. We then apply contour filtering based on the area of the detected contours.

We only select contours whose area is greater than 1000. If an object meets the criteria, we create a bounding box around it and then write these objects as separate image files. We also create a separate image and draw contours of these selected areas for visualization and a better understanding of our output.

We have used area-based contour filtering in this example. Feel free to go ahead and try contour filtering using other parameters.

Conclusion

This chapter covered a range of topics related to edge analysis and contour detection. We began by exploring the importance of edges in image processing and learned about image gradients and their computation using filters like Sobel, Scharr, and Laplacian. We then delved into contour detection, where we extracted and visualized object boundaries using various techniques. We discussed contour hierarchy, contour moments, and properties of contours, along with contour approximation and filtering methods. By the end of the chapter, we gained a comprehensive understanding of edge detection and contour analysis, equipping us with valuable skills for image processing and computer vision applications.

In the next chapter, we will dive into the application of machine learning algorithms for image classification and clustering tasks using OpenCV. The chapter will introduce popular machine learning algorithms, such as decision trees, K-means clustering and support vector machines. We will explore the principles behind these algorithms, their functioning principles, and discuss their benefits and drawbacks. Moreover, the chapter will include code examples to demonstrate the implementation of these algorithms. By the end of the chapter, readers will gain a comprehensive understanding of these machine learning techniques and how they can be effectively utilized for various applications.

Points to Remember

1. An edge refers to a significant and sudden change in intensity of color in an image. Contours are the continuous curves or boundaries representing the shape of objects inside an image.
2. Image gradient is the change in directional intensity in an image. Gradient magnitude represents the strength of the intensity change while the

Gradient Orientation denotes the direction of change in the intensity values in an image.

3. Gradient filters such as Sobel, Scharr, and Laplacian, play a crucial role in image processing by capturing and highlighting changes in pixel intensity, enabling tasks such as edge detection and feature extraction.
4. The Canny edge detector is an image processing algorithm that aims to accurately detect and locate edges in images by identifying areas of rapid intensity changes. It utilizes a multi-stage process involving noise reduction, gradient calculation, non-maximum suppression, and hysteresis thresholding to achieve robust and precise edge detection.
5. Contour hierarchy represents the hierarchical structure and relationships between detected contours, indicating connectivity and parent-child associations.
6. Contour moments are statistical measures that describe various characteristics of a contour or shape. These moments provide valuable information about the spatial distribution, size, shape, and orientation of objects in an image.
7. Contour properties provide quantitative information about the shape, size, and spatial characteristics of objects within an image, allowing for tasks such as object classification, shape analysis, and measurement in computer vision and image processing applications.
8. Contour approximation is a technique used to simplify complex contours by representing them with a reduced number of line segments or curves, enabling efficient shape representation and analysis in image processing.

Test your understanding

1. Which of the following best describes an edge in image processing?
   A. A region with uniform pixel values
   B. A transition or boundary between different image regions
   C. A specific pixel intensity value
   D. A continuous curve representing the shape of objects

2. The Sobel filter operates on an image by performing which operation(s)?
   A. Convolution with a kernel
   B. Median filtering
   C. Thresholding
   D. Histogram equalization
3. Extent is calculated as the ratio of:
   A. (Contour Area) / (Bounding Rectangle Area)
   B. Width / Height
   C. (Contour Area) / (Convex Hull Area)
   D. (Convex Hull Area) / (Bounding Rectangle Area)
4. What is the solidity property in computer vision?
   A. The ratio of the contour perimeter to its area
   B. The ratio of the contour area to the convex hull area
   C. The measure of compactness of a shape
   D. The measure of irregularity of a contour
5. Why is contour filtering used in image processing?
   A. To remove noise and smooth contours
   B. To enhance the contrast of contour edges
   C. To highlight and extract specific contours based on certain criteria
   D. To resize and reshape the contours

Chapter 8
Machine Learning with Images

Machine Learning has enabled computers to learn from data and make intelligent decisions without explicit programming. It has become a powerful tool for solving complex problems and we will explore some fundamental algorithms commonly used in image classification and clustering tasks. We will begin our exploration by introducing the basics of Machine Learning with its principles and techniques. We will then delve into algorithms used in image analysis.

We'll begin with KMeans Clustering, grouping similar data points to reveal patterns. Then, we'll cover k-Nearest Neighbors Classification, predicting classes based on neighboring samples. Logistic Regression will be discussed for binary classification, while Decision Trees and Random Forests will be examined for intuitive rule learning and improved accuracy, respectively. Finally, we'll introduce Support Vector Machines, which separate data using hyperplanes. With practical implementations in OpenCV, you'll gain valuable skills for computer vision projects.

Structure

In this chapter, we will discuss the following topics:

- Introduction to Machine Learning
- KMeans Clustering
- k-Nearest Neighbors Classification
- Logistic Regression
- Decision Trees
- Random Forests
- Support Vector Machines

Introduction to Machine Learning

Machine learning involves the use of statistical techniques and computational algorithms to enable computers to learn from and make sense of data. We will be applying these algorithms to images for a multitude of image processing applications.

By using machine learning, we aim to enhance image classification, image segmentation, and various other image-related tasks. This enables us to automate processes, extract valuable information, and make intelligent decisions based on visual data.

Machine learning can be categorized into:

- **Supervised Learning**: In supervised learning, the machine learning algorithm learns from labeled training data, where the input data is associated with corresponding labels or target values. The algorithm's objective is to learn a mapping function that can accurately predict labels for unseen data. Image classification is an example of supervised learning.
- **Unsupervised Learning**: Unsupervised learning involves learning from unlabeled data, where the algorithm aims to discover patterns, structures, or relationships within the data without any predefined labels. It focuses on finding hidden patterns or clustering similar data points based on their inherent characteristics. Clustering is a common example of unsupervised learning.
- **Semi-Supervised Learning**: Semi-supervised learning is a combination of both supervised and unsupervised learning. It utilizes a small amount of labeled data along with a larger amount of unlabeled data for training. For example, in scenarios where labeling a large dataset is not possible, semi-supervised learning can be employed to leverage both labeled and unlabeled images. By utilizing the labeled data for initial training and the unlabeled data for further fine-tuning, the model can improve its accuracy.

Terminologies associated with Machine Learning:

- **Features** refer to the individual measurable characteristics or properties of the data that are used as inputs for machine learning models. While working with images, these can be the pixel values or some information extracted from the images such as image moments or histograms.
- **Labels** represent the desired outputs that the machine learning model aims to learn or predict. In supervised learning, the labels are the known

and provided outputs for the training data. In image classification tasks, labels will refer to the class that the object belongs to.

- **Training, validation, and testing sets**: When developing machine learning models, the available data is typically split into three subsets: the training set, the validation set, and the testing set.
    - The training set is the data subset used to train the model. This generally contains a major portion of the dataset.
    - The validation set is used to fine-tune hyperparameters and assess model performance during model training and development.
    - The testing set contains images that are never seen by the model before and is used to evaluate the final model's performance on unseen data.
- Bias refers to the error introduced by using a simplistic model that consistently misses the true relationship between features and the target output. Models with high bias are too simple and underfit the data, performing poorly both on training and unseen data.
- Variance represents a model's sensitivity to noise or fluctuations in the training data. Models with high variance fit the training data closely, potentially capturing noise, but they struggle to generalize to new data. They perform excellently on training data but poorly on unseen data.

Overfitting and Underfitting

Overfitting occurs when a machine learning model becomes overly specialized to the training data. It learns the training set too closely and memorizes the noise or irrelevant details along with the underlying patterns. This limits its ability to perform well on new data, resulting in poor generalization.

It occurs when a model learns the training data too well, capturing not just the underlying patterns but also the noise or random fluctuations in the data. As a result, the model becomes overly complex and performs poorly on unseen or new data because it has essentially memorized the training data instead of generalizing from it.

Causes: Overfitting often happens when a model is too complex for the problem at hand. Complex models, such as those with a large number of parameters, can fit the training data very closely but struggle to generalize. It might also occur because the model may learn noise because there isn't enough real data to learn from. Including too many features or irrelevant features in the model can also lead to overfitting.

Overfitting happens when variance is too high, and bias is too low leading to a model that fits the training data too closely and fails to generalize.

Some of the methods to avoid overfitting are:

- **Increasing the data**: One of the most effective ways to combat overfitting is to collect more data. A larger dataset can help the model learn true patterns and reduce the influence of noise.
- **Simplifying the Model**: Choose a simpler model architecture with fewer parameters will help avoid overfitting.
- **Feature selection**: Carefully select relevant features and remove irrelevant ones through feature engineering to improve model generalization.
- **Regularization**: Apply techniques like L1 and L2 regularization or weight decay to penalize large parameter values reducing the risk of overfitting.
- **Ensemble methods**: Combine predictions from multiple models to improve generalization by reducing overfitting.

Underfitting occurs when a model fails to capture the essential patterns in the data, leading to poor performance even on the training set.

Underfitting occurs where a model is too simple to capture the underlying patterns in the data. It occurs when the model is overly generalized and performs poorly both on the training data and new and unseen data. Essentially, it fails to learn the complexities and nuances of the data.

Causes: Underfitting takes place when the chosen model is too simple or lacks the capacity to represent the relationships in the data. Insufficient Data is another reason for underfitting. When we have a small dataset it becomes challenging for the model to learn complex patterns. If there are Inadequate Features that don't capture the essential characteristics of the data, the model may struggle to fit the data well.

Underfitting occurs when bias is too high, and variance is too low resulting in a simplistic model that doesn't fit the data well.

Some of the methods to avoid underfitting are:

- **More complex model**: Select a more complex model architecture with more parameters will help solve underfitting.
- **Increase data volume**: Collect more data to give the model a better chance to learn from diverse examples and capture complex relationships.
- **Feature Engineering**: Enhance your feature set by including relevant information or creating new features that better represent the underlying patterns in the data.

- **Reduce regularization**: If you're using regularization techniques like L1 or L2 regularization, reduce the strength of regularization to allow the model more flexibility.
- **Ensemble methods**: Combine predictions from multiple models might help solve underfitting as well.

The right balance between overfitting and underfitting is important to develop a model that can accurately generalize to unseen data.

Evaluation Metrics

Evaluation metrics are used to assess the performance of train models in machine learning:

- **Confusion Matrix**: A confusion matrix summarizes the performance of a classification model. A confusion matrix consists of:
    - **True Positives (TP)**: Instances that are correctly predicted as positive by the model.
    - **True Negatives (TN)**: Instances that are correctly predicted as negative by the model.
    - **False Positives (FP)**: Instances that are incorrectly predicted as positive by the model when the actual class is negative (Type I error).
    - **False Negatives (FN)**: Instances that are incorrectly predicted as negative by the model when the actual class is positive (Type II error).

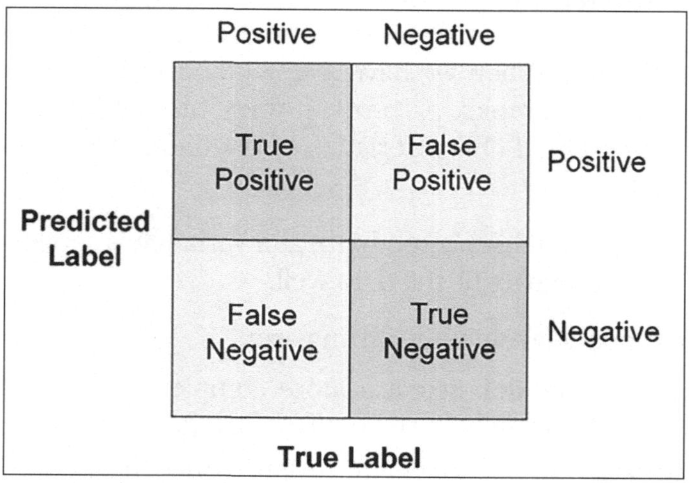

***Figure 8.1**: Confusion Matrix*

Based on the values in the confusion matrix, several evaluation metrics can be derived, including accuracy, precision, recall, and F1-score, which provide a more comprehensive assessment of the model's performance across different classes.

- **Accuracy**: Accuracy measures the overall correctness of predictions made by a classification model. It is the ratio of correctly predicted samples to the total number of samples. Accuracy is calculated as:

  Accuracy = (TP + TN) / (TP + TN + FP + FN)

- **Precision**: Precision focuses on the accuracy of positive predictions made by a classification model. Precision is calculated as:

  Precision = TP / (TP + FP)

- **Recall** or sensitivity is the true positive rate which measures the proportion of true positive predictions out of the total actual positive instances. Mathematically, recall is calculated as:

  Recall = TP / (TP + FN)

- **F1-Score**: The F1-score is the harmonic mean of precision and recall. It provides a balanced measure of a model's performance by considering both precision and recall. F1-Score can be calculated as:

  F1-score = 2 * (Precision * Recall) / (Precision + Recall)

Hyperparameters and Tuning

Hyperparameters are settings that determine how a machine learning model learns and makes predictions. These parameters are not learned from the data but are predefined by the user and significantly influence the model's performance and behavior. Properly tuning hyperparameters is essential to optimize a model's performance for a specific task.

Hyperparameter tuning is a crucial aspect of machine learning model development. Hyperparameters are settings that we must specify before training a model, and they significantly impact a model's performance. Tuning involves finding the best combination of hyperparameters to optimize a model's performance.

The process typically starts with selecting a range of hyperparameter values, and then various techniques such as grid search, random search, or Bayesian optimization are employed to systematically explore these values. Cross-validation is often used to evaluate model performance for different hyperparameter configurations, ensuring that the model generalizes well to unseen data.

Let us start implementing some machine learning algorithms with our images. We will go through machine learning concepts as we go along the chapter.

KMeans Clustering

KMeans is an iterative unsupervised machine learning algorithm used for clustering data points into k different groups or clusters. It divides the data points into clusters such that all the points in the same cluster have similar properties.

KMeans is a centroid-based algorithm. Each cluster is associated with a centroid which is the center point of the cluster. The centroid of a cluster is calculated by taking the mean values of all the data points in a cluster. The k value specifies the number of clusters needed from the operation and has to be selected by the user.

K-means clustering starts by randomly initializing K cluster centroids. After assigning each data point to the nearest centroid, the algorithm recalculates the centroids by taking the average position of all the data points assigned to each cluster. It continues this process until the centroids stabilize, optimizing the clustering by minimizing the total squared distance within each cluster:

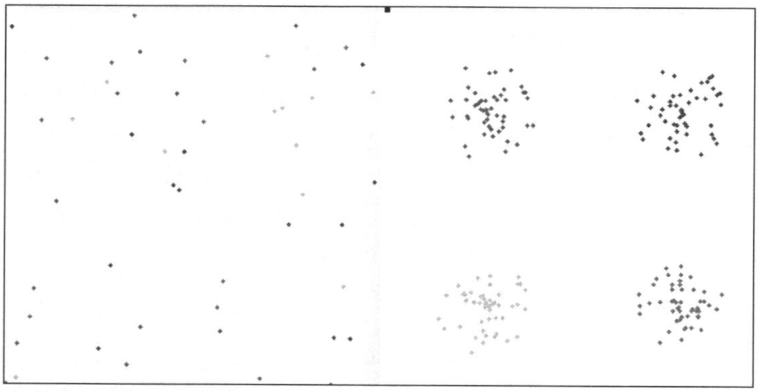

***Figure 8.2**: Left: Random dots in 4 colors, Right: Dots organized after clustering*

The step-by-step explanation of the KMeans algorithm is as follows:

1. **Initialization**: The algorithm requires the user to specify the number of clusters (k) needed in the output. The algorithm will automatically select *k* initial points from the data as the starting centroids, which represent the centers of each cluster.
2. **Cluster assignment**: Each data point in the dataset is assigned to the nearest centroid. This is done by using a distance function to calculate

the distance from each point to each of the centroids and the data point is then assigned to the nearest centroid. Distance functions such as the Euclidean distance are used to calculate the distances. The data points have been grouped into *k* clusters now.

3. **Update centroids**: Now that we have k clusters, we recalculate the centroids of each cluster by taking the mean value of all the data points in the cluster.

4. **Convergence**: After updating centroids, it is possible that some of the data points in a cluster might be closer to some centroids of another cluster. Steps 2 and 3 are repeated to assign these data points to updated clusters. The process continues till there are no more changes in the centroids indicating that the algorithm has converged. The process can also be stopped if a certain criterion has been met such as the maximum number of iterations allowed.

Output: Once the algorithm has converged, the final centroids represent the center of k clusters. New data points can be assigned to a cluster by finding the nearest cluster centroid from the data point.

As we know by now, an image is essentially a two-dimensional grid of pixels. We can use KMeans in image processing to partition the pixels in an image into various colors based on their intensity values. This clustering of pixels will allow us to group pixels together with similar intensities.

Some of the common applications that we can use clustering on images are:

- **Image segmentation**: which as you might recall was dividing images into similar regions and color quantization. By clustering similar pixels together, it can aid in tasks such as object recognition, image compression.
- **Image retrieval**: Color quantization aims to reduce the number of colors needed to represent an image which is something we can use image clustering for by replacing some colors with the color of the centroid of its cluster.
- **Content-Based Image Retrieval**: Large image databases can be organized by grouping images with similar properties together. This enables efficient retrieval and browsing of images effectively making it easier to search for specific images.
- **Image Annotation**: Clustering can be employed to automatically categorize and annotate images based on their properties. By grouping

visually similar images, it can help in automatically generating tags or annotation for images.

OpenCV provides us with a predefined function **cv2.kmeans()** to implement KMeans algorithm without having to manually code the whole algorithm.

cv2.kmeans()

Syntax:

```
retval, labels, centers = cv2.kmeans(data, K, bestLabels, criteria,
attempts, flags, centers)
```

Parameters:

- `data`: Input array consisting of float type data points for clustering
- **K**: Number of clusters needed from the clustering operation
- **bestLabels**: Optional Output integer array that stores the cluster indices for every sample.
- **criteria**: Algorithm termination criteria for the k-means algorithm. This argument is a tuple consisting of three values (type, max_iter, epsilon).
  - **type**: Specifies the type of termination criteria. It has three possible values:
    - **cv2.TERM_CRITERIA_EPS**: The algorithm stops iterating when the desired accuracy (epsilon) is reached.
    - **cv2.TERM_CRITERIA_MAX_ITER**: The algorithm stops iterating when the specified maximum number of iterations (**max_iter**) is reached.
    - **cv2.TERM_CRITERIA_EPS + cv2.TERM_CRITERIA_MAX_ITER**: The algorithm stops iterating when either of accuracy or maximum number of iterations is reached.
  - **max_iter**: The maximum number of iterations allowed for the *k*-means algorithm. The algorithm will terminate when the number of iterations reaches this value regardless if it has converged or not.
  - **epsilon**: Desired accuracy for algorithm convergence.
- **attempts**: Number of times the algorithm executes using different initial labelings
- **flags**: Used to control the behavior of the k-means algorithm. Possible values are:
  - **cv2.KMEANS_RANDOM_CENTERS**: This flag indicates that the initial cluster centers should be generated randomly.

- `cv2.KMEANS_PP_CENTERS`: This flag enables the k-means++ algorithm for initialization of cluster centers. The k-means++ algorithm provides a more effective initialization compared to random centers, leading to potentially better convergence.

Output:

- `retval`: The compactness value, that is, sum of squared distances from each point to their corresponding centers.
- `labels`: The cluster indices assigned to each sample.
- `centers`: The cluster centers.

One of the main use cases of clustering on images is image segmentation. We went through a detailed chapter on image segmentation earlier in the course. In the clustering-based segmentation topic we went through an introduction on how clustering algorithms work on images for segmentation. Let's try some code to segment our images using KMeans clustering now.

We will use the following figure for segmentation. The image provides a distinct contrast between the cloudy sky and the trees, which aids in enhancing our comprehension of the k-means algorithm.

Figure 8.3: *Input image for segmentation*

```
import numpy as np
import cv2

image = cv2.imread('image.jpg')
```

```
# Reshape the image to a 2D array of pixels
pixels = image.reshape(-1, 3).astype(np.float32)

# Define the criteria for k-means clustering
criteria = (cv2.TERM_CRITERIA_EPS + cv2.TERM_CRITERIA_MAX_ITER, 10, 1.0)

# Set the k values
k_values = [2, 3, 7]

cv2.imshow('K-Means Segmentation', image)
cv2.waitKey(0)

# Perform k-means clustering for each k value and display the segmented
images
for k in k_values:
    # Perform k-means clustering
    _, labels, centers = cv2.kmeans(pixels, k, None, criteria, 10, cv2.
KMEANS_RANDOM_CENTERS)

    # Convert the centers to integers
    centers = np.uint8(centers)

    # Replace each pixel value with its corresponding cluster center
value
    segmented_image = centers[labels.flatten()]
    segmented_image = segmented_image.reshape(image.shape)

    cv2.imshow('K-Means Segmentation', segmented_image)
    cv2.waitKey(0)

cv2.destroyAllWindows()
```

Output:

Figure 8.4: *Image Segmentation Output. Left: Input Image, Three images showing clustering into K = 2,3 and 7 clusters respectively*

The preceding code produces three outputs using different *k* values. The first value for k is 2 specifying that the image has to be divided into two clusters. From the output, we can clearly observe that the image has been segmented into two regions with each region representing sky and tree respectively. Next, by utilizing a *k* value of 3, the image is effectively divided into three distinct regions, segregating the sky, clouds, and trees. Lastly, we apply a k value of 7 to observe a more detailed segmentation of the image into seven distinct clusters allowing us to discern finer details and variations within the image.

The code begins by loading the input image and reshaping it to a 2D array of pixels. This is done to enable a 2D representation of the data, which is necessary in the cv2.kmeans function to treat each pixel as an individual data point with multiple features, facilitating distance calculations and clustering based on these features. We then initialize a list of *k* values we want to use on our image.

The next step initializes the criteria parameter to be used in the **`cv2.kmeans()`** function. The criteria parameter is a tuple which requires three values (**`type, max_iter, epsilon`**). We use the **`cv2.TERM_CRITERIA_EPS + cv2.TERM_CRITERIA_MAX_ITER`** value for type argument indicating that the algorithm will stop terminating when either of the desired accuracy or the maximum number of iterations allowed value is reached. The **`max_iter`** value is kept at 10 indicating that the algorithm can iterate a maximum of ten times before convergence. The value of epsilon is set to 1 meaning that the algorithm will consider convergence when the centroids' positions have changed by a very small amount, specifically less than 1.

Next, we iterate through each *k* value from the list initialized earlier. For each value of k, we use the **`cv2.kmeans()`** function to implement the KMeans algorithm. In the function, we pass the **`pixels`** variable consisting of a 2D array of data points and the *k* value. We then specify **`None`** value to the **`bestLabels`** output parameter followed by the criteria variable we defined earlier. The 'attempts' variable is set to 10 specifying that the algorithm can start ten times with different data point random initializations. Lastly, we use the **`cv2.KMEANS_RANDOM_CENTERS`** flag to specify random initialization of initial centroids.

Now that we have the cluster for each data point or the pixel, we need to convert our 2D array into an image again to be able to visualize it. The **`cv2.kmeans()`** function returns three outputs: **`retval`**, **`labels`** and **`centers`**. The code then assigns the corresponding cluster center value to each pixel based on the labels obtained from *k*-means clustering, resulting in a segmented image. The **`labels.flatten()`** converts the 2D array of labels into a 1D array, which is then used to index the centers array, effectively replacing each pixel value with its corresponding cluster center value. We then reshape the segmented image to the original image shape and use **imshow** to display the final output.

k-Nearest Neighbors (k-NN)

k-Nearest Neighbors is a popular supervised learning algorithm that is used for classification and regression applications. k-NN predicts the class or value of a new data point based on the majority or average of its K nearest neighbors in the training dataset.

k-NN is a non-parametric algorithm. This means that it does not make any assumptions about the underlying data and instead makes predictions based on the similarity between the input data points and the train labeled data. k-NN is also an instance-based algorithm meaning that it does not use the dataset for training, instead, it uses the entire dataset during the prediction phase of the operation:

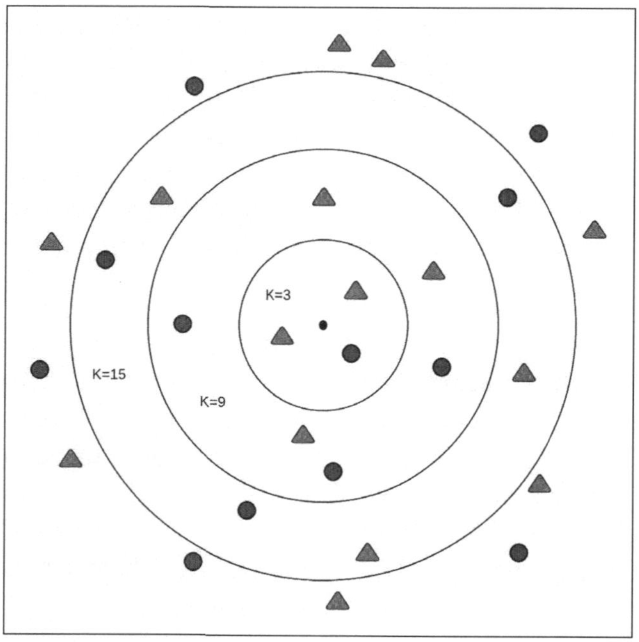

***Figure 8.5**: Data points with* K=3, 9 AND 15 *neighbors for consideration*

The KNN algorithm takes an unlabeled data point and finds the K nearest neighbors in the training dataset based on a distance metric, typically Euclidean distance. The K nearest neighbors are the data points that are most similar to the input data point. For classification tasks, the predicted class for the input data point is determined by majority voting among the K nearest neighbors.

The k-NN classification algorithm works by implementing the following steps:

1. The user chooses the number of neighbors(represented by K) to be considered for classification. Load the dataset and apply any preprocessing such as feature scaling as per the requirements.
2. Split this data into training and test sets. The test set will be used to evaluate the performance of the algorithm.
3. For each data point in the dataset, calculate its distance to all data points in the training set. Any distance metric such as Euclidean distance or the Manhattan distance can be used for calculating the distance between data points.
4. The next step is to select the K nearest neighbors to the data point. The K nearest points to the data point will be selected.
5. Among the selected K nearest neighbors the class label is assigned to the data point based on the majority voting in its selected neighbors.
6. Steps 4 and 5 are repeated for all the data points in the test set.
7. The model is then evaluated using various evaluation metrics such as accuracy or precision. Depending on the results obtained, the performance of the model can be improved by changing the K value or the distance metrics used in the operation.

Feature Scaling

Feature scaling is a preprocessing technique used in machine learning to standardize or normalize the range of features in a dataset. It aims to bring all features onto a similar scale to avoid bias towards features with larger magnitudes.

Commonly used methods for feature scaling are:

- **Normalization (Min-Max scaling)**: Normalization involves scaling each feature value to a range of 0 to 1. Min-Max scaling is a common normalization technique that is implemented by subtracting the minimum value of the feature from each data point and then dividing it by the range (maximum value minus minimum value):

$$X_{scaled} = \frac{X - X_{min}}{X_{man} - X_{min}}$$

Figure 8.6: *Normalization Formula*

where X is the original feature value, X_{min} and X_{max} are the minimum and maximum values of the feature respectively and X_{scaled} are the updated values in the range between 0 to 1.

- **Standardization (Z-score normalization)**: In this method, each feature is transformed such that it has a mean of 0 and a standard deviation of 1. It is achieved by subtracting the mean of the feature from each data point and then dividing it by the standard deviation. Standardization preserves the shape of the distribution and is suitable for features that have a normal distribution:

$$X_{scaled} = \frac{X - \mu}{\sigma}$$

***Figure 8.7**: Standardization Formula*

where X is the original feature value, μ is the mean of the feature, σ is the standard deviation of the feature and X_{scaled} is the scaled value of the feature with mean value of 0 and a standard deviation of 1.

The choice between standardization and normalization depends on the specific requirements of the dataset and the machine learning algorithm being used.

Hyperparameters

In KNN the main hyperparameter is the K value. It represents the number of nearest neighbors to consider for classification or regression. It determines the level of complexity and generalization of the model. A smaller value of K makes the model more sensitive to noise and outliers, while a larger value of K makes the model more biased and less flexible.

The distance metric is another hyperparameter that is important in KNN algorithms. The choice of distance metric, such as Euclidean distance or the Manhattan distance affects how the neighbors are identified and the similarity between data points.

MNIST dataset: The MNIST dataset is a widely known dataset often used for machine learning applications. The MNIST dataset consists of 70,000 images of handwritten grayscale images of written characters from 0 to 9 in equal amounts. Each image in the dataset is in square shape of the size 28*28. The dataset is divided into training and test sets with training sets containing 60,000 images and the test set containing 6000 images.

The goal of the MNIST dataset is to train machine learning models to accurately classify digits of the provided images and the dataset for evaluating the performance of various machine learning algorithms, particularly for image classification tasks.

The simplicity and size of the MNIST dataset make it suitable for beginners for understanding and implementing various machine learning algorithms for image classification tasks.

The MNIST dataset looks like this:

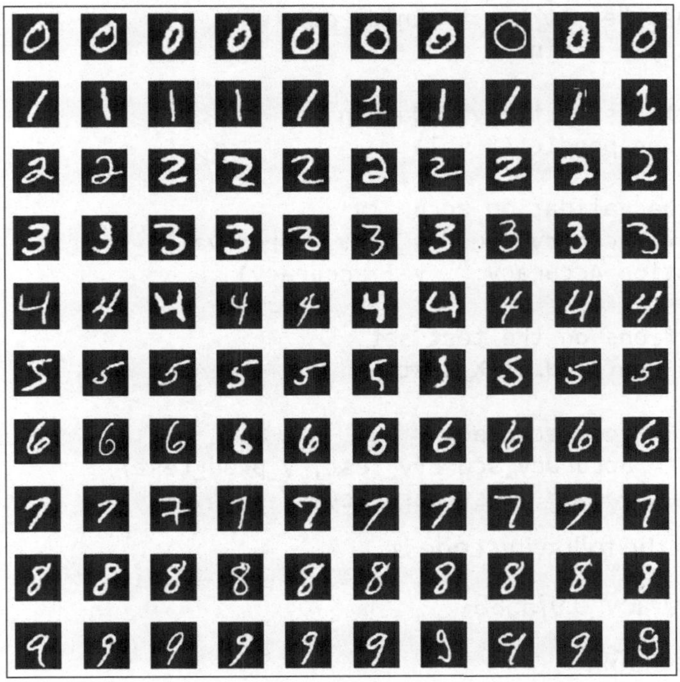

Figure 8.8: *MNIST Dataset Sample*

The dataset can be found at http://yann.lecun.com/exdb/mnist/:

```
from sklearn.neighbors import KNeighborsClassifier
from sklearn.metrics import accuracy_score
from sklearn.model_selection import train_test_split
import tensorflow as tf

mnist = tf.keras.datasets.mnist

# Load the Fashion-MNIST dataset
(X_train, y_train), (X_test, y_test) = mnist.load_data()
```

```
# Flatten the images
X_train = X_train.reshape((X_train.shape[0], -1))
X_test = X_test.reshape((X_test.shape[0], -1))

# Split the data into training and testing sets
X_train, X_val, y_train, y_val = train_test_split(X_train, y_train,
test_size=0.2, random_state=42)

# Define the KNN classifier
knn = KNeighborsClassifier()

# Fit the classifier to the training data
knn.fit(X_train, y_train)

# Make predictions on the validation set
y_pred_val = knn.predict(X_val)

# Calculate the validation accuracy
val_accuracy = accuracy_score(y_val, y_pred_val)
print("Validation Accuracy:", val_accuracy)

# Make predictions on the test set
y_pred_test = knn.predict(X_test)

# Calculate the test accuracy
test_accuracy = accuracy_score(y_test, y_pred_test)
print("Test Accuracy:", test_accuracy)
```

The output for the following code is:

Validation Accuracy: 0.973583

Test Accuracy: 0.9691

Now let us make some predictions on our images. In the preceding code we can add the following lines:

```
# Select three random test images
indices = np.random.randint(0, len(X_test), size=3)
images = X_test[indices]
predicted_labels = y_pred_test[indices]

# Preprocess the images
reshaped_images = [cv2.cvtColor(image.reshape(28, 28), cv2.COLOR_
GRAY2BGR) for image in images]

# Concatenate the images horizontally
concatenated_image = np.hstack(reshaped_images)
```

```
cv2.imshow("Images", padded_image)
cv2.waitKey(0)
cv2.destroyAllWindows()

print("Predicted Labels:", predicted_labels)
```

The output for the code is:

***Figure 8.9**: MNIST images considered for prediction*

Predicted Labels: [1 7 8]

The code begins with importing the necessary modules. We import KNeighborsClassifier and a few more helper functions from the scikit-learn library. We use the MNIST dataset which can directly be imported from TensorFlow. The **`load_data`** returns the dataset into four variables, **`X_train`**, **`y_train`**, **`X_test`**, **`y_test`**. We use the variables for training and testing respectively.

The dataset has to be split into training and validation sections. We keep the testing dataset separately to test our images on unseen images. We use the **`train_test_split`** function from the scikit-learn library to split our dataset and provide it with the X and y labels containing images with their respective labels. We specify the **`test_size`** values as 0.2 denoting that the dataset will be divided into 80% and 20% for training and validation dataset respectively.

The dataset has to be converted into the correct format for input to out classifier function. The function expects the training data to be in the form of (number of images, features) and validation dataset as (number of images,). To convert the dataset into that format we flatten the images to convert them into a one-dimensional array.

Then the code initializes the KNeighborsClassifier and passes it the training datasets and labels using the **`fit`** method. We then use the **`predict`** method to make our predictions on the validation dataset. We then use the **`accuracy_score`** method to evaluate our model and pass it the predicted values array along with the array containing real values and then print the accuracy results.

We get the validation accuracy of 0.9735 and do the prediction on the training datasets which outputs an accuracy of 0.969. We can see that accuracy is approximately 97% on the testing dataset meaning that the model is performing well and we can use it to predict classes for our images. The accuracy can be further enhanced by optimizing different hyperparameters. Incorporating techniques such as cross-validation and grid search can help identify the optimal hyperparameter values for maximizing accuracy. We will be discussing these techniques in detail as we move along the chapter.

Now that we have a trained model, we move on to the second portion of our code which displays the images with the predicted results. This portion simply takes the images and their predicted classes and displays the images and prints the predicted classes for them respectively. We randomly selected three images and use **hconcat** function to concatenate them into a single image and then print the predicted results for these images.

It is important to note that the KNN algorithm is considered to be a *lazy algorithm*. The term *lazy* in this context refers to the fact that KNN does not explicitly build a model during the training phase. Instead, it stores the entire training dataset, which can require significant memory resources, especially for large datasets.

Additionally, because KNN does not make any assumptions about the underlying data distribution, it requires more data storage and computational power compared to other algorithms. As a result, KNN can be time-consuming and resource-intensive, particularly when dealing with large datasets.

Logistic Regression

Logistic regression is a popular and widely used algorithm in machine learning used for binary classification of data into categories. While initially developed for binary classification (Two categories, marked as 0 and 1), it can be used to handle multiclass classification using some different strategies.

Logistic regression is a supervised machine learning algorithm that works by modeling the relationship between the input features and the output category variable by assuming a linear relationship.

The logistic regression algorithm uses the following steps:

1. **Input features**: Logistic regression takes input features that describe the characteristics or attributes of the data we want to classify. For example, in a dog and cat classification problem, the input features could be extracted from images, such as the color distribution, texture patterns, or shape features. These features provide information about the distinguishing characteristics of dogs and cats, and they are used as the input variables for the logistic regression model.

Let's assume that for now we are considering full images as input features. Each image is flattened to create a one-dimensional array by converting the 2D pixel values into a single vector. Each image is assigned a categorical variable (0 or 1) depending if it is a cat or a dog. This allows us to map the images to their corresponding labels and use them as training examples for logistic regression.

Let's say we have a dataset of 100 images. Each image is flattened into a one-dimensional array of length 4096 (assuming the image size is 64x64). We can represent the input features as a matrix or array with the shape (100, 4096), Additionally, we have an output variable, represented as a vector of length 100, containing the corresponding class labels (0 or 1)for each image in the dataset.

Each image comprising of 4096 input features can be represented as:

$$x = [x_1, x_2, x_3 \dots x_{4096}]$$

There are 100 images in the input data, collectively they can be represented in a single array as:

$$\begin{bmatrix} X11 & \cdots & X1m \\ X21 & & X2m \\ \vdots & \iddots & \vdots \\ Xn1 & \cdots & Xnm \end{bmatrix}$$

Figure 8.10: *Image array representation*

Where $m = 4096$, representing the number of features in each image and n = 100, representing the total number of images.

The output vector Y can be represented as:

$$\begin{bmatrix} Y1 \\ Y2 \\ \vdots \\ Yn \end{bmatrix}$$

Figure 8.11: *Image labels*

The value of Y = 0 if the image corresponds to a cat and Y = 1 if the image corresponds to a dog.

2. **Initialize weights**: To perform logistic regression, each input feature vector is multiplied by a weight 'w', and the weighted features are summed

up. This weighted sum represents the influence of each feature on the prediction. The weights are initialized to small random values or set to zeros and serve as starting points for the training process:

$$\sum_{i=1}^{n} wixi + b$$

***Figure 8.12**: Logistic regression formula*

In logistic regression, a bias term 'b' is also added. The bias term allows the logistic regression model to make predictions even when all the input features are zero.

3. **Train the Model**: Now that our data is ready, we can proceed to train our logistic regression model. During the training process, the algorithm will try to learn the boundary that will separate the two classes effectively. The boundary is a hyperplane that will divide the features space into two categories, one for cats and the other for dogs in our case.

The algorithm works by adjusting the weights assigned to each input feature iteratively to minimize the error between the predicted probabilities and the actual labels. The optimization process tries to find the most optimal values for the weights by minimizing a cost or loss function such as cross entropy loss. Logistic regression commonly uses optimization algorithms such as gradient descent, stochastic gradient descent (SGD), or variants of SGD like mini-batch gradient descent.

By adjusting the weights during training, the logistic regression model learns the importance of each input feature in predicting the probability of an image belonging to a specific class (cat or dog).

Ultimately, the trained logistic regression model finds the optimal decision boundary that separates the cat I;mages from the dog images in the feature space using the weights and bias terms

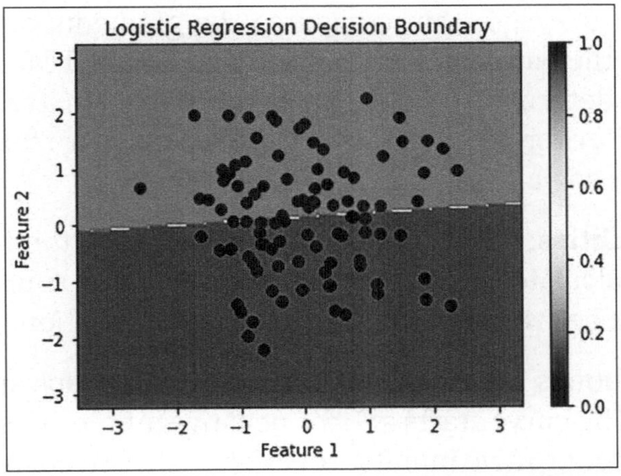

***Figure 8.13**: Logistic regression boundary used to separate classes*

The preceding figure indicates the decision boundary of a logistic regression model. It shows how the model separates the two classes based on the input features. The contour plot represents the regions where the model predicts each class, and the scatter plot displays the actual data points with different colors representing their true class labels.

4. **Gradient descent**: Gradient descent is an iterative optimization algorithm that aims to find the optimal set of parameters (weights) that minimize the cost function associated with logistic regression.

In gradient descent, the algorithm starts with an initial set of parameter values and updates them iteratively by taking steps proportional to the negative gradient of the cost function. The gradient tells us the direction in which the cost function increases the most. By taking steps in the opposite direction, we move towards the direction where the cost function decreases the most, eventually helping us find the minimum of the cost function:

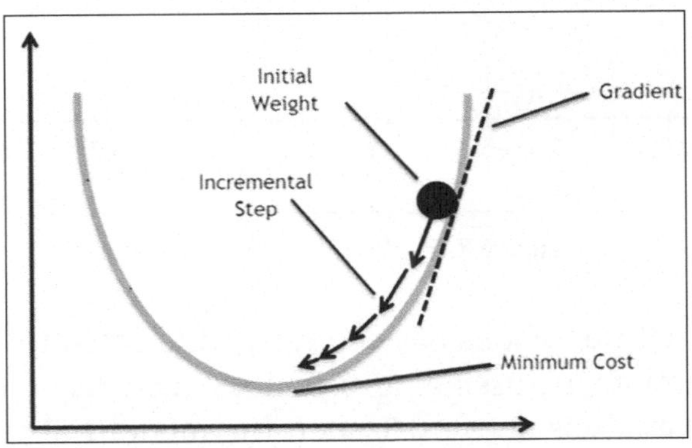

***Figure 8.14**: Gradient Descent*

At each iteration, the algorithm computes the gradients of the cost function and then updates the parameters by subtracting a scaled value of the gradients. The learning rate determines the step size taken in each iteration. The process continues until a criterion is met, such as reaching a maximum number of iterations or achieving a desired level of convergence.

Calculate probabilities: After training, the model uses the input features and their weights to calculate a weighted sum. The weighted sum is then mapped to a probability value between 0 and 1 using a sigmoid function.

The sigmoid function is a mathematical function that maps any value to a value between 0 and 1. The curve starts at 0 for negative infinity, rises steeply near 0.5, and approaches 1 for positive infinity. It has an S-shaped curve and is defined as:

$$\sigma(x) = \frac{1}{1 + e^{-x}}$$

Figure 8.15: *Sigmoid function formula*

The sigmoid curve is represented as:

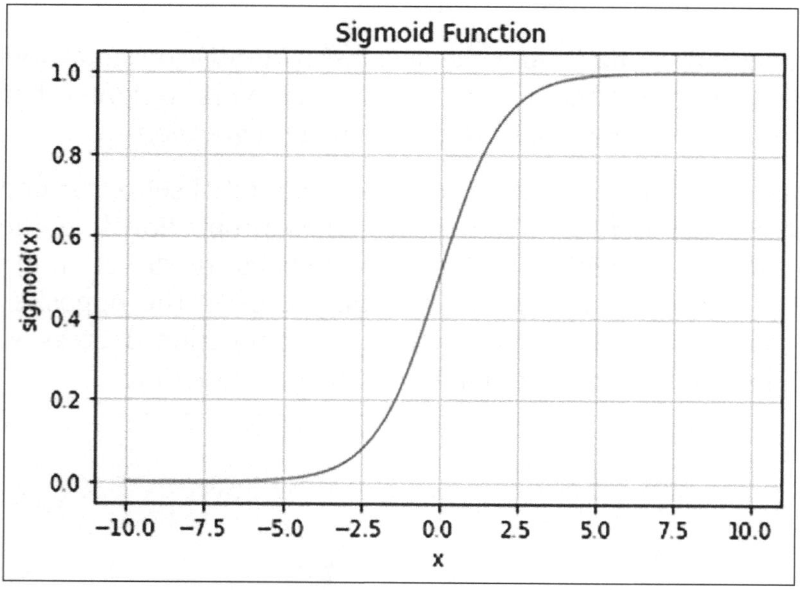

Figure 8.16: *Sigmoid Function Plot*

Prediction: Now that our values have converged in the 0 to 1 range, the model makes class predictions by assigning the most likely label (cat or dog) to the image. If the probability is above 0.5, then the model will assign it to the dog class and if it is below 0.5, the image will be assigned to the cat class.

Hyperparameters

Some of the key hyperparameters in logistic regression are as follows:

- **penalty**: This hyperparameter determines the regularization used in logistic regression to prevent overfitting. It can take different values:
    - **l1**: L1 regularization, also known as Lasso regularization, adds the absolute value of the coefficients as a penalty term.
    - **l2**: L2 regularization, also known as Ridge regularization, adds the squared magnitude of the coefficients as a penalty term.
    - **none**: No regularization is applied.

C: This parameter denotes the inverse of regularization strength. It controls the amount of regularization applied on the images. Smaller values of C will result in stronger regularization, while larger values will reduce the amount of regularization in the dataset.

max_iter This hyperparameter sets the maximum number of iterations for the algorithm to converge. It determines the maximum number of iterations taken for the algorithm to converge to the optimal solution.

Let's try to get our hands on some logistic regression code. First, we will be coding the discussed dogs and cats binary classification. After that we will be using the CIFAR-10 dataset and try to classify 10 different classes in the dataset.

We will be using the Scikit-learn library discussed in the first chapter for implementing logistic regression. The Scikit-learn library contains a lot of algorithms for data preprocessing, model training and a wide range of statistical functions:

```
import numpy as np
from sklearn.linear_model import LogisticRegression
from sklearn.model_selection import train_test_split
from sklearn.metrics import accuracy_score
import os
import cv2

# Initialize empty lists for dataset and labels
dataset = []
labels = []

train_folder = "train"

# Load images from the "dogs" folder
dog_folder = os.path.join(train_folder, 'dogs')
```

```
for filename in os.listdir(dog_folder):
    if filename.endswith('.jpg'):
        image = cv2.imread('train/dogs/'+filename,0)
        if image is not None:
            image = cv2.resize(image,(64, 64))
            k = image.flatten()
            dataset.append(k)
            labels.append(0)  # Label 0 for dog images

# Load images from the "cats" folder
cat_folder = os.path.join(train_folder, 'cats')
for filename in os.listdir(cat_folder):
    if filename.endswith('.jpg'):
        image = cv2.imread('train/cats/'+filename,0)
        if image is not None:
            image = cv2.resize(image,(64, 64))
            k = image.flatten()
            dataset.append(k)
            labels.append(1)  # Label 1 for cat images


# Convert the dataset and labels to NumPy arrays
dataset = np.array(dataset)
labels = np.array(labels)

# Split the dataset into train and test
X_train, X_test, y_train, y_test = train_test_split(dataset, labels,
test_size=0.2)

# Create a logistic regression model
logreg = LogisticRegression()

# Train the model
logreg.fit(dataset, labels)

# Evaluate the model on the training set
train_predictions = logreg.predict(X_train)
train_accuracy = accuracy_score(y_train, train_predictions)
print("Training Accuracy:", train_accuracy)

# Evaluate the model on the testing set
test_predictions = logreg.predict(X_test)
test_accuracy = accuracy_score(y_test, test_predictions)
print("Test Accuracy:", test_accuracy)
```

The output for the preceding code is:

Training Accuracy: 1.0

Test Accuracy: 1.0

In the preceding code, we follow a similar process form earlier to process the dataset accordingly and train the mode. This time instead of using images directly from a tensorflow import, we import our images from the local file directory. We add some checks in between to verify that the file read is indeed an image file with the ".jpg" extension and the image is not blank. We then preprocess it accordingly and append it to the dataset variable along with their respective class label in the label variable.

We then use the **LogisticRegression()** function, train our model and print the accuracy scores. We can see that the training and test accuracy is 1 meaning that the model has successfully being trained and can reliably predict classes for these images. 100% accuracy is almost impossible to achieve in most cases and the simplicity of the dataset enables it in this code. However, in most of the use cases we cannot expect the model to have this accuracy.

Now let us try to select some random images from out directory and make predictions on them:

```
# Select three random images
image_files = np.random.choice(os.listdir("test"), size=5, replace=False)

images = []
# Iterate over the selected image files
for image_file in image_files:
    image_path = os.path.join("test", image_file)

    # Read the image
    image = cv2.imread(image_path)

    # Preprocess images
    gray_image = cv2.cvtColor(image, cv2.COLOR_BGR2GRAY)
    image = cv2.resize(gray_image, (64, 64))

    flattened_image = image.flatten()
    reshaped_image = flattened_image.reshape(1, -1)

    # Make a prediction on the image
    predicted_label = logreg.predict(reshaped_image)[0]

    # Get the class name based on the predicted label
```

```
    class_names = ['dog', 'cat']  # Update with your class names
    predicted_class = class_names[predicted_label]

    # Draw the predicted class on the image
    font = cv2.FONT_HERSHEY_SIMPLEX
    font_scale = 0.7

    cv2.putText(image, predicted_class, (20, 20), font, font_scale,
(255,255,255), 1, cv2.LINE_AA)

    # Add the image with the predicted class to the list
    images.append(image)

output_image = np.hstack(images)

cv2.imshow("output", output_image)
cv2.waitKey(0)
cv2.destroyAllWindows()
```

Output is as follows:

***Figure 8.17**: Image Classification output images along with predicted labels*

We read some images randomly from the directory, predict classes from them and visualize the results by drawing the class labels on top of the image.

We will use the CIFAR-10 dataset for multiclass classification using logistic regression.

The CIFAR-10 dataset is a widely used benchmark dataset in computer vision and machine learning. The dataset consists of 60000 32x32 color images in 10 classes, with 6000 images per class. The dataset is divided into a training set of 50,000 images and a test set of 10,000 images. CIFAR-10 is often used for tasks such as image classification and feature extraction providing a diverse set of images, making it suitable for evaluating different machine learning algorithms.

The classes in the CIFAR-10 dataset are as follows with 10 sample images from each class:

***Figure 8.18**: Cifar-10 Dataset Sample*

The CIFAR-10 dataset with all the details is available at https://www.cs.toronto.edu/~kriz/cifar.html . However, TensorFlow contains an inbuilt API that allows for easy access and downloading of the CIFAR-10 dataset directly within the library, simplifying the data acquisition process for users:

```
import numpy as np
from sklearn.linear_model import LogisticRegression
from sklearn.model_selection import train_test_split
from sklearn.metrics import accuracy_score
from tensorflow.keras.datasets import cifar10

# Initialize empty lists for dataset and labels
dataset = []
labels = []

# Load CIFAR-10 dataset
(x_train, y_train), (_, _) = cifar10.load_data()

# Select the desired classes
selected_classes = [0, 1, 2, 3, 4, 5, 6 , 7, 8, 9]
num_images_per_class = 100
num_classes = len(selected_classes)

selected_images = []
```

```
test = []
# Iterate over the dataset and extract the desired images
for class_idx in selected_classes:
    class_images = x_train[y_train.flatten() == class_idx]
    selected_images.extend(class_images[:num_images_per_class])

# Convert the list of selected images to a NumPy array
selected_images = np.array(selected_images)

# Reshape the images to a flattened shape
flattened_images = selected_images.reshape(-1, np.prod(selected_images.
shape[1:]))

# Initialize these values to the dataset list created earlier
dataset = flattened_images

# Initialize labels for each class
labels = [0]*1000
labels = [i // 100 for i in range(1000)]

# Convert the dataset and labels to NumPy arrays
dataset = np.array(dataset)
labels = np.array(labels)

# Split the extracted images into Train and Test data
X_train, X_test, y_train, y_test = train_test_split(dataset, labels,
test_size=0.2)

# Create a logistic regression model
logreg = LogisticRegression(C=0.1)

# Train the model
logreg.fit(dataset, labels)

# Evaluate the model on the training set
train_predictions = logreg.predict(X_train)
train_accuracy = accuracy_score(y_train, train_predictions)
print("Training Accuracy:", train_accuracy)

# Evaluate the model on the testing set
test_predictions = logreg.predict(X_test)
test_accuracy = accuracy_score(y_test, test_predictions)
print("Test Accuracy:", test_accuracy)
```

The output for the preceding code is as follows:

Training Accuracy: 0.9425

Test Accuracy: 0.915

In the preceding code, we use the Cifar-10 dataset and can see that the test accuracy is close to 91%. This is a decent accuracy which can be increased by further processing and hyperparameter tuning.

We will now take an image at random from the CIFAR-10 dataset and make a prediction on that image:

```
import cv2
import numpy as np
from tensorflow.keras.datasets import cifar10

# Function to draw predicted class on the image
def draw_predicted_class(image, predicted_class):
    class_names = ['airplane', 'automobile', 'bird', 'cat', 'deer',
'dog', 'frog', 'horse', 'ship', 'truck']
    label = class_names[predicted_class]
    font = cv2.FONT_HERSHEY_SIMPLEX
    font_scale = 0.7
    color = (255, 255, 255)
    thickness = 2
    text_size, _ = cv2.getTextSize(label, font, font_scale, thickness)
    text_x = (image.shape[1] - text_size[0]) // 2
    text_y = (image.shape[0] + text_size[1]) // 2
    cv2.putText(image, label, (text_x, text_y), font, font_scale, color,
thickness, cv2.LINE_AA)
    return image

# Load CIFAR-10 dataset
(_, _), (x_test, y_test) = cifar10.load_data()

# Select one random test image
index = np.random.randint(len(x_test))
image = x_test[index]
true_label = y_test[index]

# Make a prediction on the selected image
selected_image = image.reshape(1, -1)
predicted_label = logreg.predict(selected_image)

# Draw predicted class on the image
image_with_label = draw_predicted_class(resized_image, predicted_label[0])
```

```
cv2.imshow("log_final_res.jpg", image_with_label)
cv2.waitKey(0)
cv2.destroyAllWindows()
```

Output:

***Figure 8.19**: Output image with predicted class label*

We take a random image in the above example from the Cifar-10 dataset and predict its accuracy. The image is then displayed with the predicted class for visualization.

Decision Trees

Decision trees are a type of machine learning algorithm that mimics the way humans make decisions by considering multiple factors and conditional control statements like if-else conditions. The decision tree algorithm learns decision rules from the data to make predictions.

Decision trees have a tree-like structure consisting of nodes and branches. A decision tree has the following components:

- **Root Node**: The starting points of a decision tree. The root node represents the entire dataset and serves as the initial point for branching.
- **Internal Nodes**: The internal nodes in a decision tree correspond to specific features or attributes in the dataset. These are the decision points for various features and conditions in the dataset. Each internal node evaluates the value of a particular feature and decides which branch to follow based on a predefined splitting criterion.
- **Branches**: The branches are used to connect the internal nodes in a decision tree. These branches represent the decisions and possible outcomes based on the decision from each node in the decision tree. Each branch corresponds to a specific value of the feature and leads to another node.
- **Leaf Nodes**: Terminal nodes of decision trees. These represent the final predicted outcome of the decision trees. Each leaf node contains the final decision based on the path followed from the root node through the internal nodes:

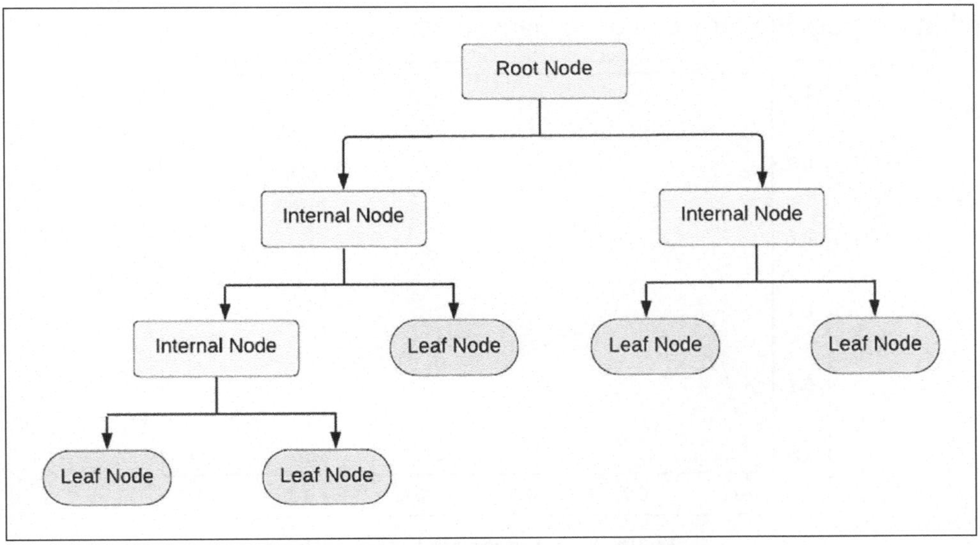

Figure 8.20: *Structure of a decision tree*

The algorithm uses a splitting criterion to make decisions in the decision trees. The criteria determine how to divide the dataset at a given node. The criteria used generally is entropy in classification problems and mean squared error in regression problems:

Entropy: Entropy is used to measure impurity or uncertainty of a set of data. Entropy measures the amount of randomness in a data. In simpler terms, entropy tells us how mixed or diverse the data is with respect to the target classes.

Entropy is calculated by examining the distribution of different categories within the dataset. If all the objects in the dataset belong to the same category, the entropy is low (zero), indicating perfect purity. However, if the objects are evenly distributed among multiple categories, the entropy is high, indicating higher uncertainty or impurity.

The entropy is calculated as:

$$E = -\sum_{i=1}^{n} p_i \log_2(p_i)$$

Figure 8.21: *Entropy Function Formula*

Where p_i is the probability of an instance belonging to class i.

The binary class entropy can be visualized as:

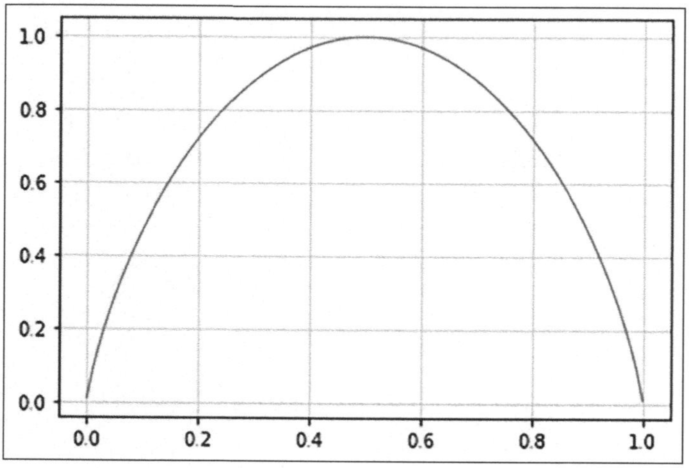

***Figure 8.22**: Entropy Function Plot*

In the context of decision trees, entropy is used as a criterion for determining the optimal splits during the tree-building process. The goal is to find features or attributes that minimize the entropy and maximize the purity of each resulting subset.

By using entropy as a measure, decision trees can systematically evaluate and choose the best splits to create a tree structure that effectively classifies the data based on the given features.

In image classification, entropy helps the algorithm decide which image features to consider when splitting the data. The goal is to find the features that provide the most information to distinguish between different classes of images.

For example, in a dataset of dogs vs cats, The decision tree algorithm looks at the features of these images, such as color, texture, or shape, and calculates the entropy for each feature. The entropy tells us how well a particular feature separates the dogs from cats.

The algorithm begins by selecting the feature that provides the most useful information for distinguishing between the two classes. This feature could be something like color, where images are divided into groups based on similar colors. Let's say the algorithm chooses a feature involving the tail length. The algorithm then splits the data based on this feature, creating branches where images with large tail lengths are grouped together. It continues this process, selecting features that bring more clarity to the classification task, such as fur color. The algorithm continues this process, creating a tree-like structure where each node represents a feature and the branches represent different values of that feature:

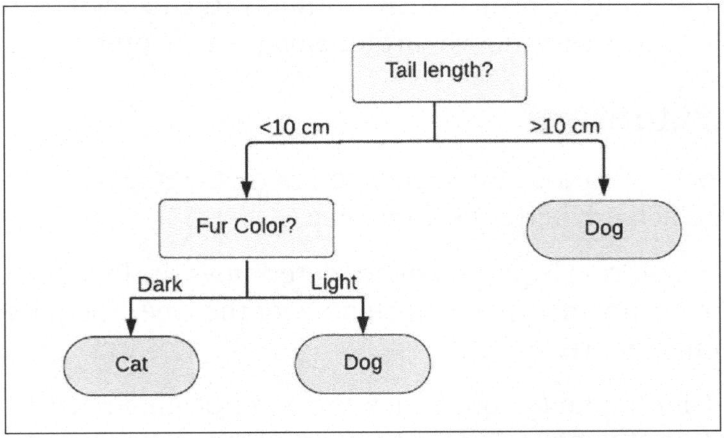

***Figure 8.23**: Decision trees workflow sample using Dog and Cat classification example*

Pruning: Decision trees are prone to overfitting. The goal of pruning is to improve the tree's generalization ability and prevent overfitting, where the tree becomes too specific to the training data and performs poorly on new, unseen data. Pruning in the context of decision trees refers to the process of reducing the complexity of a tree by removing unnecessary branches or nodes.

Overfitting: Occurs when a machine learning model learns too much from the training data and performs poorly on new, unseen data due to capturing noise or irrelevant patterns. It reflects an overly complex model that lacks generalization. It is unable to generalize the dataset and just learns the training data too closely resulting in poor results on new data points.

There are two types of pruning:

- **Pre-pruning**: This approach involves stopping the growth of the tree before it becomes fully expanded. It applies certain conditions or criteria to determine when to stop splitting nodes based on measures like depth of the tree or minimum number of samples required in a node.
- **Post-pruning**: This method involves building the full decision tree and then selectively removing or collapsing certain branches or nodes. The nodes or branches that do not contribute significantly to the overall accuracy or performance of the tree are pruned or removed.

In traditional decision tree algorithms, a single tree is constructed to make predictions based on a set of input features. However, ensemble methods take this concept further by constructing an ensemble, or a group, of decision trees.

Each tree in the ensemble independently learns patterns and makes predictions, and the final prediction is determined by aggregating the outputs of all the trees. One of the most common ensemble algorithms is the Random Forest algorithm which we will discuss as we move further along the chapter.

Hyperparameters

Decision trees have various hyperparameters that can increase their accuracy helping models achieve better performance.

`Criterion`: The criterion hyperparameter determines the function to be used for measuring the quality of a split at each node of the tree. The possible value for this hyperparameter are:

1. `Gini`: Gini impunity quantifies the level of impurity or disorder in a collection of samples. It is the measure of the probability of misclassifying a randomly chosen element in a set.
2. `entropy`: The information gain based on entropy is used as the criterion.

`splitter`: This hyperparameter determines the strategy used to choose the split at each node. It can take two values:

- `best`: It selects the best split based on the chosen criterion.
- `random`: It selects the best random split. This is used to add randomness in the model and prevents overfitting.

`max_depth`: This hyperparameter sets the maximum depth of the decision tree. It helps limit the complexity of the model by decreasing the tree sizes and thus prevents overfitting. Setting it to None will allow the tree to grow until end or contain minimum samples defined by `min_samples_split`.

`min_samples_split`: This hyperparameter sets the minimum number of samples required to split an internal node. If a node has fewer samples than `min_samples_split`, it will not be split further, effectively creating a leaf node.

`min_samples_leaf`: This hyperparameter sets the minimum number of samples required to be at a leaf node. It defines the minimum size of leaf nodes.

`max_features`: This hyperparameter controls the number of features to consider when looking for the best split at each node. The `None` value will consider all features.

We will be implementing decision trees on the Caltech-101 dataset. The Caltech-101 dataset is a widely used benchmark dataset in computer vision, consisting of 101 object categories with diverse images. We download the dataset from the website (https://data.caltech.edu/records/mzrjq-6wc02) and use some classes from the dataset for our classifier.

Let us try to use decision trees to classify these images:

```
import os
import cv2
import numpy as np
from sklearn.metrics import accuracy_score
from sklearn.model_selection import train_test_split,GridSearchCV
from sklearn.tree import DecisionTreeClassifier

# Set the paths to the image folders
folder_paths = ['airplanes', 'car_side', 'helicopter','motorbikes']

# Set the number of bins for the histogram
num_bins = 256

# Initialize lists to store the features and labels
features = []
labels = []

# Iterate over the image folders
for folder_index, folder_path in enumerate(folder_paths):
    # Get the class label from the folder name
    class_label = folder_index
    print(len(os.listdir(folder_path)))
    # Iterate over the images in the folder
    for filename in os.listdir(folder_path)[:50]:

        image_path = os.path.join(folder_path, filename)
        image = cv2.imread(image_path)
        gray_image = cv2.cvtColor(image, cv2.COLOR_BGR2GRAY)

        gray_image = cv2.resize(gray_image, (200,200))
        # Compute the histogram
        histogram = cv2.calcHist([gray_image], [0], None, [num_bins],
[0, num_bins])

        # Flatten the histogram and append it to the features list
        features.append(gray_image.flatten())

        # Append the class label to the labels list
        labels.append(class_label)

# Convert the lists to NumPy arrays
```

```
features = np.array(features)
labels = np.array(labels)

# Split the data into training and testing sets
X_train, X_test, y_train, y_test = train_test_split(features, labels,
test_size=0.2)

# Initialize a Random Forest classifier
classifier = DecisionTreeClassifier()

# Define the parameter grid for grid search
param_grid = {
    'criterion': ['gini', 'entropy'],
    'max_depth': [None, 5, 10,15],
    'min_samples_split': [2, 5, 10],
    'min_samples_leaf': [1, 2, 5],
    'max_features': [5,10,15,20,25]
}

# Perform grid search with cross-validation
grid_search = GridSearchCV(classifier, param_grid, cv=5)
grid_search.fit(X_train, y_train)

# Get the best parameters and best score from grid search
best_params = grid_search.best_params_
best_score = grid_search.best_score_
print("Best Parameters:", best_params)
print("Best Score:", best_score)

# Use the best model from grid search for prediction
best_model = grid_search.best_estimator_
train_predictions = best_model.predict(X_train)
test_predictions = best_model.predict(X_test)

# Calculate accuracy
train_accuracy = accuracy_score(y_train, train_predictions)
test_accuracy = accuracy_score(y_test, test_predictions)
print("Training Accuracy:", train_accuracy)
print("Test Accuracy:", test_accuracy)
```

The output for the preceding code is as follows:

Best Parameters: {'criterion': 'gini', 'max_depth': 5, 'max_features': 15, 'min_samples_leaf': 1, 'min_samples_split': 2}

Best Score: 0.8

Training Accuracy: 0.95

Test Accuracy: 0.775

Similar to what we did earlier, we load the dataset, preprocess the images, and this time we pass the images to the `DecisionTreeClassifier` function. In this code, we do not use the pixel values directly, but instead use the histogram values of images of our images. This time we use grid search to try to optimize our hyperparameter values:

Grid Search: Grid search is a hyperparameter tuning technique that iteratively searches for the best combinations of hyperparameters for training a machine learning model.

A grid of predefined hyperparameter values is supplied to the model and the model is trained on all the possible combinations of hyperparameters on the dataset. The combination of hyperparameters providing the best performance is selected as the optimal choice.

Overall, Grid search provides a systematic approach to fine-tune hyperparameters and improve the model's performance by exploring different hyperparameter combinations.

On obtaining the best-fit parameters from our grid search we see that the decision tree classifier has only been able to give an underwhelming ~78% accuracy on the test dataset. Clearly, the decision tree classifier has not been able to accurately predict this specific use case, and we will explore ensemble methods such as random forest which uses multiple decision trees to come up with a better result.

Note: Using other input features such as HOG (Histogram of Oriented Gradients) or LBPs (Local Binary Pattern) can help us achieve better accuracy. We will be discussing these in detail in the next chapter.

Ensemble Learning

Ensemble learning is a machine learning technique that involves combining multiple individual models to create a stronger and more accurate predictive model.

The main idea behind ensemble learning is to create multiple models of varying configurations on the same dataset. Each model is trained independently and generates their own predictions. Then these models are combined to make the final prediction by aggregating the results from each model using methods such as averaging or weighted averaging.

This results in better results than individual models since the collective knowledge of all the models trained under different conditions produces an overall more comprehensive and robust approach. The ensemble combines the strengths and compensates for the weaknesses of the individual models, leading to improved accuracy and generalization to make good predictions.

There are two types of ensemble learning methods:

- **Bagging**: In bagging multiple models are trained independently on different subsets of the dataset. Each model is trained on a random subset and the results of all the models are combined to come up with the final prediction. Bagging also helps reduce overfitting during training and improves the accuracy of the model. Random Forest is a popular algorithm that uses bagging in its operation.
- **Boosting**: Boosting is an iterative process that boosts the performance of the model sequentially. First, the base model is trained on the entire dataset and then using the outputs from the initial models, subsequent models are trained based on the weaknesses of the base model. Boosting assigns higher weights to the misclassified instances to emphasize their importance in subsequent iterations. The predictions of all the models are then combined through weighted averaging to make the final prediction. Gradient Boosting and AdaBoost are popular boosting algorithms.

To summarize, Bagging combines predictions from independently trained models, while boosting iteratively improves model performance by emphasizing misclassified instances, both enhancing accuracy and robustness of ensemble models.

Random Forest

Random Forest is an ensemble learning algorithm that combines multiple decision trees to make predictions. Decision trees are the building blocks of random forest classifiers. Each decision tree is constructed using a subset of the training data, and it makes predictions based on a series of binary decisions on the input features:

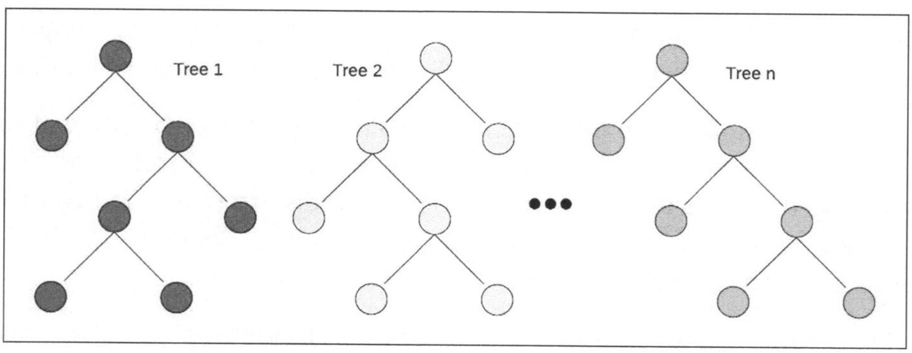

***Figure 8.24**: Random Forest: Collection of multiple decision trees*

Steps involved in Random Forest Algorithm:

1. Randomly select a subset of the dataset to create multiple samples ensuring diversity in the data for each decision tree.
2. For each tree, a random subset of features is selected from the available features. The maximum number of features to be considered are specified and a random subset is selected accordingly.
3. A decision tree is constructed using the randomly selected data subsets and features and a splitting criteria is used to construct the tree.
4. Steps 1 to 2 are repeated till the required amount of trees are constructed forming a random forest.
5. To make a prediction, input data is passed through all the trees and each tree produces an output. All the outputs are then combined and a final prediction is reached based on majority voting or averaging.

Randomness

Random Forests introduce randomness in two ways:

- As mentioned earlier, random forest is an ensemble method that uses bagging. Subsets of training dataset with replacements are used in decision trees. This means that each tree is trained on a slightly different data. This introduces variations in the dataset effectively introducing randomness and diversity in the dataset.

  This also helps to reduce overfitting since each tree has its unique training data effectively reducing the correlation between the trees. This helps the trees capture different variations and patterns in the dataset. As a result, the ensemble model is less likely to overfit to any specific pattern or noise present in the training data.

- At each split decision of the tree, a random subset of features is selected randomly for finding the best split. By limiting the features to consider at each split, the algorithm ensures that no single feature dominates the decision-making process. This is beneficial because it encourages the ensemble to consider a wider range of features and capture different aspects of the data.

  Additionally, by reducing the influence of individual features, the algorithm becomes less susceptible to noisy or irrelevant features that may exist in the dataset. This feature selection mechanism helps to focus on the most informative and discriminative features, leading to more effective and accurate decision trees.

In summary, by limiting the features to consider at each split, the Random Forest algorithm promotes diversity among the trees and reduces the risk of overfitting to specific features, resulting in a more reliable and accurate ensemble model.

Important features of Random Forest Classifier:

- **Voting and Aggregation**: As discussed beforehand, Random Forest Classifier combines predictions from multiple decision trees in the ensemble. Random Forest Classifier uses majority voting for classification tasks and averaging for regression tasks to obtain the final prediction. This voting and aggregation process helps in reducing the impact of individual noisy or biased predictions, leading to more robust and accurate results.
- **Lesser Overfitting**: Since the algorithm uses multiple trees with varying subsets of data and features, the algorithm is less prone to overfitting reduces the variance and biasBy averaging the predictions of multiple trees, it diminishes the influence of outliers and individual tree biases, resulting in more reliable and stable predictions. of the predictions.
- **Feature Importance**: Random Forest Classifier provides a measure of feature importance, indicating the relevance of each feature in making predictions. The algorithm analyzes the usage frequency and the impact of each feature across the decision trees. This feature importance analysis aids in identifying the most influential features in the dataset, enabling better outputs.

Hyperparameters

Random Forests have several hyperparameters that can be adjusted to find the right balance between model complexity and generalization ability. A Random Forest algorithm has the following hyperparameters:

- `n_estimators`: This is one of the key parameters in random forests representing the number of decision trees to be created in the ensemble. There is a trade-off between accuracy and the computational time as we increase the number of trees. White the accuracy of the algorithm will increase; the computational time will also increase with the number of trees. It is important to find an optimal value for this parameter which results in a good accuracy with acceptable amount of computational time needed for the operation.
- `max_features`: The max features parameter determines the number of features randomly selected at each split point of a tree. Setting it to a lower value reduces the correlation between trees and increases diversity, while setting it to a higher value may lead to more correlated

trees. Choosing the appropriate value for **max_features** is crucial in achieving a balance between model complexity and performance.

- **max_depth**: The max depth parameter specifies the maximum depth for each decision tree in the random forest ensemble. A deeper tree with a large depth will allow the algorithm to capture more complex features from the dataset. However, increasing the maximum depth also increases the chances of overfitting for the model. Setting an appropriate value for this parameter helps control the complexity of the model and prevents overfitting.
- **max_leaf_nodes**: The **max_leaf_nodes** hyperparameter in Random Forest Classifier determines the maximum number of leaf nodes allowed in each decision tree. It controls the depth and complexity of the trees and helps prevent overfitting. Setting a lower value restricts the tree growth, while a higher value allows for more complex trees.
- **criterion**: The **criterion** parameter specifies the splitting criteria used to evaluate the quality of a split in each decision tree. For regression tasks, other metrics such as mean squared error (MSE) or mean absolute error (MAE) are more commonly used as the splitting criteria. The two commonly used criteria are **gini** and **entropy** for classification tasks. The **gini** criterion measures the impurity or the degree of mixture of different classes in a node, while the **entropy** criterion measures the information gain or the reduction in uncertainty after the split.

In addition to these, there are other hyperparameters such as **min_samples_split** and **min_samples_leaf** that control the minimum number of samples required to split an internal node or to be considered as a leaf node, respectively. These parameters influence the tree's structure and can be adjusted to balance the bias-variance trade-off.

First, let us try to run Random Forest Classifier on the MNIST dataset and see if the accuracy has been increased:

```
import tensorflow as tf
from sklearn.metrics import accuracy_score
from sklearn.metrics import confusion_matrix
from sklearn.ensemble import RandomForestClassifier

# Load the MNIST dataset from TensorFlow
mnist = tf.keras.datasets.mnist
(x_train, y_train), (x_test, y_test) = mnist.load_data()

# Preprocess the image data
x_train = x_train.reshape(-1, 784) / 255.0
x_test = x_test.reshape(-1, 784) / 255.0
```

```
# Initialize Decision Tree classifier
classifier = RandomForestClassifier(criterion = “entropy”)

# Train out Decision Tree model
classifier.fit(x_train, y_train)

# Evaluate the model on the training set
train_predictions = classifier.predict(x_train)
train_accuracy = accuracy_score(y_train, train_predictions)
print(“Training Accuracy:”, train_accuracy)

# Evaluate the model on the testing set
test_predictions = classifier.predict(x_test)
test_accuracy = accuracy_score(y_test, test_predictions)
print(“Test Accuracy:”, test_accuracy)

# Generate confusion matrix
cm = confusion_matrix(y_test, test_predictions)
print(“Confusion Matrix:”)
print(cm)
```

The preceding code outputs the following results:

```
Training Accuracy: 1.0

Test Accuracy: 0.9706

Confusion Matrix:
[[ 972    0    1    0    0    1    2    1    3    0]
 [   0 1123    3    3    0    2    2    0    1    1]
 [   4    0 1004    3    4    2    4    8    3    0]
 [   0    0   11  973    0    7    0    9    9    1]
 [   1    1    2    0  953    0    5    0    3   17]
 [   2    0    2   13    3  858    5    2    5    2]
 [   6    3    0    0    2    4  941    0    2    0]
 [   1    6   21    0    3    0    0  986    2    9]
 [   5    0    4    7    5    4    4    4  932    9]
 [   3    6    2   10   10    5    1    3    5  964]]
```

In the preceding code, we use random forest on the MNIST dataset and see that the model has been able to achieve a 97% accuracy on the dataset.

We also print the classification matrix for the obtained results. The provided matrix represents the confusion matrix obtained from a classification task on the MNIST dataset. The diagonal elements of the matrix represent the correctly classified instances for each class, while the off-diagonal elements indicate misclassifications.

Overall, the model achieved high accuracy, as indicated by the relatively large values along the diagonal. However, there are some instances of confusion between certain classes. For example, classifying digit 4 seems to be challenging, as there are a relatively high number of misclassifications with digits 9 and 7.

Now let us try to run Random Forest Classifier on some classes from the Caltech-101 dataset and see how the accuracy is:

```
import os
import cv2
import numpy as np
from sklearn.ensemble import RandomForestClassifier
from sklearn.metrics import accuracy_score
from sklearn.model_selection import train_test_split,GridSearchCV


# Set the paths to the image folders
folder_paths = ['airplanes', 'car_side', 'helicopter','motorbikes']

# Set the number of bins for the histogram
num_bins = 256

# Initialize lists to store the features and labels
features = []
labels = []

# Iterate over the image folders
for folder_index, folder_path in enumerate(folder_paths):
    # Get the class label from the folder name
    class_label = folder_index
    print(len(os.listdir(folder_path)))
    # Iterate over the images in the folder
    for filename in os.listdir(folder_path)[:80]:
        # Read the image
        image_path = os.path.join(folder_path, filename)
        image = cv2.imread(image_path)

        # Convert the image to grayscale
        gray_image = cv2.cvtColor(image, cv2.COLOR_BGR2GRAY)

        # Compute the histogram
```

```
        histogram = cv2.calcHist([gray_image], [0], None, [num_bins],
[0, num_bins])

        # Flatten the histogram and append it to the features list
        features.append(histogram.flatten())

        # Append the class label to the labels list
        labels.append(class_label)

# Convert the lists to NumPy arrays
features = np.array(features)
labels = np.array(labels)

# Split the data into training and testing sets
X_train, X_test, y_train, y_test = train_test_split(features, labels,
test_size=0.2)

# Initialize a Random Forest classifier
classifier = RandomForestClassifier(n_estimators=200, max_depth=25, max_
features=30)
# Train the classifier
classifier.fit(X_train, y_train)

# Make predictions on the training set
train_predictions = classifier.predict(X_train)
train_accuracy = accuracy_score(y_train, train_predictions)
print("Training Accuracy:", train_accuracy)

# Make predictions on the testing set
test_predictions = classifier.predict(X_test)
test_accuracy = accuracy_score(y_test, test_predictions)
print("Test Accuracy:", test_accuracy)


# Display images with predicted class
num_images = 8
selected_indices = np.random.choice(len(X_test), num_images, replace
=False)
selected_images = X_test[selected_indices]
selected_labels = [folder_paths[label] for label in test_predictions
[selected_indices]]

for i, image_index in enumerate(selected_indices):
    folder_index = int(y_test[image_index])
    folder_path = folder_paths[folder_index]
    filename = os.listdir(folder_path)[image_index % 80]
    image_path = os.path.join(folder_path, filename)
```

```
    image = cv2.imread(image_path)

    # Draw the predicted class on the image
    cv2.putText(image, str(selected_labels[i]), (10, 30), cv2.FONT_
HERSHEY_SIMPLEX, 1, (0, 255, 0), 2)

    cv2.imshow(f"Image {i+1}", image)
    cv2.waitKey(0)
    cv2.destroyAllWindows()
```

The accuracy for the above code is :

Training Accuracy: 1.0

Test Accuracy: 0.953125

***Figure 8.25**: Random Forest Output along with the predicted class labels*

We use the same classes from the Caltech-101 dataset that we tried training out model using decision trees and achieved an underwhelmingly low accuracy. Using random forest classifier, we have been able to achieve 95% accuracy on the same dataset. We then display some images with their predicted classes for better visualization of our model results.

Support Vector Machines

Support Vector Machines is a supervised machine learning algorithm used for both regression and classification tasks. SVMs are a powerful set of algorithms known for their ability to handle complex datasets.

SVMs work by finding an optimal hyperplane that best separates the data points belonging to different classes. In binary classification problems, the goal is to find a decision boundary that maximizes the distance between the hyperplane and the nearest data points of each class.

The main idea behind SVMs is to transform the input data into a higher-dimensional feature space, where it becomes easier to find a hyperplane that linearly separates the data.

Before going into further details about SVMs, let us go through some of the terminologies used in SVM:

- **Hyperplane**: The hyperplane represents a decision boundary that separates the classes in SVM. The key characteristic of a hyperplane in SVMs is that it maximizes the margin, which is the distance between the hyperplane and the nearest data points of each class.

In a two-dimensional feature space, a hyperplane is simply a line that divides the data points. In three-dimensional feature space, the hyperplane is simply a plane and in higher dimensions it is a hyperplane:

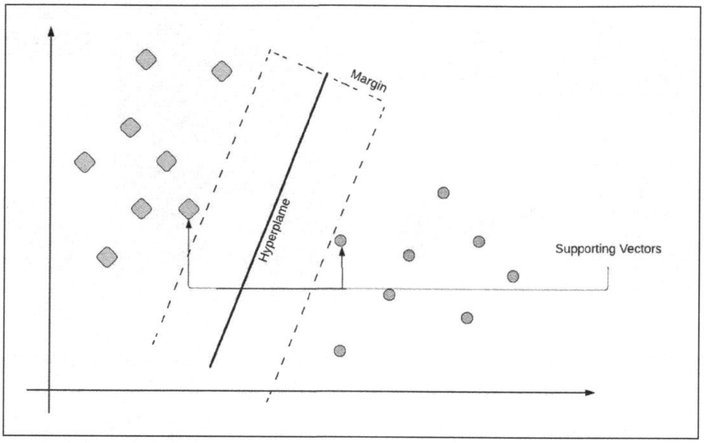

***Figure 8.26**: Support Vector Machine Components showing the hyperplane, margin and supporting vectors*

- **Margin**: Margin refers to the distance between the hyperplane and the support vectors. The margin is calculated as the perpendicular distance from the decision boundary to the closest support vectors.

A wide margin signifies a more robust decision boundary that is less susceptible to misclassifications and noise in the data while a narrow margin may indicate a higher chance of overfitting, where the model becomes too specific to the training data and may not generalize well to new data.

- **Support Vectors**: Support Vectors are the data points that lie closest to the hyperplane. During training, these support vectors have the highest influence on the placement and orientation of the decision boundary. If these support vectors are changed or removed, the boundary position and orientation will change.

Support vectors have certain properties that distinguish them from other data points. For example, they are the only data points that contribute to the construction of the decision boundary. The remaining data points that are not support vectors, have no impact on the decision boundary and can be ignored during classification.

SVM is a machine learning algorithm that finds the optimal line or curve to separate different classes of data points. It maximizes the margin between the classes, creating a clear boundary. It aims to create a clear boundary between classes, similar to drawing a line on paper to separate different shapes. It then uses this decision boundary to classify new, unseen data. Once SVM finds the decision boundary, it assigns new, unseen data points to different classes based on which side of the boundary they fall on.

The detailed steps for SVM are as follows:

1. **Data Preprocessing**: First prepare the dataset by applying necessary pre-processing techniques such as data cleaning and feature scaling. Select the input features and the target variables from the dataset and split the dataset into train and test data subsets.

2. **Select the SVM kernel**: The kernel function maps the original input data into a multi-dimensional feature space. This helps the SVM models find an optimal hyperspace that separates the classes with maximum margin. This kernel transformation helps capture non-linear relationships between the data points.

   Kernel Trick: The kernel trick is a technique used in SVM to handle non-linearly separable data. The basic idea behind the kernel trick is to replace the dot product between two data points in the higher-dimensional space with a kernel function.

   The kernel function calculates the similarity between two data points in the original feature space and maps them to a higher-dimensional space implicitly. This allows SVM to find a linear decision boundary in the transformed space, which corresponds to a non-linear decision boundary in the original feature space.

   The choice of a kernel depends on the data and the problem in consideration. Some of the popular kernels are:

   - **Linear Kernel**: A linear kernel creates a linear decision boundary and is thus helpful in datasets that can be separated linearly.
   - **Polynomial Kernel**: Polynomial functions are used in this kernel

which makes the data nonlinear mapping it into higher dimensional space. The decision boundary can be controlled by changing the degree of the polynomial in use.

- **Radial Basis Function (RBF) Kernel**: This type of kernel transforms the data into an infinite dimensional feature space which allows for more flexible boundary decisions making it a popular algorithm to capture complex non-linear relationships in the data.

3. **Train the SVM model**: In the training process, the algorithm tries to find the most optimal hyperplane that maximizes the margin between the classes. This is done by solving a convex optimization problem. The algorithm identifies the support vectors, which are the data points that lie closest to the decision boundary. It calculates the corresponding weights for these support vectors to define the hyperplane. By determining the support vectors and their weights, SVM creates a decision boundary that can accurately classify new, unseen data.

4. **Hyperparameter tuning**: The performance of the model is evaluated using various metrics such as accuracy, precision or F1 score. The hyperparameters are fine-tuned to optimize the model performance. One of the main hyperparameters in SVM is the Regularization Parameter (C). SVM uses a regularization parameter C that controls the trade-off between maximizing the margin and minimizing the misclassification error. A smaller C value allows for a larger margin but may lead to misclassifications, while a larger C value reduces the margin but focuses more on correctly classifying training examples.

   Another hyperparameter is the kernel selection hyperparameter mentioned in Step 2. The degree (polynomial kernel) of the polynomial function is a hyperparameter that controls the flexibility of the decision boundary.

   Gamma is another hyperparameter that defines the influence of each training example on the decision boundary. A smaller gamma value indicates a larger influence range, resulting in a smoother decision boundary, while a larger gamma value focuses on closer data points, resulting in a more complex decision boundary.

   In some cases, the data may be imbalanced, with one class having significantly fewer samples than the other. Setting class weights can help balance the influence of each class during training and improve the performance of the minority class.

5. **Evaluation and Prediction**: The performance of the model is evaluated using various metrics such as accuracy, precision or F1 score. Once the SVM model is trained and evaluated, it can be deployed to make predictions on new, unseen data. The model maps the new data points into the same feature space as the training data and assigns them to the appropriate class based on their position relative to the decision boundary.

This concludes our discussion on machine learning concepts. In the next chapter, we will delve into more advanced feature extraction techniques such as **Histogram of Oriented Gradients** (**HOG**) and **Local Binary Patterns** (**LBP**). These techniques are widely used in computer vision tasks and can provide further insights into image characteristics, leading to improved classification performance. We will be using these machine learning algorithms in conjunction with these advanced feature extraction methods to further enhance our understanding and performance in various computer vision tasks.

Conclusion

This chapter has provided an introduction to Machine Learning and explored fundamental algorithms in image classification and clustering, including KMeans Clustering, k-Nearest Neighbors Classification, Logistic Regression, Decision Trees, Random Forests, and Support Vector Machines. By gaining practical experience with OpenCV, you have acquired valuable skills for computer vision projects. Armed with this knowledge, you are well-equipped to apply these algorithms to tackle real-world challenges in image analysis and make informed decisions.

In the next chapter, we will delve into advanced techniques for feature detection and extraction in computer vision. Our focus will be on exploring the Histogram of Oriented Gradients (HOG) method, which captures gradient information to represent and detect object features. Additionally, we will delve into Local Binary Patterns (LBP), Hough Transforms and Bag of Visual Words. Lastly, we will explore methods such as SIFT, and SURF for feature representation and matching.

Points to Remember

- Machine learning is the field of study that enables computers to learn and make predictions or decisions without being explicitly programmed.
- Supervised learning involves training a model using labeled data,

unsupervised learning involves discovering patterns in unlabeled data, and semi-supervised learning combines both labeled and unlabeled data for training.

- Logistic Regression is a binary classification algorithm that predicts the probability of an event occurring. The algorithm works by modeling the relationship between the input features and the output category variable by assuming a linear relationship.
- Entropy is used to measure impurity or uncertainty of a set of data. Entropy measures the amount of randomness in a data. In other words, entropy tells us how mixed or diverse the data is with respect to the target classes.
- k-Nearest Neighbors (KNN) is an algorithm that predicts the class of a new data point based on its proximity to neighboring samples. It is a non-parametric algorithm that doesn't make assumptions about the underlying data distribution.
- Decision Trees are intuitive algorithms that learn decision rules from labeled data to make predictions.
- Ensemble learning combines multiple models or algorithms to improve prediction accuracy and robustness. Random Forest is an ensemble learning algorithm that combines multiple decision trees to make predictions.
- Support Vector Machines (SVM) are powerful algorithms that separate data into different classes using hyperplanes in high-dimensional spaces. SVMs transform the input data into a higher-dimensional feature space making it easier to find a hyperplane that linearly separates the data.

Test your understanding

1. What is the term for instances wrongly predicted as positive when they actually belong to the negative class?

   A. True Positives

   B. True Negatives

   C. False Positives

   D. False Negatives

2. The logistic regression model uses which function to map the input to the output:
   A. Sigmoid function
   B. Linear function
   C. Entropy
   D. Gaussian Function
3. Which of the following is not a node in decision trees?
   A. Root node
   B. Leaf Node
   C. Decision Node
   D. Branch Node
4. Boosting is a technique in ensemble learning that:
   A. Aggregates model predictions
   B. Combines weak models iteratively
   C. Trains models independently
   D. Focuses on misclassified instances
5. Which of the following is not a part of Support Vector Machines?
   A. Hyperplane
   B. Supporting Vectors
   C. Nodes
   D. Margin

Chapter 9

Advanced Computer Vision Algorithms

In this chapter, we will explore key feature detection and description techniques widely used in image processing. We will learn about different methods for detecting and describing local features in images. Local features are distinctive regions or points in an image that can be used for various applications. We will delve into the intricacies of several state-of-the-art algorithms, including FAST, Harris Keypoint Detector, BRIEF, ORB, SIFT, RootSIFT, SURF, Local Binary Patterns, and Histogram of Oriented Gradients.

By the end of this chapter, you will have a solid understanding of the theory and implementation of these methods.

Structure

In this chapter, we will discuss the following topics:

- FAST (Features from Accelerated Segment Test)
- Harris Keypoint Detector
- BRIEF (Binary Robust Independent Elementary Features)
- ORB (Oriented FAST and Rotated BRIEF)
- SIFT (Scale-Invariant Feature Transform)
- RootSIFT (Root Scale-Invariant Feature Transform)
- SURF (Speeded-Up Robust Features)
- Local Binary Patterns
- Histogram of Oriented Gradients

FAST (Features from Accelerated Segment Test)

FAST is a popular and widely used keypoint detection algorithm used in computer vision and image processing. The algorithm is designed to identify the corners or the key points in an image quickly with high accuracy. The algorithm works by analyzing the intensity variations in pixels of an image to detect key points or corners.

The algorithm works by taking a pixel as a candidate for a corner pixel and analyzing the points in its neighborhood. The intensity values of the center pixel are compared with these points in the neighborhood, and a threshold value is chosen to classify each neighborhood pixel as lighter or darker. A score is calculated based on these values and is used to classify if the pixel in consideration is a corner pixel or not.

One of the main advantages of using the FAST algorithm is its computational efficiency. The algorithm is able to deliver real-time performance as it minimizes the number of intensity comparisons required in its implementation and is thus a suitable algorithm for use in various applications such as object recognition and image stitching.

The FAST algorithm implements the following steps to detect keypoints in an image:

1. **Candidate Pixel Selection**: The algorithm begins by selecting a pixel for consideration. Running the algorithm for each pixel might be computationally expensive and thus the algorithm can choose to select pixels at a certain interval.

   A threshold value is selected to classify the neighboring pixels as darker or brighter. A radius value is also chosen for the circular neighborhood, which determines the number of pixels to be used to compare intensity values. Commonly used number of pixels is 16, which corresponds to a radius value of 3:

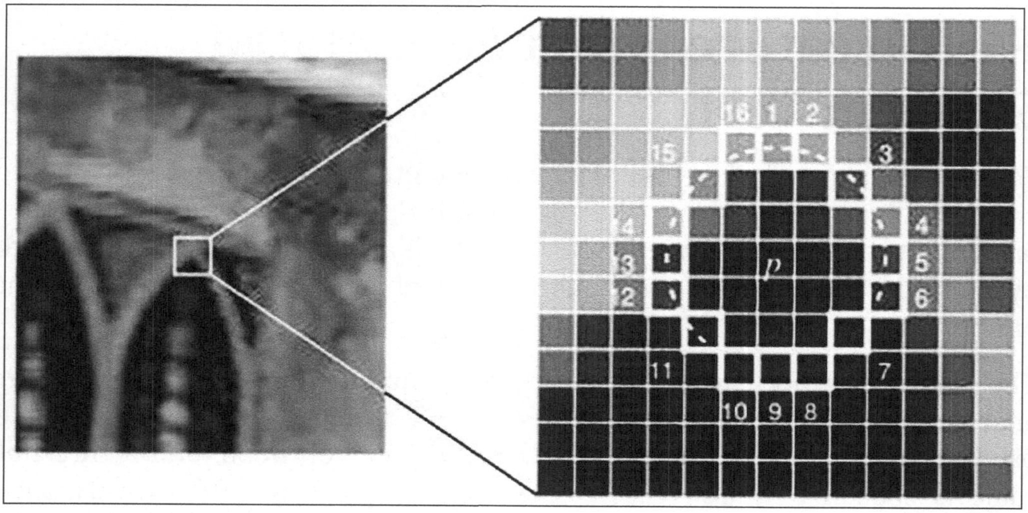

***Figure 9.1**: Neighborhood of the center pixel with radius 3 indicating 16 pixels for consideration. Img src:* https://docs.opencv.org/3.4/df/d0c/tutorial_py_fast.html

2. **Pixel Intensity Comparison**: The intensity values of the center pixel (p) are compared with the pixels in the neighborhood.

   If a pixel value is greater than the intensity of the center pixel (p) plus the threshold value (t), it is classified as a brighter pixel. If the intensity value is lesser than the center pixel(p) minus the threshold value (t), it is classified as a darker pixel.

3. **Pixel classification**: After classifying each neighborhood pixel, a value (n) is chosen, which represents the number of contiguous pixels that are brighter (> p+t) or darker (< p-t) than the center pixel. If there are at least 'n' contiguous pixels that are either brighter or darker, the candidate pixel is selected as a corner pixel or a key point.

The algorithm repeats this process for all the pixels it needs to analyze.

Let us consider both the cases with contiguous pixels being brighter or darker. Let's suppose our threshold value(t) is 10 and the number of contiguous pixels required(n) is chosen as 9.

In the following image, the left image has nine contiguous pixels that satisfy the condition where their value is greater than t+p, indicating they are brighter. Hence, the candidate pixel can be chosen as a corner pixel. Similarly, the contiguous pixels in right image are darker and thus it can be classified as a corner pixel:

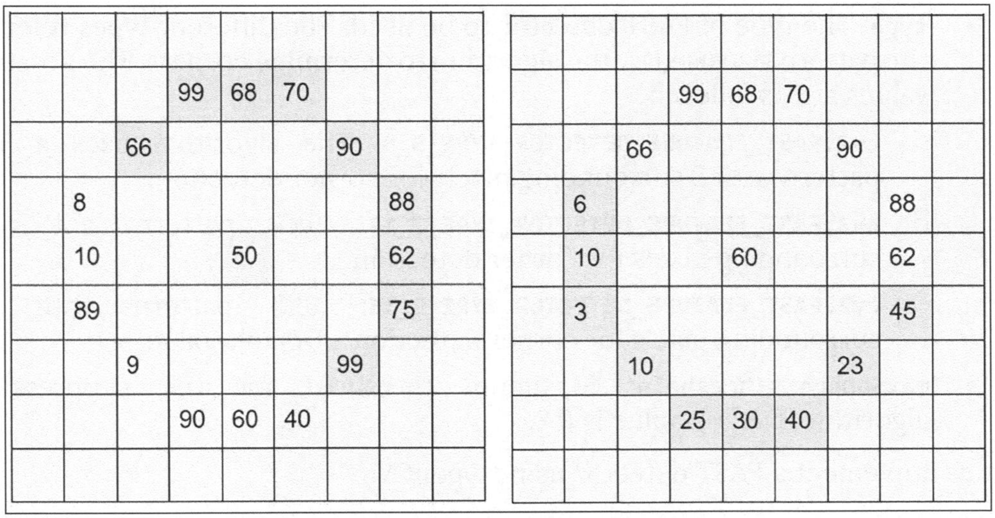

***Figure 9.2**: Contiguous pixels for selection*

Non-Max Suppression: One issue that might arrive of the operation is that multiple nearby points might be chosen as corner pixels.

Non max suppression is applied to address this problem and the corners are sorted based on scores. This score is typically based on the number of contiguous pixels (n) in the circular neighborhood that are brighter or darker. The pixels with lower scores that are within a certain distance of higher-scoring corners are discarded.

In OpenCV, we will use the **`cv2.FastFeatureDetector_create`** function to implement FAST keypoint detection. The function eliminates the need to manually code all the steps just like the case for most of the algorithms that will be discussed in this chapter.

cv2.FastFeatureDetector_create

Syntax:

```
cv2.FastFeatureDetector_create(threshold=10, nonmaxSuppression=True,
type=cv2.FAST_FEATURE_DETECTOR_TYPE_9_16, maxSuppressThreshold=0.2)
```

Parameters:

- **`threshold`**: Threshold value on the difference between intensity of central pixel and pixels of circle around it. The default value is 10.
- **`nonmaxSuppression`**: Boolean value to determine if NMS has to be applied or not. By default this value is **`True`**.

- **type**: The type of FAST detector to be used. The different types refer to the pattern size used by the algorithm to determine corners. The possible values are as follows:
  - **cv2.FAST_FEATURE_DETECTOR_TYPE_5_8**: The algorithm uses a 5x5 pattern with 8 surrounding pixels for corner detection.
  - **cv2.FAST_FEATURE_DETECTOR_TYPE_7_12**: 7x7 pattern with 12 surrounding pixels for corner detection.
  - **cv2.FAST_FEATURE_DETECTOR_TYPE_9_16**: 9x9 pattern with 16 surrounding pixels for corner detection - Default Value.
- **maxSuppressThreshold**: Maximum threshold for the suppression algorithm. Default value is 0.2.

Let us implement a FAST detector using OpenCV.

```
import cv2

image = cv2.imread(image.jpg')
gray = cv2.cvtColor(image, cv2.COLOR_BGR2GRAY)

# FAST detector object
fast = cv2.FastFeatureDetector_create()

# Detect keypoints using FAST
keypoints = fast.detect(gray, None)

# Draw detected keypoints on the image
image_with_keypoints = cv2.drawKeypoints(image, keypoints, None, color=(0, 255, 0))

cv2.imwrite(output.jpg', image_with_keypoints)
```

Following are the outputs for some of the images from the preceding codes:

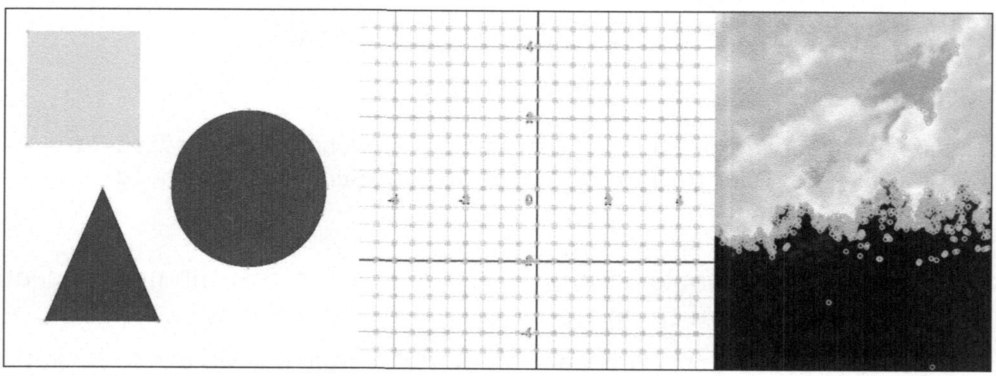

Figure 9.3: *Outputs of the FAST keypoint detector visualized on some images*

The code implements the FAST algorithm on the input image for keypoint detection. First, the images are loaded and converted into grayscale. Next, a fast detector object is created using the `cv2.FastFeatureDetector_create` function, as discussed earlier.

The `detect` method of the FAST detector object is then used to detect keypoint in an image. The method takes two arguments: the image and the mask. We pass our input image and leave the mask as blank.

cv2.drawKeypoints function is then used to draw the detected points on the image.

Harris Keypoint Detection

Harris corner detection is a popular algorithm used to identify keypoint locations in an image. It is based on the concept of corner points, which are areas where the image intensity changes significantly in multiple directions.

These corner points are considered distinctive features that can be used for various computer vision tasks, such as image matching and object recognition.

The Harris Keypoint Detector involves the following steps:

1. **Gradient Calculation**: An image gradient operator such as the Sobel operator is applied to compute image gradients orientation and magnitudes.
2. **Structure Tensor Calculation**: The structure tensor is generated by calculating the products of the gradients at each pixel and summing them over a local neighborhood. It provides information about the image's local structure and orientation.
3. **Corner Response Calculation**: The corner response is computed using the structure tensor. It measures the likelihood of a pixel being a corner point based on the variations in intensity and gradient direction. It is calculated using the eigenvalues of the structure tensor. High eigenvalues indicate corners, while low eigenvalues represent flat or edge regions.
4. **Non-Max Suppression**: To eliminate multiple corner responses in close proximity, non-maximum suppression is applied. This step ensures that only the strongest corner responses are selected as keypoints.

5. **Thresholding**: Finally, a threshold is applied to the corner responses to filter out weak corners. Only corners with response values above a certain threshold are considered as keypoints:

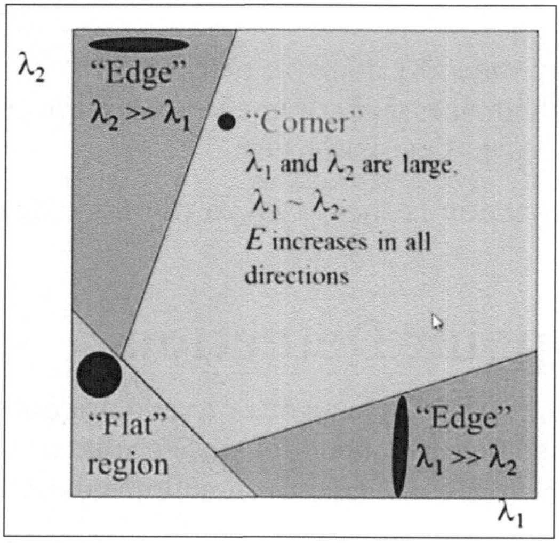

***Figure 9.4**: Thresholding for Harris Corner Detection. Img src:*
https://docs.opencv.org/3.4/dc/d0d/tutorial_py_features_harris.html

cv2.cornerHarris

Syntax:

```
cv2.cornerHarris(src, blockSize, ksize, k, borderType=cv2.BORDER_DEFAULT)
```

Parameters:

- **`src`**: Input Grayscale image.
- **`blockSize`**: Neighborhood size to be considered for corner detection. Commonly used values are 2, 3, or 5.
- **`ksize`**: It determines the size of the Sobel kernel for computing image derivatives. The value of **`ksize`** is typically taken as 3, which corresponds to a 3x3 Sobel kernel.
- **k**: The Harris detector free parameter. This parameter affects the sensitivity of the corner detection. Smaller values of k result in more corners being detected, while larger values make the detection stricter. It is a value in the range of [0.04, 0.06].

```
import cv2

image = cv2.imread('image.jpg')
gray = cv2.cvtColor(image, cv2.COLOR_BGR2GRAY)
```

```
# Harris corner detector parameters
block_size = 2
ksize = 3
k = 0.04

# Harris corner detection
corners = cv2.cornerHarris(gray, block_size, ksize, k)

# Threshold and mark the detected corners
threshold = 0.01 * corners.max()
marked_image = image.copy()
marked_image[corners > threshold] = [0, 0, 255]

cv2.imwrite(output.jpg', marked_image)
cv2.waitKey(0)
cv2.destroyAllWindows()
```

The output for this code is as follows:

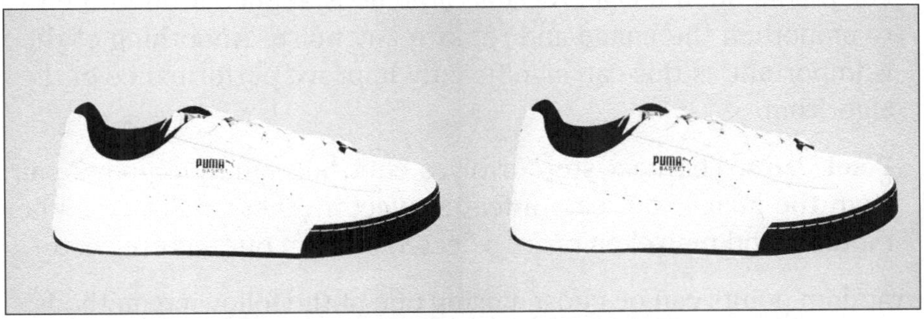

***Figure* 9.5**: *Harris keypoint detection input image with the output*

In the preceding code, we load our image and initialize parameters for the Harris keypoint detector. The code then performs thresholding on the corners array using a threshold vale calculated as 0.01 times the maximum value. Then, it creates a copy of the image and marks the pixels where corners are above the threshold by setting them to the color [0, 0, 255] (red).

BRIEF (Binary Robust Independent Elementary Features)

BRIEF is a binary descriptor used in computer vision for matching features of images. The algorithm focuses on describing key points or features such as corners or edges in an image.

The goal of BRIEF is to create a simple and compact representation of these features, known as descriptors, which can be compared and matched efficiently. BRIEF achieves this by comparing pairs of pixel intensities within a localized patch around each key point. The result of these comparisons is a binary code or string that represents the feature descriptor. This binary string captures the spatial relationships between the pixel pairs and encodes the distinctive characteristics of the feature.

BRIEF is a highly efficient binary descriptor since a small string can be used to describe the features, making the processing much simpler. BRIEF is, however, sensitive to image transformations such as rotation and scaling; thus, the algorithm is often used in conjunction with other algorithms such as SIFT or ORB.

The detailed steps involved in the BRIEF algorithm are as follows:

1. **Keypoints**: BRIEF uses keypoint detectors such as FAST to retrieve the key points of an image. A Gaussian blue is applied around the keypoint to smoothen the image and remove any noise. Smoothing of the image is important as this can significantly improve performance of the BRIEF algorithm.

2. **Pixel Pairs**: The next step involves choosing multiple points pairs (x,y) from the image to create a feature vector. These points are chosen at random, and n pixel pairs are selected to form our feature vector.

These random points can be chosen using one of the following methods:

- **Uniform Sampling**: In Uniform sampling, each pixel pair (x and y) is selected randomly and uniformly from the keypoint region without any specific pattern or bias.
- Gaussian Sampling: A Gaussian distribution is used to sample pixel pairs (both x and y) from the keypoint region. The pixel locations are chosen based on a Gaussian distribution centered around the keypoint. Pixels x and y are chosen using a Gaussian distribution with a standard deviation of 0.04 * N^2, where N represents the patch size, around the key point.
- **Gaussian Sampling (II)**: In this method, both points are sampled separately. The x-coordinate is sampled using a Gaussian distribution with a standard deviation of σ = 0.04 * N^2, where N represents the patch size. The y-coordinate is then sampled using a Gaussian distribution centered around the x-coordinate with a standard deviation of σ = 0.01 * N^2 In this method, both points are sampled separately. The x-coordinate is sampled using a Gaussian distribution with a standard deviation of σ = 0.04 * N^2, where N represents the patch size. The y-coordinate is then

sampled using a Gaussian distribution centered around the x-coordinate with a standard deviation of σ = 0.01 * N^2.

- **Coarse Polar Grid Sampling**: In this method, the x and y point locations are randomly sampled from a coarse polar grid, introducing spatial quantization. A coarse polar grid is like a grid of predefined circles and lines that help us pick specific points in a circular area around an object or point of interest. The grid represents discrete locations, and the sampling is performed within this grid structure.
- **Centered Polar Grid Sampling**: In this method, the x pixel is fixed at (0,0) and the y is sampled across a polar grid to cover all possible values.

3. **Intensity Comparison**: Now that we have n pixel pairs, the algorithm uses these pixel pairs to compare intensity values between them. In each pixel pair, the intensity value is extracted for each pixel and compared to the other pixel in the pair.

   Based on the intensity comparison results, we generate a binary string or descriptor. Each element of the binary descriptor corresponds to the result of a specific intensity comparison between the two patches. If the intensity at xi is greater than the intensity at yi, the corresponding element of the binary descriptor is set to 1; otherwise, it is set to 0.

   The end result is a vector consisting of 1s and 0s representing the output from the binary descriptor.

cv2.ORB_create

Syntax:

```
cv2.ORB_create(nfeatures=500, scaleFactor=1.2, nlevels=8, edgeThreshold=
31, firstLevel=0, WTA_K=2, scoreTypecv2.ORB_HARRIS_SCORE, patchSize=31,
fastThreshold=20)
```

Parameters:

- `nfeatures`: The maximum number of features to detect and retain in the image.
- `scaleFactor`: The ratio used for constructing the image pyramid. It determines the size of the image at each pyramid level.
- `nlevels`: The number of pyramid levels to use. More levels will detect more features but will increase the computational cost.
- `edgeThreshold`: The size of the border where features are not detected.
- `firstLevel`: The level of the pyramid at which to put the source image.

Setting it to 0 means the original image is used at the first level.

- **WTA_K**: The number of points that contribute to each element of the oriented BRIEF descriptor.
- **scoreType**: The score type used by ORB. It can be either **cv2.ORB_HARRIS_SCORE** or **cv2.ORB_FAST_SCORE**. The former indicates the Harris corner score is used, while the latter approximates the BRIEF descriptor behavior.
- **patchSize**: The neighborhood around each keypoint used for descriptor computation.
- **fastThreshold**: The threshold used by the FAST algorithm.

Let us try to use a BRIEF detector with some code. In this code, we will be taking two images. The second image will be a cropped-out part of the first image. We will use the BRIEF detector to perform feature matching on the two images and check if the features are being able to correctly match by the algorithm:

```
import cv2

image1 = cv2.imread('dog.jpg', cv2.IMREAD_GRAYSCALE)
image2 = cv2.imread('dog2.jpg', cv2.IMREAD_GRAYSCALE)

# Initialize the ORB detector
orb = cv2.ORB_create()

# Set the ORB score type to BRIEF
orb.setScoreType(cv2.ORB_FAST_SCORE)

# Detect keypoints and compute descriptors using ORB
keypoints1, descriptors1 = orb.detectAndCompute(image1, None)
keypoints2, descriptors2 = orb.detectAndCompute(image2, None)

# Create a BFMatcher object
matcher = cv2.BFMatcher(cv2.NORM_HAMMING, crossCheck=True)

# Match descriptors
matches = matcher.match(descriptors1, descriptors2)

# Sort matches by score
matches = sorted(matches, key=lambda x: x.distance)

# Draw top matches
matched_image = cv2.drawMatches(image1, keypoints1, image2, keypoints2,
matches[:10], None, flags=cv2.DrawMatchesFlags_NOT_DRAW_SINGLE_POINTS)

cv2.imwrite('brief.jpg', matched_image)
```

```
cv2.waitKey(0)
cv2.destroyAllWindows()
```

The code produces the following output:

Figure 9.6: BRIEF *feature matching output (we can observe that the algorithm has been able to match similar features together)*

The code loads the two images and initializes the descriptor.

The method **`setScoreType(cv2.ORB_FAST_SCORE)`** sets the score type of the ORB (Oriented FAST and Rotated BRIEF) feature detector to prioritize speed and efficiency during keypoint detection.

The **`orb.detectAndCompute(image, mask)`** method detects keypoints and computes their descriptors using the ORB (Oriented FAST and Rotated BRIEF) algorithm (explained in detail below) for the provided **`image1`** without specifying a mask.

cv2.BFMatcher is a class in OpenCV that represents the Brute-Force Matcher. It is a simple matcher that compares every descriptor from one set to every descriptor from another set and finds the best matches based on a specified distance measurement. We use hamming distance to compare distances and use the **`crossCheck=True`** flag to perform cross-checking when matching descriptors. We initialize the object and pass our descriptor values to the 'match' method of this object, which returns the best matches between the descriptors.

We then sort these matches based on the distance and use the function **`cv2.drawMatches`** to visualize these on the image.

ORB (Oriented FAST and Rotated BRIEF)

ORB is a feature detection and description algorithm that combines the FAST algorithm for keypoint detection and the BRIEF algorithm for feature description.

The steps involved in using the ORB algorithm are as follows:

1. **Keypoint Detection**: The algorithm first uses the FAST algorithm to detect key points in an image.

   After applying the FAST algorithm to identify potential keypoints, ORB applies the Harris corner measure to evaluate the quality of each detected corner. The Harris corner measure assesses the local image structure around each corner candidate and assigns a score based on the corner's uniqueness and saliency. ORB then selects the top N points with the highest scores among the corner candidates, ensuring that only the most relevant keypoints are retained for further processing.

   Additionally, a pyramid approach is used to generate key points at multiple scales, enabling the detection of keypoints across different levels of image details.

2. **Orientation Assignment**: This step is introduced to add rotational invariance to the algorithm. This step computes the intensity weighted centroid of the patch with the located corner at the center. By determining the direction of the vector from this corner point to the centroid, the orientation of the keypoint is established.

   Moreover, moments are computed using the x and y coordinates within a circular region of radius r, which corresponds to the size of the patch.

3. **BRIEF Descriptor**: Once the orientations are assigned, the BRIEF descriptor computation takes place. As discussed earlier, in the BRIEF descriptor, random pixel pairs within the patch centered at each keypoint are selected, and the intensities of these pairs are compared. The result is a binary descriptor that captures the local image features around the keypoints.

By combining the FAST keypoint detection algorithm for finding keypoints, the orientation assignment step, and the subsequent computation of the BRIEF descriptor, ORB achieves a comprehensive feature detection and description pipeline. This allows for reliable and efficient matching of keypoints in images, making ORB a popular choice for various computer vision applications.

The following code uses the ORB algorithm to detect and draw keypoints on an image:

```
import cv2

image = cv2.imread('image.jpg', cv2.IMREAD_GRAYSCALE)

# Initialize ORB detector
orb = cv2.ORB_create()

# Detect keypoints and compute descriptors
keypoints, descriptors = orb.detectAndCompute(image, None)

# Draw keypoints on the image
image_with_keypoints = cv2.drawKeypoints(image, keypoints, None, flags=0)

cv2.imwrite('orb.jpg', image_with_keypoints)
cv2.waitKey(0)
cv2.destroyAllWindows()
```

The output for this code is as follows:

Figure 9.7: *Keypoint detection output using ORB algorithm*

SIFT (Scale-Invariant Feature Transform)

SIFT is a widely used feature detection and description algorithm used in computer vision and image processing. SIFT is a local invariant descriptor, implying that it describes local image features that are invariant to changes in image transformations such as rotation and image scaling.

The SIFT algorithm is also robust to changes in lighting and can handle noise and the occlusions in an image, making it a popular algorithm to be used for various applications such as object recognition, image matching, and image stitching amongst many others.

The SIFT algorithm works by following the given steps:

1. **Scale-Space Extrema Detection**: The SIFT algorithm starts by creating a scale space pyramid. The scale space pyramid is a series of images obtained by applying Gaussian blurring and downsampling repeatedly, effectively capturing the image at different scales:

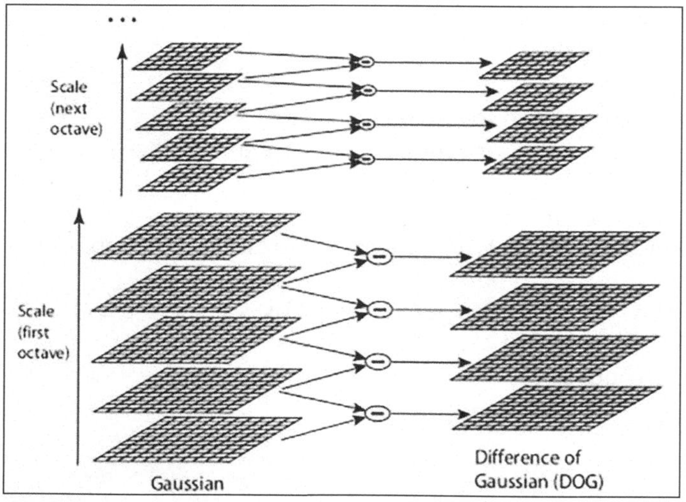

***Figure 9.8**: Difference of Gaussian used in the SIFT algorithm. Img src:* https://docs.opencv.org/4.x/da/df5/tutorial_py_sift_intro.html

   The **Difference of Gaussian (DoG)** pyramid is constructed by taking the difference of adjacent scale images from the pyramid. This pyramid highlights the areas with significant intensity changes in an image, representing the significant key points in an image.

   A pixel in an image is compared to its neighboring 8 points and 9 points each from the previous and the next scales. Keypoint candidates are identified as local extrema in the DoG pyramid, where a pixel has a higher or lower intensity compared to its neighboring pixels in both scale and space.

2. **Keypoint Localization**: Once the potential keypoints are found, they need to be refined to ensure only the stable key points remain in our image.

   The keypoints are refined by fitting a quadratic function to the nearby DoG samples, which helps to increase the accuracy of the keypoint positions.

The process starts by considering each potential keypoint and defining a local neighborhood around it. Within this region, SIFT fits a quadratic function to understand how the brightness and changes in brightness occur. This curve allows SIFT to pinpoint the precise location of the keypoint, even if it falls between two pixels, increasing accuracy.

Additionally, keypoints with low contrast or located on edges are eliminated to ensure that only distinctive and stable keypoints are retained.

3. **Orientation Assignment**: Now an orientation is assigned to each keypoint in the image to achieve rotational invariance.

   To do this, a neighborhood is taken around the keypoint and gradient magnitudes and orientations are computed. SIFT constructs a histogram to capture the distribution of gradient orientations within the neighborhood. SIFT observes which direction changes happen (like getting brighter or darker) and how much they change in that direction.

   It creates a special chart with 36 bars representing all the possible directions in a full circle (360 degrees). An orientation histogram with 36 bins covering 360 degrees is created.

   The highest peak in the histogram indicates the most common orientation. SIFT selects that direction as the orientation for the keypoint.

4. **Keypoint Descriptor**: A descriptor is now created to describe each keypoint to capture its local appearance. A 16x16 neighborhood around the keypoint is considered and the area is divided into 16 sub-blocks of 4×4 size:

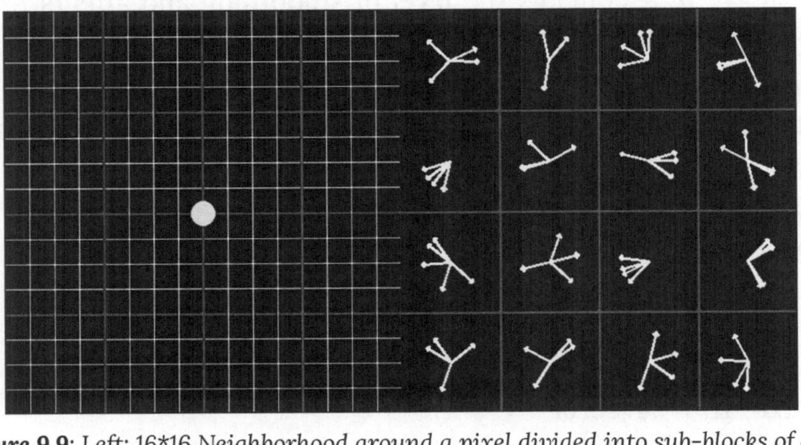

Figure 9.9: *Left: 16*16 Neighborhood around a pixel divided into sub-blocks of 4x4. Right: Gradient representation of each sub-block*

For each subregion, SIFT calculates gradient orientations and magnitudes. These gradient values are then weighted by a Gaussian function centered at the keypoint location. The 16 histograms of 8 bins each are then concatenated to form a 128-dimensional feature vector. This vector is then normalized to improve its robustness to changes in illuminations and contrast.

Output: This 128 feature vector can now be used for applications such as image matching by comparing it to other SIFT vectors.

cv2.SIFT_create

Syntax:

```
cv2.SIFT_create(nfeatures=0, nOctaveLayers=3, contrastThreshold=0.04,
edgeThreshold=10, sigma=1.6)
```

Parameters:

- `nfeatures`: The maximum number of keypoints/features to detect and retain in the image.
- `nOctaveLayers`: The number of layers per octave in the scale space. More layers allow for more precise scale variations to be captured while also increasing the computation time.
- `contrastThreshold`: Minimum contrast between a keypoint and its surrounding region for it to be retained as a feature. Lower values may result in more keypoints being detected.
- `edgeThreshold`: The minimum edge threshold. Keypoints with edge responses above this threshold are retained.
- `sigma`: The sigma value for Gaussian filtering applied to the input image at octave 0. It controls the level of smoothing and affects the scale of detected features.

We will be using SIFT to match features of two images. Just like BRIEF, we will use the same image set, which will help us to verify how our descriptor is performing:

```
import cv2
import numpy as np

image1 = cv2.imread('dog.jpg', cv2.IMREAD_GRAYSCALE)
image2 = cv2.imread('dog2.jpg', cv2.IMREAD_GRAYSCALE)

# Initialize SIFT detector
sift = cv2.SIFT_create()
```

```
# Detect keypoints and compute descriptors
keypoints1, descriptors1 = sift.detectAndCompute(image1, None)
keypoints2, descriptors2 = sift.detectAndCompute(image2, None)

# Create a BFMatcher object
matcher = cv2.BFMatcher()

# Match descriptors
matches = matcher.knnMatch(descriptors1, descriptors2, k=2)

# Apply ratio test to filter good matches
good_matches = []
for m, n in matches:
    if m.distance < 0.75 * n.distance:
        good_matches.append(m)


# Draw matches
matched_image = cv2.drawMatches(image1, keypoints1, image2, keypoints2,
good_matches, None, flags=cv2.DrawMatchesFlags_NOT_DRAW_SINGLE_POINTS)

# Display the matched image
cv2.imwrite(output.jpg', matched_image)
cv2.waitKey(0)
cv2.destroyAllWindows()
```

The output for the code is as follows:

Figure 9.10: *Feature matching output using the SIFT algorithm. Left: All the features are visualized. Right: Few features only are displayed for better visualization.*

In this code, we initialize our SIFT descriptor object and use the **`detectAndCompute(image, mask)`** to extract keypoint and descriptors for both of our images.

We then create a brute force matcher object and use the **knnMatch** method to perform k-nearest neighbor matching between descriptors1 and descriptors2, with k set to 2. The **knnMatch** method computes the k-best matches for each descriptor in descriptors1 by comparing them to the descriptors in **descriptors2**. In this case, as k is set to 2, the method returns the two best matches for each descriptor.

We then apply a small logic to filter good matches. The code iterates over each pair of matches (m, n) in the matches list. It selects only the matches where the distance of the first match m is less than 0.75 times the distance of the second match n.

These matches are then visualized using **cv2.drawMatches** function. For better understanding and comparison, an additional output showing only ten matches has been generated.

RootSIFT (Root Scale-Invariant Feature Transform)

RootSIFT is a variation of the SIFT algorithm that enhances the original SIFT descriptor by applying an additional normalization step.

In the SIFT algorithm, we saw that the final descriptor is created by taking the gradient magnitudes and orientations in the image. However, the gradients can sometimes vary in different images overall affecting the performance of the algorithm. To address this issue, RootSIFT takes the square root of the gradient magnitudes overall, reducing the effect of large gradient magnitudes on the output.

The final vector is then normalized for introducing intensity invariance and can now be used for various computer vision applications:

```
import cv2
import numpy as np

image1 = cv2.imread('2211.jpg', cv2.IMREAD_GRAYSCALE)
image2 = cv2.imread('22.jpg', cv2.IMREAD_GRAYSCALE)


# Rotate image

angle = 45

rows, cols = image1.shape[:2]

rotation_matrix = cv2.getRotationMatrix2D((cols / 2, rows / 2), angle, 1)
```

```
rotated_image = cv2.warpAffine(image1, rotation_matrix, (cols, rows))
image1 = rotated_image.copy()

# Initialize the SIFT detector
sift = cv2.SIFT_create()

# Detect keypoints and compute descriptors
keypoints1, descriptors1 = sift.detectAndCompute(image1, None)
keypoints2, descriptors2 = sift.detectAndCompute(image2, None)

# Compute RootSIFT descriptors
epsilon = 1e-7  # Small constant to avoid division by zero
descriptors1 /= (descriptors1.sum(axis=1, keepdims=True) + epsilon)
descriptors1 = np.sqrt(descriptors1)

descriptors2 /= (descriptors2.sum(axis=1, keepdims=True) + epsilon)
descriptors2 = np.sqrt(descriptors2)

# Create a BFMatcher object
matcher = cv2.BFMatcher()

# Match descriptors
matches = matcher.knnMatch(descriptors1, descriptors2, k=2)

# Filter good matches
good_matches = []
for m, n in matches:
    if m.distance < 0.75 * n.distance:
        good_matches.append(m)

good_matches = good_matches[:15]

# Draw matches
matched_image = cv2.drawMatches(image1, keypoints1, image2, keypoints2,
good_matches, None, flags=cv2.DrawMatchesFlags_NOT_DRAW_SINGLE_POINTS)

cv2.imwrite('root2.jpg', matched_image)
cv2.waitKey(0)
cv2.destroyAllWindows()
```

Output:

***Figure 9.11**: Feature matching output using the RootSIFT algorithm on a rotated image. Top: All the features are visualized. Bottom: Few features only are displayed for better visualization*

The code uses RootSIFT to compare features in two images. This time we take the second image with rotation to check our algorithm invariant to rotation. The code is similar to the code of the SIFT algorithm; however, as specified for the RootSIFT algorithm, we take the square root of the gradient magnitudes overall.

SURF (Speeded-Up Robust Features)

SURF is another feature detection and description algorithm used in computer vision and image processing. SURF is an alternative to the SIFT algorithm, which provides a faster computation and requires less space than the SIFT algorithm, while also maintains the important properties of the SIFT algorithm such as scale and rotational invariance.

Both SIFT and SURF use common steps similar to each other but also differ in some ways such as methods used for localization, orientations assignment, and descriptor generation. SURF focuses on speed and efficiency by using approximations and efficient computations, while SIFT provides more robustness at the cost of higher computational complexity.

1. **Scale-Space Extrema Detection**: SURF also creates a Difference of Gaussian pyramid. In SURF, this involves using box filters that are applied to the input image at multiple scales to create a series of blurred and downsampled images.

The DoG pyramid is then constructed by taking the difference between adjacent blurred and downsampled images effectively, highlighting the areas with significant intensity changes and thus using local extrema to detect keypoints:

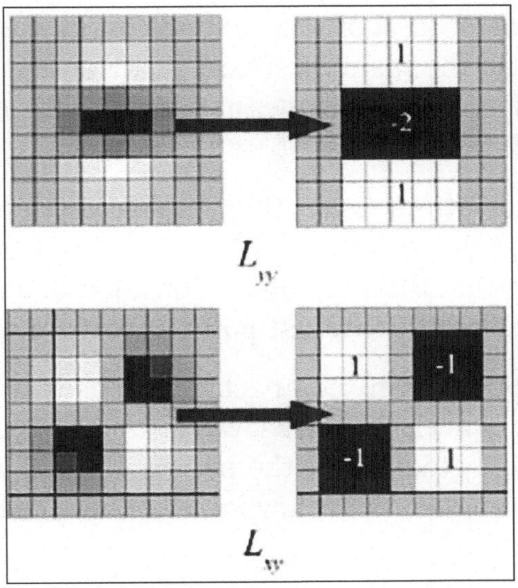

Figure 9.12: *Hessian Matrix for SURF algorithm.*
Img Src: https://docs.opencv.org/3.4/df/dd2/tutorial_py_surf_intro.html

2. **Keypoint Localization**: Similar to SIFT, precise location of keypoints need to be determined to increase performance of the algorithm.

   SURF uses the concept of Hessian matrix to determine the keypoint location. The Hessian matrix represents the second-order derivatives of the image intensities, which helps understand how the brightness changes in the image. By analyzing the Hessian matrix, SURF finds the exact spot for the keypoint that gives the strongest or weakest response in the image.

   SURF eliminates low-intensity key points by looking at the Hessian matrix again and checking how much the brightness changes around each keypoint. If the change is too small, SURF removes that keypoint because it might not be very useful.

3. **Orientation Assignment**: To determine the dominant orientation, SURF utilizes Haar wavelets. Haar wavelets are simple mathematical functions that can efficiently analyze the image's local structure. Gaussian weights are applied to enhance the accuracy of orientation estimation. The

weighted wavelet responses are plotted in a specialized space, revealing the distribution of gradient orientations.

The size of this neighborhood is determined based on a scaling factor, denoted as 6s, where 's' represents the scale of the keypoint. The size of the area that SURF looks at depends on how big or small the object is. To determine the main direction, SURF adds up the details within a 60-degree range. Integral images are used to efficiently compute wavelet responses at different scales.

4. **Keypoint Description**: Once the dominant orientation is assigned to each keypoint, SURF proceeds to extract a descriptor for the keypoint. A local region around the keypoint is considered, and a set of rectangular sub-regions, called the **interest point** or **feature window**, is defined.

To make this description more compact, SURF uses a special mathematical function called **Haar wavelets**. These wavelets help capture the important features of the image. By looking at the patterns in different directions, SURF creates a vector that represents the keypoint's unique characteristics:

```
import cv2

image = cv2.imread('image.jpg', cv2.IMREAD_COLOR)
gray = cv2.cvtColor(image, cv2.COLOR_BGR2GRAY)

# Initialize the SURF detector and descriptor
surf = cv2.SURF_create()

# Detect keypoints and compute descriptors
keypoints, descriptors = surf.detectAndCompute(gray, None)

# Get the total number of keypoints
num_keypoints = len(keypoints)

# Print the number of keypoints
print("Number of keypoints:", num_keypoints)

# Print the size of the descriptors
descriptor_size = descriptors.shape[1]
print("Descriptor size:", descriptor_size)
```

Local Binary Patterns

Local Binary Patterns is a texture descriptor that describes the local features of an image by comparing the intensity of a pixel by its neighboring pixels.

A binary pattern is created based on the comparisons of the central pixels with its neighboring pixels. Each bit in this pattern represents whether a particular neighboring pixel is higher or lower in value compared to the central pixel in consideration. The local pattern is then described by encoding this binary pattern value into a decimal image.

A histogram is then constructed of these patterns, which effectively summarizes the texture information contained in these images.

The algorithm is invariant to changes in light and another major advantage of this algorithm is that it is computationally inexpensive, making it simple to implement as it only involves only calculating the intensities of the image and comparing it to neighboring values.

The detailed steps required to implement local binary patterns are as follows:

1. **Grayscale Conversion**: The first step in calculating local binary patterns is converting our image into grayscale. Since we only need the texture information from our images, color values are not required, and we can convert our image to grayscale. Grayscale values containing values representing only the brightness of a pixel and LBPs work on these intensity values to capture local information.
2. **Pixel Neighborhood**: For each pixel in the grayscale image, a circular neighborhood of pixels around the center pixel in consideration is defined. The radius for the neighbor pixels around the center pixels is also defined. A circular boundary from the center pixel of the decided radius is drawn and the points lying on this circle will be in consideration for the algorithm:

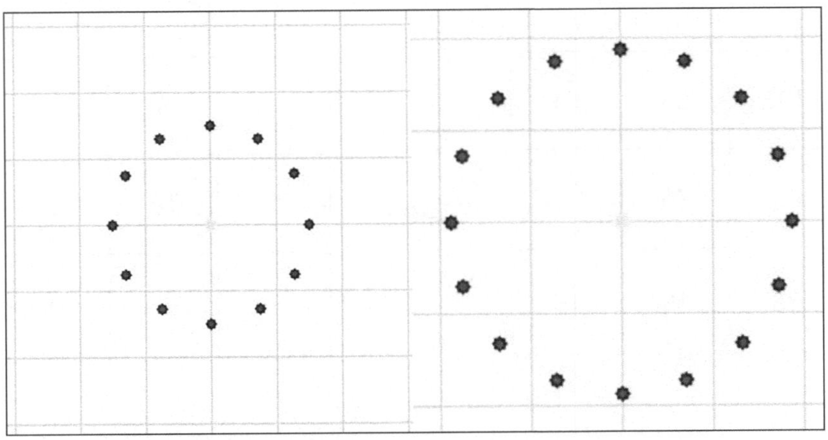

Figure 9.13: *Examples of circular boundaries drawn center point and the number of pixels in consideration*

The number of pixels and their distance from the center pixel determines the pixel neighborhood to be considered for the local binary pattern algorithm. A smaller radius focuses on capturing fine-grained local patterns, while a larger radius considers a broader region surrounding the pixel. The choice of the neighborhood size is also important as it balances the level of detail and computational complexity. A larger neighborhood includes more neighboring pixels and captures broader contextual information, while a smaller neighborhood focuses on localized patterns.

3. **Pixel Comparison**: Now that we have defined the neighborhood, we can start performing some operations using the chosen points.

   From the chosen neighborhood pixels, we compare each pixel's intensity value with the intensity of the center pixel. This comparison is done by applying a simple thresholding process. If the intensity of the neighboring pixel is greater than or equal to the intensity of the central pixel, it is assigned a value of 1. On the other hand, if the neighboring pixel's intensity is lower than the central pixel's intensity, it is assigned a value of 0.

   This process is repeated for all the pixels in the neighborhood and a binary pattern is obtained. Each bit in the binary pattern represents a specific pixel in the neighborhood and indicates whether its intensity is lower or higher. The overall binary pattern indicates the local texture or intensity variations with respect to the center pixel in consideration, providing a compact representation of the pixel neighborhood's intensity relationships.

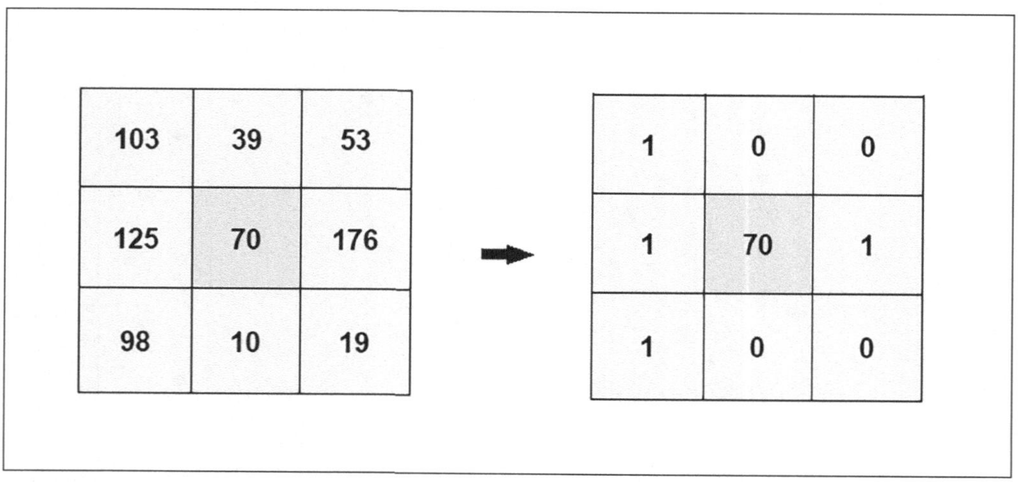

Figure 9.14: *Binary values assigned to each pixel based on comparison with center pixel*

Note: Binary patterns obtained here can be of two types: Uniform and non-uniform binary patterns.

A uniform binary pattern is a pattern that contains at most two bitwise transitions (0 to 1 or 1 to 0) when reading the pattern in a circular manner. It contains at most two 0-1 or 1-0 transitions when reading the binary pattern in a circular order. A binary pattern that does not meet this criterion is called a non-uniform binary pattern and contains more than two 0-1 or 1-0 transitions.

The need for categorizing our binary pattern arises because uniform binary patterns represent well-defined texture structures such as edges and corners and can be used for appropriate use cases. Non-uniform binary patterns on the other hand contain more complex variations in the textures and can be used when we need more fine-grained details and irregular texture details from the image.

4. **Pattern Encoding**: The binary pattern obtained from the previous step is now encoded into a decimal value. The binary pattern is treated as a binary number and corresponding values are converted from 0's and 1's into the decimal form. This value is then assigned to the center pixel:

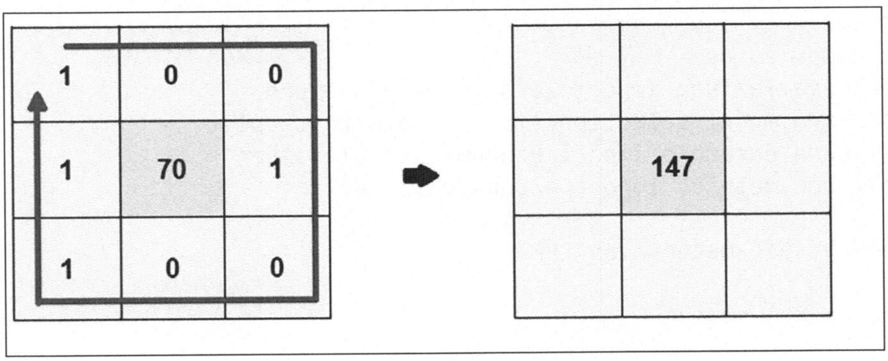

Figure 9.15: *Decimal value of the binary pattern assigned to the center pixel.*

For example, a value of 10010011 will be converted to 147 in decimal form.

5. **Histogram**: After obtaining the local binary values from the image, we will use these values to create a histogram. The histogram captures the number of occurrences of each pattern in the image. The histogram serves as a texture descriptor and summarizes the spatial distribution of local texture patterns present in the image.

To construct the histogram, we first consider each unique binary pattern as a bin, and the frequency of its occurrence is counted across the entire image. A histogram is created using all the values and represents the distribution of local textures in an image. Bins with higher counts indicate more prevalent patterns, while bins with lower counts represent less frequent patterns.

It is important to keep in mind that creating histograms using 256 bins will eliminate all the spatial information from the image. Each pixel's LBP code is treated as an independent feature and assigned to a specific bin in the histogram based on its pattern. As a result, the spatial information, such as the arrangement of patterns in the image or their spatial context, is not preserved.

To address this and retain spatial information, alternative approaches such as dividing the image into regions or using a sliding window/grid-based approach can be employed. One of the ways to do this is to divide our image into a grid and create a histogram using values for each cell in the block. This will help preserve the spatial information and capture the local texture variations within different regions of the image.

In the following code, we will be creating a classifier using LBP features. We will be using three types of images of different textures for our classification code:

```
import cv2
import numpy as np
from skimage.feature import local_binary_pattern
from sklearn.model_selection import train_test_split
from sklearn.ensemble import RandomForestClassifier
from sklearn.metrics import accuracy_score

# Define the parameters for LBP
radius = 3
n_points = 8 * radius

# Initialize lists to store features and labels
features = []
labels = []

# Iterate through the folders
folder_paths = ['line',  'dotted','honey']
for folder_path in folder_paths:
    class_label = folder_path.split('/')[-1]

    for image_name in os.listdir(folder_path):
        image_path = os.path.join(folder_path, image_name)
```

```
        image = cv2.imread(image_path, cv2.IMREAD_GRAYSCALE)

        # Compute LBP features
        lbp = local_binary_pattern(image, n_points, radius)

        # Calculate histogram of LBP features
        hist, _ = np.histogram(lbp.ravel(), bins=n_points+3, range=(0,
n_points+2))

        # Append the features and labels
        features.append(hist)
        labels.append(class_label)

# Convert features and labels to numpy arrays
features = np.array(features)
labels = np.array(labels)

# Split the data into training and testing sets
X_train, X_test, y_train, y_test = train_test_split(features, labels,
test_size=0.2)

# Initialize and train the Random Forest classifier
random_forest = RandomForestClassifier(n_estimators=300)
random_forest.fit(X_train, y_train)

# Make predictions on the test data
y_pred = random_forest.predict(X_test)

# Calculate accuracy
accuracy = accuracy_score(y_test, y_pred)
print("Accuracy:", accuracy)


def predict_image_class(image_path):

    image = cv2.imread(image_path, cv2.IMREAD_GRAYSCALE)

    # Compute LBP features
    lbp = local_binary_pattern(image, n_points, radius)

    # Calculate histogram of LBP features
    hist, _ = np.histogram(lbp.ravel(), bins=n_points+3, range=(0, n_
points+2))

    # Reshape the feature vector to match the input shape of the classifier
    feature_vector = hist.reshape(1, -1)
```

```
    # Predict image class
    predicted_class = random_forest.predict(feature_vector)[0]

    # Draw predicted label on the image
    image_with_text = cv2.putText(image.copy(), predicted_class, (10,
30), cv2.FONT_HERSHEY_SIMPLEX, 1, (255, 255, 255), 2, cv2.LINE_AA)

    # Display the image with the predicted label
    cv2.imshow('Image with Predicted Class', image_with_text)
    cv2.waitKey(0)
    cv2.destroyAllWindows()

predict_image_class("line/banded_0002.jpg")
```

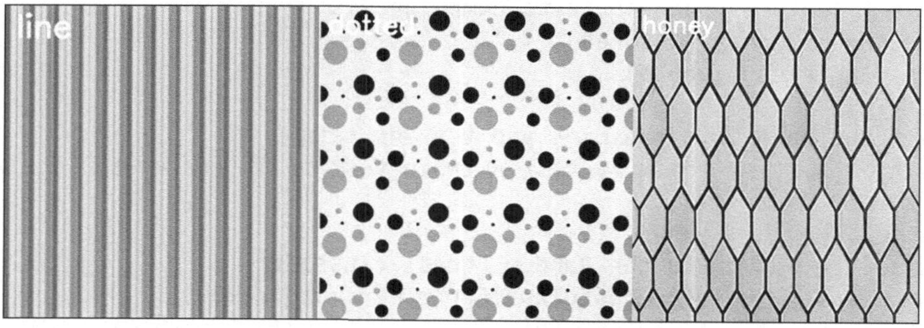

Figure 9.16: *Output of image classifier using Local Binary Patterns (the algorithm has been able to correctly classify the images to their respective classes)*

In this code, we use Local Binary Pattern features to create a classifier for our images. First, the code reads a set of images from different folders, where each folder represents a different class of a specific texture.

For each image, the code computes Local Binary Pattern (LBP) features using the **local_binary_pattern** function of the scikit-image library, which captures texture information. We specify the number of points and the radius to be considered for calculating LBPs.

After computing the Local Binary Pattern (LBP) features for each image, the code calculates a histogram of the LBP features. This histogram represents the distribution of different LBP patterns in the image, providing a compact representation of the texture information.

We then append these features along with their corresponding labels and split this dataset into train and test sets to train our RandomForestClassifier. The histogram is used as the feature vector for training the Random Forest classifier, capturing the characteristic texture patterns of each class in a condensed form.

The trained classifier is used to predict the class of a new input image specified by **`image_path`**. The image is then visualized along with the predicted label.

Histogram of Oriented Gradients

Histogram is a commonly used and a powerful feature descriptor often used in computer vision and image processing applications. Histogram of Oriented Gradients (HoG) works to capture the shape of the objects in an image.

Histograms of Oriented Gradients work on the principle that the intensity gradients can be used to describe the appearance and shape of the local object. This allows them to be useful for applications such as object detection or classification. HoG's make for good texture detectors because they are able to capture local intensity variations in an image and this can also be used for applications such as edge detection.

Histogram of Oriented Gradients describes an object based on the changes in local gradients in an image. As you might recall from earlier chapters, gradients in an image are used to describe change in pixel intensities in an image. HoG works by capturing the shape and structure of objects by measuring the magnitude and directions of gradients in an image.

Histogram of Oriented Gradients algorithm works by using a sliding window on the image. It works by moving the window across the image and calculating the gradients for each region. A histogram is then created on these image gradients capturing the local information from each cell. Blocks are formed by combining the nearby cells, and the histograms for underlying cells are concatenated. Normalization techniques are then used to handle light variations in the image.

The detailed steps for Histogram of Oriented Gradients are as follows:

1. **Image Preprocessing**: Processing an image before calculating gradients helps improve performance of the algorithm. As, we are working on image gradients, the image can be converted into grayscale since we do not require colors. Additional normalization techniques can then be used for further processing.

   One common technique used for normalization is gamma correction. Gamma correction is used to adjust the brightness or contrast of an image and is useful for correcting image intensities affected by lighting conditions. This helps to enhance the visibility of gradients, overall improving the performance of our feature descriptor.

Gamma correction can be applied by using the given formula. The choice of γ depends on the specific requirements of the use case. Common values for γ range between 0.5 and 2.0, with 1.0 representing no gamma correction.

Another technique that can be used is contrast normalization. Contrast normalization is a preprocessing technique that increases the dynamic range of an image by spreading out the intensity values over a wider range. One of the ways of achieving contrast normalization is called linear stretching, which is also known as min-max normalization, we have discussed in earlier chapters. Another way of achieving contrast normalization is using histogram equalization, which also has been a part of our discussion earlier in the course.

2. **Gradient Computation**: After preprocessing, we can use the image for computing gradients. We can use various filters such as Sobel or Scharr to compute the gradients in an image. The gradient magnitudes and directions are computed horizontally and vertically for the image:

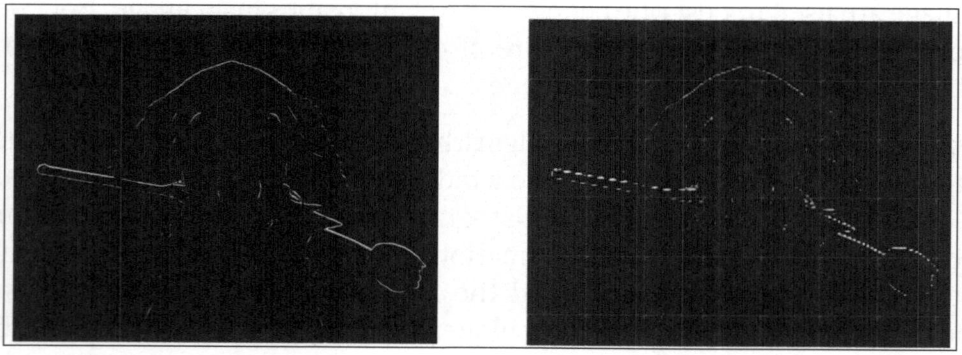

Figure 9.17: *Left: Gradient Image, Right: Gradient Image divided into equal cells*

3. **Histogram Calculation**: The gradient image is then used to compute histograms for our algorithm. We divide our gradient image into cells for calculating histograms. The image is divided into cells of a fixed size such as 4*4 or 8*8, the number of bins is decided, and the respective histogram is constructed for each cell in the image.

   Since we are creating histograms on the gradient image, the histogram bins represent gradient orientations. So, as an example, one bin might represent gradients oriented from 0 to 20 degrees, another bin from 20 to 40 degrees, and so on. The gradient magnitude will be used to compute the contribution of each gradient orientation to the histogram.

4. **Block Normalization**: One of the salient features of HoG's is their ability to work reliably under various light and illumination conditions. In this step, we take a certain amount of neighboring cells and combine them to form blocks in the image.

   Blocks are constructed such that there is some overlap in the cells constituting each block. This helps capture the spatial information and increases the overall contribution of the cell in the final result. Histograms for each constituting cell are concatenated, effectively producing a block histogram. This is done for each block in the image:

   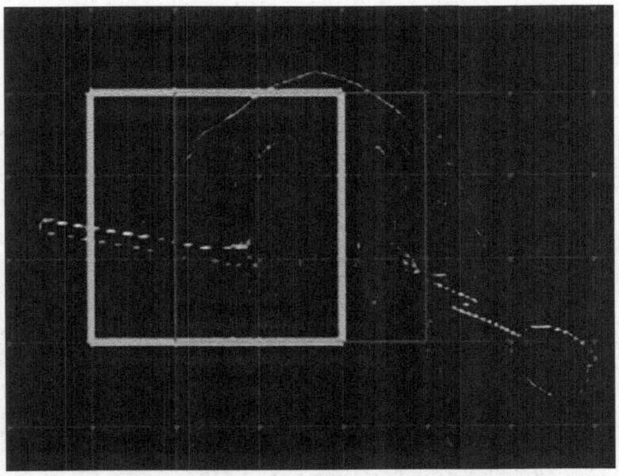

   ***Figure 9.18**: Blocks by combining cells (the green and blue boxes represent a block each of 4 cells, also indicating that certain cells in both blocks are overlapping)*

   We then again perform some type of normalization such as L1 or L2 on these blocks to ensure robustness to lighting changes in the image.

5. **HOG Descriptor**: The final step involves forming the HOG descriptor by concatenating the normalized block histograms. The resulting HOG descriptor is a high-dimensional feature vector that encodes the local gradient information of the image.

   The length of our output will depend on the various parameters we chose during the algorithm such as the number of cells, the block size, and the number of bins or gradient orientations used in the histogram.

   By quantizing gradients into histograms, normalizing blocks of histograms, and concatenating them into a final feature vector, the HOG descriptor captures the local structure and is robust to variations in lighting, contrast, and viewpoint:

```
import cv2
from skimage.feature import hog
```

```
from skimage import exposure

image = cv2.imread('dog.jpg', cv2.IMREAD_GRAYSCALE)

# Compute HOG features
hog_features, hog_image = hog(image, visualize=True)

# Display the HOG image
hog_image = exposure.rescale_intensity(hog_image, out_range=(0,
255))
hog_image = hog_image.astype("uint8")
cv2.imshow("HOG Image", hog_image)
cv2.waitKey(0)
cv2.destroyAllWindows()
```

Figure 9.19: *HOG features of the image*

In the code, the **hog** function from **skimage.feature** is applied to compute the HOG features of the image.

The resulting HOG features are then visualized by rescaling the intensity using **exposure.rescale_intensity** to enhance the visibility of the gradients. The **exposure.rescale_intensity** function is used to enhance the contrast and visibility of the HOG image. The HOG features represent the gradients of the image, which can vary in intensity. By rescaling the intensity values to the full 8-bit intensity range (0-255), it ensures that the full range of intensities is effectively utilized, leading to a more visually informative representation of the HOG features.

These HoG features can now be used for various computer vision applications.

Conclusion

In this chapter, we learnt about different methods for detecting and describing local features in images. We explored how keypoint detectors, such as FAST, Harris, SIFT, and SURF, can find distinctive and salient points in images. We also learned how descriptors, such as BRIEF, ORB, RootSIFT, Local Binary Patterns, and Histogram of Oriented Gradients, can represent the local appearance and shape of the keypoints. You should now be able to apply these methods to your own images and understand their advantages and limitations.

In the next chapter, we will dive into the fascinating world of neural networks, one of the most powerful and popular techniques in machine learning and computer vision. We will learn what a neural network is, how it works, and what are the different types of neural networks. We will also learn about the basic components of a neural network, such as layers, loss functions, activation functions, and metrics. We will also explore some of the challenges and best practices in working with neural networks, such as overfitting, regularization, and optimization.

Points to Remember

- The FAST keypoint detector is a high-speed algorithm that efficiently detects distinctive keypoints by evaluating corner responses in an image.
- BRIEF is a feature descriptor that represents keypoints using binary strings, enabling efficient matching and recognition in computer vision tasks.
- ORB is a fusion of the FAST keypoint detector and the BRIEF descriptor, offering robustness to rotational changes and real-time performance.
- SIFT is used to extract and describe key points. It is invariant to changes in scale, rotation, and affine transformations, effectively enabling robust feature matching.
- RootSIFT is a modification of SIFT that applies square root normalization to SIFT descriptors, which enhances their discriminative power.
- SURF is a feature detector and descriptor that captures interest points using image derivatives and approximations, enabling efficient and robust image recognition.
- Local Binary Patterns are texture descriptors that encode local image patterns by comparing pixel intensities with neighboring pixels.
- Histogram of Oriented Gradients is a feature descriptor that calculates the distribution of gradient orientations in an image, providing a robust representation for analyzing local image structures and patterns.

Test Your Understanding

1. The FAST algorithm works by:

   A. Evaluating corner responses in an image

   B. Calculating the distribution of gradient orientations

   C. Comparing pixel intensities with neighboring pixels

   D. Capturing local image patterns using image derivatives

2. Which of the following is not a method used to choose pixel pairs in BRIEF?

   A. Random Selection

   B. Uniform Sampling

   C. Gaussian Sampling

   D. Probability Sampling

3. Which of the following statements is true about SIFT (Scale-Invariant Feature Transform)?

   A. SIFT is a corner detection algorithm

   B. SIFT is only applicable to grayscale images

   C. SIFT descriptors are invariant to changes in scale, rotation, and affine transformations

   D. SIFT is primarily used for texture analysis

4. Which of the following is a key characteristic of the SURF (Speeded-Up Robust Features) algorithm?

   A. Scale invariance

   B. Color sensitivity

   C. Edge detection

   D. Histogram computation

5. Which of the following descriptors is computed by HoG?
    A. Binary patterns
    B. Gradient orientations
    C. Color histograms
    D. Corner responses

CHAPTER 10
Neural Networks

In this chapter, we'll dive into Neural Networks, the building blocks of modern AI. We'll cover how these networks are designed, including activation functions and training methods like Backpropagation and Gradient Descent. With a focus on Convolutional Neural Networks, we'll unravel their layers and explore popular models like LeNet, AlexNet, VGGNet, GoogleNet, and ResNet. Additionally, we'll learn about Transfer Learning, a technique to leverage existing networks, paving the way for creating smart systems.

Structure

In this chapter, we will discuss the following topics:

- Introduction to Neural Networks
- Design of a Neural Network
- Activation Functions
- Training a Neural Network
    - Forward Propagation
    - Backpropagation
- Gradient Descent
- Convolutional Neural Network
- Layers in a CNN
- First Neural Network Model
- Convolutional Neural Network Architectures
    - LeNet
    - AlexNet
    - VGGNet
- Transfer Learning
- Advanced CNN Architectures
    - GoogleNet
    - ResNet

Introduction to Neural Networks

Neural networks are machine-machine models designed in a way to mimic how the human brain works. The human brain is a large number of neurons connected to form a large network that processes information, performs complex computations, and supports various cognitive functions.

Neural networks are inspired by the structure and the functioning of these neurons in the brain and are designed in a way to recognize patterns and relationships in the input data to be able to make predictions from it.

The basic concept of a neural network involves passing input data through a series of computational layers to produce an output. Each layer consists of multiple neurons that perform computations on the data. The neurons receive inputs, apply mathematical operations to them, and produce an output that is typically passed to the next layer.

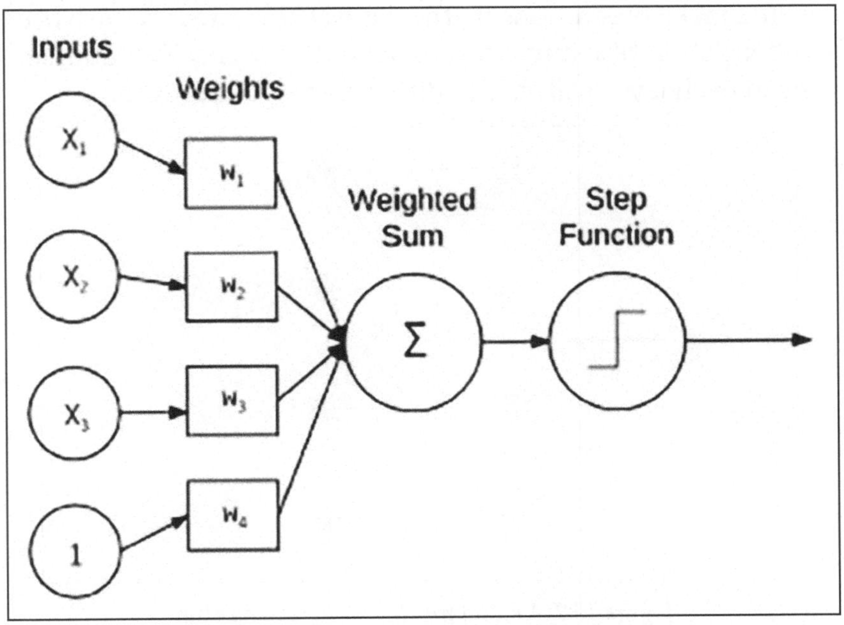

Figure 10.1: *Basic architecture of a neural network*

During the training process, neural networks learn by repeatedly showing them examples of the problem they need to solve. They compare their predictions to the correct answers and adjust their internal settings to improve. Neural networks can be trained to solve different types of problems. by changing their structure, the mathematical functions used, and the parameters used during training.

Neural networks have proven to be superior to traditional machine learning algorithms in various ways. Unlike traditional algorithms that rely on the manual selection of relevant attributes, neural networks can automatically learn and extract useful features from raw data effectively saving a lot of time, and effort and often providing a higher accuracy.

In computer vision, neural networks are employed for tasks such as image classification, object detection, and segmentation. They can accurately identify and classify objects within images, detect their precise boundaries, and even understand the context and relationships between different objects. Neural networks have also enhanced image processing techniques, enabling tasks such as image denoising, super-resolution, and image generation.

Design of a Neural Network

A neural network consists of a network of artificial neurons that learns to understand and make predictions on the dataset. A Network consists of multiple layers each consisting of many interconnected neurons. The number of layers and neurons in each layer will vary in different neural networks:

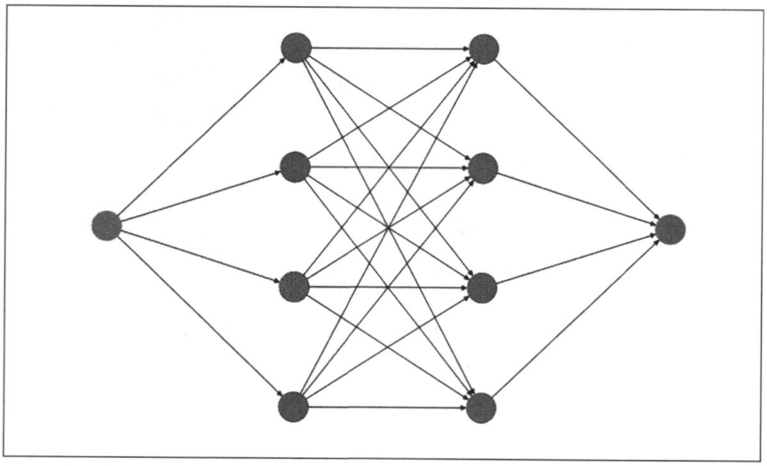

***Figure 10.2**: A standard Neural Network design*

The neurons in a layer are connected to neurons in another layer. These interconnections between each node are the weights of the neural networks which denote the strength of connection between the neurons. They determine how much influence the output of one neuron has on the inputs of the neurons in the subsequent layer. By adjusting the weights, the neural network can learn and adapt to better capture the underlying patterns and relationships in the data.

Activation Functions

The activation function decides whether a neuron should be activated or not. It takes the weighted sum of inputs and applies a mathematical operation. The resulting value from this function determines the output from that particular neuron.

Activation functions are used to introduce nonlinearity in a neural network. This non-linearity allows the neural network to model complex relationships in the data, enabling it to learn and represent more intricate patterns. Without non-linearity, the network will struggle to understand complex relationships in the network.

In a network without non-linearity, the consecutive linear operations can be combined into a single linear function. As a result, the network would lose its ability to learn and represent complex patterns. It would essentially behave in the same way as before like a single-layer linear model and would thus not be able to capture the non-linear relationships and would be unable to learn any complex patterns.

Different activation functions allow us to produce varied results from our network. Activation functions can be divided into three main types:

- **Step function**: Step functions are simple functions that have a binary output used to decide if a neuron should be activated or not. A threshold is selected and if the value from the neuron is greater than this threshold, the neuron is activated otherwise the neuron is deactivated. These are primarily used for binary classification problems.
- **Linear functions**: The output of linear activation functions can be expressed as a linear function of the input. As the name suggests, these functions do not introduce any non-linearity in the neural network and thus are only used to scale the inputs by a value.

  All layers of the linear activation function will however combine to form a single linear function and thus the model will not be able to learn any complex relationships from the dataset. Linear activation functions are primarily used in tasks like regression where the output is related to the input values directly.
- **Non-Linear Functions**: Non-linear activation functions are used to introduce non-linearity in the network. This allows the model to learn complex relationships in the dataset thus allowing it to have a good understanding of the patterns in the data eventually producing reliable outputs and predictions.

Therefore, we will primarily utilize non-linear activation functions in our neural networks to empower them to effectively capture and learn complex patterns and relationships in the data.

Some of the commonly used nonlinear activation functions are:

- **Sigmoid**: The sigmoid activation function is widely used, primarily because it compresses the values into the 0 to 1 range. It is a nonlinear function meaning that it can be used to capture complex relationships in the model.

  Sigmoid activation is used when we need to predict the probability of an event and is typically used in applications such as binary classification of images. The sigmoid function is generally used in the output layer of a neural network.

  The formula for the sigmoid activation function is:

  $$f(x) = \frac{1}{1 + e^{-x}}$$

  Figure 10.3: *Sigmoid Activation function formula*

  The drawbacks of the sigmoid function are that it is not zero-centered. This can lead to imbalanced updates during the model training and thus it impacts the distribution of activations eventually and slows down convergence in neural networks.

  Another drawback is the vanishing gradient problem, where the gradients can become extremely small for inputs far from the origin, hindering the learning process in deep neural networks.

- **TanH**: The tanh function maps the output in the range of -1 to 1. The tanh function has similar properties to the sigmoid function but differs in its range. This is also a nonlinear function and can be used to capture complex relationships.

  The function outputs values towards -1 when the input value approaches negative infinity and towards 1 when the input value approaches positive infinity. For an input of 0, the tanh function yields an output of 0.

  Unlike the sigmoid function, the tanh function is zero-centered. The function is also generally used in the hidden layers of the neural network.

The tanh activation function can be mathematically defined as:

$$f(x) = \frac{e^x - e^{-x}}{e^x + e^{-x}}$$

Figure 10.4: *TanH Activation function formula*

Similar to the sigmoid function, tanH is also susceptible to the vanishing gradients problem. However, Despite the drawbacks, the tanh activation function is still used in various neural network architectures,

- **ReLU**: ReLU or Rectified Linear Unit is a nonlinear function that introduces non-linearity by outputting the input directly if it is positive, and 0 otherwise. The function allows the values above 0 to pass unchanged through the function and any values that are below 0 are capped at 0.

  ReLu can be implemented using:

$$f(x) = \max(0, x)$$

Figure 10.5: *ReLu Activation function formula*

One of the main advantages of the ReLU function is its computational efficiency, as the function only involves simple thresholding operations. Additionally, the ReLU function helps mitigate the vanishing gradient problem that occurs in deeper networks by allowing gradients to flow more effectively.

The dying ReLU problem is a particular drawback of the ReLU activation function. Once there is a zero-value introduced in the model via ReLu, the neuron has died permanently and there is nothing that can be done to reactivate it later on. This can lead to a large number of neurons dying and thus never updating during the training process.

To address this, Leaky ReLU was introduced which allows a small non-zero output for negative inputs (instead of 0), preventing neuron death.

- **Leaky ReLU**: Leaky ReLU is an improved version of the ReLU function that solves the dying ReLU problem by adding a small positive slope in the negative areas of the graph.

LeakyReLU can be implemented using the formula:

$$f(x) = \begin{cases} x, & if\ x \geq 0 \\ \alpha x, & if\ x < 0 \end{cases}$$

***Figure 10.6**: LeakyReLU Activation function formula*

By allowing a non-zero output for negative inputs, Leaky ReLU helps mitigate the dying ReLU problem. It ensures that even if a neuron has negative inputs, it can still contribute during model training thus allowing the network to continue learning and preventing the issue of dead neurons:

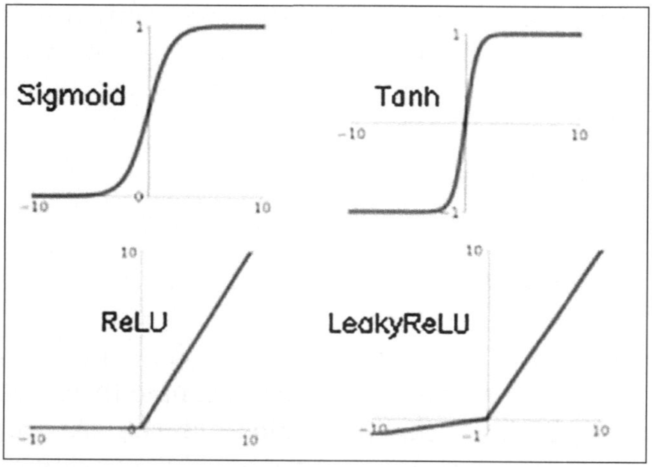

***Figure 10.7**: Graphs for various activation functions*

- **Softmax**: The softmax function is commonly used in the outer layer of the neural network. The function takes a vector of numbers as an input and transforms them into a probability distribution over multiple class.

  The function normalizes the inputs ensuring that the sum of outputs of all the class probabilities equates to 1. This makes it a primary function to be used in multiclass classification use cases. If the problem at hand is binary classification, sigmoid is used in the last layer, and sigmoid is used if the task is for multiclass classification.

Training a Neural Network

Forward Propagation Forward propagation is the process by which input data is passed through the layers of a neural network to compute predictions or outputs. It begins with the initial input and sequentially calculates the activations of neurons in each layer until the final output is obtained.

Steps for Forward Propagation:

- **Input**: The input layer receives the initial data or features and serves as the entry point for information.
- **Feature** Processing: In this step, the neural network processes the received features by calculating a weighted sum of inputs. The network incorporates learned weights (to emphasize important features) and biases (to introduce flexibility) during this computation. This is followed by applying an activation function to generate neuron activations.
- **Weights**: Weights are parameters in a neural network that determine the strength of connections between neurons and are adjusted during training to learn patterns in the data.
- Biases: Biases are adjustable parameters in a neural network that enable neurons to offset their activation functions enabling the network the flexibility to capture and represent complex relationships within the data by accounting for shifts and offsets in the input data.

  For a neuron 'j' in layer 'l', the weighted sum (Z) and activation (a) are calculated as follows:

  $$\text{Weighted Sum (Z)}: Z_j^l = \sum_i^{n[l-1]} W_{ji}^{[l]} \cdot a_i^{[l-1]} + b_j^{[l]}$$

  $$\text{Activation (a)}: a_j^{[l]} = \sigma(Z_j^{[l]})$$

- **Output Layer**: The output layer computes final predictions based on the activations from the last hidden layer. It transforms the encoded information into a format suitable for the specific task such as classification or regression.
- **Final Prediction**: The final prediction represents the output of the neural network and can vary depending on the problem type. For instance, in binary classification the prediction may be obtained by using a sigmoid activation for the last neuron.

  For the sigmoid activation (σ), the final prediction can be calculated as follows:

  $$y\_pred = \sigma(z)$$

  where 'z' is the weighted sum of inputs to the last neuron and 'σ(z)' is the sigmoid activation function applied to 'z'.

Backpropagation is a fundamental algorithm used in the training of neural networks. It enables the network to update its weights and biases by propagating the error gradients from the output layer back to the input layer. This process allows the network to learn and adjust its parameters, leading to improved performance.

Once the forward propagation step has been done and the network has predicted its outputs, the error is computed by comparing the predicted output of the network with the actual target output. The error represents the discrepancy between the network's predictions and the desired output.

A loss function is used to quantify the overall error of the network's predictions. The objective is to minimize this error by adjusting the network's parameters. The primary purpose of a loss function is to provide a measure of how well or poorly a model is performing, guiding the optimization process during training to improve the model's accuracy.

During training the goal is to minimize the loss function by adjusting the model's parameters. Optimization algorithms like gradient descent iteratively update these parameters based on the gradient of the loss function. A well-chosen loss function ensures that the model converges to a solution that best fits the data.

A loss function must be differentiable because as seen earlier, these algorithms rely on derivatives to update model parameters iteratively. Differentiability ensures that you can calculate gradients providing the necessary information about how small changes in each parameter affect the loss. This information is crucial for guiding the optimization process towards finding the optimal set of parameters that minimizes the loss.

Non-differentiable points or functions would lead to undefined gradients making it impossible to determine the appropriate direction for parameter updates and traditional gradient-based optimization methods would fail. The differentiability of the loss function is a fundamental requirement for efficient and effective model training using gradient-based optimization techniques.

Some of the loss functions commonly used are:

- **Mean Squared Error**: MSE calculates the average squared difference between the predicted and target values and is widely used for regression tasks.
- **Binary Cross-Entropy**: This measures how different the predicted probabilities are from the actual labels and is used for binary classification tasks. It measures the dissimilarity between the predicted probabilities and the true binary labels.
- **Categorical Cross-Entropy**: Categorical cross-entropy is used for multi-class classification tasks. It measures the difference between the predicted class probabilities and the true class labels. It helps the network

assign high probabilities to the correct classes and penalizes deviations from the true distribution.

Once the error is calculated, backpropagation proceeds by propagating the error gradients backward through the layers of the neural network. During the backward pass, the algorithm starts from the output layer and moves toward the earlier layers of the network. It calculates the gradients for each layer, one by one. This helps the algorithm understand how each weight and bias affects the overall error.

By propagating the error gradients backward, the algorithm figures out which directions the weights and biases should be adjusted to reduce the error and make the network perform better.

A Closer Look at the Working Mechanism of Backpropagation:

- The chain rule from calculus is at the heart of backpropagation. It allows us to compute the gradients of the loss function with respect to the parameters of the neural network layer by layer. It starts from the output layer and moves backward through the network.

  The chain rule states that if you have two functions, say, f(g(x)), then the derivative of f with respect to x is given by (df/dg) * (dg/dx).

- Next, we calculate the local gradient at each layer, which represents how sensitive the loss is to changes in the output of that layer.

  This is done using the gradient of the activation function and the gradient of the weighted sum. To compute the local gradient at a neuron in a neural network, you typically have the following components:

  - **Weighted Sum (Z)**: This is the weighted sum of inputs to the neuron before applying the activation function.
  - **Activation Function (σ)**: This function introduces non-linearity into the model and transforms the weighted sum into the neuron's output
  - **Loss Function (L)**: The loss function that measures the error between predicted and actual values.

The local gradient (∂L/∂Z) at a neuron with respect to the loss is computed as follows:

$$\partial L/\partial Z = (\partial L/\partial a) * (\partial a/\partial Z)$$

Where 'a' represents the output of the neuron after applying the activation function and ∂L/∂a is the gradient of the loss with respect to the neuron's output.

- The local gradients are then used to compute the gradients of the loss with respect to the layer's parameters (weights and biases).

The gradients of the loss with respect to the layer's parameters can be represented as:

$$\partial L/\partial weight = (\partial L/\partial Z) * (\partial Z/\partial weight)$$

$$\partial L/\partial bias = (\partial L/\partial Z) * (\partial Z/\partial bias)$$

- These gradients are used to update the parameters in the direction that reduces the loss, typically using an optimization algorithm like gradient descent.

The update rule for gradient descent is as follows:

$$New\_weight = Old\_weight - learning\_rate * \partial L/\partial weight$$

$$New\_bias = Old\_bias - learning\_rate * \partial L/\partial bias$$

- The process continues backward through the layers until we have computed the gradients for all the parameters in the network.

Gradient descent

Gradient descent is an optimization algorithm used in conjunction with backpropagation. It utilizes the calculated gradients to update the weights and biases of the neural network. By iteratively adjusting the parameters in the direction opposite to the gradients' values, gradient descent aims to minimize the error. This iterative process continues for multiple epochs, gradually reducing the error and enabling the network to learn and improve its predictions.

Imagine you are at the top of a hill, and your goal is to reach the lowest point. Gradient descent is a technique used to find the lowest point, or minimum, of a hill by taking small steps in the steepest downhill direction. You start at a random position and measure the slope of the hill at that point. Based on the slope, you take a small step downhill. You repeat this process, measuring the slope and taking steps in the direction of steepest descent until you reach a point where the slope becomes very small. This indicates you have reached a local minimum, the lowest point in that area of the hill:

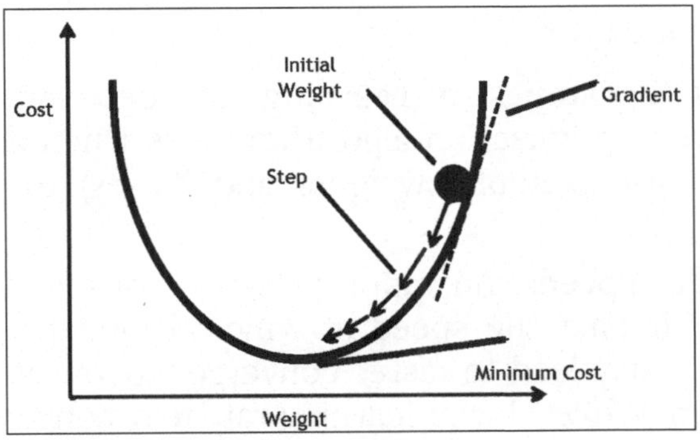

Figure 10.8: *Gradient Descent curve*

In machine learning, gradient descent is used to minimize the error or loss of a neural network. Instead of a physical hill, the "hill" represents the space of possible parameter values for the network. The goal is to find the set of parameter values that minimizes the error. The gradient, which represents the slope, indicates the direction of steepest descent in this parameter space. By iteratively adjusting the parameters in the opposite direction of the gradient, the network gradually moves towards the optimal set of parameters that minimize the error.

There are multiple types of gradient descents that can be used:

- **Batch Gradient Descent**: In batch gradient descent, the entire training dataset is used to compute the gradient of the cost function. The parameters are updated after evaluating the gradients of all training examples.
- **Stochastic Gradient Descent (SGD)**: In stochastic gradient descent, the parameters are updated after processing each training example individually. The gradients are estimated based on a single training example at a time, making it computationally efficient. However, this approach introduces more noise into the parameter updates and may require more iterations to converge.
- **Mini-Batch Gradient Descent**: Mini-batch gradient descent is a compromise between batch gradient descent and stochastic gradient descent. It updates the parameters by computing the gradients on a small subset of the training data called a mini batch. This approach combines the efficiency of stochastic gradient descent with the stability of batch gradient descent, making it a popular choice in practice.

The learning rate in gradient descent describes how large the steps are taken in each iteration. The learning rate is important for a loss function because it plays a critical role in the training of machine learning models.

Importance of learning rate:

- **Controlling the step size**: Learning rate determines the size of the steps that the optimization algorithm takes when adjusting the model parameters (for example, weights and biases) to minimize the loss function.
- **Convergence speed**: An appropriately chosen learning rate can significantly impact the speed at which a model converges. A higher learning rate may lead to faster convergence, but it risks overshooting the minimum. While a lower learning rate may converge more slowly but with greater stability.
- **Stability and Robustness**: The learning rate can affect the stability and robustness of the training process. An excessively high learning rate can result in unstable training with loss values oscillating or diverging. A moderate learning rate usually strikes a balance between convergence speed and stability.
- **Generalization**: Learning rate can also influence a model's ability to generalize to unseen data. A well-tuned learning rate can lead to a model that generalizes better as it is more likely to find a smoother and more generalizable solution.
- **Avoiding Local Minima**: Learning rate can help the optimization algorithm escape local minima or saddle points in the loss landscape. Adaptive learning rate methods such as Adam or RMSprop adjust the learning rate dynamically based on the gradient information.

A large learning rate might get the network training to converge quickly but it might also be a big enough step to overshoot the optimal solution. This might cause the loss function to oscillate and never properly convergeA small learning rate will allow for small steps resulting in more precise updates to the steps taken in each iteration. However, if the learning rate is low enough, it will result in the network taking a long time to converge or not being able to reach the optimal solution at all.

Selecting an appropriate learning rate is crucial. It often involves experimentation and finding a balance. There are adaptive learning rate techniques that automatically adjust the learning rate during training based on how the training is going. Techniques such as learning rate decay and Adam are widely used to provide an efficient learning process to the model.

Learning rate optimizers are algorithms used in training neural networks to efficiently adjust model parameters during learning. They control the step size and direction of parameter updates in order to converge to the optimal solution more quickly. Popular optimizers, like Adam and RMSProp, adapt the learning rate dynamically based on the gradients of the loss function, ensuring effective and stable training.

The preceding steps are repeated for each training example or batch in the dataset. This constitutes one iteration or one training epoch. The process of forward propagation, loss calculation, backpropagation, and weight update is performed multiple times, allowing the network to learn from the data and refine its predictions.

The training process continues for multiple epochs until the network's performance converges or reaches a satisfactory level. The convergence is typically determined by evaluating the network's performance on a validation set.

Convolutional neural networks

Convolutional neural networks are a type of deep learning models designed specifically for analyzing visual data such as images and videos. CNNs can analyze and understand visual data by extracting meaningful patterns from the data.

CNNs can learn intricate features from the image data such as the edges, textures, and patterns, and are thus able to understand complex patterns from the underlying data which makes them a powerful tool for making predictions. CNNs have been successfully applied to various computer vision tasks, including image classification, object detection, image segmentation, and facial recognition.

The fundamental operation in CNNs is the convolution operation where filters are applied to the data. These filters slide across the inputs enabling them to capture all the information. The values for these kernels are updated through the training process. Pooling functions are another important aspect of CNNs which are used to downsample the data to extract the most important features and reduce the complexity of the network.

Layers in a CNN

The layers of a CNN are as follows:

Convolutional Layer

The convolutional layer is the fundamental component of convolutional neural networks. The layer is designed to process and extract visual information from images or videos.

The convolutional operation is the fundamental operation of convolutional layers in a CNN. The convolutional operation involves sliding a filter across the input data and at each position the filter is multiplied to the corresponding values of the input data. The dot product of the operation results in a scalar value which is then combined with a bias term and passed to a non-linear activation function:

3	2	10	4	6	6	8
0	2	6	5	5	10	6
10	10	1	7	9	9	10
0	3	1	0	5	4	4
1	6	2	5	4	0	6
0	6	7	8	2	2	5
9	10	9	0	0	4	8

X

0	1	-1
-1	1	-2
-2	0	2

=

1	-12	6	-23	-8	-9	-8
4	-18	-16	2	-17	-10	-1
-4	-20	-34	-3	-19	-22	12
-22	25	-3	-20	-4	-16	20
-11	6	-8	-10	-20	-12	17
-9	-2	-12	-21	-6	-7	5
-13	-31	-15	-8	8	-10	4

Figure 10.9: *Convolution Operation using a 3×3 filter on a 7,7 matrix*

The kernel or filter is a matrix, typically of size 3×3, 5×5 but can vary depending on the operation. The kernel is applied to the input data at each convolutional operation and each kernel is designed to capture specific information such as edges or textures from the data. The values of kernels are initialized randomly when the convolutional neural network is created. During the training process, these weights are adjusted and optimized to capture relevant patterns and features in the input data.

The network learns from labeled training examples and uses an optimization algorithm, such as gradient descent, to update the weights iteratively. The goal is to minimize the error or loss between the predicted outputs and the true labels:

- **Stride**: Stride determines the step size at which the filter slides across the input data. It is the number of steps the kernel takes between each operation. For example, a stride of 2 will make the kernel move two pixels at a time as it slides over the input data, skipping every other pixel in the process. This results in a downsampled output with reduced spatial resolution.

A larger stride reduces the size of the feature maps, resulting in down-sampling and less spatial information. On the other hand, a smaller stride preserves more spatial information, leading to larger feature maps.

- **Padding**: Padding involves adding extra border pixels to the input data before applying the convolution operation. Without padding, the filter may not be able to slide over the entire input, especially at the corners and edges. Padding helps to prevent the shrinking of the feature maps after convolution.

It can be "valid" (no padding), "same" (pad the input to keep output size the same as input), or "full" (maximum padding to keep all elements in the feature maps).

The formula to calculate the size of the output in a convolutional operation is:

$$W_{out} = \frac{W - F + 2P}{S} + 1$$

Figure 10.10: *Formula to compute the size of the output of a convolutional operation*where:

- W is the spatial size of the input
- F is the spatial size of the filter
- S is the stride
- P is the amount of padding

Pooling Layer

The pooling layers are a key component of CNNs designed specifically to downsample the dimensionality of feature maps produced by the convolutional layers. This helps to reduce the memory requirements and the computational complexity of the model while retaining important information.

The pooling layer downsamples the data by aggregating information within small regions. The most commonly used pooling operations are max pooling and average pooling. In max pooling, the maximum value within the sub-region is selected thereby retraining the most prominent feature in the window. The averaging pooling operation selects the average value within the area under the window resulting in a more smoothed-out operation:

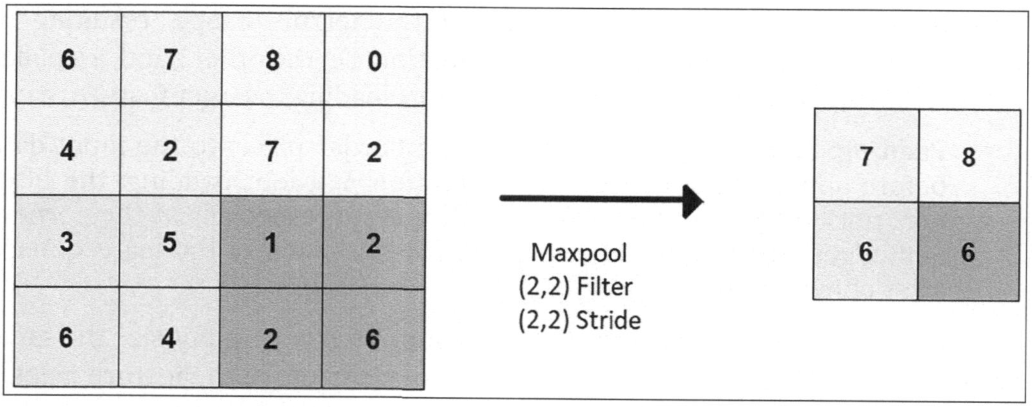

Figure 10.11: *Using Max pooling operation on a 4,4 matrix with 2,2 filter and a 2,2 stride*

As defined earlier, stride determines the number of steps to skip between each operation. The filter size determines the area to be considered for each operation. Common filter sizes used are 2x2 and 3x3 but values can be changed depending on the operation. It is important to note that using too large values for the filter might result in information loss as values under a large area will be minimized.

While pooling layers reduce the spatial resolution, they retain the most salient features of the input. This allows the network to focus on the essential characteristics of the data while discarding less critical information, leading to more efficient and meaningful feature representations.

The formula for the output of a pooling layer is:

$$W_{out} = \frac{W-F}{S} + 1$$

Figure 10.12: *Formula to calculate output size from a pooling operation*

Fully Connected Layer

The fully connected layer, also known as the dense layer, is a type of neural network layer found in the latter part of a Convolutional Neural Network (CNN) architecture. Unlike the convolutional and pooling layers that extract local features, the fully connected layer is responsible for learning global patterns and making final predictions based on the features learned from earlier layers.

The flatten layer reshapes the output from the previous layers into a 1D vector. This is often required before connecting to a fully connected layer.

In a fully connected layer, each neuron is connected to every neuron in the previous layer. This means that every element in the output of the previous layer contributes to the calculation of each neuron in the fully connected layer. The final output of the fully connected layer represents the network's prediction for the given input data.

The fully connected layer adds a level of abstraction and decision-making to the CNN architecture, enabling it to leverage the learned features to perform tasks like image classification, object detection, and other tasks involving pattern recognition and prediction.

Activation Layer

As discussed earlier, activation layers are applied after every convolutional or fully connected layer to introduce non-linearity, which helps the network learn complex patterns and make final predictions.

First Neural Network Model

Let us create our first neural network now. We will be creating a basic neural network architecture and training it on the dogs vs cats dataset:

```
import tensorflow as tf
from tensorflow.keras.preprocessing.image import ImageDataGenerator
from tensorflow.keras.models import Sequential
from tensorflow.keras.layers import Conv2D, MaxPooling2D, Flatten, Dense,
Dropout
import matplotlib.pyplot as plt

# Fix image dimensions
img_width, img_height = 256, 256

# ImageDataGenerator
train_datagen = ImageDataGenerator(
    rescale=1.0/255,
    shear_range=0.2,
    zoom_range=0.2,
    horizontal_flip=True,
    validation_split=0.2
)
```

```
# Training Set
train_set = train_datagen.flow_from_directory(
    'train',
    target_size=(img_width, img_height),
    batch_size=32,
    class_mode='binary',
    subset='training'
)


# Validation Set
validation_set = train_datagen.flow_from_directory(
    'train',
    target_size=(img_width, img_height),
    batch_size=32,
    class_mode='binary',
    subset='validation'
)

# Create CNN model
model = Sequential()
model.add(Conv2D(32, (3, 3), activation='relu', input_shape=(img_width,
img_height, 3)))
model.add(MaxPooling2D((2, 2)))
model.add(Conv2D(64, (3, 3), activation='relu'))
model.add(MaxPooling2D((2, 2)))
model.add(Conv2D(128, (3, 3), activation='relu'))
model.add(MaxPooling2D((2, 2)))
model.add(Flatten())
model.add(Dense(128, activation='relu'))
model.add(Dropout(0.5))
model.add(Dense(1, activation='sigmoid'))

# Compile
model.compile(optimizer='adam', loss='binary_crossentropy', met-
rics=['accuracy'])

# Train model
model.fit(train_set, epochs=10, validation_data=validation_set)

# Save model for future references
model.save('dog_cat_classifier.h5')
```

The code produces the following output:

```
…
Epoch 8/10
```

```
625/625 [==============================] - 292s 468ms/step - loss: 0.3939
- accuracy: 0.8253 - val_loss: 0.3899 - val_accuracy: 0.8328
Epoch 9/10
625/625 [==============================] - 298s 476ms/step - loss: 0.3780
- accuracy: 0.8345 - val_loss: 0.3775 - val_accuracy: 0.8350
Epoch 10/10
625/625 [==============================] - 294s 471ms/step - loss: 0.3657
- accuracy: 0.8372 - val_loss: 0.3736 - val_accuracy: 0.8314
```

First let us understand the various imports, data loaders, the different components used in the code, and how layers are added to a model:

We start by importing essential components from the TensorFlow library to facilitate our tasks. We import components necessary for building and training neural network models, including Sequential for creating a linear stack of layers, and various layer types like Conv2D, MaxPooling2D, Flatten, Dense, and Dropout.

Data Loading

The ImageDataGenerator is a tool in TensorFlow that helps us efficiently handle and augment image data for training deep learning models. It simplifies the process of preparing and feeding image data into the model by providing automatic data augmentation and preprocessing.

Note: Data augmentation is a clever technique that helps us get more out of our existing images, especially when we have a limited number of pictures. By applying small transformations like flipping, rotating, or zooming to our images, we can create new versions, effectively increasing our dataset. This expanded dataset allows our computer to learn from a wider variety of images, enhancing its accuracy in recognizing and understanding different visual patterns.

We can define all the augmentation parameters that we want to apply to our dataset in the ImageDataGenerator parameter and the function will take care of it for us without having to explicitly code each of the transformations.

There is also a rescale parameter defined in the ImageDataGenerator. Rescaling the images by dividing each pixel value by 255 helps ensure that the pixel values are in a normalized range (between 0 and 1), which improves the training process of neural networks.

The **ImageDataGenerator** function initialized our data generator; now we employ the **Flow_from_directory** function to utilize this object for reading and augmenting images from directories during neural network training.

The **Flow_from_directory** function is used to dynamically load, augment, and organize image data from directories for neural network training. It acts as a bridge between your image data stored in directories and the neural network training process. We specified the data parameters in the **ImageDataGenerator**. **Flow_from_directory** uses it to generate image batches for effective neural network training.

The **Flow_from_directory** function will process images from the specified directory (**train**). It will apply the required transformations and store the augmented data in the designated format for our network training. The **target_size** here specifies the size to which the images will be resized to.

The batch size refers to the number of training examples that are used in one iteration of updating the neural network's weights during training.

- A larger batch size means the network learns from more examples at once, potentially speeding up training, but it also requires more memory.
- A smaller batch size might provide more accurate weight updates, but training could take longer due to frequent updates.

The choice of batch size involves a trade-off between training speed and memory usage, influencing the learning process and convergence of the neural network. In this code, we specify the batch size to be 32, effectively meaning that during each training iteration, the model will learn from 32 images, and this process will repeat until all the images have been processed, contributing to the gradual improvement of the model's performance.

The **class_mode** is set to binary since it is a binary classification problem and in the case of multiple classes, it would have been categorical.

The **subset** parameter is used to specify whether the **flow_from_directory** function should focus on a particular subset of the dataset, such as *training* or *validation*.

A validation subset is required to set aside a portion of the data specifically for validation purposes during training, helping to monitor the model's performance on unseen data and prevent overfitting by providing an independent evaluation.

Now that our data loaders have been initialized, we can move forward to creating our model.

Model Instantiation

Creating a Sequential model means we are organizing the layers of a neural network like stacking building blocks one on top of the other. Data linearly flows through these layers, each layer processing and transforming the information. This linear flow of the data in a sequential model helps us create network architectures by establishing a clear input-to-output data flow.

We will specify the layers of our neural network now:

- **Convolutional layers**: We begin by using the Conv2D function to initialize the first convolutional layer. This layer will learn 32 different features or patterns from the input images. The filter size is set to (3, 3), which means each filter scans a 3x3 grid of pixels at a time. The 'relu' activation function is applied to introduce non-linearity and enhance the network's ability to capture intricate details.
- **Pooling layers**: After each convolutional layer, we employ the MaxPooling2D function with a pool size of (2, 2). This pooling operation reduces the spatial dimensions of the feature maps, effectively downsampling the information. It helps the network focus on important features and reduces computation while preserving essential patterns.
- **Flattening**: The Flatten layer serves as a transition, converting the 2D feature maps into a 1D vector. This step is crucial for connecting the convolutional layers to the fully connected layers that follow.
- **Fully connected layers**: Next, we add a Dense layer with 128 neurons and a 'relu' activation function. This layer helps the network grasp more advanced details from the flattened features, making it better at recognizing complicated patterns in images.
- **Dropout layer**: To prevent overfitting, a Dropout layer is added with a rate of 0.5. This layer randomly deactivated 50% of its neurons during each training iteration, encouraging the network to be more robust and generalize better.
- **Output layer**: Finally, we include an output layer with a single neuron and 'sigmoid' activation function. This neuron produces the model's prediction and is suitable for binary classification tasks.

There are multiple convolutional layers added sequentially in the code. Each layer learns from simple to complex features, like going from lines to patterns. Adding multiple layers makes it understand basic and advanced ideas, similar to how our brain processes information. This helps the network grasp intricate details and do well on complex tasks. The early layers see simple stuff, and the later layers put them together to understand tricky things. We use pooling to keep our network size from getting too large.

Here, we've created a basic code for training a classifier to distinguish between dogs and cats. However, as we tackle more intricate tasks, the network architecture will expand and evolve to handle the increased complexity. This adaptability ensures our model's effectiveness across a range of challenges.

Now that we have created the architecture of our model. We will compile it and then start training the model.

Before we start training our model, we need to prepare it for learning. This is where the compile step comes in. When we call **model.compile**, we're configuring essential aspects of the learning process:

Compile is used to set up the learning rules for our neural network. We choose how the model should adjust its parameters to make better predictions (learning rate optimizer), specify the loss function we want to use, and track how well the model is doing during training using metrics like accuracy or loss.

'Adam' is a popular optimizer known for its efficiency and adaptability. We're unable to go into an in-depth explanation of the Adam optimizer due to the limitations of this book. Feel free to explore and learn more about the topic on your own.

We specify loss as **binary_crossentropy** because it measures the difference between predicted and actual outcomes for binary classification tasks such as our dog vs cat classification here. The metrics as 'accuracy' meaning we want to track how often the model's predictions match the true labels during training. Instead of accuracy, we could also have tracked the "loss" metric meaning how well the model is minimizing the error between its predictions and the actual outcomes.

We can finally start training our model now. The fit function trains our neural network using the provided training dataset (**train_set**) for a specified number of epochs (10 in this case). During each epoch, the model adjusts its parameters to better match the training data.

The **fit** function will start training the model and produce the results as shown in the output earlier. This function provides insights into various aspects such as the number of batches processed, the loss and accuracy calculated for each batch, and the time taken for an epoch to finish.

After every epoch, the fit function automatically evaluates the model's performance on validation data, computing validation loss, and accuracy. We can use these metrics to see how well our model is learning and improving over time.

Results

Analyzing the output from this code, we can deduce that our model underwent 10 epochs, signifying that all training images were processed 10 times by the model. In each epoch, the dataset was divided into 625 iterations of 32 images (batch size), and it takes roughly 294 seconds for each epoch to conclude.

On the 10th epoch, we have been able to achieve a training loss of 0.3657 and a training accuracy of 0.8372. The validation loss is at 0.3736 while keeping an accuracy of 0.8314. This remarkable performance suggests that our model has reached a promising level of understanding after just 10 epochs.

The consistency of the results over the last few epochs indicates that the model's learning has likely plateaued. Achieving an impressive 83% accuracy after just 10 epochs, especially for our initial model, is quite remarkable. As we delve into more advanced models, we'll have the opportunity to explore further improvements and witness the model's enhanced performance.

We ultimately save the model for future use and deployment.

Now that our model has been trained, let us use this model and see if it can predict results on new images:

```
import numpy as np
from tensorflow.keras.preprocessing import image

def predict_image_class(model, image_path, class_names):
    img = image.load_img(image_path, target_size=(img_width, img_height))
    img_array = image.img_to_array(img)
    img_array = np.expand_dims(img_array, axis=0)
    img_array /= 255.0

    # Predict
    prediction = model.predict(img_array)
    predicted_class = class_names[int(prediction[0][0])]

    plt.imshow(img)
    plt.title(f'Predicted Class: {predicted_class}')
    plt.axis('off')
    plt.show()
```

```
# Load model
loaded_model = tf.keras.models.load_model('dog_cat_classifier.h5')

class_names = ['Cat', 'Dog']

image_path_to_predict = 'path_to_your_image.jpg'
predict_image_class(loaded_model, image_path_to_predict, class_names)
```

Results for a few images are as follows:

***Figure 10.13**: Model predictions on some images with the predicted class label*

In this code, we use the **predict** method to use our model on the input image. We load our image and preprocess it according to the model requirements. We then use the matplotlib library to print the class along with the original image.

We use **np.expand_dims** to adjust how our model processes images, whether it's just one image or many. We convert our input data to 4 dimensions using **np.expand_dims** to prepare it for processing by the neural network model. (1,256,256,3 here) Adding that extra dimension helps the model work smoothly in both cases. So, when we're predicting, we can use the same approach for a single image as well as for multiple images all at once. This makes things simpler and more consistent in our code.

We can observe that the model has been successfully able to classify these images correctly. However, it is important to note that our model has an accuracy of ~83% meaning that we can expect some incorrect predictions as well.

Dropout Regularization

Dropout is a regularization technique widely employed in neural networks to enhance their generalization performance and prevent overfitting. Using dropout allows the network to learn more robust and diverse representations from the data.

It operates by randomly switching off or *dropping out* a fraction of neurons during each training iteration, effectively making the network less reliant on any single neuron's output. During training, dropout will deactivate some neurons with a probability generally around 0.2 to 0.5. This will prevent the network from overfitting on the training set as different subsets of neurons are activated for each forward pass.

Dropout is only used during training, However, during inference dropout is not used and the whole network is utilized to make predictions. Dropout is integrated into neural network architectures by adding dropout layers, a technique utilized in many modern designs.

Neural network architectures

In the previous example, we created our own very basic neural network architecture containing a few layers. As datasets grow larger and more intricate computer vision problems emerge, the limitations of this straightforward network architecture become apparent. It struggles to handle the expanding number of complexities and intricate details that require capturing.

As a result, we turn to more complex network architectures to address these challenges. Models with deeper layers, such as deep convolutional neural networks (CNNs), have demonstrated significant advancements in handling intricate features and extracting valuable patterns from massive datasets. These sophisticated architectures empower computer vision systems to effectively tackle a wide array of challenging tasks, including image recognition, segmentation, object detection, and even autonomous driving, with unparalleled accuracy and efficiency.

Depending on the use case, we have the option to either design our custom architecture or leverage commonly used architectures, which have demonstrated their ability to yield impressive results. Crafting our own architecture allows us to tailor it to specific requirements with respect to the use case at hand thus providing greater flexibility and potential for optimizing the performance of our model. However, Using commonly used well-established models is effective in various scenarios, providing a faster and more reliable way to construct model architectures thus making it a good choice for various complex computer vision applications.

Let us discuss some of the commonly used architectures and explore how they can be implemented to produce impressive results.

LeNet

LeNet or Lenet-5 is one the earliest and most influential convolutional neural network architectures. Designed in 1998 by Yann LeCun along with some colleagues, it was primarily designed to handle handwritten digit recognition tasks. The network not only received remarkable success but also laid the foundation for the widespread adoption of CNNs in computer vision.

LeNet-5 is a convolutional neural network architecture with seven layers. It consists of two convolutional layers followed by activation functions and average pooling layers. The feature maps are then flattened and passed through two fully connected layers, ending with a softmax activation for digit classification.

Let us use Python to code and understand the LeNet architecture properly. The model LeNet model can be constructed as follows:

```
import tensorflow as tf
from tensorflow.keras import layers, models

def lenet():


    # Initialize LeNet model
    model = models.Sequential(name="LeNet")

    # LeNet architecture
    model.add(layers.Conv2D(6, (5, 5), activation="tanh", input_
shape=(32, 32, 1), name="Conv1"))
    model.add(layers.MaxPooling2D((2, 2), name="MaxPool1"))

    model.add(layers.Conv2D(16, (5, 5), activation="tanh", name="Conv2"))
    model.add(layers.MaxPooling2D((2, 2), name="MaxPool2"))

    model.add(layers.Flatten(name="Flatten"))

    model.add(layers.Dense(120, activation="tanh", name="Dense1"))
    model.add(layers.Dense(84, activation="tanh", name="Dense2"))
    model.add(layers.Dense(10, activation='softmax', name="Output"))

    return model

lenet_model = lenet()

# Display the summary of the model
lenet_model.summary()
```

The preceding code initializes the LeNet model architecture and uses the **`model.summary()`** function to print model details. The output for the preceding code is as follows:

```
Layer (type)                  Output Shape               Param #
=================================================================
Conv1 (Conv2D)                (None, 28, 28, 6)          156

MaxPool1 (MaxPooling2D)       (None, 14, 14, 6)          0

Conv2 (Conv2D)                (None, 10, 10, 16)         2416

MaxPool2 (MaxPooling2D)       (None, 5, 5, 16)           0

Flatten (Flatten)             (None, 400)                0

Dense1 (Dense)                (None, 120)                48120

Dense2 (Dense)                (None, 84)                 10164

Output (Dense)                (None, 10)                 850

=================================================================
Total params: 61,706
Trainable params: 61,706
Non-trainable params: 0
```

Figure 10.14: *LeNet model Summary*

The result displays the summary of the model architecture. The summary function has provided us with essential information such as layer type, the output shape from each layer and the number of trainable parameters in each layer.

Note: Trainable parameters are learned and updated during model training, contributing to the optimization process. Non-trainable parameters are fixed and do not change during training, serving as constants. These parameters are typically introduced when using pre-trained models or when certain layers are frozen during fine-tuning.

From the preceding output, we can understand the LeNet architecture. LeNet is a convolutional neural network architecture with seven layers. LeNet uses a kernel size of 5 during its convolutional operations and a kernel size of 2 during the average pooling operations. The number of filters for both the convolution layers are 6 and 16 respectively based on the original architecture of the model.

Note: The number of filters in a convolutional layer is determined by design choices and the complexity of the features to be captured. Generally, as we

go deeper into the network, the number of filters increases to detect more intricate and abstract features, building on the simpler ones learned earlier. This helps the network understand the data better and improves its ability to recognize patterns in images or other inputs.

The network consists of two convolutional layers followed by activation functions and average pooling layers. Tanh is the activation function used in the original architecture of LeNet and average pooling is done to reduce the dimensionality of the network.

The feature maps are then flattened into a 1D array by the flattened layer in the network and then passed through two fully connected layers also known as dense layers. The dense layers contain the specified number of neurons (120 and 84 in LeNet). The final layer uses the softmax activation to give the probabilities of each possible class, allowing the network to make predictions on the input data. The original architecture is used for handwritten digit recognition hence the softmax layer has 10 neurons in the model.

Now that we have understood the LeNet architecture, let us try to train the CIFAR 10 dataset on this network:

```
import tensorflow as tf
from tensorflow.keras import datasets, layers, models

(train_images, train_labels), (test_images, test_labels) = datasets.
cifar10.load_data()
train_images, test_images = train_images / 255.0, test_images / 255.0

# Create the LeNet model using the Lenet function defined earlier
model = lenet()

model.compile(optimizer='adam',
              loss='sparse_categorical_crossentropy',
              metrics=['accuracy'])

history = model.fit(train_images, train_labels, epochs=50, batch_size=32,
validation_data=(test_images, test_labels))

# Evaluate the model
test_loss, test_acc = model.evaluate(test_images, test_labels)
print("Test accuracy:", test_acc)


# Visualize accuracy and loss
plt.plot(history.history['accuracy'], label='Training Accuracy')
plt.plot(history.history['val_accuracy'], label='Validation Accuracy')
```

```
plt.xlabel('Epoch')
plt.ylabel('Accuracy')
plt.legend()
plt.show()

plt.plot(history.history['loss'], label='Training Loss')
plt.plot(history.history['val_loss'], label='Validation Loss')
plt.xlabel('Epoch')
plt.ylabel('Loss')
plt.legend()
plt.show()
```

The training ends with the following results:

```
Epoch 14/15
1563/1563 [==============================] - 8s 5ms/step - loss: 0.5283
- accuracy: 0.8176 - val_loss: 1.2572 - val_accuracy: 0.6207
Epoch 15/15
1563/1563 [==============================] - 7s 5ms/step - loss: 0.4721
- accuracy: 0.8390 - val_loss: 1.2717 - val_accuracy: 0.6247


Test accuracy: 0.6247000098228455
```

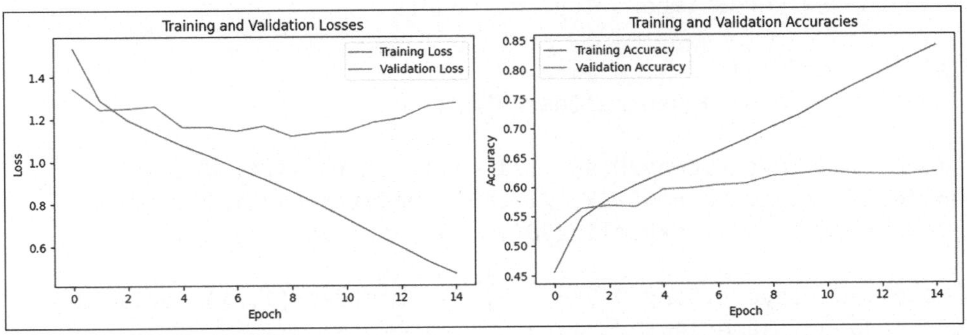

Figure 10.15: *Output graphs from the model training*

Now, we initialize the model and train it as we did in the earlier example. We have used the Cifar-10 dataset this time meaning that we are doing a multi-class classification this time.

Looking at these graphs helps us to better understand how the training process is going and if the model is not overfitting. If the validation loss is not decreasing while the training loss is, this generally means that the model might be overfitting to the training data and not generalizing well to unseen data.

AlexNet

AlexNet is a seminal neural network architecture introduced in 2012 by Alex Krizhevsky, Ilya Sutskever, and Geoffrey Hinton. The model came to light when it competed in the **ImageNet Large Scale Visual Recognition Challenge** (**ILSVRC**) challenge and won it by a significant margin.

The success of AlexNet was partly attributed to its parallel processing implementation on **Graphics Processing Units** (**GPUs**). This parallelization significantly accelerated model training and enabled the efficient use of large datasets.

AlexNet also introduced revolutionary techniques such as dropout and data augmentation which helped increase the performance of deep learning models significantly. AlexNet also used the ReLu activation function which played a significant role in solving the vanishing gradient problem effectively paving the way for the popularization of the ReLu activation function in deep learning applications.

Let us look at the architecture of AlexNet with the help of Python just like we did in LeNet:

```
import tensorflow as tf
from tensorflow.keras import layers, models

def alexnet_model():
    model = models.Sequential(name="AlexNet")

    model.add(layers.Conv2D(96, (11, 11), strides=(4, 4), activa-
tion='relu', input_shape=(227, 227, 3), padding='valid'))
    model.add(layers.MaxPooling2D((3, 3), strides=(2, 2)))

    model.add(layers.Conv2D(256, (5, 5), strides=(1, 1), activation='
relu', padding='same'))
    model.add(layers.MaxPooling2D((3, 3), strides=(2, 2)))

    model.add(layers.Conv2D(384, (3, 3), strides=(1, 1), activation='
relu', padding='same'))

    model.add(layers.Conv2D(384, (3, 3), strides=(1, 1), activation='
relu', padding='same'))

    model.add(layers.Conv2D(256, (3, 3), strides=(1, 1), activation='
relu', padding='same'))
    model.add(layers.MaxPooling2D((3, 3), strides=(2, 2)))
```

```
    model.add(layers.Flatten())

    model.add(layers.Dense(4096, activation='relu'))
    model.add(layers.Dense(4096, activation='relu'))
    model.add(layers.Dense(1000, activation='softmax'))

    return model

alexnet = alexnet_model()

alexnet.summary()
```

The model summary resulting from the previous code is shown as follows:

```
Model: "AlexNet"
_________________________________________________________________
 Layer (type)                Output Shape              Param #
=================================================================
 conv2d (Conv2D)             (None, 55, 55, 96)        34944

 max_pooling2d (MaxPooling2D  (None, 27, 27, 96)       0
 )

 conv2d_1 (Conv2D)           (None, 27, 27, 256)       614656

 max_pooling2d_1 (MaxPooling  (None, 13, 13, 256)      0
 2D)

 conv2d_2 (Conv2D)           (None, 13, 13, 384)       885120

 conv2d_3 (Conv2D)           (None, 13, 13, 384)       1327488

 conv2d_4 (Conv2D)           (None, 13, 13, 256)       884992

 max_pooling2d_2 (MaxPooling  (None, 6, 6, 256)        0
 2D)

 flatten (Flatten)           (None, 9216)              0

 dense (Dense)               (None, 4096)              37752832

 dense_1 (Dense)             (None, 4096)              16781312

 dense_2 (Dense)             (None, 1000)              4097000

=================================================================
Total params: 62,378,344
Trainable params: 62,378,344
Non-trainable params: 0
```

***Figure 10.16**: AlexNet model Summary*

The AlexNet model consists of five convolutional layers which are followed by the ReLU activation function. Some of the layers also use max pooling to downscale the network. The network also contains three fully connected layers which serve as the decision-making part of the network, producing the final output predictions based on the extracted features from the earlier layers.

The layers contain parameters and filters of varying sizes, which help in learning hierarchical and increasingly complex features from the input data. The smaller filters focus on capturing finer details, while larger filters help identify broader patterns. The final fully connected layer in AlexNet has 1000 parameters corresponding to the number of output classes in the ImageNet dataset.

Since the model has around 62 million parameters, overfitting was a major concern in the AlexNet model and thus Dropout and Data Augmentation techniques were introduced as a measure to prevent overfitting and effectively improve the training performance of the model.

Using the AlexNet architecture with a 32×32×3 input size will not be feasible as the original AlexNet architecture was designed for a 227*227*3 image size. AlexNet was optimized for larger images and downsizing the input may lead to the loss of important information. The architecture's convolutional layer design will not translate well to the smaller input causing poor performance and overfitting. We can consider alternative architectures like VGG or increase the size of our input images to fit AlexNet architecture. Feel free to try other datasets with larger image sizes to implement AlexNet as well

VGGNET

VGGNET is a popular convolutional neural network architecture that was released in 2014 and achieved remarkable results in the **ImageNet Large Scale Visual Recognition Challenge (ILSVRC)** by achieving high accuracy on various image recognition benchmarks. It is still one of the most preferred architectures for various computer vision tasks.

The key characteristic of VGGNet is its uniform architecture, which primarily consists of 3x3 convolutional layers stacked on top of each other. These small-sized filters enabled the network to learn intricate features and deep hierarchies of representations, making it robust and capable of recognizing complex patterns.

There are various variations of the VGGNet differing on the number of layers present in the model. VGG16 (the original VGGNET model) and VGG19 are commonly used VGGNet architectures comprising 13 and 16 convolutional layers respectively and each comprising 3 fully connected layers. The extra layers in VGG19 allow it to learn even more complex representations often leading to better performance however also means higher computational requirements.

MiniVGG is a lightweight version of the original VGGNet, designed to strike a balance between model complexity and efficiency. It typically consists of fewer convolutional layers and smaller filter sizes, making it suitable for less computationally powerful devices or smaller datasets. Due to its smaller size, it might not be able to achieve similar performance compared to the larger VGG models, however, when a smaller model is needed due to space or time limitations MiniVGG is the preferable option:

```
import tensorflow as tf
from tensorflow.keras.models import Sequential
from tensorflow.keras.layers import Conv2D, MaxPooling2D, Flatten, Dense

def VGGNet(input_shape):
    model = Sequential()

    model.add(Conv2D(64, (3, 3), activation='relu', padding='same', in-
put_shape=input_shape))
    model.add(Conv2D(64, (3, 3), activation='relu', padding='same'))
    model.add(MaxPooling2D((2, 2), strides=(2, 2)))

    model.add(Conv2D(128, (3, 3), activation='relu', padding='same'))
    model.add(Conv2D(128, (3, 3), activation='relu', padding='same'))
    model.add(MaxPooling2D((2, 2), strides=(2, 2)))

    model.add(Conv2D(256, (3, 3), activation='relu', padding='same'))
    model.add(Conv2D(256, (3, 3), activation='relu', padding='same'))
    model.add(Conv2D(256, (3, 3), activation='relu', padding='same'))
    model.add(MaxPooling2D((2, 2), strides=(2, 2)))

    model.add(Conv2D(512, (3, 3), activation='relu', padding='same'))
    model.add(Conv2D(512, (3, 3), activation='relu', padding='same'))
    model.add(Conv2D(512, (3, 3), activation='relu', padding='same'))
    model.add(MaxPooling2D((2, 2), strides=(2, 2)))

    model.add(Conv2D(512, (3, 3), activation='relu', padding='same'))
    model.add(Conv2D(512, (3, 3), activation='relu', padding='same'))
    model.add(Conv2D(512, (3, 3), activation='relu', padding='same'))
    model.add(MaxPooling2D((2, 2), strides=(2, 2)))

    model.add(Flatten())
    model.add(Dense(4096, activation='relu'))
    model.add(Dense(4096, activation='relu'))
    model.add(Dense(1000, activation='softmax'))
    return model

input_shape = (224, 224, 3)
```

```
model = VGGNet(input_shape)

model.summary()
```

This will print the VGGNET model summary as follows:

Model: "sequential"

Layer (type)	Output Shape	Param #
conv2d (Conv2D)	(None, 224, 224, 64)	1792
conv2d_1 (Conv2D)	(None, 224, 224, 64)	36928
max_pooling2d (MaxPooling2D)	(None, 112, 112, 64)	0
conv2d_2 (Conv2D)	(None, 112, 112, 128)	73856
conv2d_3 (Conv2D)	(None, 112, 112, 128)	147584
max_pooling2d_1 (MaxPooling2D)	(None, 56, 56, 128)	0
conv2d_4 (Conv2D)	(None, 56, 56, 256)	295168
conv2d_5 (Conv2D)	(None, 56, 56, 256)	590080
conv2d_6 (Conv2D)	(None, 56, 56, 256)	590080
max_pooling2d_2 (MaxPooling2D)	(None, 28, 28, 256)	0
conv2d_7 (Conv2D)	(None, 28, 28, 512)	1180160
conv2d_8 (Conv2D)	(None, 28, 28, 512)	2359808
conv2d_9 (Conv2D)	(None, 28, 28, 512)	2359808
max_pooling2d_3 (MaxPooling2D)	(None, 14, 14, 512)	0
conv2d_10 (Conv2D)	(None, 14, 14, 512)	2359808
conv2d_11 (Conv2D)	(None, 14, 14, 512)	2359808
conv2d_12 (Conv2D)	(None, 14, 14, 512)	2359808
max_pooling2d_4 (MaxPooling2D)	(None, 7, 7, 512)	0
flatten (Flatten)	(None, 25088)	0
dense (Dense)	(None, 4096)	102764544
dense_1 (Dense)	(None, 4096)	16781312
dense_2 (Dense)	(None, 1000)	4097000

***Figure 10.16**: VGG16 model Summary*

Total params: 138,357,544

You might have realized that writing architectures from scratch can be a long and tedious process. Thankfully, tensorflow provides us with the functionality to load the model architectures directly without having to write any lines manually:

```
import tensorflow as tf
from tensorflow.keras.applications import VGG16

# Load VGG16 model without weights
vgg_model = VGG16(weights=None, include_top=True)

vgg_model.summary()
```

This will load the VGG16 model directly without having to write any lines of code. This especially comes in handy when large networks such as GoogleNet and ResNet need to be implemented. We will discuss these architectures as we move along the chapter.

The **`include_top=True`** parameter in the VGG16 model indicates that the pre-trained architecture includes the original fully connected layers designed for image classification tasks allowing us to utilize the entire model for predictions. Setting **`weights=None`** means that the model will be initialized with random weights instead of using any pre-trained weights. We will be using these parameters when we discuss transfer learning in the next section.

You can go ahead and try to train the VGGNet on any dataset of your choice. Training the VGGNet on CIfar10 results in ~75% which is a significant improvement over the 62% accuracy from the LeNet model. As models grow deeper, they learn increasingly complex and abstract features, allowing for further accuracy improvement by fine-tuning hyperparameters, employing data augmentation techniques, and exploring advanced optimization algorithms:

Results for VGG16 training for 15 epochs:

```
Epoch 14/15
782/782 [==============================] - 34s 44ms/step - loss: 0.1469
- accuracy: 0.9503 - val_loss: 1.0631 - val_accuracy: 0.7604
Epoch 15/15
782/782 [==============================] - 34s 44ms/step - loss: 0.1214
- accuracy: 0.9590 - val_loss: 1.1230 - val_accuracy: 0.7460
```

Another thing to notice in the preceding code is the **`weights`** and **`include_top`** parameters. We will discuss these in the next section where we will delve into transfer learning, a technique utilizing pre-trained models such as VGG16 to enhance performance on new tasks by reusing learned features and using them in different computer vision applications.

Transfer Learning

Transfer learning is a popular technique used in deep learning for training models by leveraging knowledge from other pre-trained models and using that information to solve new computer vision tasks.

In transfer learning, we begin by loading the weights of a pre-trained model, from which we extract features. Subsequently, these extracted features are utilized to fine-tune the new model for the target task

The key approach to using transfer learning is to use pre-trained models as feature extractors. The idea is to remove the last layer or more than one layer of the pre-trained model and use the output from the preceding layers as input features to a new model. By doing this, the new model can benefit from the generic features learned by the pre-trained model. We can also use only a certain part of the pre-trained model and fine-tune it using another dataset to get the desired results.

For example, an image classification model trained on imagenet can be used for a dog-vs-cat classification problem by loading the weights and removing the last layer. The last layer can be rewritten to provide a classification between two categories and the model can be further trained on the dog vs cat dataset.

There are various advantages of using transfer learning as the training time for the models is reduced significantly. The network doesn't have to learn all the features from scratch and the features learned during the initial training can be reused and just fine-tuned according to the new problem at hand.

Also, using transfer learning can help while training models with only small datasets. The information encapsulated in the pre-trained models can be used in training new models and thus when we have small datasets only, we can use transfer learning to train deep learning models. Transfer learning also improves the generalization and thus overall improves the performance of models.

Other Network Architectures

Let us discuss some advanced neural network architectures and explore how we can use transfer learning to use these networks to our advantage.

GoogleNet

GoogleNet, also known as Inception-v1 is an architecture developed by researchers at Google in 2014 and was the winner of the **ImageNet Large Scale Visual Recognition Challenge** (**ILSVRC**) that year.

The network primarily introduced the inception module which utilizes multiple convolutional filter sizes in parallel within a single layer. The Inception module is the key component of GoogleNet which allows the model to capture information at different scales while speeding up the training process as well.

Before going into the details about the network, let's discuss another concept used by the architecture. The Inception Module introduced another important concept used a lot in deep learning i.e. the use of 1v1 convolutions.

A 1×1 convolution, also known as a pointwise convolution applies filters of size 1x1 to the input feature maps, unlike traditional convolutions that use larger filter sizes like 3x3 or 5x5. The primary

The 1v1 convolution is primarily used for dimensionality reduction in a network. It reduces the number of channels in the input feature maps, making the data more compact and computationally efficient. However, if needed the 1v1 convolution operation can also be used to increase the number of channels allowing the model to learn more complex patterns and representations.

The 1v1 convolution can also be used to combine and integrate features from different parts of the network. This enables the model to learn and capture more diverse features from the network effectively enabling the network to learn better overall increasing the performance of the network.

Inception Module

Inception Module was a revolutionary addition to deep learning models as the module was able to capture multi-scale information effectively while maintaining a balance between the computational requirements and the model performance.

The main innovation of the Inception module is its ability to capture features at multiple spatial scales by incorporating multiple filters of different sizes (1×1, 3×3, and 5×5) in parallel within a single layer. This parallel approach enables the model to extract both fine-grained details and larger-scale patterns effectively. A max-pooling layer is also included in parallel to perform spatial downsampling, reducing the spatial dimensions of the feature maps while preserving important information:

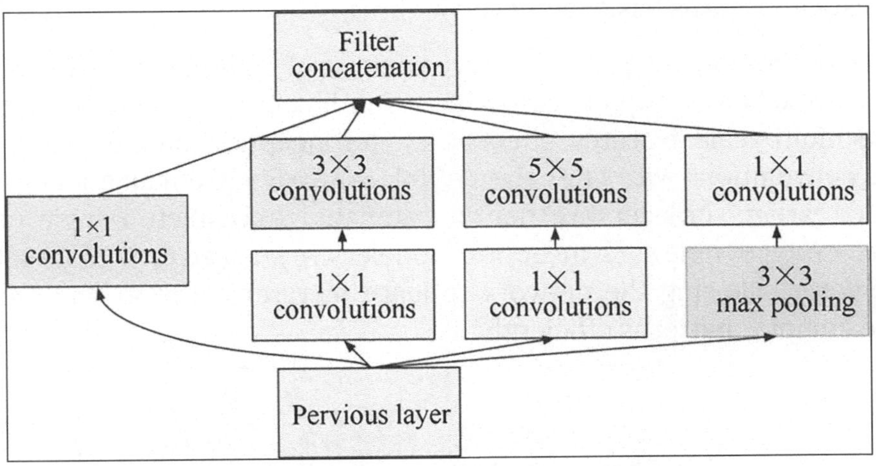

Figure 10.17: *Inception Module*

The outputs of all these parallel layers are then concatenated creating a merged set of features representing diverse information from various scales.

Another thing to notice here is that each parallel layer uses a 1×1 convolution operation along with the normal operation which helps with the dimensionality reduction thus reducing the size of the network significantly.

The max pooling layer complements the feature extraction process in the inception module and is included in parallel to efficiently downsample the feature maps. This downampling operation is performed to reduce the spatial dimensions of the feature maps while keeping the most significant information. This allows the model to focus on more critical information while managing computational complexity.

Multiple Inception modules can be stacked on top of each other to create a deep and hierarchical model architecture. Each module can learn a different set of features building an overall hierarchy of features. For example, The first Inception module might learn simple features like edges and textures, and then pass the learned features to the next module which would build upon those features to recognize more complex patterns.

Architecture

The architecture of GoogleNet starts with an input layer that takes an image of fixed size, typically 224×224 pixels. The initial layer is a standard convolutional layer with 64 filters of size 7×7. It is followed by a ReLU activation and a max-pooling layer to reduce the spatial dimensions. This first layer processes the raw image data and learns basic low-level features.

The core of the GoogleNet architecture consists of multiple Inception modules, which are stacked on top of each other. Each Inception module is designed to capture multi-scale features effectively. The inception module incorporates parallel convolutions with filter sizes of 1×1, 3×3, 5×5 and a max pooling layer as discussed earlier. The layers are then concatenated to complete a single inception module. A total of nine such inception modules are stacked on top of each other in GoogleNet allowing the network to learn hierarchical representations and capture complex patterns efficiently:

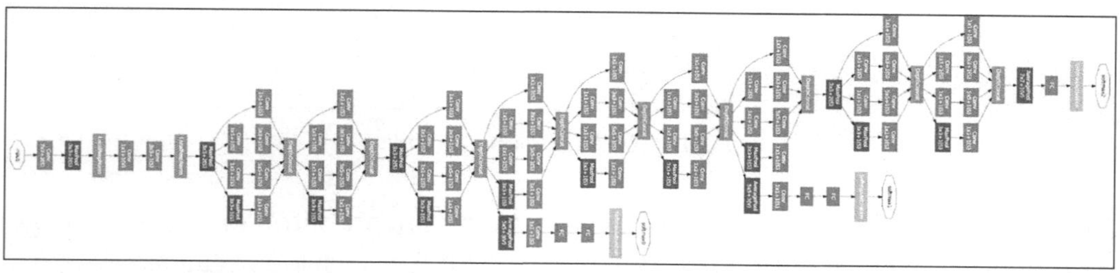

Figure 10.18: *The GoogleNet model architecture as described in the original paper*

To improve training and combat the vanishing gradient problem, GoogleNet also includes auxiliary classifiers after some of the Inception modules. These classifiers provide additional gradients during backpropagation, which aids in training the network effectively. These auxiliary classifiers consist of average pooling, followed by 1x1 convolutions and softmax layers. The predictions made by these auxiliary classifiers are not used for the final decision of the network but serve as intermediate supervision points during training. The overall loss function used for training GoogleNet is a combination of the loss from these auxiliary classifiers and the final loss from the main classifier.

GoogleNet also adds a global average pooling layer at the end, which reduces the spatial dimensions of the feature maps to a 1D vector before passing through fully connected layers for classification. This pooling helps drastically reduce the number of parameters and provides a more computationally efficient and effective approach for image recognition:

```
import numpy as np
import tensorflow as tf
from tensorflow.keras.applications import InceptionV3
from tensorflow.keras.preprocessing.image import ImageDataGenerator
from tensorflow.keras.layers import Dense, GlobalAveragePooling2D
from tensorflow.keras.models import Model

# Parameters
num_classes = 101
input_shape = (224, 224, 3)
batch_size = 32
epochs = 10

# Using InceptionV3 model pre trained on ImageNet data
base_model = InceptionV3(weights='imagenet', include_top=False, input_
shape=input_shape)

# Freeze layers in base model
for layer in base_model.layers:
    layer.trainable = False

# Add custom classification layers on top
x = base_model.output
x = Dense(1024, activation='relu')(x)
predictions = Dense(num_classes, activation='softmax')(x)

model = Model(inputs=base_model.input, outputs=predictions)

model.compile(optimizer='adam', loss='categorical_crossentropy',
metrics=['accuracy'])

data_gen = ImageDataGenerator(
    rescale=1.0 / 255,
    rotation_range=20,
```

```
    width_shift_range=0.2,
    height_shift_range=0.2,
    horizontal_flip=True,
    fill_mode='nearest',
    validation_split=0.2)

data_generator = data_gen.flow_from_directory(
    'images',
    target_size=input_shape[:2],
    batch_size=batch_size,
    class_mode='categorical',
    subset='training')

val_generator = data_gen.flow_from_directory(
    'images',
    target_size=input_shape[:2],
    batch_size=batch_size,
    class_mode='categorical',
    subset='validation')

model.fit(
    data_generator,
    steps_per_epoch=data_generator.samples // batch_size,
    epochs=epochs,
    validation_data=val_generator,
    validation_steps=val_generator.samples // batch_size,
    callbacks=[early_stopping])

model.save('caltech101_inceptionv3.h5')
```

Output:

```
Epoch 5/5

218/218 [==============================] - 88s 405ms/step - loss: 0.2455
- accuracy: 0.9226 - val_loss: 0.4703 - val_accuracy: 0.8810
```

Here, we're initializing the **base_model** using the InceptionV3 architecture. By setting **weights='imagenet'**, we're loading pre-trained weights from the ImageNet dataset, which helps our model start with learned features. The parameter **include_top=False** means we're excluding the original fully connected layers, making it suitable for feature extraction. This approach allows us to attach our specialized layers for classifying our specific dataset.

We then loop through the layers in the model and freeze them. We freeze certain layers to avoid training them all over again, which saves time and resources. This also helps preserve the valuable knowledge already captured by the pre-trained model. In case we want to further refine the model's understanding for our specific task, we can unfreeze specific layers and fine-tune them as needed.

By utilizing pre-trained models and applying transfer learning, we have achieved an impressive accuracy of 88% within only five epochs. This highlights the effectiveness of transfer learning in enhancing model performance.

ResNet

ResNet, abbreviated from Residual Network, was introduced by Kaiming He, Xiangyu Zhang, Shaoqing Ren, and Jian Sun in 2015. ResNet has become a fundamental building block for various tasks in artificial intelligence due to its ability to train deep neural networks and their ability to handle the vanishing gradient problem.

ResNet introduced a novel architecture in the form of residual blocks which are the building blocks of ResNet networks. These residual blocks allow for the training of much deeper networks while avoiding the vanishing gradient problem.

Residual Blocks

Residual blocks are a critical architectural element introduced in the Residual Neural Network (ResNet) architecture:

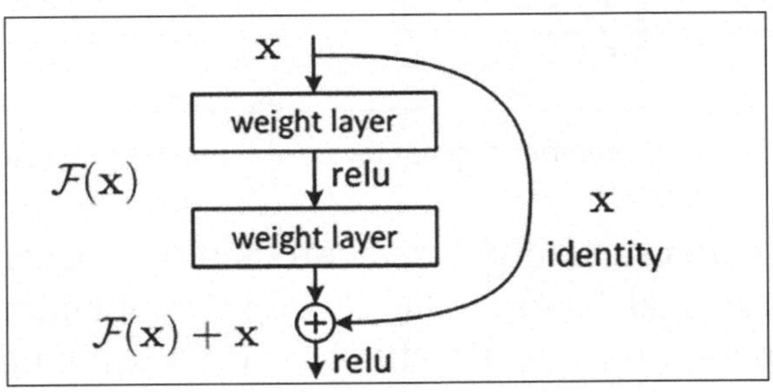

***Figure 10.19**: Residual Block*

As we increase the size of a neural network, ideally it should improve its performance and accuracy. However, in practice, as the network gets deeper, it often becomes harder to train.

One of the main reasons for this difficulty is the vanishing gradient problem. As the network goes deeper, the gradients (values that help the network learn) become extremely small as they backpropagate through the layers. These vanishing gradients prevent the network from effectively adjusting the initial input to reach the desired output during the learning process.

Residual blocks were introduced to address this issue. A residual block is a special building block that introduces a "shortcut" connection, also known as a **skip connection** or **identity mapping**. This shortcut connection allows the output of one layer to be added directly to the input of another layer, bypassing some intermediate layers.

By using this approach, the network can focus on learning the incremental adjustments (residuals) rather than trying to learn the entire transformation from input to output. This makes it easier for the network to optimize its weights and allows us to train very deep networks effectively. Overall, residual blocks help neural networks to "skip" some layers and learn the residual changes efficiently.

Architecture

The main idea behind ResNet is to stack multiple residual blocks on top of each other to create a deep neural network. This allows the network to take advantage of the various skip connections and overcome the vanishing gradient problem:

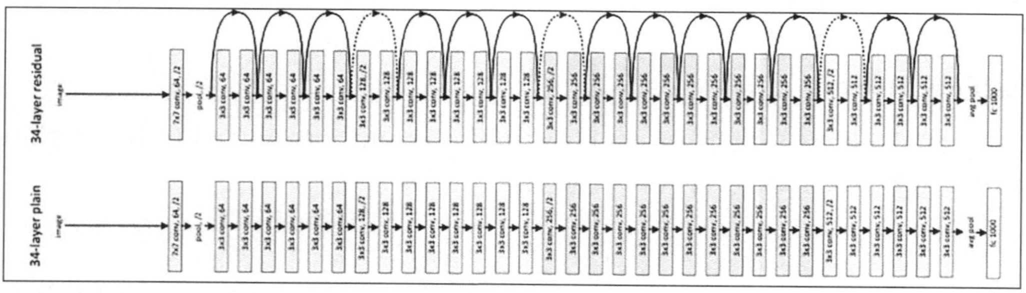

Figure 10.20: *ResNet-34 model showing skip connections compared to a standard 34-layer model*

In a ResNet, the network is organized into multiple layers, and each layer contains several residual blocks. The shortcut connections in the residual blocks help information to flow directly from the beginning to the end of the network, enabling the network to retain and learn from earlier representations effectively.

There are several variants of ResNet's depending on the number of layers in the network. Some of the common variations of ResNet include ResNet-18,

ResNet-34, ResNet-50, and ResNet-152 with the number representing the layers in each architecture:

- **ResNet-18**: ResNet-18 is a shallow variant of the ResNet architecture consisting of 18 layers. It introduced the concept of residual blocks helping mitigate the vanishing gradient problem and allowing for the training of deeper networks.
- **ResNet-34**: ResNet-34 is a slightly deeper variant with 34 layers. It follows the same principle of residual blocks but offers increased model capacity compared to ResNet-18. This architecture is suitable for a wide range of computer vision tasks and is known for its simplicity and effectiveness.
- **ResNet-50**: ResNet-50 is a deeper model with 50 layers, making it more powerful in capturing complex patterns and features in data. It is commonly used in image classification and transfer learning tasks, thanks to its ability to learn rich representations from large datasets.
- **ResNet-152**: ResNet-152 is the deepest among the mentioned variants with 152 layers. This architecture is capable of achieving state-of-the-art results in various computer vision tasks including image recognition, object detection, and segmentation by leveraging its immense capacity to capture hierarchical features.

Apart from these, there are other variants of ResNet such as ResNet-101 and ResNet-110, which offer increased model depth and capacity for tackling more complex tasks in computer vision and deep learning. All of these ResNet variants have made significant contributions to the field of deep learning enabling the training of very deep neural networks that excel in various computer vision tasks while mitigating issues related to training depth. The selection for the type of architecture will be dependent on the type of problem at hand.

ResNet 50,101 and 152 models can be loaded directly via TensorFlow. Other Resnet models such as 18 and 34 need to be coded separately:

```
import tensorflow as tf
from tensorflow.keras.applications import ResNet50, ResNet101, ResNet152


# Load ResNet models
resnet18 = ResNet50()
resnet34 = ResNet101(weights='imagenet')
resnet50 = ResNet152(weights='imagenet')
```

You can go ahead and try to explore ResNet models and try to train the models on different datasets according to your choice.

Conclusion

In this chapter, we learned about Neural Networks' basics, design, activation functions, and training methods like Backpropagation and Gradient Descent. Additionally, we trained our neural networks on various datasets, explored Convolutional Neural Networks (CNNs) and their layers, and studied prominent models like LeNet, AlexNet, VGGNet, GoogleNet, and ResNet. Transfer Learning was introduced as a tool for leveraging existing networks, providing a comprehensive foundation for understanding and creating intelligent systems.

In the next chapter, we will delve into the basics of object detection, which involves identifying specific objects within images or videos. We'll then explore various techniques used for object detection, such as sliding windows, image pyramids, and object tracking. Additionally, we will also explore how deep learning can be harnessed for effective object detection.

Points to remember

- A neural network is a computational model inspired by the human brain that processes information through interconnected nodes, enabling it to learn and make predictions.
- An activation function is a mathematical operation in a neural network that determines the output of a neuron based on its input, introducing non-linearity and enabling the network to capture complex patterns in data.
- Backpropagation is a process that involves calculating and propagating errors backward through a neural network's layers and adjusting connection weights to enhance prediction accuracy.
- Gradient descent is an optimization algorithm used in training neural networks, which involves iteratively adjusting the model's parameters by moving in the direction of the steepest descent of the loss function to find the optimal values.
- A Convolutional Neural Network (CNN) is a specialized type of neural network designed for image and spatial data, using convolutional layers to automatically learn hierarchical features from the input and enabling effective pattern recognition.
- Existing neural network architectures, like LeNet, AlexNet, and VGGNet, provide frameworks that can be utilized to construct specialized models for various tasks.

- Transfer learning makes use of pre-trained models to improve the performance of neural networks on new, similar tasks.
- ResNet is a neural architecture that addresses deep network training by using shortcut connections for improved feature learning in layers.

Test your understanding

1. Which activation function is more suitable for preventing the dying ReLU problem?

   A. ReLU

   B. Leaky ReLU

   C. Both

   D. Neither

2. How does dropout regularization work?

   A. Adds noise to the input data to improve generalization.

   B. Increases the number of layers in the network.

   C. Applies data augmentation to the input images.

   D. Sets a fraction of neurons to zero during each iteration.

3. Which layer is responsible for reducing dimensionality in a CNN?

   A. Convolutional layer

   B. Activation layer

   C. Pooling layer

   D. Fully connected layer

4. The primary components of a pre-trained model in transfer learning are?

   A. Input data and activation functions

   B. Weights and biases

   C. Activation functions and loss functions

   D. Optimization algorithm and activation functions

5. What is the main purpose of the Inception module in a CNN?
    A. To reduce the depth of the network and improve training efficiency.
    B. To increase the number of parameters for better feature extraction.
    C. To process input data using only fully connected layers.
    D. To capture and process information at multiple scales using different kernel sizes.

Chapter 11

Object Detection Using OpenCV

In this chapter, we will explore the fundamentals of object detection and the process of identifying objects within images and videos. It covers various techniques like sliding windows, image pyramids, and template matching using OpenCV. This chapter will explore training our very own object detection algorithm from scratch. We will explore the effectiveness and ease of use of pre-trained algorithms such as Haar Cascades and DLIB for object detection. The chapter also explains feature extraction for object detection, highlights facial landmarks using DLIB and touches on object tracking methods using OpenCV.

Structure

In this chapter, we will discuss the following topics:

- Introduction to object detection
- Detecting objects using sliding windows
- Template matching using OpenCV
- Haar cascades
- Feature extraction for object detection
- Facial landmarks with DLIB
- Object tracking using OpenCV

Introduction to object detection

Object detection is a fundamental task in computer vision that enables machines to understand and detect objects in images or videos. Using computer vision, computers have been able to detect objects in real time which has given way to a wide number of applications in the field.

With the advancement in technology in recent years, object detection has seen remarkable progress. A substantial amount of research has been conducted to enhance the accuracy of these systems while also optimizing their performance in terms of space and time efficiency. The availability of large datasets, high computational chips and the need for intelligent systems have driven object detection to be one of the most extensively researched topics in computer vision.

Object detection helps systems capable of not only recognizing and identifying the presence of a certain object in an image, but object detection systems are able to accurately predict the exact location of an object in an image. Object Detection systems generally work by drawing bounding boxes around the predicted objects to accurately localize and identify them within an image or a video sequence.

Object recognition systems are capable of performing various tasks and have found their way into transforming numerous industries. Object detection systems have enabled us to develop a wide range of applications such as video surveillance, augmented reality, retail analytics, and industrial automation, among others.

One of the remarkable applications of object detection systems has been autonomous driving capabilities. Object recognition has enabled vehicles to identify and respond to traffic signs, pedestrians, and other vehicles. This has led to enhanced safety and improved efficiency in transportation systems.

Traditional computer vision techniques such as Haar cascades and HOG have been instrumental in the evolution of object detection. These techniques leverage meticulously crafted features and classifiers, enabling effective detection in specific contexts. However, recently deep learning techniques have emerged as a powerful tool harnessing the capacity to automatically learn and generalize features.

There are also multiple challenges with object detection. These challenges can be due to variations in object appearance such as scale variations, cluttered backgrounds, and or object occlusion. Objects may also appear different due to variations in lighting conditions, camera viewpoint and improper picture resolution. As we continue researching object detection, numerous techniques have been developed to handle these problems, effectively creating state-of-the-art solutions.

Let's start by discussing a rudimentary approach towards object detection using Python.

Detecting objects using sliding windows

To start with object detection, imagine how humans perceive objects in their surroundings. First, we survey each object and angle using our eyes and then we attempt to locate the desired item by comparing its distinct characteristics with those present in their environment. If we discover an object that matches, we have found the item. The first approach we will use for object detection will build on this process.

Just like humans scan their environment, we will use sliding windows to *scan* and traverse through objects in the hope of finding the object we want to detect. By incrementally shifting the window and analyzing each subregion we can effectively detect objects of interest within the image. We will use a comparison mechanism, such as Euclidean distance between our object and frame in consideration. The frame with the lowest value will contain our object:

Figure 11.1: *Sliding Window operation on an image to detect objects. The window is moved through the image until an object of matching characteristics is found.*

The code will better help understand the process:

```
import cv2
import numpy as np

source_image = cv2.imread('scene.jpg')
template = cv2.imread('house.jpg')

# Define a range of scales to consider
scales = np.linspace(0.5, 1.5, 5)


# Variables to store best case values
```

```
best_match_value = float('inf')
best_match_location = (0, 0)
best_scale = 1.0

for scale in scales:
    print(scale)
    # Resize the template according to the current scale
    scaled_template = cv2.resize(template, None, fx=scale, fy=scale)

    template_height, template_width = scaled_template.shape[:2]

    for y in range(0, source_image.shape[0] - template_height):
        for x in range(0, source_image.shape[1] - template_width):
            region = source_image[y:y + template_height, x:x + template_
width]

            # Mean squared difference between the region and template
            diff = np.sum((region - scaled_template)**2)

            if diff < best_match_value:
                best_match_value = diff
                best_match_location = (x, y)
                best_scale = scale

# Actual size of the detected object
detected_width = int(template.shape[1] * best_scale)
detected_height = int(template.shape[0] * best_scale)

cv2.rectangle(source_image, best_match_location, (best_match_location[0]
+ detected_width, best_match_location[1] + detected_height), (0, 255,
0), 2)

cv2.imshow('Object Detection Result', source_image)
cv2.waitKey(0)
cv2.destroyAllWindows()
```

The source image used here is:

Figure 11.2: *Source Image*

In the preceding code, we use sliding windows to find our target object from a large image. We start by loading the original image and the image of the object (house in this case) we want to detect in the source image. The template for this will be an image of the house, that we try to detect from the preceding image:

Figure 11.3: *Template Image. We will try to detect this object from the source image*

Since we don't know the size of the target object inside our image, we will resize our template image to a range of scales. We use the **`np.linspace`** function to define a scale range between 0.5 to 1.5. We keep the third parameter as 5 which will generate 5 evenly spaced range values between 0.5 and 1.5.

We define three variables that will store the best values as we iterate through the image with the sliding window. As we will loop through the values, these values will store the best match value, the location of the best match and the scale at which we received that match. The **`best_match_value`** starts as infinity as any calculated difference will be smaller. The variable will store and update the lowest difference value for identifying the best template match.

Now we can start using the sliding window to find the object in the image. The first loop runs through all the scale values we defined earlier, and we resize our template image to this scale using the resize function. We store the dimensions of this image in variables which will help us to define the size of the sliding window in the respective scale.

Next, we loop through the image using the sliding window. The loops iterate through valid starting points (y, x) in the source image, where the template can fit entirely without going out of bounds. Subtracting template height and width ensures that the loops stay within these valid ranges for accurate matching.

We extract the necessary region from the image and store the result in the **`region`** variable as we slide through the image. This region acts like a sliding window, moving across the image to compare its content with the template during the process of template matching for object detection. We use the mean squared difference metric to compare the extracted region with the scaled template image. If this difference is lower than the previous values, we store the best values in the variables we defined earlier.

Once we have gone through the result, our lowest distance value, along with its position and scale, is now stored in the variables. We use the rectangle function to draw the bonding box at this point and, as we can see, the logic has been able to correctly identify the house from the image:

Figure 11.4: *Output: Object found and visualized with a bounding box*

It is important to note that, while the algorithm has been able to identify our object properly, it has a lot of caveats. For one, it takes a lot of computational time to compare objects at each position and each scale in the original image. Also, we are not sure of the scale of the object in the original image and this logic might fail to identify the object properly if the scales variable here is not initialized properly. This method is not robust with variations in scale, rotations, lighting, or occlusions.

Let's explore alternative methods that can identify objects while mitigating some of these challenges.

Template matching using OpenCV

Template matching is a fundamental concept in object detection that involves using a predefined template image and searching the target image to find instances that match its characteristics.

The sliding window we discussed in the last code can also be considered a template matching code, as it involves the basic process of searching for a template image in the target image and finding the best match.

Here, we will use OpenCV's in-built function for template matching. This function eliminates the need to build custom sliding windows and while the function also slides the template over the target image, it works much faster in comparison.

cv2.matchTemplate

Syntax:

```
cv2.matchTemplate(image, template, method=cv2.TM_SQDIFF, mask=None)
```

Parameters:

- **`image`**: Source Image
- **`template`**: Template Image
- **`method`**: The comparison method calculates similarity scores. The options for this parameter are:
  - **`cv2.TM_SQDIFF`**: Sum of squared differences. - Default Value
  - **`cv2.TM_CCORR`**: Cross-correlation.
  - **`cv2.TM_CCOEFF`**: Cross-correlation coefficient.
  - **`cv2.TM_CCORR_NORMED`**: Normalized cross-correlation.
  - **`cv2.TM_CCOEFF`**: Cross-correlation coefficient.
  - **`cv2.TM_CCOEFF_NORMED`**: Normalized cross-correlation coefficient.
- **`mask`**: Optional mask

Let us use this function to detect some objects. We will use the coin image we used earlier in the course of this book and try to detect a specific coin from it.

The image we will be using is:

Figure 11.5: *Source Image*

Let us try to detect this coin from the image. This is a rotated image of one of the coins present in the preceding pictures:

Figure 11.6: *Template Image*

```
import cv2
import numpy as np

source_image = cv2.imread('coin.jpg')
template = cv2.imread(template.jpg')

# Save width and height of template
template_height, template_width = template.shape[:2]

# Template matching
result = cv2.matchTemplate(source_image, template,
cv2.TM_CCOEFF_NORMED)
min_val, max_val, min_loc, max_loc = cv2.minMaxLoc(result)

# Get the top-left corner of the detected area
top_left = max_loc

# Get the bottom-right corner of the detected area
bottom_right = (top_left[0] + template_width, top_left[1] + template_
height)

cv2.rectangle(source_image, top_left, bottom_right, (0, 255, 0), 2)

cv2.imwrite(Output.jpg', source_image)
cv2.waitKey(0)
cv2.destroyAllWindows()
```

Figure 11.7: *Output with detected object*

Output:

The preceding code loads the source and template images just like we did before. This time we use the `cv2.matchTemplate` function to easily detect our objects without having to explicitly code sliding windows and best match comparison.

To illustrate our findings, we locate the minimum and maximum values using the `cv2.minMaxLoc` function on the resulting image. We get the upper-left value and use it to compute the coordinates for the lower-right corner of the bounding box that we intend to draw.

This was a very simple way to detect objects in our images. However, it is important to remember that template matching will struggle with significant variations in scale, rotation, lighting conditions, and complex scenes. The comparison method used might also influence the detection results.

Haar cascades

Haar cascade detection, also known as the Viola-Jones algorithm after its inventors Paul Viola and Michael Jones revolutionized real-time object detection. The algorithm gained prominence in face detection for its ability to rapidly detect faces in images. Owing to its versatility and capabilities, the applications for this algorithm have since expanded to meet various demands.

One of the main reasons for its popularity is the efficiency and the speed it promises. This is primarily due to the use of Haar-Like features and cascade of classifiers.

Haar-like features: Haar-like features are simple rectangular patterns used in the Haar Cascade algorithm for object detection. Inspired by the Haar wavelet transform, these features capture basic visual patterns, such as edges, lines, and corners in an image.

Haar-like features consist of rectangular regions of different sizes and positions within an image. These features focus on differences in pixel intensities between light and dark subregions in each rectangle. The Haar Cascade algorithm uses three main types of Haar-like features: edge features, line features, and four-rectangle features:

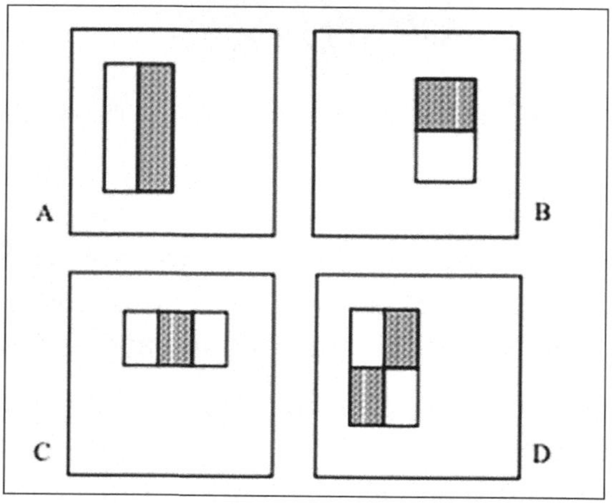

***Figure 11.8**: Haar-Like Features example, Image source: https://www.cs.cmu.edu/~efros/courses/LBMV07/Papers/viola-cvpr-01.pdf*

By combining these patterns Haar Cascade algorithms can spot objects by noticing the unique ways they stand out from their surroundings. By calculating the difference in pixel intensities within these rectangular regions, the algorithm can efficiently capture important visual characteristics of objects. This makes them good at detecting objects in images.

Cascade of classifiers: A cascade of classifiers is a smart strategy used in object detection to quickly find objects while efficiently using computer resources. Each filter in the cascade eliminates parts of the image that are less likely to contain the object. It starts with quick and simple checks to reject obviously non-object areas, saving time. As the image goes through each filter, the computer becomes more confident about whether it found the object or not. This step-by-step process makes object detection faster and more accurate.

These features are aggregated and combined using machine learning techniques like AdaBoost to create a strong classifier capable of distinguishing between objects and non-object regions. Haar classifiers are now used for techniques like face detection and object recognition.

Training our own Haar cascade is a complex task that involves intricate processes like AdaBoost techniques and NMS. These concepts are beyond the scope of this book and do not need to be explored in-depth, as we can conveniently utilize pre-trained models provided by OpenCV. We can use these pre-trained cascades that simplify the process and allow us to directly use them for object detection.

There are several pre-trained Haar cascades available as an open-source for various object detection tasks. Some of the commonly available options are:

- Face detection:
  - **haarcascade_frontalface_default.xml**: Detects frontal faces.
  - **haarcascade_smile.xml**: Detects smiles within faces.
  - **haarcascade_eye.xml**: Detects eyes within faces.
- Full body and pedestrian detection:
  - **haarcascade_fullbody.xml**: Detects full human bodies.
  - **haarcascade_upperbody.xml**: Detects upper human bodies.
  - **haarcascade_lowerbody.xml**: Detects lower human bodies.
  - **haarcascade_pedestrian.xml**: Detects pedestrians.
- Car detection:
  - **haarcascade_car.xml**: Detects cars.

The XML files represent the trained Haar cascade classifiers and can be found at OpenCV's GitHub repository (https://github.com/opencv/opencv/tree/master/data/haarcascades) and other online sources. These files can be downloaded and used for our applications without any restrictions.

Haar also has a pre-trained model to detect frontal cat faces. For our example, let's try detecting a cat face from an image. The file name for the trained cat face detector is **haarcascade_frontalcatface.xml**.

```
import cv2

# Loading pre-trained cat face cascade
cat_face_cascade = cv2.CascadeClassifier('haarcascade_frontalcatface.xml')

image_path = cat.png'
image = cv2.imread(image_path)
gray_image = cv2.cvtColor(image, cv2.COLOR_BGR2GRAY)

# Perform cat face detection
cat_faces = cat_face_cascade.detectMultiScale(gray_image, scaleFactor=1.1,
minNeighbors=5, minSize=(30, 30))
```

```
for (x, y, w, h) in cat_faces:
    cv2.rectangle(image, (x, y), (x + w, y + h), (255, 0, 0), 2)

cv2.imshow('Cat Face Detection', image)
cv2.waitKey(0)
cv2.destroyAllWindows()
```

The output for the code is as follows:

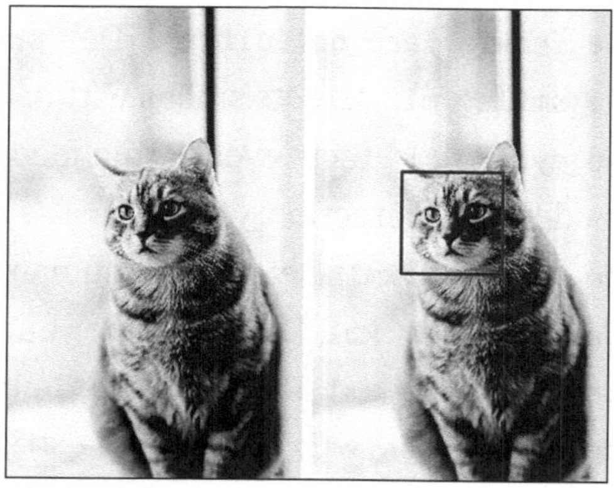

***Figure 11.9**: Left: Input Image, Right: Detected Face*

We can see that the Haar cascade has been able to easily detect the face of our cat in the image. Why don't you try to run cat face detection on a video?

To demonstrate Haar Cascades on a video, we will use another model and see how the Haar pedestrian model works and if it is able to accurately detect pedestrians walking on the road:

```
import cv2

pedestrian_cascade = cv2.CascadeClassifier('haarcascade_fullbody.xml')

# Open a video capture object
video_path = 'pedestrian_video.mp4'
cap = cv2.VideoCapture(video_path)

while cap.isOpened():
    ret, frame = cap.read()
    if not ret:
        break

    gray = cv2.cvtColor(frame, cv2.COLOR_BGR2GRAY)
```

```
    # Perform pedestrian detection
    pedestrians = pedestrian_cascade.detectMultiScale(gray,
scaleFactor=1.1, minNeighbors=5, minSize=(50, 100))

    for (x, y, w, h) in pedestrians:
        cv2.rectangle(frame, (x, y), (x + w, y + h), (0, 255, 0), 2)

    cv2.imshow('Pedestrian Detection', frame)

    if cv2.waitKey(1) & 0xFF == ord('q'):
        break

cap.release()
cv2.destroyAllWindows()
```

In the preceding code, we used a video of pedestrians and tried to detect them using the **haarcascade_fullbody.xml** model. Some of the frames from the output video are as follows:

Figure 11.10: *Results of people detection using the Haar model*

We can observe that Haar has generally provided accurate results in the video. However, it's important to note that in some cases, Haar missed detecting one or two people. This is due to its sensitivity to factors like complex backgrounds and variations in pose and scale, thus highlighting its limitations in challenging scenarios.

One of the widely used applications of Haar is face detection in computer vision. The Haar Cascade Classifier is effective in locating human faces within images and videos. **haarcascade_frontalface_default.xml** is one of the models used for face detection. Feel free to explore the mentioned model or other Haar models and utilize them for various other applications.

Feature extraction for object detection

Feature extraction involves transforming image data into representations that better represent essential patterns and information present in the image. We can use these features to detect objects in our images.

By using features extracted using techniques such as Histogram of Oriented Gradients or Local Binary Patterns, we can implement robust and effective object detection algorithms. These features can help us facilitate accurate and reliable identification and localization of objects within images.

Object detection using feature extraction operates by training a machine learning algorithm on these features of the objects we want to detect. We can utilize this model to predict and identify objects within new images.

In this section, we will create our very own face detector to identify and locate human faces within images. We will be using HoG to extract features from the dataset and SVM model for our classification.

The steps for creating an object detection algorithm using features are as follows:

1. **Dataset preparation**: The first step involves gathering a dataset containing positive and negative examples of the object we want to detect. Positive examples will have images containing the object that we want to detect (in this case face images) and negative examples are images without the object.

2. **Feature extraction using HOG**: For each image in your dataset, we will compute the Histogram of Oriented Gradients. HoG will help us to capture the distribution and intensity of gradients within the image. These HoG features will help our model to understand the characteristics of the object we want to detect.

3. **Training the classifier**: HOG features obtained from the previous step are then used to train our classifier. Support Vector Machines (SVM) are a good choice for this application. The SVM model will learn to separate positive and negative examples based on the extracted HOG features.

4. **Sliding window**: Once the model is trained, we will use a sliding window for testing new images. For each window position HOG features are computed, and the trained classifier is used to determine whether the object is present in the window or not.

5. **Non-maximum suppression**: Since multiple overlapping windows might detect the same object, apply non-maximum suppression to eliminate redundant detections. This involves keeping only the most confident detection in each area of overlap.
6. **Object localization and visualization**: After non-maximum suppression, we have the final detected bounding boxes for the objects in the image. These bounding boxes are then drawn on the original image to visualize the detected objects.

Before we proceed to implement this using code, there is another important concept that needs to be discussed.

Image pyramids

Image pyramids are a technique used in image processing and computer vision to create a series of images at different scales. An image pyramid consists of a level of images where each level represents the same image but at a different scale. The original image forms the base level and subsequent levels are obtained by resizing (upscaling or downscaling) to the previous level:

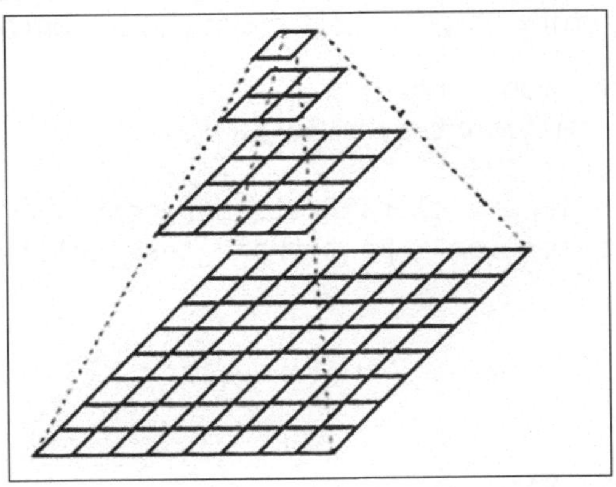

Figure 11.11: *Image Pyramid*

We will be using these image pyramids in object detection. They will help us to analyze images in different sizes, enhancing our ability to detect objects of varying scales. This will ensure that objects can be accurately identified regardless of their size in the image.

Image pyramids are of two types:

- **Gaussian pyramids**: The Gaussian pyramid is built through a series of operations on the original image. It starts with applying Gaussian smoothing and then the image is downsampled effectively reducing its size while maintaining its overall appearance. Each level of the Gaussian pyramid captures the image at a different scale, with increasing levels representing images that are progressively more blurred.

- **Laplacian pyramids**: The Laplacian pyramid is derived from the Gaussian pyramid only. It is used to capture the details that are lost during downsampling. Each level of the Laplacian pyramid contains the difference between the corresponding level in the Gaussian pyramid and the next level. Laplacian pyramid images are like edge images only and essentially represent the fine details and high-frequency components of the image.

We can move on to creating our very own object detection application now.

We will be using the LFW (Labeled Faces in the Wild) dataset for face images in our application. The LFW dataset is an open-source and widely used collection of facial images. It contains thousands of images of individuals collected from the web with variations in lighting, pose, and facial expressions.

For our negative images, that is, images not containing a face, we will be using images from various backgrounds containing various objects. The objective is to make this dataset as wide as possible. We are using background images so that the model can successfully classify faces from the backgrounds:

```
from skimage.feature import hog
from skimage.transform import pyramid_gaussian
from sklearn.svm import SVC
from sklearn.metrics import classification_report
from sklearn.model_selection import train_test_split
import numpy as np
import cv2
import os

orientations = 9
pixels_per_cell = (8, 8)
cells_per_block = (2, 2)

postitive_data= []
positive_labels = []

positive_folder='lfw'
positive_features = []

for folder in os.listdir(positive_folder):
    if not os.path.isdir(os.path.join(positive_folder, folder)):
        continue
```

```
    subfolder_path = os.path.join(positive_folder, folder)
    for filename in os.listdir(subfolder_path):
        img = cv2.imread(os.path.join(subfolder_path, filename), cv2.
IMREAD_GRAYSCALE)
        img = cv2.resize(img,(64,64))
        feature = hog(img, orientations, pixels_per_cell, cells_per_block,
block_norm='L2', feature_vector=True)
        postitive_data.append(feature)
        positive_labels.append(1)

negative_data= []
negative_labels = []

negative_folder='scene'
negative_features = []

for folder in os.listdir(negative_folder):
    if not os.path.isdir(os.path.join(negative_folder, folder)):
        continue

    subfolder_path = os.path.join(negative_folder, folder)
    for filename in os.listdir(subfolder_path)[:200]:
        img = cv2.imread(os.path.join(subfolder_path, filename), cv2.
IMREAD_GRAYSCALE)
        img = cv2.resize(img,(64,64))
        feature = hog(img, orientations, pixels_per_cell, cells_per_block,
block_norm='L2', feature_vector=True)
        negative_data.append(feature)
        negative_labels.append(0)

data = postitive_data+negative_data
labels = positive_labels+negative_labels

(train_data, test_data, train_labels, test_labels) = train_test_split(
      np.array(data), labels, test_size=0.2)

model = SVC(kernel='linear', C=1.0)
model.fit(train_data, train_labels)

predictions = model.predict(test_data)
print(classification_report(test_labels, predictions))
```

This produces the following classification report:

```
              precision    recall  f1-score   support

           0       1.00      1.00      1.00       539
           1       1.00      1.00      1.00       621

    accuracy                           1.00      1160
   macro avg       1.00      1.00      1.00      1160
weighted avg       1.00      1.00      1.00      1160
```

Amongst other metrics, we can observe that the precision and accuracy are 1.0 indicating that the model has been able to accurately classify all the images properly from the test dataset.

In the code, we begin by importing all the necessary libraries. We will be using the scikit-learn HoG function and define the parameters to be used for HoG feature extraction.

We define our positive image dataset path and loop through the images in the folder. For all images, we convert them to grayscale and resize them to a fixed size of (64,64) for HoG feature extraction. We extract the features for each image and append the **positive_data** list with the parameters. We append a value of 1 for each positive image to our **positive_label** list. We do the same for our negative images and combine positive and negative lists for our model training.

The data is split into train and test with a test dataset of 20%. Next, an SVM model is initialized and trained on the training data extracted earlier. The model is then tested on the test data and a classification report is printed to analyze our model performance. From the resultant classification report, it is evident that the model has good accuracy and is able to accurately classify our images.

Now that our model is trained with good accuracy, let us try to detect objects on new images.

This is a brief overview of how the inference pipeline will operate. We load an image and use sliding windows to traverse through the image. The model trained earlier is used to make predictions for each frame. If the model outputs a value of 1, that is, there is a face present in the frame, we save the box values in a list. The model generates overlapping detections on the same object. We use non-maximum suppression to address this and display the final results:

```
img= cv2.imread("coco1.jpg")
final = img.copy()


detections = []
confidences = []

(width, height)= (64,64)
windowSize=(width,height)
downscale=1.5

for scale, resized in enumerate(pyramid_gaussian(img, downscale=1.5)):
    for y in range(0, resized.shape[0] - height, 10):
        for x in range(0, resized.shape[1] - width, 10):
            window = resized[y: y + height, x: x + width]

            if window.shape[0] == height and window.shape[1] == width and
window.shape[2] == 3:

                window = cv2.cvtColor((window*255).astype(np.uint8),
cv2.COLOR_BGR2GRAY)
                features = hog(window, orientations, pixels_per_cell,
cells_per_block, block_norm='L2')
                features = features.reshape(1, -1)
                pred = model.predict(features)

                if pred == 1 and model.decision_function(features) > 0.8:
                    print("Detection:: Location -> ({}, {})".format(x, y))
                    detections.append((int(x * (downscale**scale)), int(y
* (downscale**scale)),
                                       int(width * (downscale**scale)),
                                       int(height * (downscale**s-
cale))))
                    confidences.append(model.decision_function(features))

for box in detections:
    x, y, w, h = box
    cv2.rectangle(img, (x, y), (x + w, y + h), (0, 0, 255), thickness=2)

# Convert detected boxes NumPy array
boxes = np.array([[d[0], d[1], d[2], d[3]] for d in detections],
dtype=np.int32)
indices = cv2.dnn.NMSBoxes(boxes, np.array(confidences).ravel(), 0.5,
0.3)

for idx in indices:
    x, y, w, h = boxes[idx]
```

```
    cv2.rectangle(final, (x, y), (x + w, y + h), (0, 0, 255), thickness=2)

# Display the image with bounding boxes
cv2.imshow("All Detections", img)
cv2.imshow("After NMS", final)
cv2.waitKey(0)
cv2.destroyAllWindows()
```

Figure 11.12: *Left: Original Output with multiple overlapping bounding boxes, Right: Output after applying non-max suppression*

In this code, we create two empty lists, one to store the frames that the model predicts as having our face and the second list to store the confidence score for each detection for the corresponding frames. We also initialize the width and depth variables. These are the image sizes that we trained our model on. The sliding windows to be used will have the same size so that each frame can directly be predicted by the model without having to resize the frame.

Now, since the faces inside the input image can be of any size, there might be a possibility that a face is significantly larger than our frame size. In this case, our model will not be able to correctly predict the occurrence of a face inside the frame. To address this by applying Gaussian pyramids, which will allow us to create multiple scaled versions of the input image. For the Gaussian pyramids, we set the downscale value to 1.5 This signifies that each successive pyramid level is 1.5 times smaller than the previous one making our image smaller by 1.5 times in each iteration.

We start iterating through the image using sliding windows and use scikit-learn' s Gaussian pyramid function which handles the downsizing automatically and returns the resized image. The 'scale' variable is used to keep track of the number of times an image has been downsized. We apply a shape check to verify that the frame is of the accurate size. This helps handle any size errors, and the code doesn't stop executing if there is any incorrect sized frame.

We convert the image to grayscale to preprocess it for model prediction. One important thing to note here is that the scikit-learn Gaussian pyramid returns our image in 0-1 format. Our model has been trained on images with pixel values ranging from 0 to 255. To accommodate this, we scale the values by multiplying them by 255. We then calculate the HoG features for the image and use the outputs for model prediction.

If the model predicts a value of 1, that is, the frame contains a face, we take this frame into consideration, otherwise the sliding window moves on to the next frame. We also need to make sure that the model is confident about the prediction. A low prediction score can be eliminated as the detections might not be correct. We save any values higher than 0.8 and discard frames that the model is unsure about. The 0.8 value is subjective and has to be adjusted depending on the application.

Now if the frame has passed the checks, we save the box values to our detections list. The values (x, y) corresponding to the top left values of the frame along with the width and height of the frame are stored in the list. Notice we have used the **`downscale`** and **`scale`** variables here. The Gaussian pyramid has resized our images, but we need to draw bounding boxes on the original image. To achieve this, we must rescale the coordinates of the boxes to match the dimensions of the original image.

You might remember that the scale value keeps track of how many times the image was downscaled by a factor of 1.5. For instance, if the image was downscaled twice, we multiply the values by the downscale factor raised to the power of the number of times it was downsized. For example, if we made the image smaller two times, we took the downscale factor and raised it to the power of two.

Now that we've successfully identified the frame containing a face, as shown in the left image of the result, we can observe that the model predicted two overlapping frames for the same face. To address this, we apply a technique called non-maximum suppression. This technique will assist us in completing the process by refining our results and ensuring that only the most accurate frame predictions are retained.

Non-maximum suppression is a post-processing step in object detection. It involves sorting predicted bounding boxes by their confidence scores, then sequentially selecting the highest-scored box and suppressing overlapping boxes based on a predefined threshold value. This process ensures that only the most confident and non-overlapping boxes are retained, improving the accuracy of the final detection results.

We use OpenCV's implementation of Non-max suppression using the **`cv2.dnn.NMSBoxes`** function and pass the required values to it. Boxes along with their confidence scores are passed to the function. The value of 0.5 is the IoU (Intersection over Union) threshold. It determines the level of overlap allowed between bounding boxes. If the IoU between two boxes is above this threshold, the box with a lower confidence score will be suppressed. The 0.3 is the confidence threshold. Boxes with confidence scores lower than this threshold will be discarded.

This function returns the indices of the selected boxes from the initial boxes list we passed to the function. These indices correspond to the boxes that have been retained by the non-max suppression algorithm. We plot these boxes on the image to produce the image on the right. We can see that the algorithm has been able to successfully eliminate the box with lower confidence effectively producing an accurate result.

We have successfully trained a model and created an object detection system from scratch. For a better understanding of the concepts, feel free to try this for other use cases, such as vehicle detection.

In practice, we usually don't need to start from scratch as there are pre-trained models available that have already learned a wide range of features from large datasets. One such model is the dlib 68 model for facial landmark detection. Let us explore this highly useful model in the next section.

Facial landmarks with DLIB

The **`dlib`** library is a versatile toolkit in computer vision that offers a powerful 68-point face detection and landmarks model. This model is widely recognized for its robustness and accuracy in identifying facial features.

The primary attributes of the DLIB library are:

- **Face detection**: The dlib 68-point model excels at locating faces within images and video. Owing to its high accuracy and inference speed, it is often used for applications such as facial recognition and emotion analysis. Utilizing its face detection capabilities, we can efficiently identify regions of interest containing faces without having to code almost anything.
- **Facial landmarks**: A remarkable feature of this model is its ability to identify 68 distinct landmarks on a detected face. These landmarks encompass critical features like eyes, nose, mouth, and eyebrows. The precision of these landmark positions enables advanced facial analysis

such as head pose estimation and facial expression recognition among various other applications.

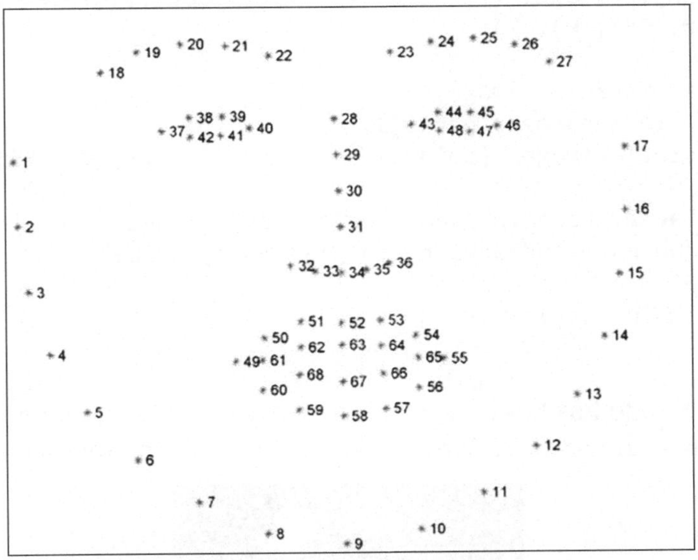

Figure 11.13: *DLIB 68 Landmark points on the face*

Facial landmarks are fixed points on a face that serve as anchors for understanding facial geometry. In the dlib 68-point model, these landmarks consistently mark features like eyes, nose, and mouth. By precisely locating them, we can assess facial expressions, head orientation, and more.

For example, tracking changes in facial landmarks allows us to analyze emotions. The positions of facial landmarks shift based on whether a person is laughing or feeling sad.

```
import dlib
import cv2

detector = dlib.get_frontal_face_detector()
predictor = dlib.shape_predictor("shape_predictor_68_face_landmarks.dat")

image = cv2.imread("face.jpg")
gray = cv2.cvtColor(image, cv2.COLOR_BGR2GRAY)

# Detect faces in the grayscale image
faces = detector(gray)

# Loop over detected faces
for face in faces:
    # Predict the facial landmarks for each detected face
```

```
    landmarks = predictor(gray, face)

    cv2.rectangle(image, (face.left(), face.top()), (face.right(), face.
bottom()), (0, 255, 0), 2)

    # Draw landmarks on image
    for point in landmarks.parts():
        cv2.circle(image, (point.x, point.y), 1, (0, 0, 255), -1)

cv2.imshow("Facial Landmarks and Rectangles", image)
cv2.imwrite("output_landmarks_rectangles.jpg", image)
cv2.waitKey(0)
cv2.destroyAllWindows()
```

The preceding code has been used to correctly identify the face in the picture, also it has drawn the 68 facial landmarks as shown in the following figure:

Figure 11.14: *Dlib 68 output on face showing face detection rectangle and 68 face landmark points*

The image needs to be in grayscale for the dlib model inference. The Dlib model file **shape_predictor_68_face_landmarks.da**' can be downloaded from the official dlib website 'http://dlib.net/files/'. A simple Google search with the filename can also be used to download the file.

In the preceding code, the line **get_frontal_face_detector** function initializes a face detector object using dlib' s pre-trained model for frontal face detection. This detector is able to locate faces within images or video frames.

In the next line, we load the pre-trained model for facial landmark detection. This model specifically identifies 68 landmarks on a detected face.

We first use the face detector to detect faces in the image. For each of the faces found in the image, the predictor is used to detect the 68 landmarks on the face. We then draw these points and the rectangle for visualization.

Dlib is versatile and applicable across various scenarios. In the upcoming chapter, we'll delve into a practical application that makes use of this model.

Object tracking using OpenCV

Object tracking is a task in computer vision that involves locating and following a specific object as it moves within a video. Object tracking involves identifying an initial target object in the first frame and then intelligently predicting its whereabouts in subsequent frames. Unlike object detection which identifies objects within a single frame, object tracking refers to following objects as they move in a video.

Object tracking plays a vital role in various real-world applications. Some key areas where object tracking are:

- **Surveillance Systems**: Object tracking is used to monitor and analyze the movement of people and objects in security cameras.
- **Autonomous Vehicles**: Autonomous cars use object tracking to detect and follow other vehicles, pedestrians and obstacles on the road.
- **Robotics**: Robots employ object tracking for tasks like picking and placing objects, navigation, and human-robot interaction.
- **Augmented Reality (AR)**: AR applications use object tracking to overlay virtual objects on real-world scenes, enhancing the user experience.

OpenCV provides efficient tools and algorithms that make tracking objects easier and more accessible without having to explicitly code these from scratch. There are a lot of tracking algorithms built in the OpenCV library, each having its own merits.

The object tracking process typically consists of two steps:

- **Initialization**: First we specify the initial bounding box that surrounds the object that we want to track. The object can be either manually defined by the user or an object detection technique can be used for the same.
- **Tracking Loop**: Once the object is initialized, we enter a tracking loop. In each iteration of the loop we process a new frame from the video. The tracking algorithm updates the position of the object based on its previous location and appearance. The tracked object can be visualized by drawing a bounding box around it in each frame.

It is not practical to cover all the trackers in detail. However, we will be using the MIL (Multiple Instance Learning) Tracker today for our example of object tracking using OpenCV. This will help us understand and demonstrate how object tracking works using OpenCV. Feel free to try other trackers on your own.

The MIL (Multiple Instance Learning) Tracker is an algorithm that pays attention to different patches of the target object in each video frame. By observing these patches over time, the tracker learns the various appearances of the object. This helps the tracker maintain accurate tracking of the object even when the object's appearance changes due to factors like angles or occlusions.

Some of the other object tracking algorithms in OpenCV are KLT (Kanade-Lucas-Tomasi) Tracking, CSRT (Discriminative Correlation Filter with Channel and Spatial Reliability) and MOSSE (Minimum Output Sum of Squared Error). The choice of algorithm depends on the specific use case. Feel free to explore these algorithms on your own accord.

The MIL Tracker can be implemented using the **cv2.TrackerMIL_create()** function in OpenCV:

```
import cv2


# Initialize our tracker object
tracker = cv2.TrackerMIL_create()

video = cv2.VideoCapture('car.mp4')
ret, frame = video.read()


# Custom bounding box
bbox = cv2.selectROI(frame)

# Initialize tracker with first frame and the drawn bounding box
tracker.init(frame, bbox)

while True:
    ret, frame = video.read()
    if not ret:
        break

    # Update the tracker to get the new bounding box
    success, bbox = tracker.update(frame)

    # Draw the bounding box
    if success:
        x, y, w, h = [int(val) for val in bbox]
        cv2.rectangle(frame, (x, y), (x + w, y + h), (0, 255, 0), 2)
```

```
    cv2.imshow('Object Tracking', frame)

    if cv2.waitKey(0):
        break

# Release video
video.release()
cv2.destroyAllWindows()
```

In the preceding code, we use the **cv2.TrackerMIL_create()** function to track our object. In this example, we are tracking a moving car and using OpenCV to read the video:

Figure 11.15: *Left: First frame from the video. Right: Manually drawn bounding box on the frame to specify the object to be tracked*

The tracking function works by taking input from the user to specify the object that needs to be tracked. The **cv2.selectROI** function takes the first frame of the video and asks the user for an input corresponding to the bounding box of the target object. It opens a window where we can drag a rectangle to define the ROI. The first frame is displayed to the user, and the custom bounding has to be drawn manually by the user to specify the object that needs to be tracked.

The bounding box is saved, and the tracker is initialized using the first frame and the corresponding bounding box of the object to be tracked.

We then iterated through the video frame by frame and updated the latest frame on the tracker object. The tracker object returns a Boolean variable **success** that indicates whether the object tracking was successful in the current frame and a bounding box bbox tuple containing the coordinates of the tracked object's bounding box.

For each frame, if the tracker object was successfully able to detect an object, we display the corresponding frame with the bounding box drawn using the rectangle function. The operation continues until the video has been completed.

From the outputs, we can observe that the tracker has been successfully able to track our car.

Some of the output frames from the video are as follows:

***Figure 11.16**: Four frames from the video displaying object tracking as it moves*

The preceding images display four instances from the video as our car is being tracked. Our tracker has been able to accurately track our car as it traverses in the video. An interesting thing to notice here is that the tracker was able to accurately track our car accurately even when it was occluded behind the tree.

This is just a single instance of a tracker in OpenCV for a rudimentary understanding of how object tracking works in OpenCV. As mentioned earlier, there are various trackers in OpenCV. You can try these trackers on your own with various other use cases.

Conclusion

In this chapter, we gained insight into object detection fundamentals, including techniques like sliding windows, image pyramids, and OpenCV's template matching. We explored both self-training and pre-trained methods like Haar Cascades and DLIB for effective object detection. Additionally, we delved into feature extraction, facial landmarks with DLIB, and the basics of object tracking using OpenCV.

We have now reached the culmination of our journey through the theoretical concepts covered in this book. Throughout this journey, we delved into

OpenCV exploring its various components including morphological operations, histograms, HOG (Histogram of Oriented Gradients), LBP (Local Binary Pattern), and more. Along the way we undertook numerous projects, applying machine learning techniques in conjunction with OpenCV. Additionally, we introduced the foundational concepts of neural networks.

In this final chapter, we'll leverage the skills we've acquired to create and delve into more projects. This hands-on approach will enhance your comprehension of how projects are developed and executed using OpenCV.

Points to remember

- Object detection involves identifying items within images or videos, enabling tasks like tracking and recognition.
- Sliding windows is an object detection technique that works by moving a window through an image. This window varies in size and scans the image, helping identify objects of different scales.
- Template matching involves comparing a smaller template image to different sections of a larger image. The goal is to find areas where the template closely matches the larger image to enable the detection of specific objects.
- Haar cascades utilize patterns of intensities to detect objects within images. These cascades are composed of multiple stages, each refining the object detection process by progressively narrowing down areas of interest based on intensity thresholds.
- Feature extraction for object detection entails transforming raw image data into meaningful features that capture distinct patterns or characteristics. These features serve as input to machine learning algorithms, enabling them to learn and distinguish between different objects or classes during the detection process.
- An image pyramid is a multi-scale representation of an image, consisting of progressively downsampled versions. This pyramid enables object detection algorithms to identify objects of various sizes by analyzing different levels of detail in the image.
- Non-maximum suppression is a technique used in object detection to eliminate redundant and overlapping bounding boxes. It helps refine the results by selecting the most relevant bounding box for an object and discarding others.
- Object tracking is the process of following and monitoring the movement of objects across a sequence of images or frames in a video.

Test your understanding

1. In template matching, what does the term “template” refer to?
   A. The source image where an object is located
   B. A small image or pattern that is used for comparison
   C. The background of the image
   D. The noise present in the image
2. What does each stage of a Haar cascade involve?
   A. Applying a specific filter
   B. Removing noise from the image
   C. Enhancing color contrast
   D. Calculating image gradients
3. What is the primary purpose of a Gaussian pyramid in image processing?
   A. Enhancing image contrast
   B. Applying edge detection
   C. Generating multiple resolutions of an image
   D. Removing noise from an image
4. What is the primary purpose of the DLIB 68 facial landmarks model?
   A. Recognizing objects in images
   B. Detecting facial emotions
   C. Identifying facial features and landmarks
   D. Enhancing image resolution
5. What is the main objective of object tracking in computer vision?
   A. Detecting objects within images
   B. Identifying facial landmarks
   C. Following the movement of objects across consecutive frames
   D. Enhancing image resolution

Chapter 12
Projects Using OpenCV

In this final chapter, we'll leverage the skills we've acquired to create and delve into more projects. This hands-on approach will enhance your comprehension of how projects is developed and executed using OpenCV.

We'll begin by exploring the Automatic Book Inventory system, a practical application that will automate the process of cataloguing and extracting book information automatically. Next, we'll delve into the Document Scanning project Using OpenCV and OCR, where we'll learn to extract text from images, opening up a world of possibilities for digitizing paper documents.

Moving on, we'll delve into the fascinating realm of Face Recognition, where we'll unlock the potential of facial recognition technology. Finally, we'll wrap up by exploring Drowsiness Detection, a project that has critical applications in driver safety.

These projects will not only consolidate your OpenCV skills but also equip you with valuable tools to tackle real-world challenges in computer vision.

Structure

In this chapter, we will explore the following projects:

- Automated book inventory system
- Document scanning using OpenCV and OCR
- Face recognition
- Drowsiness detection

Automated book inventory system

In this project, our goal is to create an efficient book management system. We will achieve this by employing a Python library to capture book data through QR code scanning. This approach will streamline the process of gathering book information automatically. The project will take a picture and all the necessary information about the book will be retrieved and stored automatically.

We will harness the power of an external API to fetch comprehensive details about each book, including titles, authors, publication dates, and more. The retrieved data will allow us to maintain an organized and up-to-date inventory of our books. To enhance usability, we will store this valuable information in a user-friendly spreadsheet, making it accessible and manageable for our team.

We will utilize the PyZbar library for QR code decoding in our project. This library efficiently locates QR codes within an image and scans them to extract valuable information, simplifying the process of data retrieval.

The library can be installed using pip by using the command:

```
pip install pyzbar
```

We will start by importing this and OpenCV and the decode function from the **pyzbar** library. The **decode** function is used to identify and extract data from QR codes and barcodes within an image.

Let us use this image for our code:

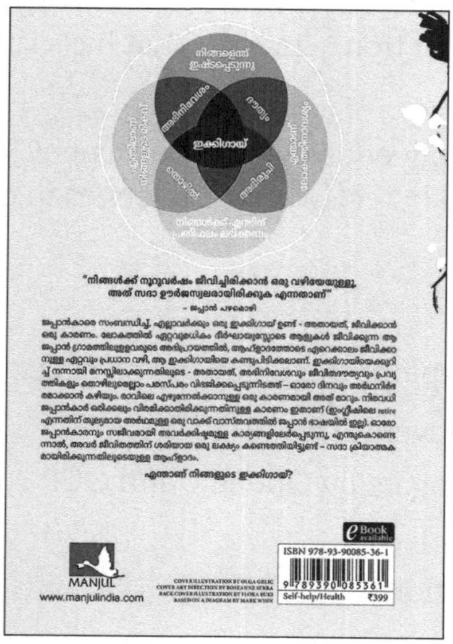

Figure 12.1: *Input image of a book with QR code*

```
from pyzbar.pyzbar import decode
import cv2

img = cv2.imread("book.jpg")
decoded_objects = decode(img)
```

The decoded objects contain data about the detected QR codes and barcodes including their content, type, and location within the image. We print the barcode type and data to verify if the barcode was scanned properly or not:

```
for obj in decoded_objects:
    barcode_data = obj.data.decode('utf-8')
    barcode_type = obj.type
    print(f"Barcode Type: {barcode_type}, Data: {barcode_data}")
```

Output: **`Barcode Type: EAN13, Data: 9789390085361`**

Notice how we did not have to do any manual segmentation or extraction of the QR code from the image. The **`pyzbar`** library took care of everything for us.

Next, we use the Open Library API for retrieving book information based on an **ISBN (International Standard Book Number)**. This is the number we extracted from the bar code in the previous step. The **`requests`** library is used to send HTTP requests to the API and retrieve data from it.

On passing the ISBN to the API, it returns a lot of information about the book. We extract certain parameters such as book title, author, and publication information here and return these values from the function. If any of the parameters is not available, we return a not found value for that parameter:

```
def get_book_info(isbn):
    url = f'https://openlibrary.org/api/books?bibkeys=ISBN:{isbn}&
jscmd=data&format=json'
    response = requests.get(url)

    if response.status_code == 200:
        book_data = response.json().get(f'ISBN:{isbn}')
        if book_data:
            title = book_data.get('title', 'Title not found')

            # Retrieve author information
            authors = book_data.get('authors', [{'name': 'Author not
found'}])
            author_names = [author['name'] for author in authors]

            # Retrieve publication information
```

```
            publish_date = book_data.get('publish_date', 'Publication
date not found')
            publisher = book_data.get('publishers', [{'name': 'Publisher
not found'}])

            return {
                'Title': title,
                'Authors': author_names,
                'Publish Date': publish_date,
                'Publisher': publisher[0]['name']
            }

    return {
        'Title': 'Book not found',
        'Authors': ['Author not found'],
        'Publish Date': 'Publication date not found',
        'Publisher': 'Publisher not found'
    }
```

Next, we pass the barcode-generated ISBN value to the preceding function and print the extracted information:

```
book_info = get_book_info(barcode_data)
print(f"Book Title: {book_info}")
```

The output from the code is as follows:

```
Book Title: {'Title': 'Ikigai The Japanese secret to a long and hap-
py life', 'Authors': ['Héctor García', 'Francesc Miralles'], 'Publish
Date': 'Jun 24, 2017', 'Publisher': 'Total Kannada'}
```

We can see that by just taking a single code, the system has been able to extract a lot of information about the book. We can store this information in a spreadsheet or database for further organization and reference.

In this code, we will use the Pandas library, which is a powerful Python library for data manipulation and analysis. You are free to use any other technology according to your choice.

The **pandas** library will create a spreadsheet of the extracted columns and save the information as a csv file on our local disk.

The **pandas** library can be installed by using pip:

```
Pip install pandas
```

```
import pandas as pd

# Function to store book details in a CSV file using Pandas
def store_to_csv(book_info, isbn):
    try:
        df = pd.read_csv(‘books.csv’)
    except FileNotFoundError:
        df = pd.DataFrame(columns=[‘ISBN’, ‘Title’, ‘Authors’, ‘Publish
Date’, ‘Publisher’])

    book_info[‘ISBN’] = isbn

    # Append book information to DataFrame
    df = pd.concat([df, pd.DataFrame([book_info])], ignore_index=True)

    df.to_csv(‘books.csv’, index=False)

store_to_csv(book_info, barcode_data)
```

The results will look like this.

	A	B	C	D	E	F
1	ISBN	Title	Authors	Publish Date	Publisher	
2	9789390085361	Ikigai The Japanese secre	['Héctor García', 'France	Jun 24, 2017	Total Kannada	
3	9788172234980	The Alchemist	['Paulo Coelho']	2018	HarperCollins	
4	9781408855652	Harry Potter and the Philos	['J. K. Rowling']	September 1, 2014	Bloomsbury	
5	9789387944862	How to Win Friends and In	['Dale Carnegie']	Feb 19, 2018	Jaico Publishing House	
6						
7						
8						

We have successfully developed a system that captures book information from an image with remarkable speed and automation. This process requires minimal effort and time, offering a highly efficient way to obtain and save book details in a CSV file.

Document scanning using OpenCV and OCR

Document scanning is a crucial task in various applications, from digitizing paper documents to automating data extraction from text-heavy materials. OpenCV (Open Source Computer Vision Library) and OCR (Optical Character Recognition) technologies are powerful tools that can be combine to perform efficient document scanning and text extraction.

In this project, OpenCV is utilized to enhance and transform images of sheets of paper. The process begins by loading an image and applying several image processing techniques, including grayscale conversion, Gaussian blur, and edge detection using the Canny algorithm.

The code then identifies the largest contour in the edged image, which represents the sheet of paper. By approximating the four corners of this contour, a perspective warp is applied to obtain a corrected view of the paper.

Once we have a clearer image of the paper we can use **Tesseract OCR** (**Optical Character Recognition**) to extract text from the image. Tesseract OCR is a powerful tool for recognizing text in images and converting it into machine-readable text.

To install Tesseract OCR, we need to download the Tesseract installer for Windows from the official GitHub repository: 'https://github.com/UB-Mannheim/tesseract/wiki'. Once the installation is complete, we can use Tesseract OCR from the command line or integrate it into your Python code using the Pytesseract library (Python wrapper for Tesseract).

The `pytesseract` library can be installed using pip.

```
Pip install pytesseract
```

We load the necessary libraries, load the image and apply some basic image transformations followed by edge detection using the Canny Edge Detector. The edged image will help us extract the contours from the image representing the paper.

The image we will be using for our code is:

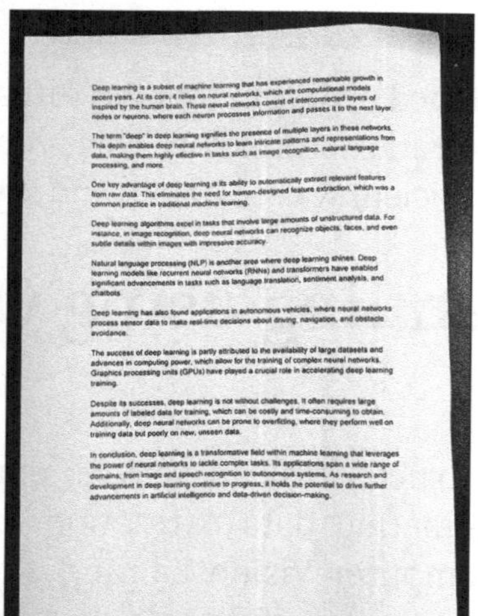

Deep learning is a subset of machine learning that has experienced remarkable growth in recent years. At its core, it relies on neural networks, which are computational models inspired by the human brain. These neural networks consist of interconnected layers of nodes or neurons, where each neuron processes information and passes it to the next layer.

The term "deep" in deep learning signifies the presence of multiple layers in these networks. This depth enables deep neural networks to learn intricate patterns and representations from data, making them highly effective in tasks such as image recognition, natural language processing, and more.

One key advantage of deep learning is its ability to automatically extract relevant features from raw data. This eliminates the need for human-designed feature extraction, which was a common practice in traditional machine learning.

Deep learning algorithms excel in tasks that involve large amounts of unstructured data. For instance, in image recognition, deep neural networks can recognize objects, faces, and even subtle details within images with impressive accuracy.

Natural language processing (NLP) is another area where deep learning shines. Deep learning models like recurrent neural networks (RNNs) and transformers have enabled significant advancements in tasks such as language translation, sentiment analysis, and chatbots.

Deep learning has also found applications in autonomous vehicles, where neural networks process sensor data to make real-time decisions about driving, navigation, and obstacle avoidance.

The success of deep learning is partly attributed to the availability of large datasets and advances in computing power, which allow for the training of complex neural networks. Graphics processing units (GPUs) have played a crucial role in accelerating deep learning training.

Despite its successes, deep learning is not without challenges. It often requires large amounts of labeled data for training, which can be costly and time-consuming to obtain. Additionally, deep neural networks can be prone to overfitting, where they perform well on training data but poorly on new, unseen data.

In conclusion, deep learning is a transformative field within machine learning that leverages the power of neural networks to tackle complex tasks. Its applications span a wide range of domains, from image and speech recognition to autonomous systems. As research and development in deep learning continue to progress, it holds the potential to drive further advancements in artificial intelligence and data-driven decision-making.

Figure 12.2: *Input image of a document*

```
import cv2
import numpy as np

img = cv2.imread(‘document.jpg’)

height, width, channels = img.shape

gray_img = cv2.cvtColor(img.copy(),cv2.COLOR_BGR2GRAY)
blur_img = cv2.GaussianBlur(gray_img,(5,5),0)
edged_img = cv2.Canny(blur_img,75,200)
cv2.imshow(‘edged’,edged_img)
cv2.waitKey(0)

contours, hierarchy = cv2.findContours(edged_img,cv2.RETR_TREE, cv2.
CHAIN_APPROX_NONE)
```

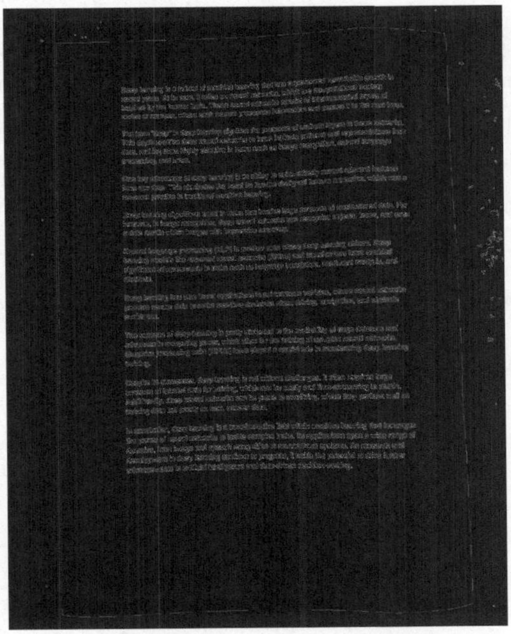

Figure 12.3: *Image with Edges, will serve as an input to contour detection to determine the corners of the document*

From the contours extracted, we will select the most prominent one that corresponds to the sheet of paper in the image. To achieve this, we first calculate the areas of all the contours found using the **`cv2.contourArea()`** function and store these areas in the areas list. Then, we identify the index of the contour with the largest area.

Next, we use contour approximation to approximate the shape of the largest contour found in the image. We calculate the contour's perimeter using **`cv2.arcLength()`** and **`cv2.approxPolyDP()`** is used to create a quadrilateral approximation of the contour based on the specified precision, resulting in the **approx** variable:

```
areas = [cv2.contourArea(c) for c in contours]
max_index = np.argmax(areas)
print(max_index)

epsilon = 0.1 * cv2.arcLength(contours[max_index], True)
approx = cv2.approxPolyDP(contours[max_index], epsilon, True)
```

Using the contours extracted in the earlier step, we perform a perspective transformation to crop and straighten the image. We define two sets of points (**pts1** and **pts2**) in which pts1 represents the corners of the approximated paper and pts2 represents the desired rectangular output. The **cv2.getPerspectiveTransform()** function calculates a transformation matrix (matrix) to map **pts1** to **pts2**.

Then, we apply this transformation using **cv2.warpPerspective()** to obtain the result, which is a modified image with the paper aligned and cropped for better visualization and analysis. Finally, the result is displayed with a horizontal flip for improved visualization:

```
pts1 = np.float32(approx)
pts2 = np.float32([[0, 0], [width, 0], [width, height], [0, height]])
matrix = cv2.getPerspectiveTransform(pts1, pts2)
result = cv2.warpPerspective(img, matrix, (width, height))

flip = cv2.flip(result, 1) cv2.imshow('Result',flip)

cv2.waitKey(0)
cv2.destroyAllWindows()
```

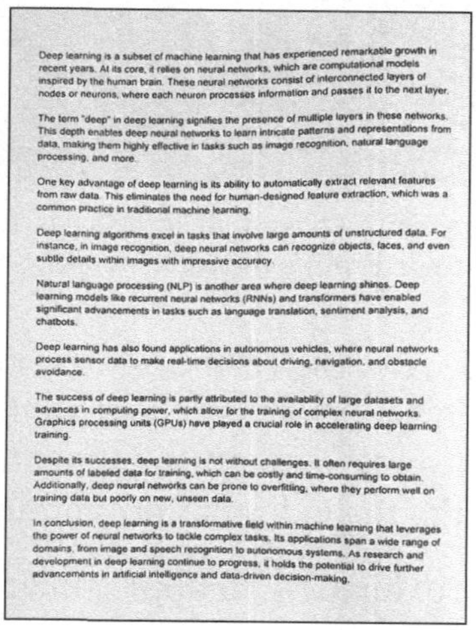

Deep learning is a subset of machine learning that has experienced remarkable growth in recent years. At its core, it relies on neural networks, which are computational models inspired by the human brain. These neural networks consist of interconnected layers of nodes or neurons, where each neuron processes information and passes it to the next layer.

The term "deep" in deep learning signifies the presence of multiple layers in these networks. This depth enables deep neural networks to learn intricate patterns and representations from data, making them highly effective in tasks such as image recognition, natural language processing, and more.

One key advantage of deep learning is its ability to automatically extract relevant features from raw data. This eliminates the need for human-designed feature extraction, which was a common practice in traditional machine learning.

Deep learning algorithms excel in tasks that involve large amounts of unstructured data. For instance, in image recognition, deep neural networks can recognize objects, faces, and even subtle details within images with impressive accuracy.

Natural language processing (NLP) is another area where deep learning shines. Deep learning models like recurrent neural networks (RNNs) and transformers have enabled significant advancements in tasks such as language translation, sentiment analysis, and chatbots.

Deep learning has also found applications in autonomous vehicles, where neural networks process sensor data to make real-time decisions about driving, navigation, and obstacle avoidance.

The success of deep learning is partly attributed to the availability of large datasets and advances in computing power, which allow for the training of complex neural networks. Graphics processing units (GPUs) have played a crucial role in accelerating deep learning training.

Despite its successes, deep learning is not without challenges. It often requires large amounts of labeled data for training, which can be costly and time-consuming to obtain. Additionally, deep neural networks can be prone to overfitting, where they perform well on training data but poorly on new, unseen data.

In conclusion, deep learning is a transformative field within machine learning that leverages the power of neural networks to tackle complex tasks. Its applications span a wide range of domains, from image and speech recognition to autonomous systems. As research and development in deep learning continue to progress, it holds the potential to drive further advancements in artificial intelligence and data-driven decision-making.

Figure 12.4: *Extracted document from the image. We will pass this document to the tesseract OCR in the next step.*

Now that we have a clearer image of the paper, we can use tesseract to convert this image into text format.

We import the **Pytesseract** library and pass the paper image to it for text extraction. The tesseract installation path containing the **tesseract.exe** file has to be specified for **Pytesseract**. This is the path where we installed the Tesseract in the first step:

```
import pytesseract

# Set the Tesseract executable path
pytesseract.pytesseract.tesseract_cmd = r'C:/Program Files/Tesser-
act-OCR/tesseract.exe'

# Use Tesseract to extract text
text = pytesseract.image_to_string(flip)

print(text)
```

Output:

Deep learning is a subset of machine learning that has experienced remarkable growth in recent years. At its core, it relies on neural networks, which CT are inspired by the human brain.

As research and development in deep learning continue to progress, it holds the potential to drive further advancements in artificial intelligence and data-driven decision-making.

Tesseract does an excellent job of converting the images to text, and from the result, it's evident that it has accurately extracted the text.

Face recognition

Face recognition enables the identification and verification of individuals based on their facial features. The fundamental idea behind face recognition is to analyze and compare unique facial characteristics such as the arrangement of eyes, nose, mouth and other facial landmarks to establish a person's identity. We can use these characteristics to compare and verify whether a face matches a known identity.

Face recognition technology has a wide range of applications. It is used for access control and security in buildings and security areas. Faces are scanned on the entrance and only people authorized for access are allowed inside the premises. Similarly, face recognition is widely used in mobile phones and other electronic devices for user authentication.

While deep learning techniques are often used for robust face recognition, OpenCV also offers functions that can assist in face recognition tasks. OpenCV provides tools and methods to detect faces, extract facial features, and even train basic face recognition models.

In the last chapter, we discussed face detection using various techniques. In this exercise, we will take that a step further and build our very own face recognition model using OpenCV.

We will be using the LFW (Labeled Faces in the Wild) dataset for our face recognition application. The LFW is an open-source dataset containing a collection of face images of individuals obtained from the internet. We will use these images to train and test our face recognition model.

We start the code by importing the necessary libraries and specifying the path to our LFW directory. Next, we create our face recognition model object using the **LBPHFaceRecognizer_create** function.

We will be using the **LBPHFaceRecognizer_create()** function in OpenCV to create a face recognition model based on Local Binary Pattern Histograms (LBPH). LBPH is a widely used face recognition algorithm known for its simplicity and effectiveness in recognizing faces in images.

The algorithm computes a histogram of the binary patterns obtained from comparing each pixel to its neighbors. This histogram of patterns is then used as a feature vector to represent and recognize faces based on the distribution of these patterns in the image:

```
import cv2
import os
import numpy as np

data_dir = 'LFW/'

recognizer = cv2.face.LBPHFaceRecognizer_create()
```

The LFW dataset contains face images of 5749 people, with approximately 10 images of each person. The dataset is organized with a specific structure: inside the main LFW folder, there are subfolders dedicated to each person containing their respective images. We will navigate through these subfolders and collect the grayscale images into a 'faces' list. Additionally, we will create a 'label' list that will hold the names of the individuals, serving as labels for our model during training:

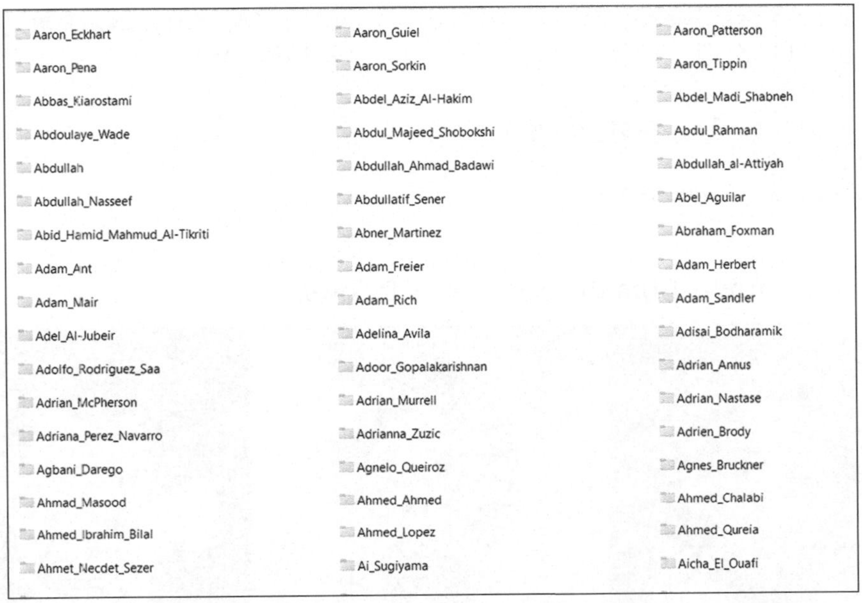

***Figure 12.5**: LFW directories structure showing subdirectories with person names containing images.*

```
for label, person_dir in enumerate(os.listdir(data_dir)):
    person_path = os.path.join(data_dir, person_dir)
    for image_name in os.listdir(person_path):
        image_path = os.path.join(person_path, image_name)
        image = cv2.imread(image_path, cv2.IMREAD_GRAYSCALE)
        faces.append(image)
        labels.append(label)
```

Now that we have our dataset ready, we will train our face recognizer model with these images:

```
recognizer.train(faces, np.array(labels))
```

Training our face recognition model with OpenCV proved to be an uncomplicated process. Let's evaluate its performance and see if it can successfully recognize faces. We will load some images from the LFW dataset and predict the results to evaluate our model:

```
test_image = cv2.imread('lfw/Tim_Welsh/Tim_Welsh_0001.jpg', cv2.IMREAD_
GRAYSCALE)

label, _ = recognizer.predict(test_image)

# Get the name corresponding to the predicted label
predicted_person = os.listdir(data_dir)[label]
```

```
cv2.putText(test_image, f"{predicted_person}", (0, 60), cv2.FONT_
HERSHEY_SIMPLEX, 1, (255, 255, 255), 1, cv2.LINE_AA)

cv2.imshow('result, test_image)
cv2.waitKey(0)
cv2.destroyAllWindows()
```

Some of the outputs from the code are as follows:

***Figure 12.6**: Outputs from the face recognition project*

After verifying the results, it is evident that the model has accurately predicted outcomes. This demonstrates that our face recognition model is functional and has been developed successfully.

Drowsiness detection

In this exercise, we will create a drowsiness detection system using OpenCV. Drowsiness detection systems aim to identify signs of driver fatigue or drowsiness, which can pose a significant risk on the road.

By analyzing the position and orientation of a driver's face, we can use OpenCV to monitor facial features and movements. Tracking eye movements such as blinking frequency and duration can be used as a crucial parameter for drowsiness detection. When signs of drowsiness are detected, an alert mechanism can be used to enhance safety and prevent accidents.

We start by loading the necessary libraries and the Dlib-68 model to identify facial features:

```
import cv2
import dlib
from scipy.spatial import distance as dist
```

```
face_detector = dlib.get_frontal_face_detector()
eye_landmark_detector =
dlib.shape_predictor("shape_predictor_68_face_landmarks.dat")
```

In our drowsiness detection system, we establish two essential variables to establish the conditions. First, we set a threshold value for the vertical eye size below which the eye is considered closed, marking the frame for potential drowsiness. We also define another parameter that specifies the number of consecutive frames in which drowsiness is detected before triggering an alert:

```
VERTICAL_EYE_THRESHOLD_PIXELS = 13
CONSECUTIVE_FRAMES_THRESHOLD = 20
```

We initialize our video capture object and create an empty variable that keeps track of the number of consecutive frames for which the eye was detected closed:

```
cap = cv2.VideoCapture(0)
consecutive_frames_closed = 0
```

For each frame of the video, we use the face detector and generate landmarks for the face using the Dlib model object we initialized earlier. In this code, we will calculate the vertical distance of the eye landmarks. We will take two vertical points from the top and two from the bottom of each eye, and then calculate the average distance between these points. If the vertical distance is reduced by our threshold, we will assume that the eye is closed for this frame:

```
while True:
    ret, frame = cap.read()
    if not ret:
        break

    gray = cv2.cvtColor(frame, cv2.COLOR_BGR2GRAY)

    faces = face_detector(gray)

    for face in faces:
        landmarks = eye_landmark_detector(gray, face)

        # Calculating the vertical distance between landmarks
        left_eye_top = dist.euclidean((landmarks.part(37).x, landmarks.
part(37).y), (landmarks.part(41).x, landmarks.part(41).y))
        left_eye_bottom = dist.euclidean((landmarks.part(40).x,
landmarks.part(40).y), (landmarks.part(38).x, landmarks.part(38).y))
        right_eye_top = dist.euclidean((landmarks.part(43).x, landmarks.
```

```
part(43).y), (landmarks.part(47).x, landmarks.part(47).y))
        right_eye_bottom = dist.euclidean((landmarks.part(46).x,
landmarks.part(46).y), (landmarks.part(44).x, landmarks.part(44).y))

        # Average vertical distance for both eyes
        avg_vertical_distance = (left_eye_top + left_eye_bottom + right_
eye_top + right_eye_bottom) / 4.0

        cv2.line(frame, (landmarks.part(37).x, landmarks.part(37).y),
(landmarks.part(41).x, landmarks.part(41).y), (0, 0, 255), 1)
        cv2.line(frame, (landmarks.part(38).x, landmarks.part(38).y),
(landmarks.part(40).x, landmarks.part(40).y), (0, 0, 255), 1)
        cv2.line(frame, (landmarks.part(43).x, landmarks.part(43).y),
(landmarks.part(47).x, landmarks.part(47).y), (0, 0, 255), 1)
        cv2.line(frame, (landmarks.part(44).x, landmarks.part(44).y),
(landmarks.part(46).x, landmarks.part(46).y), (0, 0, 255), 1)
```

We draw the lines for visualization and text to keep track of how the algorithm is working. The checks are added for drowsiness detection by comparing the threshold with the average distance calculated earlier. If the eyes are closed for 20 consecutive frames, we display an alert saying drowsiness detected:

```
        cv2.putText(frame, f"AVG Vertical Distance: {avg_vertical_
distance:.2f} pixels", (10, 30), cv2.FONT_HERSHEY_SIMPLEX, 0.5, (0, 0,
255), 2)

        cv2.putText(frame, f"Drowsiness Threshold: {VERTICAL_EYE_
THRESHOLD_PIXELS} pixels", (frame.shape[1] - 200, 30), cv2.FONT_HERSHEY_
SIMPLEX, 0.5, (0, 0, 255), 2)

        drowsiness_detected = avg_vertical_distance < VERTICAL_EYE_
THRESHOLD_PIXELS
        if drowsiness_detected:
            consecutive_frames_closed += 1
            if consecutive_frames_closed >= CONSECUTIVE_FRAMES_THRESHOLD:
                cv2.putText(frame, "Alert: Drowsiness Detected!", (10,
60), cv2.FONT_HERSHEY_SIMPLEX, 0.7, (0, 0, 255), 2)
        else:
            consecutive_frames_closed = 0

    cv2.imshow("Drowsiness Detection", frame)
```

```
    if cv2.waitKey(1) & 0xFF == ord("q"):
        break

cap.release()
cv2.destroyAllWindows()
```

The output from the preceding code is as follows:

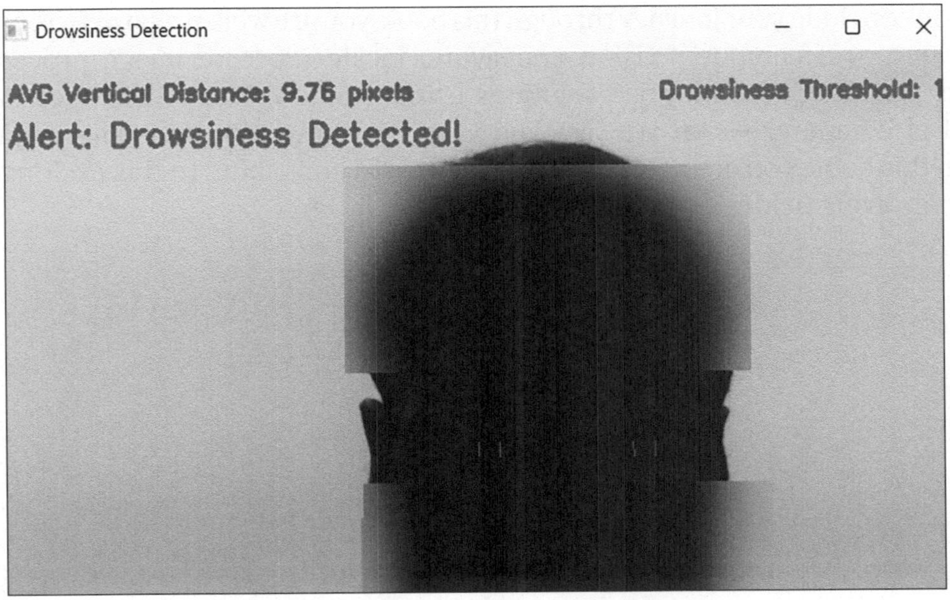

Figure 12.7: *Drowsiness Detection Output*

Our drowsiness detection algorithm is performing effectively. Please feel free to make any modifications or enhancements and don't hesitate to add new features if desired.

Conclusion

This brings us to the end of our OpenCV book. This OpenCV book has taken you on a comprehensive journey through the fascinating world of computer vision. We began by establishing a solid foundation, introducing you to practical aspects of working with image data and equipping you with the necessary tools for effective manipulation and enhancement of images.

As we progressed through the material, you explored advanced techniques for image analysis, delving into critical concepts related to shape detection and boundary extraction. Subsequently, the book ventured into the realm of machine learning and artificial intelligence, providing insights into the application of these technologies to real-world computer vision challenges.

Our journey culminated in a series of practical projects, offering hands-on experience and an opportunity to apply the knowledge gained throughout the book. These projects served as a testament to your newfound expertise in OpenCV and computer vision.

As you conclude your journey through this book, you are well-prepared to embark on your own computer vision endeavors, tackle intricate image processing tasks and develop innovative solutions using OpenCV. The possibilities in the field of computer vision are vast and with the knowledge and skills acquired from this book, you are now ready to explore and contribute to this exciting and ever-evolving field.

Index

A

B

C

N

O